Churchill

C000115785

Under Friendly Fire

WALTER REID

BIRLINN

For Callum and Elspeth

This edition first published in 2012 by
Birlinn Limited
West Newington House
10 Newington Road
Edinburgh
EH9 1QS

www.birlinn.co.uk

Copyright © Walter Reid 2008

ISBN: 978 1 84341 059 1

British Library Cataloguing-in-Publication Data
A catalogue record for this book is available from the British Library

Typeset by Hewer Text UK Ltd, Edinburgh
Printed and bound by Clays Ltd, St Ives plc

Contents

List of Illustrations

Acknowledgements

I am most appreciative of the help I received in the course of researching and writing this book and I am very glad to have this opportunity to express my thanks to those named below - and also to very many others who took an interest in the project, joined in stimulating discussions and helped me to crystallise and refine my thoughts.

Dr Paul Addison of Edinburgh University, where he was until recently Director of the Centre for Second War Studies (now the Centre for the Study of the Two World Wars), and author of the *Oxford DNB* article on Winston Churchill and of much else, very kindly read the book in draft and discussed it with me at some length. I am very grateful to him for his generous help. The book benefited greatly from his advice on structure and from his reflections on the parabolic course of Churchill's influence over the war.

David Reynolds, Professor of International Relations at Cambridge, whose many books include *In Command of History: Churchill Fighting and Writing the Second World War*, a fascinating work of analysis which sheds much light on the history of the war which Churchill wrote, and the history he took care not to write, also very kindly read the work in draft, gave most welcome advice on structure, and eliminated numerous solecisms. I am grateful to him.

A number of ideas, encounters, events and discussions combined to prompt me to write this book. Amongst them was a stimulating lecture at the Edinburgh Centre for Second War Studies, as it then was, by Sir Martin Gilbert, who also took an interest in my project at an early stage. Like everyone else who sets out to read or write about Churchill, I am hugely in Sir Martin's debt.

There are many others whose help was invaluable. Dr Daniel Scroop is not only a very dear son-in-law but also a distinguished British historian of America with a particular interest in Roosevelt and the New

Deal era. The American sections of the book (and other sections too) are much the better for his advice, though he should not necessarily be taken to agree with all aspects of my assessment of FDR.

I am grateful to Melissa Atkinson of the National Portrait Gallery, to Liz Bowers of the Imperial War Museum for her help with this and earlier books, to Professor Antoine Capet of Rouen University for letting me see both published articles and unpublished papers that illuminate Churchill's attitude to France, to David Hamill for his interest and support and for improving my ski-ing technique, to Daniel Myers of the Churchill Centre, to Doris Nisbet, as ever, for secretarial and much wider logistic backup, and to Claudia Tscheitschonigg for her friendship and help with translation.

Dr John Tuckwell commissioned the book, and I am very grateful to him and to Val for their confidence in this and earlier ventures and for their friendship. At Birlinn, Hugh Andrew, despite the demands of presiding over a constantly expanding publishing house, found time to take a personal interest in the book. Andrew Simmons moved the production process forward without apparent effort, and was also great fun to work with. My copy editor, Dr Lawrence Osborn, snuffled out and dug up potential problems with the intuitive genius that separates the truly gifted truffle-hound from the rest.

My daughters, Dr Julia Reid and Bryony Reid, read the typescript very carefully and with approaches that differed in reflection of their respective disciplines, and made innumerable suggestions that collectively resulted in enormous changes for the better. I am impressed and grateful.

Last in the order of these acknowledgements, but certainly not in the scale of her contribution, comes my wife, Janet. Her editorial input as always was sensitive and perceptive and reflected her background as a journalist. But my heart-felt gratitude to her goes beyond that to a much wider element of love, support and encouragement. Without her this book – and much else too – would not have happened and life would be much less fun.

Glenfintaig, June 2008

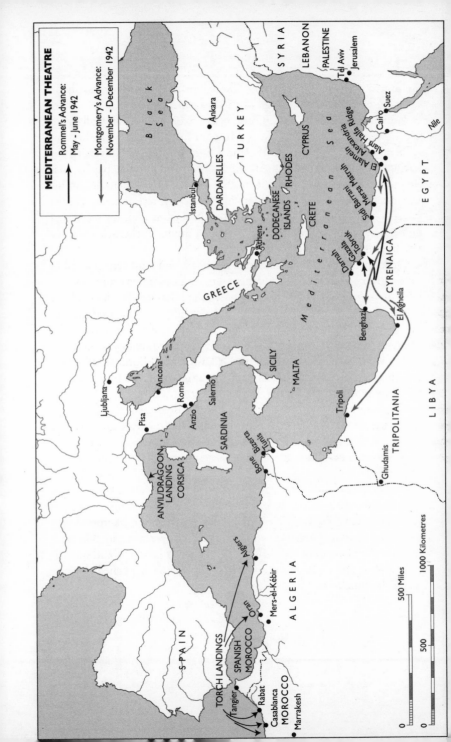

MEDITERRANEAN THEATRE

Rommel's Advance:
May – June 1942

Montgomery's Advance:
November – December 1942

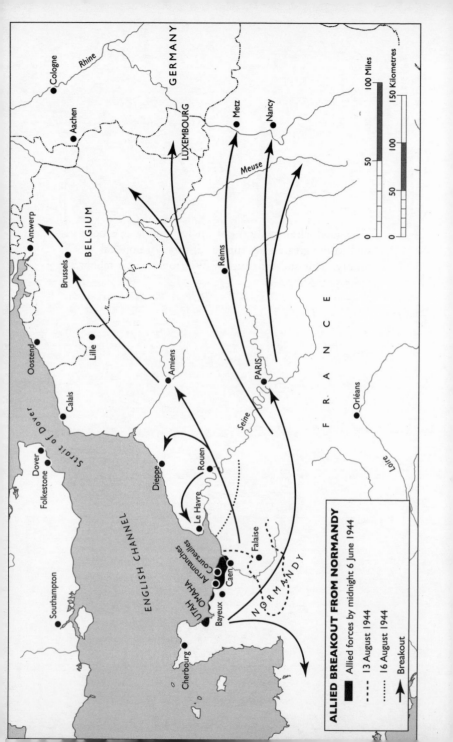

ALLIED BREAKOUT FROM NORMANDY

Allied forces by midnight 6 June 1944
13 August 1944
16 August 1944
Breakout

Part I

'The good, clean tradition of English politics has been . . .
sold to the greatest adventurer of modern political
history. This sudden coup by Winston and his rabble is a
serious disaster.'

(R.A. Butler, 10 May 1940.)

I

The War of Words

There was never any doubt that Churchill would write a history of the Second World War if he lived to see its end. Even if he had not repeatedly said he would, he had never been involved in a military enterprise without recording his experiences, either as a book or in journalism.

He was proud of the fact that throughout his life he had supported his family and an elevated lifestyle by his pen. Between 1898 and 1958 he wrote fifty-four volumes. By adding in his final speeches, a 1962 compilation of his early articles and eight books published posthumously, he produced seventy-four volumes and, including articles, published letters, speeches and books, a total output of about 15 million words.[1]

His first book, *The Story of the Malakand Field Force*, an account of his experiences on the Afghan frontier, was published when he was only twenty-three. He had already written many newspaper articles, describing his experiences as an observer of the Cuban Civil War in 1895. In India, as well as composing his story of the Field Force he was sending reports both to the *Daily Telegraph* and the *Allahabad Pioneer*. He was also writing short stories and working on his one novel, *Savrola*.

So it went on. In Egypt in 1898 he was writing for the *Morning Post* and *The Times*. The articles for the *Morning Post*, he told his mother, would 'act as foundations and as scaffolding for my book'. That book, *The River War*, was published at the end of 1899. By then he was in South Africa, which similarly provided material for publication.

All of this can be seen as preparation for his remarkable survey of the First World War, *The World Crisis*. At the Admiralty, Munitions and the War Office, Churchill had been at the centre of the direction of the war, and the history he published between 1923 and 1931 is detailed, remarkably accurate and still very well worth reading. His vivid descriptions and dramatic prose are undergirded by the authority of a mass of statistical data.

But in another respect, too, *The World Crisis* foreshadows the still more monumental history of the Second World War. He is the hero as well as the narrator, prompting Arthur Balfour's celebrated quip: 'I hear that Winston has written a book about himself and called it *The World Crisis*'. Churchill appears to be at the centre of events, dominating, directing and controlling them. His vision and his initiatives are those that count.

In the course of the Second World War he did not disguise the fact that his account of the conflict would be equally subjective. When a companion wondered what history would make of events, he famously replied, 'I know, because I intend to write the history'. On another occasion he gave the same response, though more elliptically, to the observation that it would be interesting to see what the verdict of history would be: 'That will depend on who writes the history'.

These, then, were to be the hallmarks of *The Second World War*: massive quotation of official documents, supporting a particular and skewed account of the historic events of the years 1940 to 1945. The treatment was to be noble, like the magnificent Gibbonian prose in which the story was told: the pettinesses, confusion, bungling and ignoble squabbling which are so much the essence of history are swept from his sanitised pages to give way to myth, drama and inspiration.

The Second World War, like *The World Crisis*, runs to six volumes; but the second series of volumes is bigger than the first: it extends to nearly 2 million words. Something like 12 per cent of these words is contained in appendices, in which official minutes and papers are quoted in part or whole. Churchill's approach to these papers was very simple: 'They are mine. I can publish them'. The constitutional position was much more opaque, and all that can be said with certainty is that Churchill was quite wrong. All the same, for a variety of reasons, many of them depending on rules which he himself had drawn up before surrendering office in 1945, he was able to take with him a substantial volume of his 'own' minutes and telegrams. He also had the right to consult an even bigger volume of papers, which was left in the government's hands. Furthermore, although government consent was required to quote from official documents and despite the fact that the Cabinet Secretary, Sir Edward Bridges, was anxious to avoid a repetition of the rash of memoirs based on official papers that occurred after the First World War, Churchill was accorded a very special dispensation.

The government came to think of his memoirs as having a quasi-official status and representing a statement for the historical record in the interests of the nation.

There were distortions in his narrative. The war in the Pacific is dealt with very sketchily, and there is no acknowledgement at all that it was Russia which really won the war in Europe. These faults reflect the egotistical nature of Churchill's project. His account was the sort of story that Julius Caesar told, history created by Great Men, events moulded by titans. When Eisenhower's naval assistant, Harry Butcher, published his diaries in 1946, Churchill wrote to his old colleague: 'The Articles are, in my opinion, altogether below the level upon which such matters should be treated. Great events and personalities are all made small when passed through the medium of the small mind.'[2]

The archival approach and the self-justifying process came together: because the documentary evidence more readily available consisted of Churchill's minutes and directives, not the responses to them, the picture that he painted was of events which he galvanised, and in which others' roles were minimised or completely excluded. This was resented by some, and the reaction of Sir Alan Brooke, later Viscount Alanbrooke, Chief of the Imperial General Staff for most of the war, will particularly be noted later in this narrative. Lord Reith, who had been a disappointing Minister of Information and was no friend of Churchill, complained, 'Winston prints in his war book innumerable directives and never once lets us see a single answer'.

In a fascinating piece of scholarly detective work, Professor David Reynolds has revealed the remarkable history of the writing of Churchill's history.[3] Sir Norman Brook, Bridges' successor as Cabinet Secretary, became less a censor than a co-author, and actively helped, drafting chunks of the narrative. Other public servants also made contributions. The price of government approval was a certain amount of vetting, but political control of the narrative stemmed less from the Labour government, in power when the first volumes appeared, than from Churchill himself. Even in opposition, but particularly when he was in power again after 1951, he distorted the historical record for political reasons.

In his second ministry he was greatly preoccupied by the tragic sense that the victory of 1945 would be succeeded by another war, even more terrible than the last. Nothing was to be done which might prejudice the chances of avoiding that disaster. Differences with Stalin were minimised, and in particular the tensions in the relationship with

America and the increasing divergence of the views of the two allies were
almost written out. By the time that the last volumes were appearing,
Eisenhower, the wartime Supreme Commander, was President of the
United States, and the true nature of Anglo-American relations by the
end of the war is accordingly scarcely hinted at.

There was some criticism of the history as the successive volumes
were published. Emmanuel Shinwell adapted Balfour and said that
Churchill had written a novel with himself as the chief character.
Michael Foot, though generally well disposed, spoke of Churchill
'clothing his personal vindication in the garb of history'.[4] Other
criticisms were made, both in regard to detail and to the nature of
the books, but they were overshadowed by the vast preponderance of
favourable reviews. In so far as criticism was noticed at all, it was largely
discredited because it came from those who had never been Churchill's
supporters.

The publication of the six volumes was the literary phenomenon of
the time. Each volume was published in America before Britain, and a
series of different editions was published in each country, as well as
elsewhere: concurrent Canadian, Australian, Taiwanese and book club
editions appeared with translations in almost every language in Europe,
including Russian. Editions in the remaining languages of the world
followed. Among the various printings which subsequently appeared
were paperbacks, and in addition to publication in book form, the
history was serialised in Britain, America, Australia and other countries.
The first volume appeared in forty-two editions of the *Daily Telegraph*.[5]
In Britain alone the hardback six volumes were printed in quantities of
about 250,000 each, and in the case of the early volumes they sold out
within hours.

Churchill never claimed that his book represented the whole story: 'I
do not describe this as history, for that belongs to another generation.
But I claim with confidence that it is a contribution to history which
will be of service to the future.' Those closest to the centre of affairs
knew well that Churchill had not been alone in controlling events and
that he was justifying himself before history and enhancing his personal
role. But no one wished to destroy a myth that flattered not just
Churchill, but Britain collectively – and indeed the American allies. The
story he told was one of resolve, endurance and heroism. There was a
collective collusion in perpetuating the legend that he was creating. To
do otherwise would have minimised the nation's achievement as well as
Churchill's and, particularly in the austere days of post-war Britain

when there was little else to celebrate, it would have been close to treachery to question the way in which victory had been won.

In the years that followed, many studies of component parts have altered views of aspects of the Second World War, but they have done little to dislodge from the popular mind the account of the war as Churchill gave it. It is doubtful now if the Second World War will ever be separated from the aura of heroic unity against evil that separates it from the study of other conflicts in history.

In Churchill's lifetime, publications like Brooke's diaries and those of General Sir John Kennedy made little impact on his reputation or that of his history. One or two publications in America had equally little effect, and his standing there is probably higher now than ever, and certainly higher than it is in his own country. In 1966, Lord Moran published his diaries. As his doctor, he had seen Churchill in his more vulnerable moments and the picture he drew was suggestive of weakness and doubt. In reality, although Churchill had treated Moran with great kindness and drew him into his own household, the doctor was never privy to the real secrets of the war and was not present at the meetings that mattered. Churchill talked incessantly, threw out ideas and thought aloud. Moran recorded what he claimed to have heard, sometimes in suspicious detail. He set out his story at length – although some elements were omitted: he makes no mention of the substantial financial provisions that Churchill made for his family. His account is fascinating and often informative, but is written from a limited perspective.

In the event it did more to enhance the Churchillian legend than to reduce it: Churchill's intimates, under the editorship of Sir John Wheeler-Bennett, and with the active encouragement of Clementine Churchill, published *Action this Day: Working with Churchill* in 1968, and very effectively displaced the Moran account with a picture of a vital, decisive and stimulating war leader, whose judgement and intuitive vision was the indispensable source of victory. Churchill himself could not have hoped for more.

One of the contributors to *Action this Day* was Churchill's former Private Secretary and subsequently his most devoted defender, John Colville. In his *The Churchillians* of 1981 he developed his theme and in his diaries and *The Fringes of Power: Downing Street Diaries 1939–1955*, he supplied a substantial volume of data with which to support it. His books are not the only ones on which the Churchillian legend now rests.

At a certain level serious efforts have been made to reappraise Churchill, and to assess him according to normal historical criteria.[6] There have also been more generalised attacks by David Irvine and Clive Ponting. A recent example, written with great gusto, is Gordon Corrigan's *Blood, Sweat and Arrogance, and the Myths of Churchill's War* (2006). The broadest revisionist attack was John Charmley's *Churchill, The End of Glory: A Political Biography* (1993), which received more publicity than it might have done because of a favourable review by Alan Clark. Charmley is concerned to cut Churchill down to size, determined – as Sir Michael Howard pointed out – never to give him the benefit of the doubt.[7]

While his thesis is not entirely clear, Charmley appears to favour appeasement and to think that Halifax and Chamberlain were right to wish to seek peace with Germany in 1940. He makes the point that by standing out against Hitler, Britain only won the war at the cost of financial bankruptcy and loss of world power. It was on this point that Alan Clark agreed with him, though Britain would not have retained much world power, and probably not much financial power either, if Hitler had dominated the world as he planned to do.

The fact that Britain was weak and diminished by 1945 is in itself neither particularly startling nor noteworthy. What is interesting is to consider why this was the corollary of victory and whether things could have been done better.

While it is true, as this book seeks to emphasise, that as the years went by, Churchill had less and less control over the war and increasingly became America's humiliated and ignored petitioner, that was a fate infinitely less abject than being a British Pétain. Churchill had to work within the circumstances that existed. It is clear now, as his own history never revealed, that at many levels his room for manoeuvre was limited. He had to fight to have his strategy adopted, to the extent it was. He frequently failed. He had to fight against the Americans; he had to fight against British generals and the Chief of the Imperial General Staff. The Free French alliance was often much more trouble than it was worth. The backing of his own party could not be relied upon in the House of Commons, and the War Cabinet overruled him from time to time. Sometimes he lacked even domestic support.

These various sources of obstruction have been dealt with individually: they are brought together in this volume not to emphasise Churchill's weaknesses and failures, but rather to suggest that what he did is all the more remarkable in the face of such opposition.

Churchillism may have been overdone; so has revisionism, if that consists of a bleak enumeration of the ways in which Britain's standing in the world was diminished as a result of the war. It is time for post-revisionism, by which I mean an analysis of some of the factors by which Churchill was constrained.

It is the argument of this book that in the West it was Churchill, more than anyone else, who devised the strategy that won the war, and that he succeeded in doing so despite the efforts and interventions of less far-seeing strategists who were motivated by sectional concerns or, in the case of the Americans, by a desire to mould the polity and economy of a post-war world. In the course of this narrative there will be numerous occasions where Churchill's will be seen to be the broader vision and the more inspired concept. But not always; and his short-comings are also recorded.

The book attempts to bring together the characters, events and trends that tended to limit Churchill's freedom of action, to explore the extent to which he was able to resist the impeding factors and to see how far he or others were in the right when there were differences. Other, structural constraints over which he had little or no control, such as problems of mobilisation, foreign exchange and trade, also of course bore down upon him.

I have tried to strike a balance between a discussion of themes and a sequential narrative treatment of events in order to give a comprehensible history of the war. I have sought to concentrate on the western war, and the Pacific dimension appears only when unavoidable. Relations with Russia are only slightly more prominent, and in order to contain the book within reasonable compass are not discussed at length. Stalin was in any event the ally from whom Churchill might reasonably have expected trouble, though for much of the war he proved surprisingly reliable.

In 1940 Churchill was a political outsider, widely distrusted by his own party, vulnerable and not expected to last. The Crown and what was not then called the Establishment did not greatly like him. Senior naval commanders and many senior army officers regarded him with a degree of hostility. He had to weld together a new means of political control over the service chiefs, and by slow degrees he consolidated his political position.

It was not until the outcome of the Second Battle of El Alamein in November 1942 that he was safe from imminent deposition. From then for a time he was dominant in the Atlantic Alliance and was generally able to bend his military advisers to his will. It was a period he enjoyed, but a short one. As early as the Casablanca Conference his own service chiefs were beginning to gain in confidence, and increasingly the Allied Joint Chiefs sidelined both Roosevelt and Churchill, whom they described as 'paltering' at some of the conferences. By the time of the Teheran Conference at the end of 1943 he was a relatively negligible figure in the Alliance, and even at home his own party felt able to rebel, for instance over Yalta and even over teachers' pay.

He had little time or interest for the crucial domestic political planning that was going on by this stage in the war. It involved Conservative politicians such as Sir John Anderson and Rab Butler as well as Labour Ministers, but the fact that this was not generally recognised may account for the final blow, which Churchill felt so acutely, the defeat at the 1945 general election.

It has been estimated that about 1,633 books have now been written about Churchill.[8] No apology is made for adding to that total. No one who is interested by this ever-fascinating sport of nature who emerged at a critical moment in the history of the world and affected that history for the better is disappointed to see another book about him.

One of the most moving pictures of Churchill is of him in old age, at table, despairingly saying that his whole life had been a failure. 'I have worked hard all my life, but what have I achieved? Nothing.' Of course this was the most monstrous misappreciation of his enormous achievements. His wonderful buoyancy had succumbed to age and an impaired circulation. But what lay behind this sense that all he had done for his country had been negated? That is what this book is about.

The Semblance of Power

The debate over the Norway campaign brought Churchill to power. He could equally well have been its victim. Far more than any other Minister, he had been intimately involved in the Norway campaign, and his conduct was certainly not free from fault. There were many in the Commons who would have been glad to see him fall. Fortunately for him the preoccupation of activists on both sides of the House was not Churchill but Chamberlain. Dissident Tories had finally thrown off tribal loyalties and fear of a savage Whips' office, and had nerved themselves to join with the opposition in tearing down a Prime Minister whom they believed incapable of a successful prosecution of the war. Churchill could not be allowed to get in the way. His interventions to acknowledge his own responsibility were brushed aside, and only served to emphasise his loyalty. In later life he frequently referred to the exquisite circumstances in which every avowal of culpability was met with an expression of support. He emerged from the debate with his position strengthened and not weakened.

All the same it was initially far from clear that he, or anyone else, would be replacing Chamberlain as Prime Minister. Although the proceedings in the House had assumed the character of a Vote of Censure when the Opposition declared its intention of forcing a vote, what had begun on 7 May 1940 was technically only a debate on an Adjournment Motion. And the government did secure a majority despite the strength of the vote against it on the evening of 9 May. At ten o'clock on the following morning Churchill was told that Chamberlain had decided to stay on as Prime Minister.

Hitler changed his mind for him. This was the day on which he launched his Western Offensive and entered France. At eleven o'clock Churchill was summoned to Downing Street for his momentous meeting with Chamberlain and Halifax. The accounts of that historic confrontation vary in details, and Churchill amazingly gets the date wrong; but in their essentials they hang together. Brendan Bracken and Kingsley Wood, a staunch Chamberlainite who had suddenly jumped ship, presumably because he had heard that his chief was ready to drop him as the price for staying in office, secured an undertaking that Churchill would say little or nothing, and when Halifax put the critical question to him, 'Can you see any reason, Winston, why in these days a Peer should not be Prime Minister?', he turned his back, looked out on Horse Guards Parade and maintained the silence which he described in his memoirs as seeming 'longer than the two minutes which one observes in the commemoration of Armistice Day'.[1]

Halifax, the successor that Chamberlain and the King would have preferred, broke the silence by saying that, as a peer, he could not carry out the responsibilities of Prime Minister. Well, maybe, but it seems more likely that he simply wanted to take the job at a more propitious moment. Earlier in the day he had told Rab Butler, his Parliamentary Under-Secretary, that he felt he could do it.[2] But in the current circumstances he did not have the stomach for the task: literally so – he felt sick at the prospect and when Margesson failed to make a choice between him and Churchill earlier in the day, 'my stomach ache continued'.[3] If he had wanted the job then and there he could have taken it without any great constitutional difficulty. The desperate circumstances were very different from those that had, only just, ruled out Curzon, as a peer, from the premiership as recently as 1923. Halifax would have had the support of the Labour and Liberal parties, and he was infinitely more acceptable to the Conservatives.

The King was certainly not initially a supporter of Churchill, the man who had championed his brother during the Abdication Crisis; and his mother, Queen Mary, expressed the Royal Family's views when she urged Colville to remain with Chamberlain and not to work for the new Prime Minister. When Chamberlain demitted office the King told him he had been unfairly treated, and that he thought his successor should be Halifax.[4] The King did indeed cause some problems in Churchill's early months in office: he was unnecessarily obstructive, for instance in opposing the appointment of Beaverbrook as Minister of Aircraft Production and the conferment of a privy councillorship on Bracken. For all his devoted royalism, Churchill did not allow his monarch to get in the way of waging the war, and the King soon came to realise the worth of his First Minister, and a mood of mutual respect was established.

Before the day was out Churchill was Prime Minister, and in one of the most memorable passages in his history of the war he described how as he went to bed he was 'conscious of a profound sense of relief. At last I had the authority to give directions over the whole scene.'[5] That was fiction. He was the prisoner of his enemies in his own party, sustained by his former enemies in the Opposition. He was conscious now and for a considerable time to come that his hold on power was tenuous and critically dependent on delivering results. There was a widespread view that he would not be Prime Minister for long.[6]

Even within the War Cabinet he could not be confident of getting his way. Powerful figures saw him as no more than a stopgap, and the bulk of the Conservative parliamentary party viewed him with ill-disguised distaste. At about the same time as Churchill was going to bed conscious of his profound relief, Rab Butler, Lord Dunglass, the future Sir Alec Douglas-Home ('the kind of people surrounding Winston are the scum') and John Colville, Chamberlain's Private Secretary, met to drink a champagne toast to Chamberlain, 'the King over the water'. Colville later recalled the distaste with which he and his colleagues saw the appeasers, Sir Horace Wilson, Dugdale and Lord Dunglass, replaced by the arrival of Churchill's 'myrmidons', Brendan Bracken, Lindemann and Desmond Morton. 'Seldom can a Prime Minister have taken office with "the Establishment" as it would now be called, so dubious of the choice and so prepared to find its doubts justified.'[7]

Colville had to adjust to a dramatic change in tempo as he started to work for the dynamic Churchill, rather than the dignified, correct and very traditional Chamberlain. Government business was now transacted 24 hours a day and 365 days a year, with little rest for the Private Secretaries, who followed their master wherever he might be. Chamberlain never took his Private Secretaries to Chequers, where he was connected to the rest of the world by just a single telephone – in the pantry.

A generation earlier it would have been difficult to overstate the Conservative Party's dislike for Churchill. During the First War it neither forgave nor forgot his treachery in crossing the floor to join the Liberals. As President of the Board of Trade, allied closely to Lloyd George, his speeches were intemperate and sometimes ill-judged and the Establishment, including Edward VII, found it inexcusable that someone of his background should seek, as they saw it, to tear down the institutions they prized. In the First World War, the Tories had insisted on his removal from the Admiralty as the price of coalition, and the suspicion, even hatred behind that demand was more typical of the party's sentiments than Baldwin's rehabilitation of Churchill in the 1920s.

These memories were still strong among the traditionalists; younger and more progressive Tories were unimpressed by what they had seen as antediluvian resistance to the India Bill. There was additionally a general view that despite his aristocratic, ducal connections, he was not quite a gentleman.

Even more than his policy over the India Bill, Churchill's maverick championing of Edward VIII during the Abdication Crisis, and the talk of a King's Party, did him incalculable harm. Many thought that the episode had ended his political career, and many certainly hoped that was the case.

Churchill was always too mercurial a personality, too big a persona, to be contained comfortably in any one political party, and the Conservative Party under Chamberlain was a particularly uncomfortable place. Chamberlain had considerable abilities, but the degree of his control over the party was unappealing, almost dictatorial. Independence of thought was not encouraged. The whips under Margesson were ruthless in their tactical use of spying and dirty tricks. Their behaviour in the Perth and Kinross by-election, when the Duchess of Atholl stood as an independent candidate, is a good example. Fifty Conservative MPs were sent north to tell the electorate that a vote for the Duchess was a vote for war. Local landowners were induced to bribe and threaten their employees to ensure they did not vote for her.

Chamberlain looked continuously for evidence of conspiracies, and manipulated the press shamelessly to support the government. It was not a good period for parliamentary democracy. The Conservative Party generally knuckled under, and accepted a culture in which disloyalty to the leader was regarded as tantamount to treason. It followed that Churchill was excoriated by the unthinking majority of Tory party members in and out of the Houses of Parliament. It was largely pressure from outside the party that caused Chamberlain to bring Churchill back to the Admiralty on the outbreak of war.

Churchill's loyalty to Chamberlain thereafter was total, and indeed matured into a romantic regard for his chief, but Chamberlain and those close to him did not respond in kind. In the aftermath of Norway, Chips Channon recorded that Lord Dunglass had asked him whether he thought that, 'Winston should be deflated. Ought he to leave the Admiralty?'[8] Chamberlain was said to be thinking along these lines, and Nicolson reported that the whips were briefing against Churchill and representing Norway as 'another Churchill fiasco', an allusion to a popular view of the Dardanelles.[9]

The conspirator's punishment is that he sees conspiracies where they do not exist, and Chamberlainites suspected Churchill of plotting against his leader. But he was scrupulously loyal. When asked to throw in his lot with those who wished to see Chamberlain replaced, and despite the fact that he would have been the replacement, he repeatedly replied that he had 'signed on for the voyage'. And after the vote in the Norway debate he wrote to his captain, 'This has been a damaging debate, but you have a good majority. Do not take the matter grievously to heart.'

Even after he had become the captain of the ship, he was viewed by the traditionalists as being – at best – a necessary and temporary expedient in the exigencies of the times. Nancy Dugdale, the wife of a junior whip, wrote to her husband, now in the army, 'I could hardly control myself . . . W.C. is really the counterpart of Goering in England, full of the desire for blood, "Blitzkrieg", and bloated with ego and over-feeding, the same treachery running through his veins, punctuated by heroics and hot air.' In reply her husband referred to his Prime Minister's colleagues in terms that he might have been applying to Hitler's: 'All those reptile satellites – Duff-Cooper – Bob Boothby – Brendan Bracken, etc. – will ooze into jobs they are utterly unsuited for. All we are fighting for will go out of public life. I regard this as a greater disaster than the invasion of the Low Countries'.[10]

But greatly as Churchill was hated by the Chamberlainites and the rank and file, he was far from warmly regarded by the anti-appeasers. His little group of supporters was not part of the mainstream of opposition to the government. To an extent he stood away from that opposition, partly because he had hoped for office from Chamberlain early in 1939, and then, after the outbreak of war, because of loyalty to the head of the government of which he was part.

But, more importantly, the anti-appeasers did not want him even if he were available. The main group of anti-appeasers, 'the glamour boys', was led by Eden. In the course of time Eden sometimes seemed to be Churchill's favourite son, but that was far from the case. For political reasons that were not of Churchill's making, it seemed clear for perhaps fifteen years that Eden would succeed Churchill, and Churchill did nothing to undermine that assumption, but the older man had no great enthusiasm for the younger, whom he thought weak and of limited ability. He and Eden got on well enough, and Eden married his niece, but Churchill was much more warmly disposed to others – for instance Macmillan and, strangest of all, that most enthusiastic former appeaser,

Rab Butler. The Prime Minister frequently disagreed with Eden when the latter was Foreign Secretary, particularly over France and Russia, and some of Churchill's rebukes were fairly stinging.

Eden for his part was entirely loyal to Churchill, although there were times during the war when he might just have displaced him, but the relationship was not an easy one. Eden had been Baldwin's protégé. He had benefited from Churchill's eclipse and as a contender for the succession to Chamberlain kept at a distance from the older man, his rival.

The glamour boys were vastly more numerous than the handful of Churchillites, and there was little common membership of the two groups. The mainstream anti-appeasers were also much more substantial in terms of political weight. They included Leo Amery, Ronald Tree, Bobbity Cranborne, Edward Spears, Duff Cooper and Macmillan. Macmillan was the only one of the group who was also close to Churchill.

Although Eden's personality was associated with the group, and it was probably he who lent it glamour, he was not always present at its meetings and offered little leadership. He was always willing to wound, but not to kill. Repeatedly he appeared to gear himself up for a major assault, only to back down at the last moment. Amery was a more effective leader, but collectively the group feared to bell the cat. In the period between the beginning of the war and the Norway Debate, innumerable opportunities for the anti-appeasers to ambush Chamberlain were lost, and the culture of loyalty to the leader was such that even when the Norway vote took place many Conservative members, some of them veterans of the Great War, went into the opposition lobby in tears.

The men who voted against their party at the cost of such emotional pain were all the more appalled that the man for whom they had made such a sacrifice rewarded not them but their opponents when he took office. He had never been one of them before, and he continued to stand apart. Thus Churchill entered office hated and despised by the appeasers and without the affection of their critics.

Domestic Support

Many regarded the rackety friends whose company stimulated Churchill as distasteful: Clementine Churchill was frequently a critic and often absented herself from the dinner table when she disapproved of the company, dining from a tray in her room.

Churchill married Clementine Hozier on 12 September 1908. He was thirty-three and Clementine twenty-three. He had proposed unsuccessfully to two other women and Clementine had been courted by another man for two years and was twice secretly engaged to him. She had also been left in a maze with Lord Bessborough in an unsuccessful attempt to prompt a proposal.[1] During her short engagement to Churchill, Clementine hesitated, apparently because of her fiancé's commitment to public life. Churchill sought to reassure her; and her brother Bill wrote to her to say that she could not be seen to break-off a third engagement and humiliate Churchill.

Churchill wonderfully wrote of his wedding that he 'lived happily ever after'. So he did at one level, but his use of the fairy-tale formula is revealing: he certainly loved Clementine for the rest of his life, but rather as an idealised romantic creation. The fact that so much of their communication is preserved in a vast body of correspondence points up a certain contrivance in the relationship. The correspondence is often ineffably touching. Churchill's last letters to his wife are very moving, like one of 1 April 1963 written in the frail hand of an 88-year-old husband to Clementine on her seventy-eighth birthday:

> My Darling One,
>   This is only to give you
>   my fondest love and kisses
>   *a hundred times repeated*
>   I am a pretty dull and

paltry scribbler; but my stick as it writes carries my
heart along with it.
                    Your ever & always
                              W.

Some of the later letters are poignant in other ways too. There is one
in which Churchill, the most generous, often too generous, of men,
defends himself with dignity and pain against the charge that he was
being mean to Clementine. Even at a much earlier stage she could be
thoughtless and hurtful. When Churchill was in the trenches in 1916,
Clementine wrote to him saying that she hoped she would see a little
more of him alone when he was next home: 'We are still young, but
Time flies, stealing love away and leaving only friendship which is very
peaceful but not very stimulating or warming.' Churchill, the romantic,
was upset: 'Oh my darling do not write of "friendship" to me – I love
you more each month that passes and feel the need of you and all your
beauty. My precious charming Clementine . . .'
    During this spell in the trenches in the aftermath of the Darda-
nelles, Churchill frequently talked of abandoning the military life and
coming back to London where he felt his future lay. Although he
could perfectly honourably have done so, and in so doing leave a
situation in which he was in constant danger from which he made no
effort to shelter himself, Clementine told him, again and again, that it
would be better that he stayed in France. She seemed curiously able to
appear more concerned for his place in history than his place in the
domestic circle.
    Throughout the course of their marriage she repeatedly felt it
incumbent on her to give him advice that he did not want to hear
and which on occasions he found distressing. We cannot know whether
or how often she bit her tongue or put away her pen; what can be seen is
that she frequently proffered advice and information that he would
rather not have had. As he rarely paid any attention to her advice, it
might have been thought that she would have realised that it would
have been kinder to remain silent.
    At the end of 1934 Clementine took an extended break and went on
a cruise with Lord Moyne (formerly Walter Guinness), who was going
to Indonesia on an improbable quest to capture a large reptile known as
a komodo dragon. Churchill had been invited but could not go, and
they were apart for five months. He devotedly kept in touch with her,
sending an unbroken stream of letters to tell her of events at home. Far

away, Clementine fell in love with one of her companions, a handsome
art dealer named Terence Phillip. They were constantly together. Mary
Soames, in her biography of her mother, very properly does not tell us
whether the relationship was consummated, and indeed she may not
know. Her mother described the episode to her with the words, '*C'était
une vraie connaissance de ville d'eau*', which does not take us very far
forward.[2]

But Churchill cannot have been unaware of what had happened. It is
impossible to imagine him allowing himself to be in a similar situation.
When Mrs Reggie Fellowes made a determined assault on his marital
fidelity at the Ritz in Paris he had stood firm,[3] and he must have been
very deeply pained that Clementine was not equally resolute. There is
no hint in the correspondence of any recrimination or reproach.

Throughout her life she remained a committed Liberal. She hated the
Conservative Party, except for Churchill's constituency association.[4]
But her attitude was a little confused. On 1 September 1940, Colville
recorded in his diary, 'It amused me slightly that Mrs C., who does
nothing but profess democratic and radical sentiments, should put off
inviting any of the officers to dine until the guard consists of the
Coldstream. The Oxford and Bucks Light Infantry were never invited
inside.'[5]

The list of her husband's friends of whom she approved would be
shorter than the list of those of whom she disapproved. Just a few of the
latter were F.E. Smith, Churchill's cousin, 'Sunny', Duke of Marlbor-
ough, Frederick Guest and Beaverbrook. She could be very rude even to
people who were not on the disapproved list if she thought their
behaviour unacceptable. When Montgomery, for example, made a
typical, disparaging remark about politicians, he was flayed and told to
leave her house: he was only allowed to stay after abject apologies. Even
Jock Colville, though he became a warm admirer and was to find many
complimentary things to say about Clementine, acknowledged that
'She could . . . display an acidity of tongue before which the tallest trees
would bend, and she would occasionally give vent to uncontrollable
temper. The storms were terrifying in their violence . . .'[6] Or from his
diary for 22 October 1940: 'Mrs C. considers it one of her missions in
life to put people in their place, and prides herself on being outspoken'.[7]

Many of Churchill's friends were arrivistes, a trifle shady, not serious,
undesirable in her eyes. But in some cases her objections are difficult to
understand: it is not easy to see what damage could have been done to
his career when, in old age, he enjoyed some distraction from his

increasing frailty in the hospitality and thoughtfulness of Onassis and of Emery and Wendy Reves on the Mediterranean and in the South of France. Wendy Reves, his publisher's wife, took enormous pains to make Churchill happy at La Pausa on the Côte d'Azur, when spells of happiness were becoming rare. He was fond of her: 'She is young, she is beautiful, she is kind'. There was inevitably talk, but it was foolish, uninformed and absurd. Yet Lady Churchill refused to allow Wendy Reves to attend her husband's funeral. Wendy Reves described Churchill's marriage as 'a myth' and in the lengthy periods apart, and in the correspondence, moving though it is, much of it written when both spouses were under the same roof, there is something about the relationship that seems artificial, though nurtured by romance and idealisation.

The 'lived happily ever after' description of his marriage hints at Churchill's capacity for romanticising, and the same idealisation occurs in relation to his mother. In *My Early Life*, in which he recorded her 'brilliant impression upon my childhood's eye', he said, 'She shone for me like the Evening Star. I loved her dearly – but at a distance.' That was not the fullest description of a glittering and remarkably predatory female. It is understandable that he failed to mention her reputed 200 affairs ('a suspiciously round number', said Roy Jenkins) and her various husbands, one a contemporary of her son and one younger still. But he drew a veil equally over the fact that she was a distant and neglectful mother and that his only exposure to love as a child was from his nurse, Mrs Everest.

It would be a wonderful understatement to say that marriage to Churchill was not easy. He was improvident, reckless and unpredictable. Clementine did not know how the story was to end: it could have been in bankruptcy and disgrace. Without the stimulation and excitement of her husband's career, she was perhaps more aware of their children's serious and sometimes tragic problems. She was acutely conscious of the perilous household finances. Throughout her life she suffered from debilitating and distressing periods of fatigue, anxiety and depression, for which the only treatment in these days was prolonged holidays for rest and recuperation. In other respects too her health was not strong. The index to the biography by her daughter, Lady Soames, contains references not only to nervous exhaustion, but also to miscarriage, operations, neuritis, streptococcal infection, shingles, broken shoulder and broken hips.

4

The Political Landscape

His wife felt that in the matter of his companions, and in other respects too, Churchill's judgement could be poor, and indeed the most frequent criticism, even from people who admired him in other respects, related to his judgement. Rab Butler, although a cerebral Tory, spoke for many when he described Churchill in 1940 as 'the greatest political adventurer of modern times . . . a half-breed American . . . The good clean tradition of English politics, that of Pitt as opposed to Fox, had been sold to the greatest adventurer of modern political history . . . the sudden coup of Winston and his rabble was a serious disaster and an unnecessary one'.[1] Beatrice Webb had earlier said that he had 'more of the American speculator than the English aristocrat'.

Many of his own party saw him as Butler did, and in the Commons Chamber, it was the Labour benches which cheered his early appearances as Prime Minister – largely simply because they liked him better than Chamberlain. For many weeks Churchill was received in embarrassing silence by the Tories. It was not until 4 July 1940, when Churchill had to give the news of the Royal Navy's destruction of the French fleet at Mers-el-Kébir that the Chief Whip, Margesson, decided to set an example. He stood up, turned and waved his order paper and his well-drilled minions joined him on their feet. Thereafter the Tories joined the Labour Party in cheering their chief.

His political position was extremely weak and he was aware of it. There were press campaigns against the retention of the Municheers. The *News Chronicle* and the *Daily Herald*, for instance, criticised Chamberlain and Kingsley Wood in particular ('No room for Deadweight.'[2]), and reported open discussion of resignations. But Churchill was not a free agent, and to the annoyance of the press and of some of his own small band of supporters, he retained most of his colleagues in the government, tainted though they were with appeasement. He represented this as a deliberate policy of conciliation and unity. To an extent it may have been, and he put the case against indicting the guilty men in a major speech to the House on 18 June 1940, in which he directly addressed the desire in the press and among the public for retribution against those who had left Britain so unprepared for war:

> There are many who would hold an inquest in the House of Commons on the conduct of the Governments – and of Parliaments, for they are in it too – during the years which led up to this catastrophe . . . Of this I am quite sure, that if we open a quarrel between the past and the present, we shall find that we have lost the future. Therefore, I cannot accept the drawing of any distinctions between Members of the present Government.

The retention of the men of Munich was certainly not entirely a voluntary gesture of magnanimity. He had no real choice. He privately asked the press to stop the campaign for the removal of the 'Guilty Men', explaining that given their strength in his party in the Commons, he had to rely on them. If he 'trampled on these men, as he could trample on them, they would set themselves against him, and in such internecine strife lay the Germans' best chance of victory'.

After making his key Cabinet appointments Churchill was very fully occupied in trying to stiffen French resistance, and he allowed Margesson, the personification of Chamberlain's policy of discipline and control, to allocate junior appointments, restrained with little obvious success by Bracken as the representative of the new regime. Overwhelmingly the administration was dominated by the Municheers. Churchill's hands were so tied that not only did he have to keep most of them in the Cabinet, but he had also little to offer his own loyal supporters: those who toppled Chamberlain received scant rewards. Amery, who had done more than anyone else to engineer the defenestration, was in the lowly India Office. Eden did receive the War Office, but that meant less than it sounds, as the real decisions were taken by the Minister of Defence: he was not even in the War Cabinet. Duff Cooper might have expected to do better than Minister for Information, although he did not make much of a job of it. He proved to be unpopular; sending his son, John Julius, to Canada was not a good political signal, however humanly understandable it may have been. Churchill told his old friend that he was said to be spending too much time at home and 'trying to run the Ministry of Information from

Bognor'. Butler soon reported that the 'political stockbrokers' were 'selling Duff Coopers'; he was replaced by Bracken (Churchill told Bracken that Cooper 'had failed completely. It just shows that it doesn't do to harness a thoroughbred to a dung-cart.'[3] Neither man seems to have been upset by this reflection.)

Boothby and Macmillan were disappointed not to be given offices of consequence. Bracken was only a PPS. On the other hand, even the Whips, notably Margesson and the Scottish Whip, James Stuart, the dark and oppressive enforcers of the unedifying Chamberlain days, remained in office. Boothby thought that Churchill resented those who had put him in power.

The under-rewarded supporters were far from happy. At a personal level they were disappointed, but more altruistically they were also aghast that having finally nerved themselves to dispose of an administration they thought incapable of winning the war, they now saw the same inadequate personalities continuing in office. The message seemed to be that there had been no real change of regime. They agonised about whether to accept what they were offered, until Amery counselled them to make the most of what they had. They even dared to voice their concerns to Churchill, but were told to get on with things in their menial roles. He could do nothing else. He still had no real power base in a party which did not generally like him. He knew that he was only tolerated for the moment because he might deliver results. If he did, real power might eventually come his way.[4]

Butler was a good observer, always slightly detached, amused by ironies. A tolerantly retained man of Munich himself, he summed up the government's strength (and weakness), 'If intrigue or attacks on the government grow to any great extent all we have to do is to pull the string of the toy dog of the 1922 Committee and make it bark. After a few staccato utterances it becomes clear that the government depends upon the Tory squires for its majority'.[5] That may have been satisfactory for Butler and the traditionalists, but the very source of Tory support spelled out the threat to Churchill: the backwoodsmen of the shires might have been prepared to rally round the government, but they would not necessarily rally round Churchill.

There was an example of the tensions even among ostensible loyalists on 17 June 1940 when Amery, Boothby, Macmillan and Lord Lloyd met to discuss their dissatisfaction with the way the war was being waged. Chamberlain got wind of what was happening and told Churchill. His response was that 'If there is any more of this nonsense they will go' and he told that to Amery. But his position was not as powerful as he was pretending.

There was no more loyalty among his more prominent colleagues. They still tended to regard their chief as Chamberlain, who remained the leader of the Conservative Party. Churchill was well aware of this: he wrote to Chamberlain on the day he succeeded him, 'To a large extent I am in yr hands'.[6] Chamberlain only renounced the hope of resuming the premiership after he developed cancer in October 1940 and until then remained leader of his party. He had discussed standing down in favour of Churchill in May 1940, but the new PM referred to his role as leader of a broad coalition and said that he should not lead any one political party.[7] After his illness Chamberlain wrote in his diary on 9 September 1940 that he had to 'adjust myself to the new life of a partially crippled man which is what I am. Any ideas of another Premiership after the war have gone. I know that is out of the question.'[8]

In understanding Churchill's weakness in the Conservative Party and in Parliament it helps to remember that when this question of the succession to the leadership of the Party arose, it was far from certain that the PM would even be a candidate. He was urged to take the position by Lieutenant-Colonel G.S. Harvie-Watt, an MP and government whip, when he met the Prime Minister at the Anti-Aircraft Battalion which he commanded near Redhill at the beginning of October 1940. Harvie-Watt advised him that 'it would be fatal if he did not lead the Conservative Party, as the bulk of the party was anxious that he should be Leader *now we are at war* [my emphasis].' Churchill was however still suspicious about the party and remembered how they had regarded him before the war. Harvie-Watt sought to reassure him that hostile views were now confined to a minority and that 'the mass of the party was with him. My strongest argument, however, and I felt this very much, was that it was essential for the PM to have his own party – a strong one with allies attracted from the main groups and especially the Opposition parties. But essentially he must have a majority and I was sure this majority could only come from the Conservative Party.' Harvie-Watt thought his advice had done his own career no good, but he became the PM's PPS nine months later and remained in that position until the end of the war.

Churchill was not just worried about his weakness in Parliament: he was concerned also about his weakness vis-à-vis Ministers, and he took the opportunity to sound Harvie-Watt out about this. The latter's advice was that with 'a strong army of MPs under you, Ministers would be won over or crushed.'[9]

When the leadership of the party finally fell vacant Churchill realised that he must seize it if he were not to be in the position of Lloyd George in coalition. Clementine took a different view: she argued that he would diminish his position as a national leader by accepting it. Clementine's advice was, as so often, ignored, but she urged her case vehemently. She hated the Conservatives, and her daughter recalled that that on this issue 'her latent hostility toward the Tory Party boiled over; there were several good ding-dong arguments between them'.[10]

Churchill himself was not a natural Tory. Long ago, in 1903, he had written to Lord Hugh Cecil, 'I hate the Tory Party, their men, their words & their methods', and thirty-six years later, just eighteen months before he became the party's leader, he wrote to Clementine of 'these dirty Tory hacks who would like to drive me out of the Party'.[11]

Although he became the leader of the Conservative Party at the end of 1940, he remained the prisoner of the rank and file for the following two years. Things only changed when he delivered victories. Then the Party became his prisoner, and so it remained until he resigned in 1955.

In the period before the victories started to flow Churchill had to face a great deal of criticism in the House. He was too much of a Commons man to find it demeaning, but he was very far from the Olympian leader that Roosevelt could be – and very different from the Axis warlords. From time to time he did resent the criticism that he faced when the margin between victory and defeat was very fine and he was working almost on a day-to-day basis to hold the line. He sometimes said, and he may well have meant it, that he had not realised how much time Parliament would take. He said to J.A. Spender in July 1941, 'You must remember that unlike the President I have to appear continuously before the legislature. Indeed I have had to give much more time to the House of Commons than I bargained for when the Ministry was formed.'[12]

Sir Alexander Cadogan, the Permanent Under-Secretary of State for Foreign Affairs, never overawed by Churchill (or indeed any politician), sometimes complained in his diary that the Prime Minister was absent from meetings because 'Winston is still working on his speech'. But, quite apart form the fact that an enduring part of the corpus of English literature was in the process of composition, and that public morale was being sustained, as a civil servant he overlooked the political importance of these speeches. They mattered in the House. The political observers like Channon, Duff Cooper and Nicolson, not all of them committed Churchillians, testify to the extent to which the speeches frequently turned the mood of the House and brought semi-detached back-benchers behind the government.

The great set speeches were not the only hurdles that Churchill had to surmount in the House. He also had to take part in debate, and in 1940 he had succeeded Chamberlain not only as Prime Minister, but also as Leader of the House. This combination of offices was usual, but not inevitable, until 1942. Then Churchill gave up the Leadership, and no Prime Minister has held the office since. But while he remained Leader he was obliged to attend the House and to submit to detailed questioning much more than he would have done simply as Prime Minister. Routine announcements on the business of the House opened the way for discussion of matters of procedure and convention that touched on the conduct of the war.

In addition to the brooding Municheers on the Tory Right, there was a bunch of busy backbenchers of both parties who made life difficult. Some were critical to an extent that suggested straightfor-ward ill will – Bevan may have been an example – but others acted from particular deeply held convictions, or sometimes just in response to bees in their bonnets. When Sir Roger Keyes was no longer on active service he came into the last category. He had been a great friend of Churchill and probably remained a devoted supporter, but he could be a nuisance, for example in the Secret Session after the loss of the *Prince of Wales* and the *Repulse*. Emmanuel Shinwell was constantly critical, but – from his perspective if not Churchill's – with constructive intent. There was a hard core of those who sought throughout the early years to replace Churchill at the centre of war direction with a supreme council of some sort. Their motivation lay in the fact that they continued to believe that he simply could not be trusted. The Earl of Winterton and Edgar Granville, a Liberal appeaser, were among those who regularly argued for change, and Geoffrey Mander, a Liberal, later Labour, was also vociferous until he became Sir Archibald Sinclair's PPS in 1942. Leslie Hore-Belisha, a National Liberal then Independent, who had been Secretary of State for War from 1937 to 1940, and a member of the War Cabinet until that year, never got over his removal. There were numerous others who joined with those men in making life difficult for Churchill when it was already difficult enough.

In debate and when dealing with ordinary business he was closely questioned not just on the large issues of the war, a legitimate subject of enquiry, but also on the niceties of paltry issues of alleged unconstitutional procedure, the powers of Ministers of State, the number of Ministers, and above all the constitution of the War Cabinet.

On 9 July 1941, for instance, Churchill had to put up with a lot of questioning from Hore-Belisha on the definition of the duties of a Minister of State, and the propriety of making ministerial appointments without first making a statement in the House.[13] Churchill was of course very adept at dealing with his critics, often contrasting what they said out of office with what they had said when in. He had been very good with Hore-Belisha a week earlier, when the former War Minister was querying the role of a Minister of State resident in the Middle East:

> I am sure that the House will not accuse me of wanting in respect or deference in every effort to serve them, but if the right hon. Gentleman wishes to make a criticism of what is widely accepted as a highly useful and important step in the appointment of a member of the War Cabinet to be resident at the seat of the Middle Eastern War, I daresay some Parliamentary opportunity will occur. I have no doubt that some answer will be made to him although whether the answer will satisfy his wide-ranging curiosity I cannot tell.[14]

It is hardly surprising that in a letter to Attlee and Lord Cranborne in December 1941 Churchill referred to the government's critics in the House of Commons as the 'snarlers and naggers'. It must have been a great relief when the snarlers and naggers and their tiresome questioning were followed in April 1941 by a sycophantic enquiry from his old Private Secretary, Commander Oliver Locker–Lampson: 'Is it not much better to wait and trust the Prime Minister?'[15]

There were always potential rivals. Although Halifax did not wish to be Prime Minister in May 1940, he almost certainly hoped that he would have the opportunity of taking over in more congenial circumstances before long. Chamberlain, as has been seen, envisaged returning. Even Lloyd George, Churchill's oldest parliamentary colleague and friend, hoped to displace him, telling his secretary on 3rd October 1940, 'I shall wait until Winston is bust'.[16]

In these early months of the war, particularly, there was a significant dissident block of about thirty MPs and ten peers led by the Labour

Member, Richard Stokes, which saw Lloyd George as its potential leader. At this point in the war, Lloyd George was still robust enough to be a credible leader of a much more significant body of opinion than Stokes' followers, and certainly did not rule himself out of returning to save the nation once again.

Preparation

The fact that, despite everything, Churchill was where he was rested on the undeniable recognition that he was supremely well qualified to direct the war. He was fond of reminding people that he seen active service in four continents in the course of his military career. Thus, when he went to the Front in the First World War to an active command, he reported to Clementine that he had already met most of the Staff in the course of his 'soldiering'. In 1909, after a field day with the Queen's Own Oxfordshire Yeomanry, in which he held a commission, he told Clementine that he thought he had more tactical vision than professional soldiers. 'I am sure I have the root of the matter in me – but never I fear in this state of existence will it have chance of flowering – in bright red blossom'.[1]

Between 1909 and 1939 that root had been well tended. When he became Prime Minister, he had not only been intermittently a member of the Cabinet since 1908 but also, continuously a member of the Committee for Imperial Defence from 1909. He had discharged important responsibilities at the Board of Trade, as Home Secretary, as Colonial Secretary and as Chancellor of the Exchequer, but also had experience in areas directly related to the conduct of war: First Lord of the Admiralty (twice), Minister of Munitions, Secretary of State for War and Secretary of State for Air. Few Prime Ministers had a wider experience of both government and a greater grasp of the machinery, the *business*, of government. Much of his success in getting his own way against opposition from the civil service and the military chiefs derived from the fact that he knew so well how the system worked.

As Secretary of State for War during the First World War he was able to observe the defects of the archaic machinery of military command, which he criticised afterwards in *The World Crisis* for its unbalanced nature. His comments on the undeserved status accorded to generals and admirals by the popular press were strongly expressed, but perfectly reasonable:

> A series of absurd conventions became established, perhaps in-evitably, in the public mind. The first and most monstrous of these was that the Generals and Admirals were more competent to deal with the broad issues of the war than abler men in other spheres of life. The General no doubt was an expert on how to move his troops, and the Admiral on how to fight his ships . . . but outside this technical aspect they were helpless and misleading arbiters in problems in whose solution the aid of the statesman, the financier, the manufacturer, the inventor, the psychologist was equally required.[2]

These were views formed by daily observation of the naval and military leaders throughout the First World War, and they were views from which Lloyd George, for instance, would not have dissented. They were not views of course with which the admirals and the generals would agree. Admiral Jellicoe, for instance, referred to Churchill's 'entire inability to realise his own limitations as a civilian . . . quite ignorant of naval affairs'.[3] But Generals and Admirals, like members of other closed professions, are conservative and resentful of interference from those who are in a position to give them directions without the same institutional background. During the First World War Churchill took a much more active role in running the naval war than any First Lord had previously done. Many ideas that the navy successfully adopted were his alone and there were innumerable technical advances which he pushed through in the face of resistance.

His remarks about the limitations of the military imagination must be kept in mind. They are at the heart of his relations with the generals and the general staff in the Second War. He thought he was at least as well qualified as the professionals to make judgements on professional issues. The professionals resented amateur interference, and their supporters still take that view. The truth is that war *is* far too important to be left to the generals, in the sense that no general in the Second World War at least had sufficient knowledge, let alone grasp, of the overall scene – military, economic, political – to be able to synthesise the issues. Of course Churchill made mistakes and got things wrong, sometimes at elementary levels, but while others might have been right on individual matters, they came *partis pris* with their own priorities and special interests. What is remarkable is that Churchill was so often so much more right than anyone else.

Fortunately in the perilous circumstances of the Second World War, he did not have to face the same criticism from the press that he and Lloyd George had faced in 1914–1918, when the great press barons often capriciously and irresponsibly chose to support military and naval figureheads against their political masters. Thus the *Morning Post* of 23 October 1914: 'When Mr. Churchill became First Lord he set himself directly to undermine the power of the Board and to establish himself as Dictator . . . In plain language, Mr. Churchill has gathered the whole power of the Admiralty into his own hands and the Navy is governed no longer by a Board of experts, but by a brilliant and erratic amateur.'[4]

At regular intervals Churchill's government was subjected to press criticism that limited his freedom of movement, weakened his authority and affected his policies, but he had cultivated the press barons between the wars and most of them were his close friends. Campaigns such as those that destabilised Asquith were not directed against him at a personal level – although attacks on the government in general occurred much more frequently than the subsequent myth of a country united would suggest. Churchill found these attacks unwelcome: they created dissension in Parliament, and meant that he had to turn his attention from fighting the war to managing public opinion. When for instance the *Daily Mail* campaigned in June 1941 for a reorganisation of the War Cabinet, he was resentful and irritated, and told Beaverbrook that if he could not be allowed to direct the war himself, he would resign.[5]

Criticism of Churchill for constitutional abuse was also muted, although it certainly took place. Because of the new position he created for himself as Minister of Defence, his direct intercourse with the Chiefs of Staff was perfectly legitimate. It was also unprecedented and often resented, but it was essential and productive. Churchill brought with him in 1940 an extensive knowledge, in theory and in practice, of the conduct of war. He had never been to Staff College, and had no experience as a staff officer or indeed of any sort of senior command. But he had studied the conduct of warfare across the centuries; and through his times at the Admiralty, at the War Office and at the Air Ministry, together with his intimate involvement in the developments of aerial warfare through the 1930s, he had acquired a vast amount of technical knowledge.

It was a strange feature of the 1930s that despite being on the political sidelines, Churchill was kept peculiarly well informed about military developments at home as well as in Germany. A number of courageous individuals risked their careers because of their conviction that he apprehended Britain's danger more accurately than anyone else. Major Desmond Morton, with whom Churchill had worked in the First War (when Morton survived a bullet through his heart), and who was now at the Industrial Intelligence Centre, monitoring German industrial development, supplied him with the facts which he deployed so effectively to contrast German rearmament with inaction at home. Morton was joined later by Ralph Wigram, who provided Churchill with information from the Foreign Office on German aircraft production. A year later, Squadron Leader Tore Anderson provided great detail on the inadequate personnel and equipment in the Royal Air Force. There were others, such as Brigadier Hobart of the Royal Tank Corps.

Not all the information that came to Churchill did so by unofficial routes. With Baldwin's approval, The Secretary of State for Air, Sir Philip Cunliffe-Lister, invited Churchill to join the Air Defence Research Sub-Committee in July 1935. The Chief of the Imperial General Staff supplied him with information about the tank programme. The Minister for the Co-ordination of Defence and the Secretary of State for Air allowed him to see secret installations. When Churchill asked Morton in 1929 for classified information, Ramsay MacDonald said, 'Tell him whatever he wants to know, keep him informed', and the permission was given in writing and renewed by both Baldwin and Chamberlain. It is far from clear quite what the motives for this liberal policy were: much of the ammunition given to Churchill was immediately directed against the government. It may have been altruism: Baldwin wrote to a friend, 'If there is going to be a war – and no one can say that there is not – we must keep him fresh to be our war Prime Minister'.[6]

As Minister of Munitions in the First World War, he had learned much about the material aspects of war. He had worked with the Chief of the US War Industries Board, Bernard Baruch, that six-foot five-inch giant who was the source of information not only on American military production but also on how Churchill could lose a fortune in the Wall Street crash. He was well equipped to understand the significance of the loss of equipment at Dunkirk and the need for American material support thereafter. His unique daily study of the Ultra decrypts meant that he, more than any other war leader, was aware of the detail of the daily progress of the war.

John Peck of his Private Office recorded, 'I have the clearest possible recollection of General Ismay talking to me about a meeting of the Chiefs of Staff Committee at which they got completely stuck and admitted that they just did not know what was the right course to pursue; so on a purely military matter, they had come to Churchill, a civilian, for his advice. He introduced some further facts into the equation that had escaped their notice and the solution became obvious.'[7]

Churchill knew more about the detail of intelligence than any other Prime Minister before him and probably since, and set more store by its value than any of his predecessors. He 'stood head and shoulders above his political contemporaries in grasping the importance of intelligence and harnessing it to his cause'.[8] He had been involved in the birth of the modern British intelligence services at the Home Office before the First World War, and in Room 40 at the Admiralty during that war. Between the wars he sought to maintain his connection with the Secret Service and what it learned, and during the Second World War he cherished and jealously guarded all the secrets that the Ultra decrypts provided as a result of breaking the Enigma key. He understood the huge advantage that a detailed study of Ultra gave him – not only in relation to military matters, but also as insight into international relations through a study of diplomatic traffic.

As the volume of available material grew he had to rely on pre- paratory sifting, but until then he worked through a huge volume of undigested decrypts. He took security of the material extraordinarily seriously. His secretaries were not aware of Ultra, let alone allowed access to it, and the cost in terms of time of his attention to intelligence was immense.[9]

After the war Churchill complained to Moran that people talked as if all he had done was to put heart into the British people through his magnificent speeches. What he thought far more important was that he had presided over the practical direction of the war. The sheer *effort* of doing so was incredible. Because of his insistence, as a result of experience in the First World War, on documenting all orders and instructions that he issued, the record of that effort is preserved. The ministerial boxes followed him wherever he might be in the world, in them a special file from Ismay with reports from the Chiefs, together with the Enigma decrypts. All this – and the records of these travels, the packed Engagement Diaries – testifies to the harnessing of dynamic energy. The most frequent reaction to meeting Churchill in those years is a reference to that energy. It was rigorously directed towards just one end. He told a Private Secretary, 'Each night, before I go to bed I try myself by Court Martial to see if I have done something really effective during the day – I don't mean merely pawing the ground, anyone can go through the motions, but something really effective'.[10]

6

The Greatest of the Myths

The War Cabinet initially consisted of Churchill, Chamberlain, Halifax and, for the Labour Party, Attlee and Greenwood: Churchill had one vote out of five. His most momentous battle with his colleagues occurred at the end of May 1940, a battle he chose later not simply to ignore, but rather to deny. In his memoirs, he declared that 'Future generations may deem it noteworthy that the supreme question of whether we should fight on alone never found a place upon the War Cabinet agenda'. Strictly speaking the matter was *not* on any written agenda, but he went on to say that it was not 'even mentioned in our most private conclaves'.[1] That was very far from true. There was an amazing, continuous discussion of these proposals throughout 26, 27 and 28 May 1940.[2] Roy Jenkins described the denial of these discussions as 'the most breathtakingly bland piece of misinformation in all six volumes [of the war memoirs].'[3]

Churchill would never concede that these deliberations took place, and he would certainly never admit that he himself was not *in principle* hostile to negotiations. In his wonderful declaration to the House of Commons as Prime Minister he had said: 'You ask, What is our aim. I can answer in one word: Victory – at all costs, victory in spite of all terror; victory, however long and hard the road may be, for without victory there is no survival.' There was indeed no thought in his mind of an ignoble surrender to the Germans. But he was perfectly realistic in these dark days. On 12 June 1940, for example, when he and Ismay were returning from France, and it was clear that Britain would soon be fighting on alone, Ismay confidently said 'We'll win the Battle of Britain'. Churchill stared at him and said, 'You and I will be dead in three months' time'.[4] He had said something similar a few days earlier to Baldwin. He did believe in eventual British victory: he was not made to imagine anything else. But it would probably be victory following invasion of the British Isles, and only after a long war waged from overseas. Against that likely prospect he never ruled out a negotiated peace – provided it was at the right time and on the right terms.

His confidence in eventual victory flowed in part from the fact that, like many others, Churchill took the erroneous view that the Nazi economy was brittle and overstretched and that a sudden collapse like that of 1918 could be expected. Thus he told Roosevelt on 15 June 1940 that he was not looking for an expeditionary force from the United States: indeed he wanted an American declaration for its moral force even more than for the material assistance that it would bring.

As well as believing that the German economy was on the verge of collapse, Churchill, like others, misled himself by thinking that politically the Nazi regime was vulnerable: under the stresses of war the Germans would throw off a leadership which they did not truly support. But this was not enough to encourage him, at this stage, to consider that he should be looking for outright victory. There is much evidence to show that he was not averse to a negotiated peace, provided it was 'not destructive of our independence'.[5] Indeed, he appears even to have been prepared to cede territory. Chamberlain quotes him as saying, 'If we could get out of this jam by giving up Malta and Gibraltar and some African colonies he would jump at it'.[6]

The difference between Churchill and his two Conservative colleagues in the War Cabinet in the critical discussions at the end of May 1940 was that he felt that the time for negotiation was not yet right, and that it should be postponed until talks could be conducted on more equal terms. On 26 May, pressed by Halifax, he said that he would be prepared to discuss terms, 'even at the cost of some territory', *provided that matters vital to Britain's independence were unaffected.* By 27 May he indicated he was prepared to accept a peace involving 'the restoration of German colonies and the overlordship of central Europe', although he thought that Hitler would be very unlikely to settle for that.

Far from not ruling out the possibility of participating in peace negotiations, then, Churchill saw a negotiated peace as the likeliest way in which the war would end. But the negotiations would take place with an economically broken Germany no longer ruled by Hitler. A total British victory was not realistic or conceivable at that stage in the war and had not even been policy when Britain was allied to France with her strong army.[7] 'Victory at all costs' was a misleading slogan if it implied, as most people thought it did, the total defeat of Germany.

While Churchill might have made some concessions to Germany for the sake of peace, Halifax was prepared to make substantial territorial concessions to *Italy* to keep her out of the war. In a conversation with the Italian ambassador on 15 May he dropped hints in regard to Gibraltar, Malta and Suez. In a draft that was omitted from his memoirs, Churchill declared that 'The Foreign Secretary showed himself willing to go a long way to buy off this new and dangerous enemy [Italy]'.[8]

Halifax's position was not Churchill's. He thought that there was no chance of crushing Germany: it was a question of saving as much as possible of Britain's sovereignty.[9] His Note to the War Cabinet of 27 May 1940 suggested an approach to Mussolini as an intermediary for the purpose of sounding out Germany on peace terms.

This ongoing debate continued until 28 May. That day's discussions began with a War Cabinet at 11.30 a.m., dealing mainly with operational matters. The substantive discussions of the previous days resumed at 4 p.m. and continued until 5.30. Matters were not going well for Churchill. The French wanted to meet Hitler, and Halifax said that he could not see any objection to this. Although Chamberlain was now tending to shift his position and stress the risks involved in mediation, bickering continued between Churchill and Halifax. The debate had become very heated. The PM accused Halifax of advocating capitulation; '[N]ations that went down fighting rose again, but those which surrendered tamely were finished'. Halifax responded angrily, saying that nothing he had suggested could even remotely be described as ultimate capitulation. (But remember that the Foreign Office did not abjure the Munich Settlement until 1942.[10]) The PM said that in any event the chances of decent terms being offered at the present time were a thousand to one against.[11] At this stage there was deadlock, and Churchill could have been outvoted.

There was then a break. At six o'clock Churchill addressed a meeting of those Cabinet Ministers who were not in the War Cabinet and to whom, in the press of events, he had not been able to speak. According not only to his own account, but also to Dalton and Amery, the speech he made to them was one of his most powerful: patriotic and effective. Dalton says that it contained the phrase, 'If this long island story of ours is to end at last, let it end only when each of us lies choking in his own blood upon the ground'. The reception was ecstatic, and buoyed by the support from the wider Cabinet (of whom Halifax had said, 'The gangsters will shortly be in complete control') Churchill returned to his four colleagues in the War Cabinet. He told them of the resolve of their colleagues: 'They had not expressed alarm at the position in France, but had expressed the greatest satisfaction when he had told them that there was no chance of our giving up the struggle. He did not remember having ever before heard a gathering of persons occupying high places in political life express themselves so emphatically.'

The reaction to his speech, in its effect on the War Cabinet, was a pivotal event in world history. 'Then and there', said John Lukacs, Churchill 'saved Britain, and Europe, and Western civilisation.'[12]

We cannot tell whether Churchill had contrived this *coup de théâtre*, but shamed by the resolve of their juniors and abandoned by Chamberlain the waverers capitulated without further debate. Halifax made just one final attempt, and suggested Roosevelt as a mediator, rather than Mussolini. Churchill disposed of that very briefly: 'The Prime Minister thought an appeal to the United States at the present time would be altogether premature. If we made a bold stand against Germany, that would command their admiration and respect; but a grovelling approach, if made now, would have the worst possible effect.'

On the previous day, when Halifax told Cadogan, the Permanent Under-Secretary at the Foreign Office, that he could not continue to work with Churchill, Cadogan replied, 'Nonsense: his rhodomontades probably bore you as much as they do me, but don't do anything silly under the stress of that.'[13]

Halifax did not find Churchill congenial. He said of Churchill's voice that, 'It oozes with port, brandy and the chewed cigar'. He did not do anything silly, in the sense of resigning, but he had not quite reached the end of his attempts at negotiation. At the very time that Churchill was making his 'finest hour' speech, some sort of discussions were going on between Butler, Halifax's Under-Secretary, and the Swedish minister in London, Bjorn Prytz. The documents relating to this episode are still unreleased, and that fact is highly suggestive of a further attempt by the Foreign Office to see a negotiated settlement. Indeed as late as early July Cadogan reported that Halifax was entertaining hopes of a peace negotiated through the Vatican. Churchill: 'I hope it will be made clear to the Nuncio that we do not allow any enquiries to be made as to terms of peace with Hitler'.[14] Later in that month, after Hitler's speech of 19 July, the ambassador in Washington, Lord Lothian, investigated through the intermediation of an American Quaker what German peace terms might be. He was reported as claiming that they were 'most satisfactory'.[15] It was not until the end of the year, when Churchill had strengthened his political position, that he could be confident of hearing no more about seeking terms. Indeed, as late as November in that same year, he himself was still not ruling out the possibility of a negotiated peace. So much for never considering making peace with Germany.

It was a full year before Eden signalled a move away from negotiation in a speech on 5 July 1941 in which he said that 'We were not prepared to negotiate with Hitler at any time on any subject'. Churchill brought the statement to the attention of the War Cabinet on 7 July 1941 and it was approved and accepted, as a *new* policy position. Even so, on 27 November 1941 he was minuted as saying at a War Cabinet meeting that 'We had made a public statement that we would not negotiate with Hitler or with the Nazi *régime*'; but he thought it would be going too far to say that Britain would not negotiate with a Germany controlled by the army. It was impossible to forecast what form of government there might be in Germany at a time when their resistance weakened and they wished to negotiate.[16]

The May meetings were the high-water mark of Cabinet rebellion. By January of the following year, the War Cabinet had been expanded in size to eight, four of the members being departmental Ministers. Additionally, Churchill arranged that the leader of the Liberal Party and Air Minister, Sir Archibald Sinclair, should join the War Cabinet when any matter affecting significant political or party issues were involved. Sinclair was a devoted Churchillian, his ADC on the Western Front and almost a second son. He wrote to Churchill in April 1916, expressing his ' longing to serve you in politics – more humbly but more energetically than I have been able to in war.'[17] In the Second World War according to the *Oxford Dictionary of National Biography* Churchill 'continued to treat Archie as a subaltern and social companion . . .' His recruitment was a neat way of turning the balance of power in a War Cabinet which in any event became less significant.

Halifax's wings were clipped, but Churchill was still conscious that he represented a threat. In his first reshuffle he tried to persuade him to abandon the Foreign Office and take over Chamberlain's position as Lord President. Although he failed, he was soon able to send him off to Washington as ambassador, a post he offered on another occasion to Lloyd George: a convenient place for stowing away rivals. When Lloyd George had briefly been considered for the post, Halifax reported that Churchill had felt it would be necessary to cross-examine him first to see whether he had 'the root of the matter in him . . . By this he means that any peace terms . . . offered . . . must not be destructive of our independence'.[18]

It is interesting, and indicative of just how far Churchill was from victory at any price or unconditional surrender at this stage that the formula which he proposed to use to establish whether Lloyd George did have the root of the matter in him was no more than the form of words which Halifax had used in the May 1940 Cabinet debate.[19]

The Machinery of Command

The next structural matter to which Churchill turned his attention related to the military direction of the war. As War Minister in the First War he had seen at first hand the paralysing struggles between politicians and professional soldiers, and the strange belief among the latter that even in the conditions of total, twentieth-century war, they composed a privileged and arcane profession with which the politicians had no right to interfere. Churchill had no intention of finding himself in the position of Lloyd George in his dealings with Sir William Robertson, the Chief of the Imperial General Staff, and Sir Douglas Haig. He said to Boothby: 'It took Armageddon to make me Prime Minister, but now I am there I am determined that power shall be in no other hands but mine. There will no more Kitcheners, Fishers or Haigs'.[1]

Prior to becoming Prime Minister, Churchill had already been able to use his position as First Lord of the Admiralty to deploy an unusual degree of control over the war as a whole, but he had not been impressed by the machinery he was required to use. War direction was in the hands of the Ministerial Committee for the Co-ordination of Defence, initially chaired by Chamberlain, but then by Churchill in his role as First Lord. A Chiefs of Staff Committee already existed, but met separately. The Chiefs of Staff did not like Churchill's style and he, for his part, was aware that they could always appeal over his head to the Prime Minister.

The system was inefficient and muddled. It was much improved by the model that he now established as Prime Minister, combining the premiership with the Ministry of Defence. This was a novel departure, and Churchill implemented it with great expedition. His appointment as Minister of Defence was made in the very first round of ministerial appointments on 11 May 1940, along with just his seven most senior colleagues.[2] The assumption of this dual role addressed the criticism

made of the Chamberlain government that no one Minister had
responsibility for prosecuting the war. Churchill had given the matter
much thought before his becoming Prime Minister had even been a real
prospect. The War Office, which he disliked even more than the
Foreign Office,[3] was now reduced to administrative functions. The
Ministerial Co-ordination Committee was abolished.

As Minister of Defence he presided over a non-existent Ministry. It
consisted of him, Prime Minister under a different name, and a very
small staff. It was a fiction, but a fiction that critically allowed him to
overcome the service resistance to political direction that had bedevilled
Lloyd George's conduct of the First World War. The fictional Ministry
was reinforced by Lindemann's Statistical Branch, which Churchill
brought with him from the Admiralty, and which was a device for
appraisal and statistical evaluation.

The Chiefs of Staff Committee now met with Churchill, as Minister
of Defence, on a daily basis, and a *modus vivendi* between the military
and the political was established that had never existed before. It was
certainly not without its tensions – Churchill strongly believed in
'creative tension' – and the Chiefs of Staff were frequently infuriated by
his rudeness, advocacy of hare-brained schemes and predilection for
testing arguments by prolonged and heated opposition. He sought to
assess the validity of his own arguments by forcing them on his
interlocutors at very great length, appearing to register no valid
opposition. In his history of the war, Churchill is said to have
represented the proceedings of his meetings with the Chiefs of Staff
as 'A monologue only occasionally interrupted by what were no more
than distant voices and echoes'; but that is an oversimplification. What
really took place was 'an incessant dialogue between Churchill and his
military advisers, and with his political advisers too.'[4]

Churchill, said David Stafford, talking about intelligence matters,
but in words which have a more general application, 'leaned heavily on
his advisers and listened to them carefully, but never allowed himself to
be imprisoned by them. By temperament acutely aware of the deadly
power of institutional inertia and *déformations professionnelles*, he always
valued independent and trusted sources . . .'[5]

In a post-war interview with Francis Williams, Attlee was asked
whether Churchill had too much control over the strategic planning of
the war. He said that was not the case: 'Winston was the driving force, a
great War Minister . . . but there was quite a lot of discussion at the
Defence Committee'. He conceded that there could be a great deal of

disagreement, but was asked if in the event Churchill had his way. He said that that was often the case. 'But there were quite a lot of occasions when he didn't. He'd get some idea he wanted to press, but after we had considered it the rest of us would have to tell him that there was no value in it.'

Attlee went on to say, 'Winston was sometimes an awful nuisance . . . but he always accepted the verdict of the Chiefs of Staff when it came to it, and it was a great advantage for him to be there driving them all the time . . . we always accepted their professional advice. Even Winston did after a struggle. We never moved on a professional matter without them.'[6] But he made a hugely significant caveat – 'But you needed someone to prod the Chiefs of Staff.' It is of crucial importance to remember this when one reads the diaries and memoirs of the military men.

It was a system that no one would have devised or sought to justify, and it worked remarkably well. Of course the generals were none the worse for prodding. The easiest way not to lose a battle is not to fight it. When Churchill was told that Hitler constantly interfered with his generals, his unrepentant reaction was to say 'I do the same'.[7] Churchill may have been at fault in not putting *more* pressure on the professionals. Even a commentator as critical of Churchill as Liddell Hart acknowledges that 'his minutes from 1940 on show him as being usually in advance of his official military advisers and executants' and he goes on to wonder why the PM did not push them 'along faster or replace them with more forward-thinking men'.[8]

He was more than a galvanising and inspiring catalyst in the discussions of the Chiefs of Staff. They were so burdened and preoccupied by practical considerations that lay below the level of true strategy that they were not often able to discuss that subject.[9] Churchill, taking the grander view, brought to the Chiefs of Staff a scale of vision that they individually and collectively lacked.

He also brought to his meetings with the Chiefs the great advantage of his compendious knowledge of the intelligence reports. The scale of the material he had studied meant that he could form a much broader appreciation of events than they. Intelligence was indeed one of the weapons he and they used in their battles. As Churchill insisted on his own direct access to the products of Bletchley Park he was at a great advantage against the Chiefs, whose information was at second hand. Accordingly, the Chiefs sought to establish the Joint Intelligence Committee as the repository and distributor of intelligence material with the responsibility for ensuring that intelligence underpinned strategy and operations. Eventually the JIC did come to fulfil that role, but not without some mistakes along the way, and not for some time. Until it had acquired sufficient skills and resources, Churchill was frequently able to outflank the Chiefs because of his command of intelligence. He was well aware of this and took pains not to be controlled. Reports were not 'to be sifted and digested by the various Intelligence authorities': they were to go straight to him via Desmond Morton.[10] It was not until the spring of 1941 that in this respect 'the Chiefs were able to battle with Churchill on a level playing field'.[11]

The system worked well in part because of the diplomacy of Major-General Hastings ('Pug') Ismay, who headed the skeletal defence office, supported by Colonel Leslie Hollis and Colonel Ian Jacob (both later major-generals). Ismay's role was critical and had two functions: he was Churchill's principal staff officer, an executive post, but he was also, as a member of the Chiefs of Staff Committee, involved in the formulation of policy. He had to maintain the metaphysical distinction between the two positions. Churchill once asked him his views on a decision of the Chiefs, which he had communicated to the Prime Minister. Ismay said that if his services were to be valued, the Prime Minister must never ask that question. 'And he never did.'[12]

Under these three men there were a Joint Planning Committee and the Joint Intelligence Committee, which both evolved plans of their own and evaluated those put to them by the Chiefs of Staff Committee. The whole thing was fairly fluid and organic.

Having established himself as Minister of Defence, Churchill appointed two sub-committees of the non-existent Defence Committee: Defence Committee (Operations) and Defence Committee (Supply). The former was the key one, consisting of Churchill, Attlee and the three Service Ministers, with the Chiefs of Staff always in attendance. The War Cabinet was supposed to be served by the Defence Committee (Operations) and the Defence Committee (Supply) but increasingly left the Prime Minister and the Chiefs of Staff to get on with things and came to play little part in the direction of the war. Initially its Defence Committee, consisting of Attlee, Beaverbrook and the three Service Ministers, met frequently, but the meetings took place progressively less often. The Service Ministers themselves played largely administrative roles.

The army representative on the Chiefs of Staff Committee consisted of the Chief of the Imperial General Staff. Ironside was succeeded by

Dill as CIGS in May 1940 and Alan Brooke succeeded Dill in December 1941.The navy's representative was initially Dudley Pound, who was succeeded as First Sea Lord by A.B. Cunningham in September 1943. For the Royal Air Force, Newall was succeeded by Portal in October 1940.

The changed approach at the centre of the direction of the war was dramatic. There are many descriptions of the sheer physical force that Churchill brought to bear, striding from room to room, summoning queues of Ministers and civil servants, demanding Action this Day on the famous red cards, ending the leisurely practices of peacetime and expecting the same total commitment to winning the war that he himself evinced.

He ruled from the start that his orders would be given in writing, and that only written orders were to be regarded as having his authority. His output is staggering – in its size, but in many other respects as well. Those who regard Churchill as little more than a bombastic orator should study what he wrote. Perhaps the most outstanding feature is the grasp of detail, a grasp that could be reflected in a highly intricate dissection of technical issues, but which could also extend to the no less detailed review of huge strategic issues examined at very great length in panoramic surveys. Smaller subjects were also taken in – smaller subjects that mattered to individuals: an unfairness, an abuse, a misuse of power by lowly officials.

He was particularly sensitive, patrician though he was, to injustices imposed for reasons of class or prejudice. There is always a profound sense of humanity. In the darkest of days and working crippling hours he found time to write letters of condolence and sympathy to a widow or mother of whom he had heard, often hardly known to him, and the tender, thoughtful messages he sent must have meant much to the recipients.

He found time to pursue some pet subjects. He was always interested in feeding the people and achieving a fair distribution of food resources. The Egg Production Scheme received a lot of idiosyncratic attention and it was noted that '[a]lthough rabbits are not by themselves nourishing, they are a pretty good mitigation of vegetarianism'.[13]

When Lloyd George attacked Churchill in the House of Commons on 7 May 1941 for being surrounded by yes-men, rather than people who would stand up to him and say, 'No, no, no', the Prime Minister expostulated to his oldest political ally in some frustration, 'Why, goodness gracious, has he no idea how strong the negative principle is in the constitution of the British war-making machine? The difficulty is not, I assure him, to have more brakes put on the wheels; the difficulty is to get more impetus and speed behind it.'[14] The minutes and memoranda were the attempt to generate that impetus and speed. The drive that lies behind them, the precision of the carefully chosen language in which they are couched, their logic and persuasiveness are the evidence of a powerful, disciplined and amazingly well-stocked mind.

Very soon his immediate entourage and his civil servants resigned themselves to this new regime and even found themselves swept up in its stimulating current. Initially there were reservations and complaints; and some reached Clementine. Typically, she thought it wise to relay the complaints to her husband. She wrote a letter on 23 June 1940, had second thoughts and tore it up, only to rewrite it a few days later, burdening Churchill, in these inordinately stressful days with reports that his manner was described as 'rough, sarcastic and over-bearing'. As Sir Martin Gilbert has pointed out, 'This was the same man who had been described three weeks earlier as "a mountain of energy and good nature", and within the following few weeks as "in wonderful spirits . . . full of offensive plans" and "most genial"'.[15] On the very day that Clementine wrote her letter Colville described Churchill lying in bed, gazing affectionately at his cat, Nelson, and murmuring, 'Cat, darling'.[16] She asked him to use his powers with 'urbanity, kindness and if possible Olympic calm'. It was an unnecessary letter at such a time, not thoughtless – far from that – but ill advised. Her husband was working eighteen hours a day to stave off defeat.

Churchill's self-confidence was not dented. He had achieved a great deal. He had become Prime Minister at a time when his abilities were indispensable. Despite great political weakness he had secured his position for the moment. He had improved on the machinery of waging war which had been so ineffective in 1914–18. But he had a tiny and inefficient army, which was being swept off mainland Europe and his only ally was about to sue for peace.

The Battle of France

In parallel with consolidating his position and constructing machinery for the direction of the war, every minute of Churchill's day was devoted to addressing the question of how to avoid imminent military defeat. Three weeks after he came into office he asked the Chiefs of Staff for an assessment of Britain's chances. There was little to reassure him in their reply. They reported on 26 May, concluding only *on balance* that Britain might survive; and even that depended on some fairly dodgy assumptions regarding the maintenance of the link with North America and keeping the RAF and the supply of aircraft to it in business. Churchill expected an invasion in which he would die in a heroic last stand. 'Take one with you' was to be the slogan.

All that lay between Britain and that invasion was France. His first military task therefore was to try to rally the French against the Germans with the support of the British Expeditionary Force. By the time he arrived on the scene there was in truth little he could do, and spur-of-the-moment attempts to galvanise the weak and demoralised British troops into last-minute activity irritated the army. Henry Pownall, for example, Chief of Staff to the Expeditionary Force, reacted furiously to Churchill's peremptory demand on 23 May for a counter-attack by eight divisions from three different armies at an hour's notice: 'The man's mad'.[1]

But what the British army could do in France was pretty insignificant. It was a tiny force. Nothing on a substantial scale had been planned and by the end of 1939 only five regular British divisions had arrived in France. In the spring of 1940 eight territorial divisions were sent; but their experience had been limited to guard duties. The War Office did not even have up-to-date maps of France and some divisions were not equipped with knives, forks and mugs.

The Battle of France would not be won or lost by Britain; indeed Britain's role could only be marginal. Churchill had to encourage France to try to save herself – both for her own sake and for the sake of her ally. At the cost of an enormous injection of energy – physical and emotional – he did all he could for France, the country he loved so much and whose history he knew so well,[2] and in which he chose to spend so much time, the country which he had first visited in 1883 at the age of nine, driving with his father through the Place de la Concorde, when he saw the monuments of Alsace and Lorraine draped in black crêpe after their annexation by the Germans thirteen years before.

From France he sent an urgent telegram to the War Cabinet on 16 May asking them, against the advice they were being given by Dowding, to allow six more squadrons to be used 'not for any local purpose, but to give the last chance to the French army to rally its wavering strength. It would not be good historically if their requests were denied and their ruin resulted . . . I must have answer by midnight in order to encourage the French. Telephone to Ismay at embassy in Hindustani'.[3] Beyond that, Churchill had to accept Dowding's advice, rejecting repeated requests from the French, even one as late as 16 June, when Jean Monnet flew to London (de Gaulle, who was with Monnet and, exceptionally, spoke in English, told Churchill, 'I think you are quite right').[4]

Britain and France had made a formal, mutual commitment that neither would make a separate peace. As the last days of French liberty ebbed away, the French had to confront this undertaking again and again. It soon became clear that both Pétain and Weygand were for an armistice and against continuing the war from, for instance, North Africa. Towards the end of May, France began to talk of asking for terms through Italy. While they awaited Britain's response to such an initiative, Daladier, the latest in a series of Foreign Ministers, panicked at the prospect of Italy's joining Germany in the war against France: he prepared a draft telegram offering substantial colonial concessions. Britain's lengthy and anxious Cabinet discussions on the same subject of looking for terms concluded on 28 May, with a firm but far from inevitable decision against treating. Daladier was informed, and his telegram was not sent.

Despite his later denunciation of 'the Italian jackal . . . trying to pick up an empire on the cheap', Churchill's attitude to Mussolini at the moment had to be eminently flexible. He made it known to Italy that if she were to remain neutral, she would be entitled to participate in eventual peace negotiations as a victorious co-belligerent. Unattracted by this distant reward, Italy joined the war on 10 June. France was on the brink of the surrender which was to follow just two days later, but already, and while still Britain's ally, obstructed Churchill's attempts to attack the new enemy. Ismay reported to Churchill that the French would not allow the RAF units still in France to take off on bombing raids against Italy. Churchill raised the matter at once with Reynaud and Weygand. They claimed that there was a misunderstanding, but the following morning Ismay was told that the French had now placed farm carts on the runway to make it impossible for British bombers to attack France's enemies.

Ahead of French capitulation the Prime Minister shuttled indefatigably backwards and forwards from England to France, trying to put heart into his allies. He made no less than six exhausting trips across the Channel, always at some risk of being shot down. Two of the visits involved overnight stays.

Pre-war planning had long envisaged that opposition to Germany would consist of a close alliance with France. To an even greater extent than in the First World War, the French military contribution was to exceed that of Britain, whose participation would largely be in the air. Despite the knowledge that there must be the closest cooperation between one small British Army and the eight French ones, there was in fact extraordinarily little liaison. It thus came as a chilling surprise for Churchill, on 16 May, when he asked, '*Où est le masse de la manœuvre?* to be told 'There is no reserve'. Churchill recorded,

> I admit this was one of the greatest surprises I have had in my life. Why had I not known more about it, even though I had been so busy in the Admiralty? Why had the British Government, the War Office above all, not known more about it? It was no excuse that the French High Command would not impart their dispositions to us or to Lord Gort except in vague outline. We had a right to know. We ought to have insisted.[5]

Perhaps they should have insisted, but the fact is that requests for military information from the French were usually unavailing. French officers frequently declined to tell their British counterparts what their dispositions consisted of.[6] The net result was that the British had no knowledge of their Allies' – their only Allies' – Order of Battle.

In the absence of a reserve, the British and French armies separated and Britain fell back on Dunkirk. Reynaud had drafted an order, which said that French troops were to make their way to the embarkation beaches, 'the British forces embarking first'. Churchill intervened explosively: *'Non! Partage: bras-dessus, bras-dessous'*.[7] But Weygand placed obstructions in the way of evacuation of French troops, and some ships sailed off empty.

At Calais, where British and French forces were also pinned down, the French General Fagalde threatened to use force to stop the British from embarking – a disappointing reaction in view of the fact that the British were only at Calais to demonstrate solidarity with the French. For flawed and symbolic reasons Churchill chose to compound the mistake, by ordering the British Calais troops to hold out and refrain from surrendering.

After Dunkirk there was a wave of Anglophobia in France. While that was to be expected among those who did not know the detail of events, it was not confined to such people. Weygand accused the BEF of 'a refusal to fight',[8] and Pétain, recalling the moment when the *Kaiserschlacht* threatened to break the Anglo-French line in 1918, said to the British that he had given them forty divisions then. 'Where are your forty divisions now?' There were particularly bitter attacks on Britain for not contributing a greater air element to the defence of France. Account was not taken of the fact that in just two months Britain had lost 959 aircraft and 435 pilots, and that she had only 331 modern fighters left.[9] France's plight was not the fault of Britain or France alone – it was a joint responsibility for failing to think through their preparations for a war that they knew was coming.

The series of historic meetings held in the shadow of France's collapse were of necessity rushed and ill planned. The political complexities on the French side were subtle and it was often difficult to know how far French remarks were to be taken at face value and how far they were designed to stimulate changes of position among colleagues in an uneasy coalition. Churchill was magnificent in English and in French, but the French generals, especially Weygand, the Commander-in-Chief, and Pétain and even Churchill's old friend, Georges, were full of gloom. Only Reynaud, the Prime Minister, showed much inclination to fight on.

Churchill returned to London from his 10 June excursion and wrote to Roosevelt, urging him to stiffen French resolve. He was back at Weygand's headquarters on 11 and 12 June, and left with confirmation that France would not make peace without consulting him. On 13 June, he returned to France to meet Reynaud at Tours. By this stage, the effects of war on France were very evident. Churchill's aircraft had to find a landing between craters. No one was at the airport to meet him, and the conference took time to assemble. Weygand had said that an armistice must be asked for at once. Reynaud was still resisting, but he, too, had asked Roosevelt for help and now intended to send a final request for American intervention, spelling out that otherwise the consequences would be Roosevelt's responsibility.

The British were taken aback by how fast the situation had changed, and it took them some time to realise that Reynaud was now telling them that France could resist no more. He asked them to release France from the reciprocal commitment not to make a separate peace. Churchill replied with great sympathy and understanding and did not underestimate the consequence of the loss of the British Army in the north of France, but he did not give the consent that Reynaud sought and he ended by looking hard at him and saying, 'that is my answer to your question'. Unqualified as that answer was, Reynaud asked for clarification. Churchill spoke with tears in his eyes: 'I have already said we would refrain from reproaches and recriminations. The cause of France will always be dear to us, and if we win the war we will one day restore her to all her power and dignity. But that is a very different thing from asking Great Britain to consent to a departure from the solemn undertaking binding two countries'.[10]

The meeting then broke up so that the British could talk together in the garden. When it resumed, de Gaulle had arrived uninvited and took the liberty of joining the meeting. He had not heard the earlier exchanges and does not appear to have understood what was now being said. Churchill started by saying explicitly that 'Nothing in the discussion he had just had with his colleagues had led any of them to change their views. Lord Halifax and Lord Beaverbrook had expressed their approbation with what he had said just now, and it could therefore be assumed that the Cabinet would also agree,'[11] but for some inexplicable reason de Gaulle understood Churchill to be agreeing to release France from her commitment.

All the evidence available makes it totally clear that he was wrong.[12] Churchill was of course profoundly sympathetic to the predicament of France, whose historic role he recognised and respected, and de Gaulle may have been misled by his compassion, his failure to bluster, his respect for his allies in their disaster. In any event, he was quickly told he was mistaken. Spears told him so almost immediately and when de Gaulle replied that Baudouin was saying something different, Spears ran after the Prime Minister's car. Churchill confirmed the position to

Spears: 'Churchill had said "*Je comprends*" to indicate that he understood what Reynaud was saying: not that he approved of it. "*Comprendre* means understand in French, doesn't it?" Churchill asked Spears. "Well", said Winston, "when for once I use exactly the right word in their own language, it is going rather far to assume that I intended it to assume that I meant something quite different. Tell them my French is not so bad as all that." '[13] But despite the correction, de Gaulle continued to believe that Britain had connived in a turnaround by Reynaud which he could not accept. Whatever he thought of Reynaud, he was unfair to Churchill.

In London on 16 June with Jean Monnet, de Gaulle was told by the ambassador, Corbin, that Reynaud had sent a telegram to Churchill making a final request to allow France to ask for an armistice and implying that he would resign if Britain refused.

Corbin and Monnet then told de Gaulle of the remarkable proposal for a union between France and Britain which they had worked out with Sir Robert Vansittart, Permanent Under-Secretary at the Foreign Office from 1938 to 1941 and now Chief Diplomatic Adviser to the Foreign Secretary. De Gaulle was very doubtful about the feasibility of the scheme but endorsed it in the hope that it would strengthen Reynaud's position against his less stalwart colleagues. It is interesting that the proposal originated in France – as did the similar proposal which is now known to have been made in 1956 by the French Prime Minister Guy Mollet.

When Churchill heard of the proposal he was not impressed and indeed had little opportunity to consider it as he negotiated to hold the French from capitulating. He was deeply involved in an attempt to persuade the United States to lend support to France. He had sent telegrams to Roosevelt on 13, 14 and 15 June, reminding him that without American support France would cease to resist. Eventually, however, he was persuaded by de Gaulle that the union offer should be made, and the Cabinet too agreed that the proposal might as well be issued. The proposal was relayed by Churchill to Reynaud by telephone: 'Hello, Reynaud! De Gaulle is right! Our proposal may have great consequences. *Il faut tenir!* Well, see you tomorrow! At Concarneau'. It was only when Chamberlain had an audience that evening that the King learned about the adjustment to his territories.[14]

Before Churchill could leave for Concarneau the following day he heard that Reynaud had resigned and that Pétain had been asked to form a government. Churchill was not on metropolitan French soil again until after D-Day. Pétain's response to the union proposal was 'Why fuse with a corpse?' The corpse he was referring to was Britain's. The Council of Ministers equally failed to rise to the level of events, and there were references to not wishing to be subjects of His Britannic Majesty or to see France become one of the Dominions of the British Empire. Many leading British statesmen were hardly more enthusiastic, but that did not mean that Britain was not hurt by the speedy rejection of a morally costly offer, and the *entente cordiale* died with it.[15]

That was the end of France. It had been spelled out on the evening of 16 June, when Roosevelt's response to France's pleas had arrived, essentially negative. Right up to the last minute, Britain continued to provide material support to France. It is often forgotten that after Dunkirk fresh British troops were sent back to France. But the French political and indeed military command was now in pieces. Weygand was flatly refusing to obey Reynaud's orders. There were violent rows between the two men. Reynaud was now in a minority in arguing against an armistice. He resigned and the President, Lebrun, called in the presidents of the two Chambers of Parliament for their constitutional advice on who Reynaud's successor should be. They recommended that Reynaud should be reappointed. Lebrun, however, felt there was no alternative but to appoint Pétain. France was no longer at war. George VI spoke for many of his countrymen when he reacted to the fall of France by saying that things would be a lot easier now that Britain did not have to bother about her allies.

What was Britain now to say to the renewed request that France be released from her undertaking? Churchill was aghast at the proposal: 'Tell them that if they let us have their fleet we shall never forget, but that if they surrender without consulting us we shall never forgive. We shall blacken their name for a thousand years!' Then he added 'Don't, of course, do that just yet'. The gravity of the situation did not overwhelm him: he was in particularly good spirits that evening, reciting poetry, murmuring 'Bang, bang, bang, Goes the farmer's gun, Run, rabbit, run, rabbit, Run, run, run' before taking a turn in the garden, telling one or two dirty stories to his staff and bidding them good night at 1.30: 'Goodnight, my children.'[16]

There was little point in refusing point blank to agree to what was going to happen anyway and the best that could be done appeared to be to accede, subject to the condition that the French fleet moved to British ports. The final British response to France's request that she might sue for a separate peace was given in a telegram sent on 16 June.

It pointed out that the agreement forbidding separate negotiations had been made with the French Republic, and not with any particular administration: 'It therefore involves the honour of France'. Britain wholly excluded itself from any part in an enquiry about terms but consented to France's doing so, 'provided, but only provided, that the French fleet has sailed forthwith for British harbours pending negotiations'.[17] Churchill sent a personal telegram, recording that he could not believe that 'the illustrious Marshal Pétain and the famous General Weygand will injure their ally by delivering over to the enemy the fine French fleet. Such an action would scarify their names for a thousand years of history.' For the moment, that did the trick.

The consequences of the fall of France were immense. Mussolini, who had been hesitating on the sidelines, was reassured that there were opportunities to be exploited. When he declared war on France on 10 July the Mediterranean was no longer Britain's. Indeed, with Italy in the war and the French fleet out of it, Britain had to make a choice between Mediterranean and Far Eastern strategy. As early as 28 June the Australian and New Zealand governments were told that it was not practical for Britain to send a fleet to defend Singapore. There were thus direct repercussions in both the Far East and in the Mediterranean. There was to be debate about whether Britain's Mediterranean Strategy was the creation of Brooke or of Churchill. Perhaps it was Pétain's.

The consequences of the *nature* of the fall of France were also hugely significant. Defeated France, Vichy France, remained to an extent an unknown quantity until the unoccupied area was taken over by the Germans in 1942. On several occasions Vichy came close to entering the war on the German side. Vichy France had to be humoured, principally to avoid precipitating a transfer of its fleet to Germany. America and Britain interpreted this need in different ways, and there were serious differences between the allies about who represented Free France and indeed how far Free France should be recognised.

A deficiency in French morale undercut all that had been done to prepare for war at a material level. France had rearmed strongly ahead of the war, and there was a confident belief in France as in Britain that the superior vitality of the economies of the allies would enable them to survive a prolonged war and to defeat Germany, whose economy was believed to be overstretched and precarious. In 1938 defence spending equalled a third of all French government spending and by 1940 France had more tanks (at 2,900) than Germany – even allowing for seized Czechoslovak tanks. French artillery also substantially outnumbered

German – 11,200 guns to 7,710. In aircraft she was not nearly so well off. Britain's role was to be primarily naval, but the military contribution was also expected to assist[18] – to some extent, but not a lot. At the time of the Munich Crisis the British army numbered just 180,000 men, with a Territorial Army of 130,000. Germany had 550,000, with a further 500,000 in reserve. Gort, as CIGS, said, 'In the circumstances, it would be murder to send our forces overseas to fight a first-class power'.

Diplomatic preparations for the war had been less than satisfactory: France's attempts to secure allies against the Nazi menace (in which she was not assisted by Britain) had been remarkably unsuccessful and such allies as she had were those countries which fell to Hitler in the years that led up to 1939.

The alliance between Britain and France itself was not a particularly cordial one. After the First World War the two countries had drifted apart. Among military men in Britain there were many who thought that the First World War had been a temporary aberration from the tradition of fighting *against* the French, and even among senior politicians there was often a surprisingly crude dislike of Gallic neighbours. Liberal British thinkers felt that since 1918 France had adopted a militaristic and aggressive spirit. France was equally unenthusiastic about Britain. Many Frenchmen felt that they had borne the brunt of the fighting in the First World War and that Britain was now, more than ever, prepared to fight to the last Frenchman.

Efforts had been made to overcome this mood of hostility. The King and Queen visited France for four days in 1938 and the following year President Lebrun paid a return state visit to London. 'Chips' Channon sourly referred to the visit as a 'Frog week' organised for the sake of 'pro-frog boys' like Eden and Churchill. Chamberlain was not a 'pro-frog boy', but he enjoyed the entertainment after Lebrun's speech so much that he got hiccups.[19]

Even at this distance, even with the benefit of hindsight and seventy years of research, the speed and profundity of France's collapse is difficult to understand. The reaction to the defeat of France in so short a space was generally one of amazement. Rebecca West said that it ranked as a tragedy 'as supreme in history as *Hamlet* and *Othello* and *King Lear* rank in art'. The Canadian Prime Minister, Mackenzie King said 'It is midnight in Europe'. Antoine de Saint-Exupéry was stunned: 'Surely I must be dreaming'. Churchill: 'I was dumbfounded. What were we to think of the great French Army and its highest chiefs?'[20]

The Constable of France

Although France could no longer support Britain's war, she could still affect it, especially through the agency of the man who came increasingly to personify his country. De Gaulle and Churchill first met in May 1940. The Frenchman was impressed by Churchill and made an equally good impression on him.[1] De Gaulle had no interest in making peace. He spoke of guerrilla warfare: capitulation was out of the question. As Spears put it, 'His bearing, alone among his compatriots, matched the calm, healthy phlegm of the British . . . No chin, a long, drooping, elephantine nose over a closely-cut moustache, a shadow over a small mouth whose thick lips tended to protrude as if in a pout before speaking, a high receding forehead and pointed head surmounted by sparse black hair lying flat and neatly parted. His heavily hooded eyes were very shrewd. When about to speak he oscillated his head slightly like a pendulum, while searching for words'.[2]

On one occasion, when Churchill came across de Gaulle standing apart from the others, he greeted him as '*L'homme du destin*'. Later he charged the meeting with romance, talking of de Gaulle as 'The Constable of France'. But even at the time he saw this junior officer as a significant figure.

De Gaulle was to cause immense irritation, often by extraordinarily petty obstructiveness. When he arrived in London on 17 June, calling himself the leader of the 'Free French', he presented Churchill with an immediate difficulty. De Gaulle was *persona non grata* with Vichy and indeed he was shortly to be condemned to death *in absentia* for failing to carry out orders. The joke in London at the time was that if he returned to France, all de Gaulle would again be divided into three parts.

Contact continued with the new regime at Vichy, which Britain still regarded as the best means of contesting German occupation. There was accordingly considerable hostility to de Gaulle within the

British government and Foreign Office. It was very much Churchill's personal decision to take the initiative to recognise him formally and to give military support to the Free French. Spears was the catalyst in the process of inducing Churchill to take this initiative: the Cabinet in the Prime Minister's absence had already agreed to follow the Foreign Office line: de Gaulle was not to be allowed to broadcast to France. In the event the famous broadcast of 18 June 1940, a call to arms made above the heads of the present leaders of France, and serving to underscore their ignominy, was one of the great propaganda moments of the war – not so much for its immediate effect, which was limited, but as a historic waypoint. It was also a decisive moment for de Gaulle: 'At the age of forty-nine I was entering upon adventure, like a man thrown by fate outside all terms of reference'.[3]

Outside the Foreign Office there was popular support in Britain for de Gaulle and the Free French. From the Royal Family to the scores of unknown widows who sent their wedding rings so that the gold might be used to fund his cause, there were manifestations of solidarity. Churchill was at the front of this. He made a highly supportive speech in the Commons on 20 August and in the course of the summer repeatedly pushed and prodded to ensure that the Frenchman received the supplies he needed and that his requests were not met with official obstruction. At this stage in their relationship, Churchill respected the one Frenchman whose resolution, as he saw it, matched his own. To the end of his life, even when de Gaulle was at his worst in terms of petty vindictiveness, he could be moved to tears by the idea that this man had supported him when he was alone in 1940. De Gaulle's unalterable cast of mind would not have allowed him to do anything else.

In the aftermath of Dunkirk Churchill had to consider the implications of the divorce from France. About 120,000 French troops had been rescued at the fall of France and brought back to Britain. It was hoped that they would join the fight for freedom in a Free French army; but given the choice of doing so or being repatriated in accordance with international law, almost all chose to return to their defeated homeland: only some 4,000 stayed to fight with de Gaulle, and a further 1,500 to remain in the Free French Navy. The loss of so many trained troops was a blow to Britain's war effort, and gives the lie to the Gaullist myth so sedulously propagated after the war that France had saved herself by her own efforts.

Only a small part of the French fleet was in British ports when France capitulated, two battleships and five destroyers within the UK and one battleship and four cruisers at Alexandria, plus, in both cases, a number of minor craft. The bulk of the French fleet was at Casablanca and at Mers-el-Kébir and Oran. There were also substantial numbers of cruisers in Algiers and Toulon. Pétain and Admiral Darlan had told Britain that no French warships would be allowed to fall into Axis hands, and indeed Darlan had ordered his captains to scuttle rather than surrender. But, Francophile though he was, Churchill could not rely on these promises. The terms of the French Armistice were only prised out of the French by Sir Ronald Campbell, the British ambassador, with difficulty. They were not reassuring. Article 8 provided that the fleet was to be demobilised and disarmed under German or Italian supervision, and little weight could be attached to a 'solemn assurance' that the vessels would not be used for Germany's own purposes.

The options that were offered to the French were generous: they could continue the war either as part of the Royal Navy or part of the Free French Navy, sail their ships to British or French West Indian ports with reduced crews or scuttle. The ultimatum was reported to Vichy by Gensoul, the French Admiral at Mers-el-Kébir, in crudely simplified terms: he had six hours to sink his ships or see them destroyed. Vichy declined to comply and Britain had no choice but to use force. Some 47 French officers and 1,250 sailors were killed, with 351 wounded.

The damage the incident caused has lasted for generations in the French mind. Its immediate effect was that Vichy carried out an air raid on Gibraltar and broke off diplomatic relations with Britain (though Vichy France was still not at war with Britain). Even Churchill's admirals were gratuitously unsupportive. Admiral Somerville, who had opened fire at 17.45 on 3 July described it as 'a filthy job', and Admiral Sir Andrew Cunningham, Flag Officer, North Atlantic, referred to it as a 'ghastly error'. They and Admiral Sir Dudley North, the third admiral involved, never wavered in their belief that the use of force was unnecessary and mistaken.[4]

The attitude of the admirals has to be contrasted with that of the most sensitive Frenchman in the world. De Gaulle was furious when he heard the news and he always resented what he considered to be British glorification of the event, but after only a few hours Spears found him very calm and objective, seeing things in perspective. What Britain had done was inevitable from Britain's point of view.[5] In a broadcast to

France on 8 July, de Gaulle went even further: 'There cannot be the slightest doubt that, on principle and of necessity, the enemy would have used [the French fleet] either against Britain or against our own Empire. I therefore have no hesitation in saying that they are better destroyed'.[6] In December 1940, lunching at Chequers, he went further and said that if Britain made more of the fact that she was standing alone, 'Oran would seem natural, because the world was at stake'.[7]

The matter was not well handled. Gensoul could never later explain how it came about that he relayed the British ultimatum to his superiors in such a misleading form. On the British side, too, there were strange errors. Negotiations in this most delicate of matters were entrusted to Captain C.S. Holland, an officer who had been marked out earlier as having a 'judgement about French officers [that] had become gravely impaired',[8] and a signal from Pound to Somerville authorising the acceptance of demilitarisation of the French ships was vetoed by the War Cabinet on the strange grounds that 'this would look like weakening': a decision that cost great numbers of lives and poisoned relations with the French. Gensoul had already said he too could accept demilitarisation.

There were echoes of this distance between the War Cabinet and the naval chiefs in the way that the French navy holed up in Alexandria was handled. Here the British admiral on the spot was Andrew Cunningham. He dealt with his opposite number, Admiral Godfroy, with very great skill, understanding and sensitivity. He was a man of great confidence, and that allowed him, amongst other things, quite simply to ignore one of the unhelpful signals he received from London. He described a signal which ended with the crass words, 'Do not (repeat) NOT fail', as 'a perfect example of the type of signal which should never be made'.[9] He argued and delayed and used his judgement, and at the end of the day, and despite the interventions from London, he resolved the problem without bloodshed or ill feeling. To do them justice, Pound and Alexander, the First Lord, sent him a generous tribute: 'Most sincere congratulations on complete success of your negotiations'. And the Prime Minister 'also wishes his congratulations to be sent to you'. But Churchill said later that Cunningham had been 'too pussy-foot' in his dealings with Godfroy,[10] in contrast to the more forthright approach in the case of Mers-el-Kébir.

The Mers-el-Kébir decision, which Churchill had described as a terrible one 'like taking the life of one's child to save the State', was of course a cruel necessity. The admirals on the spot who for the rest of

their lives deprecated action which they regarded as unnecessary may
have been too close to the spot to comprehend the larger implications
of events. If the French fleet had fallen into German hands, Britain
would have lost the Battle of the Atlantic and almost certainly the war
itself. The imperative was all the greater as while Gensoul was treating
with the British, the French admiralty ordered all their battleships *en
clair* to converge on Mers-el-Kébir to reinforce him.[11] 'Settle everything before dark', said Churchill, 'or you will have reinforcements to
deal with'.

The Mers-el-Kébir decision was very much Churchill's own, made
on his reading of the overall situation. It caused him great pain.[12] A
Chiefs of Staff opinion of 24 June had to be reversed at his demand, and
he ignored the unanimous view of a conference of flag officers at
Gibraltar, which followed a meeting between North and Gensoul at
Mers-el-Kébir.

Then and later the navy made much of the fact that Darlan had
ordered that the fleet would be scuttled rather than handed over to the
Germans. Churchill could not rely on a Vichy promise. Later Darlan
was to allow Germany to take military supplies across Syria to assist
opposition to Britain in Iraq. Churchill described him as 'a bad man
with a narrow outlook and a shifty eye. A naval crook is usually a bad
sort of crook.'

As had been hoped, Churchill's resoluteness convinced Roosevelt
that Britain really did intend to fight on and that material assistance
given to Britain would not ultimately be delivered to Germany. The
House of Commons was also impressed by his determination.

It was indeed when Churchill reported the incident to the
Commons that Margesson brought the Conservatives to their feet
for the first time. When Churchill told the Commons that 'we shall
not fail in our duty, however painful,' members rose to their feet in
applause. But Margesson was responding as well as directing. There
was a new mood amongst all Members of the House, who saw,
perhaps for the first time, the resolve and determination at the heart
of the direction of events. Their reaction was both unexpected and
overwhelming. The speech was punctuated by gasps of surprise and
endorsed with euphoric approval. Churchill left the House weeping,
saying, 'This is heartbreaking to me'.[13] Eric Seal, one of the Prime
Minister's Private Secretaries, wrote home the next day: 'It was a
tremendous success. The scene at the end was quite awe-inspiring –
the whole crowded House rose & cheered for a full two minutes . . .

The PM was quite upset. He went quite pink and there were
certainly tears in his eyes. What it was all about I still don't really
know. The speech was good, but not better than the others; & the
occasion – the outbreak of hostilities with our old ally – hardly one
for rejoicing.'[14]

After Mers-el-Kébir French warships in British ports were seized by
the Admiralty. The crews were given the chance of fighting alongside
the British, but as usual the majority chose to go back to France: a
disappointment always to de Gaulle.

The dubious quality of the Free French allies was shortly underlined
in Operation MENACE, the expedition to Dakar in September 1940. The
operation had originally been conceived as a blockade of French
warships at Casablanca. In the event, most of the fleet had been able
to escape to Dakar. De Gaulle misread the situation and thought that
the operation could simply be diverted to that port. When it transpired
that there were Vichy cruisers in the region Churchill decided on
cancellation, but again de Gaulle was unduly optimistic. Churchill gave
way.

The operation was a complete failure. First of all there was a woeful
lack of security on the part of the Free French before they left
England. The French officers notoriously enjoyed passing on news of
their adventures and plans in the cocktail bars of West End hotels,
and there were German agents even within their own numbers. It was
reported that in a Liverpool restaurant toasts had been given to
'Dakar', and de Gaulle publicly went off to Simpson's in Piccadilly to
buy his tropical kit. Increasingly it proved necessary to withhold
information from the French, and, to his exasperation, even from de
Gaulle.

Secondly, it emerged that at Dakar there simply was not the
sympathy for de Gaulle which he had expected. He had not helped
by broadcasting in advance and alerting the authorities to his arrival.
There were no defections to him and the Vichy forces defended the port
vigorously.

Finally, the expedition was thoroughly badly organised, and contact
was lost between the French and the British Admiral John Cunningham
(not to be confused with Admiral Andrew B. Cunningham, 'ABC', who
confuses matters further by being the brother of General Alan Cunningham).

Dakar caused much criticism of the government in the country. The
Prime Minister was so stung by coverage in the press, the *Sunday*

Pictorial and the *Daily Mirror* in particular, that he proposed to the War
Cabinet that the newspapers should be prosecuted.

> The immediate purpose of these articles seemed to be to affect the
> discipline of the Army, to attempt to shake the stability of the
> Government, and to make trouble between the Government and
> organised labour. In his considered judgement there was far more
> behind these articles than disgruntlement and frayed nerves. They
> stood for something most dangerous and sinister, namely, an attempt
> to bring about a situation in which the country would be ready for a
> surrender peace [*sic*]. It was not right that anyone bearing his heavy
> responsibilities should have to submit to attacks of this nature upon
> his Government.[15]

Fortunately the War Cabinet vetoed prosecution.

There were attacks in Parliament too, where Churchill generously
defended de Gaulle and declared that the Free French deserved Britain's
continued support. At this time the Free French were not obviously and
inevitably the image of France defiant and destined to revive. They were
rather a maverick bunch of very dubious quality. De Gaulle himself was
a very junior officer – his initial rank of brigadier-general equated to that
of a British brigadier – and with little political experience as junior
minister just before the fall of France.

Churchill's advocacy saved the Free French in Britain, but Dakar did
them great damage in the United States, where Roosevelt was not alone
in seeing de Gaulle as unreliable and unstable, and very much
Churchill's puppet. This view coloured American relations with de
Gaulle throughout the war, and also her attitude to Vichy, which she
regarded as the legitimate government of France and altogether a much
more attractive option. Dakar proved the excuse for keeping the Free
French out of the loop and at a distance.

Despite Churchill's commitment to de Gaulle and his Free French,
contacts continued with Vichy – not least because contacts also
continued between Vichy and Germany. In the summer of 1940 Laval
and Darlan threatened to transfer what remained of the French fleet,
together with French bases, to Germany: indeed, they wanted a
declaration of war on Britain. Britain responded with delicate negotiations, some direct from Churchill to Pétain, some through the intermediary contact of Professor Louis Rougier, and some via Sir Samuel
Hoare and the Madrid Embassy. All of this was profoundly unaccep-

table to de Gaulle, who believed that Darlan might well carry out his threat or even use the French fleet directly against Britain. '*La France ne marchera pas, mais la flotte peut-être.*'[16] For him, '[t]he mere fact that the Vichy government exists under the present conditions represents in the eyes of the Free French an injury to the honour and the interests of France for which there is no possible justification'.

Sailors, Airmen and Soldiers

At the Admiralty Churchill had not thought much of the senior officers he had dealt with, and they were equally unimpressed by him. Throughout the war the admirals proved to be a rather ungovernable collection, secure in their professional conservatism and always armed with what Churchill saw as technical obfuscations.

One casualty of the Dakar disaster was Admiral Sir Dudley North. He allowed the French fleet to escape through the Straits of Gibraltar on 11 September, and his stock had fallen as a result of his protest about Mers-el-Kébir. He had taken the trouble to report ill feeling about the operation at Gibraltar and within the fleet. The immediate result was to anger the First Lord, A.V. Alexander, who told Churchill that he had proposed to Pound that North be dismissed. Alexander beefed up a signal from Pound to North, to read that, 'opinions of senior officers are always of value before an operation takes place . . . [But t]heir Lordships deprecate comments on a policy which has been decided on by the Admiralty in the light of factors which were unknown to officers on the spot.' A very reasonable position. Churchill's own view was that 'It is evident that Admiral Dudley North has not got the root of the matter in him, and I should be very glad to see you replace him by a more resolute and clear-sighted officer'.[1] For the moment Pound felt that there were not adequate grounds for dismissal, but North's days were limited, and very soon he went.

The circumstances surrounding his departure post-Dakar are a little strange: he handled MENACE badly, but not that badly. His dismissal, and the refusal to allow an official inquiry into it, was resented by many fellow officers, and the admirals generally felt that Pound was altogether too ready to comply with Churchill's wishes. Suspicions persisted that he had been unfairly dismissed on Churchill's instructions, although Churchill denied this in a letter to North of 7 June 1948, and North himself pressed after the war for an inquiry into the circumstances surrounding his dismissal. Such an inquiry never took place, but Macmillan investigated the matter in 1957 and concluded that North had not been 'the victim of Service or political prejudice'.

It is probably the case that his dismissal was not directly engineered politically – at least not by Churchill. There was prejudice against him within the service, as well as specifically on the part of Pound, who was unimpressed by the fact that in MENACE North had simply waited for instructions without putting himself into a position in which he could carry them out. 'How can I continue to place reliance on a Flag Officer who does not act because he is waiting for instructions?' But mitigating factors were ignored. Pound's tendency to look for scapegoats was well known.

Some naval historians have been unduly critical of Pound. Superficially he was unimpressive and an easy target. Brooke compared him to a dormouse. Churchill referred to his 'slow, unimpressive look'. But he went on to say that the look was deceptive. On another occasion Churchill said that 'there were only four men whose minds were in tune with his own – Smuts, Beaverbrook, Bracken – and Pound'.[2] Pound had his difficulties with Churchill, but stood up to him well, and it is not clear why Roskill, for instance, regarded him as a mere cat's-paw.

Churchill inherited Sir Charles Forbes as Commander-in-Chief, Home Fleet. On Forbes rested the responsibility of the naval element of defence against invasion. It was a role which he filled uneasily. In the first place, he did not think that it was the navy's job to occupy such a defensive function. That was the army's job: the navy would win the war in other ways. Secondly, he strongly opposed the practical implication: the fact that his ships were strung out round the British Isles, their positions known to the Germans. 'It is most galling that the enemy should know just where our ships . . . always are, whereas we generally learn where his major forces are when they sink one or more of our ships.'[3] An additional result was that British convoys operated with minimal naval cover. This was the period the U-Boat commanders called 'the Happy Time', '*die glücklichen Zeiten*'.

Churchill, as First Lord, had already come across Forbes in the early stage of the war. Forbes had argued that the Fleet should be based at Scapa Flow, and not, as Churchill wished, in the Clyde. He had stood up well to Churchill, and his arguments won the day, but Churchill never liked him. In the navy, too, Forbes had many critics. He did not endear himself to the many colleagues who failed to appreciate the vulnerability of surface vessels to aircraft by complaining about the inadequacy of anti-aircraft gunnery in the service, and his misfortunes in the Norwegian campaign, when the Germans had cracked the naval cipher, meant that he was unfairly known as 'Wrong Way Charlie'. But he generally did things the right way, and if he had been allowed to support the convoys, or if his views on the threat from the air, which were in advance of his time, had been accepted, many disasters would have been avoided and many lives saved. Later Andrew Cunningham said, 'How right he was . . . He was in my opinion quite one of the soundest and best of our war admirals, and was never given credit for his doings. Winston and Brendan Bracken disliked him.'[4] Maybe they did, but so did lots of others, and there was no division between the Prime Minister and the Chiefs of Staff on naval deployment in the face of the threat of invasion.

A more fundamental problem with the Admiralty lay in its wish to abandon the eastern Mediterranean and concentrate on Gibraltar, so that the Atlantic approaches could be guarded. Churchill made a decision of enormous significance. In the face of considerable opposition from Pound he ordered that the fleet be kept at Alexandria, even if Spain and Italy joined the Axis powers. This bold move was part of a strategic shift from the pre-war concept of giving priority to Far Eastern interests, and was endorsed by the decision of the Chiefs of Staff at the beginning of July to hold the Middle East and eastern Mediterranean for as long as possible. Without Churchill's initiative, the continued British presence in North Africa, the only active theatre in the early years of the war, would not have been possible. There was to be debate about who was responsible for Britain's Mediterranean Strategy in the war. Sir Alan Brooke, who became Chief of the Imperial General Staff, claimed to have invented it. But it was overwhelmingly Churchill's brainchild. It represented the confluence of a number of his decisions and priorities, and keeping the fleet at Alexandria was the first of them.

Brooke, on the other hand, in the early stages of the war was in charge of the Home Command, and he did his best to resist the transfer of troops out of Britain. His policy was the product of his responsibilities, but if he had prevailed over Churchill's bolder vision there would have been no engagement with the enemy, no opportunity for British and American troops in North Africa to join hands with the forces in the Western Desert: no alternative to a final and hazardous assault on mainland Europe. There would have been no Mediterranean Strategy, and victory would have been deferred for two years.

As early as 27 November 1940 Churchill told Colville that he wanted to 'wage war on a great scale in the Middle East. By next spring I hope we shall have sufficient forces there.' The Mediterranean war was the result of this vision, which brought together Italy's weakness, oil interests and opportunism. The boldness of the decision to transfer resources away from the British Isles which were under great threat, and not as convention would suggest to the Far East, was his brave and personal choice.

The RAF was left alone to a great extent and indeed enjoyed a sort of quasi-independence from Chiefs of Staff control. Dowding was able to resist requests from his allies and from British forces in France that would have involved seriously depleting the limited resources that were being held for the subsequent Battle of Britain. He had told Churchill with the support of the Chiefs of Staff that with fewer than twenty-five squadrons of fighters Britain could not be defended. He knew that Churchill was under huge pressure from the French, but in his view the Battle of France was already lost, and obliging the French further risked losing the war. 'What I did was to get out of my chair, walk round the Cabinet table, lay down in front of Churchill a graph which I had prepared . . . I said, "This is my graph of the losses of Hurricanes during the past ten days; it shows that if losses continue at the same rate for the next ten days we shall not have a single Hurricane left in France or in England." This did the trick and the wastage of fighters was stopped.'[5]

Dowding's strength of character had profound implications for the outcome of the Battle of Britain. Like Harris, he was not popular with his fellows, but Churchill recognised the merits of both men. Harris was appointed to take over Bomber Command after a highly critical report on the leadership of his predecessor, Air Marshal Sir Richard Peirse, in the 7 November 1941 raids in which thirty-seven aircraft were lost.

Air Chief Marshal Sir Cyril Newall, who had been Chief of the Air Staff since 1937, emerged from the Battle of France with diminished authority and was replaced by Sir Charles Portal, who remained in place throughout the war and was a key member of the Chief of Staff Committee.

At the head of the army, Ironside was Chief of the Imperial General Staff from the outbreak of war until 27 May 1940. During the Battle of France he had gone with Gort, Commander-in-Chief of the Field Force, as the Expeditionary Force was technically referred to, to see General Billotte at Lens. Billotte was with General Blanchard, Commander-in-Chief of the First French Army. Both were in despair. Billotte was a small man. 'Tiny' Ironside was six feet four inches tall. (Gort's nickname was 'Fat Boy' because he was slim.) Ironside in frustration finally picked up Billotte by his tunic and shook him like a rag doll. These British generals seem to have been a physical bunch: Spears told Churchill that at an interview with Reynaud on 27 May 1940 'I shook the little man, in quite a friendly sort of way of course'. But the French could be physical too: after a telephone conversation with Ironside, Weygand said on one occasion that he would have liked to box the British general's ears. It was said that he would have had to climb on a chair to do so.

Ironside's intellectual ability was limited. It was possibly his sheer size rather than anything else that made Buchan choose him as his model for Richard Hannay. Brooke was not well disposed towards him, though there were not many people to whom he was well disposed. He was recalled from the governorship of Gibraltar in May 1939 to be Inspector-General of Overseas Forces. Sir John French had held this position before the First World War and combined it with the appointment, quasi-tacit, of Commander-in-Chief designate. In Ironside's case, there was no parallel appointment, not even a tacit one, but he behaved as if it were in the bag, to the extent that he sent his assistant to Aldershot to recruit headquarters staff when war seemed imminent. He was to be disappointed. Hore-Belisha, the reforming Secretary of State for War, had been getting on badly with the CIGS, Gort, and was glad to send him off to France. Gort's successor as CIGS was Ironside, whom Hore-Belisha had passed over for the appointment, rightly in Ironside's view, in 1938.

It was an appointment which Churchill, then at the Admiralty, pressed for, but it was not a good one. It would not have been wise to give him the appointment in 1938 and he was no more suitable two years later. He had never held a staff appointment at the War Office in his life. Churchill had to work with him on the Norway campaign, when the CIGS was irritated by Churchill's detailed interventions. After just a year in office Ironside was replaced by Dill and was much happier in his new position as Commander-in-Chief Home Forces. On his dismissal Gort had been shunted off to Gibraltar in April 1941, but just seven months later Churchill had the bizarre notion of reappointing him as CIGS in succession to Dill. A few months later, in March 1942, he considered using him to replace Auchinleck in the Middle East. He was dissuaded by Brooke: Gort was another officer for whom he had little time.

In command of Home Forces, Ironside's preparations against invasion consisted substantially of a 'crust' along the potential invasion coastlines, with relatively light inland defences ahead of a strong line designed to stop invaders from reaching London or the Midlands. The plans were criticised: they were thought to imply a readiness to yield considerable areas of land near the coast. With limited resources, Ironside really did not have much choice, but Brooke, who was appointed to Southern Command on 26 June 1940, was particularly keen on creating a strong reserve: a notion which Churchill supported, despite the speech about fighting on the beaches. Indeed the PM told the Chiefs of Staff on 28 June 1940 that 'the battle will be won or lost, not on the beaches, but by the mobile brigades and the main reserve'.[6] Churchill's view was that of many local commanders as well of Brooke.

The PM toured the south coast defences on 17 June 1940, when he was nobbled by Brooke and accepted that he was the man to defend Britain. Brooke replaced Ironside on 19 June 1940.

In these heroic days, invasion was not regarded simply as a possibility: it was *expected* – probably in East Anglia rather than on the south coast. There were, as always, differences between Churchill and his advisers. He was sanguine that nothing would happen as long as the Royal Air Force commanded the skies. The military tended to the view that the Germans might well move before then, possibly in a series of scattered raids. Ironside thought that 9 July was the most likely date, and Churchill was later to speak of a peak of invasion excitement 'even in high quarters during the first week of July' though rather disassociating himself from that view.[7] In reality he, as much as anyone else, expected invasion daily during the second week of July. Churchill saw the issue of whether or not invasion took place in strategic terms. On Sunday, 14 July he noted perceptively, 'Hitler must invade or fail. If he fails he is bound to go east, and fail he will.'[8]

Early in September 1940, invasion was expected from day to day, almost from hour to hour. On 4 September Eden had highlighted the risk in remarks that were reported in the *Times*. The Invasion Warning Sub-Committee heard that all leave was to be cancelled in the German Army on 8 September. On 7 September the code word 'Cromwell', which was to indicate that invasion was expected, was used – causing considerable confusion among those who inferred that invasion had already taken place. Attempts at pre-emptive bridge destruction were only stopped with difficulty.

Just three days later in a speech on the BBC, Churchill spoke in ringing terms about the risk of invasion: 'We must regard the next week or so as a very important period in our history. It ranks with the days when the Spanish Armada was approaching the Channel and Drake was finishing his game of bowls, or when Nelson stood between us and Napoleon's Grand Army at Boulogne.'[9] Stirring stuff, but by then he was privately coming to the view that invasion was increasingly unlikely. He found it helpful and indeed necessary however to maintain the notion of immediate national danger. It was good for morale and it kept his Tory enemies at bay.[10]

Similarly, and quite a bit later, he found it useful not to share with Roosevelt the fact that invasion was no longer expected. The apprehension of danger might stimulate American assistance.[11]

Churchill saw 15 September as 'the culminating date' in the Battle of Britain. That view was not entirely the product of hindsight. He had spent the day at the headquarters of No.11 Group, Fighter Command, at Uxbridge, where he had watched the direction of the air battle. In the course of the day, there were echoes of the exchange with Gamelin on 16 May, when he had asked where the strategic reserves were. A similar question to Air Vice-Marshal Park, Commander of No.11 Group about reserves received the reply: 'There are none'. But by the time Churchill had returned to London and wakened at eight o'clock from his afternoon nap, he was told that 183 German planes had been destroyed with a loss of fewer than 40 British planes. The figures were not wholly accurate, but their message was unmistakable. The Battle of France had been lost; the Battle of Britain had almost certainly been won. But if invasion and defeat were no longer imminent, how, with no allies and with a routed army and unproven commanders, could war be waged against Germany?

Carrying the War to the Enemy: The Western Desert 1940

At this stage Churchill's difficulties with Pound and the other Chiefs of Staff lay principally in the fact that they wanted total concentration on defence of the United Kingdom, while Churchill was looking increasingly for offensive opportunities. He did not believe that the war could be won in any other way. Equally, he was certain that America would not come to Britain's aid unless Britain were seen to be capable of helping herself. He was aware that the American ambassador, Joseph Kennedy, was telling Roosevelt that Britain did not have the stomach for a fight. Kennedy was not the only American pessimist. General Raymond E. Lee, the United States Military Attaché said in September 1940: 'On a cold-blooded appraisal, one might say that the betting on Britain's beating off an invasion this fall is now about three to one.'[1]

Churchill knew that his personal and political position depended on delivering results. By the end of September 1940, the month in which Dakar – his first offensive operation and an unmitigated disaster – had taken place, 6,954 civilians had been killed and in the first week of October alone, a further 2,000 died.

Consequently, the moment the imminent risk of invasion had passed – or even before that moment – Churchill wished to see resources moved overseas. Only thus could the Axis be beaten. Only thus would America be convinced that Britain meant business. 'The completely defensive habit of mind which has ruined the French must not be allowed to ruin all our initiative.' The offensive spirit was distilled into the various cloak-and-dagger organisations he now set up: a Special Operations Executive, Commandos, paratroops and a Directorate of Combined Operations. These organisations were to be used to make the sort of random strikes that had been a traditional part of British strategy in the eighteenth century. They were also, however, the product of a personal weakness for unconventional warfare that ties in with an exaggerated view of the value of the Boer commandos that Churchill had seen forty years earlier. A favourite target was always Norway; the French Atlantic coast and German islands were also favoured. This scattered opportunism did not appeal at all to conventional military planners. It was the sort of approach that infuriated Brooke when he became Chief of the Imperial General Staff in December of the following year. He saw no merit in what he regarded as an uncoordinated series of adventures. 'If you're going to the barbers,' he expostulated to Churchill, 'you decide where you're heading for before you go out the door.' Churchill in reply was as silly as he sometimes could be: 'No I don't'.

The lack of judgement argument is too glib an explanation for mistakes. From the outset of his political life there had been attacks on his judgement. When, for instance, he became First Lord for the first time, in 1911, the *Spectator* wrote, 'He has not the loyalty, the dignity, the steadfastness and the good sense which makes the efficient head of a great office'; and this sort of complaint was the commonest criticism over the years. Chamberlain and Halifax said the same thing, and the point was made most famously, and gently, by Baldwin, in a put-down that he prepared but never used, the story of the fairies that attended Churchill's birth. They gave him courage, wit, eloquence and every other gift that could be wished for, until the last one said that this would not do, he must have a fault, and she bestowed on him a fatal want of judgement.

His judgement certainly could sometimes look woefully erratic. In argument and particularly when in opposition he was inclined to throw out a mass of extreme propositions, some of which were simply designed to shock, some of which were not thought through at all, and some of which he would seek to defend to the end. But when he was in a position of authority his approach was quite different. He had learned from the Dardanelles the danger of pursuing a policy on which he did not have the wholehearted backing of his department and his colleagues. His approach a few years later at the Treasury showed just how seriously he had taken that lesson; and when he had supreme power he exercised it with infinite caution. His language and his arguments could still be extreme, but at the end of the exchanges he submitted to unanimous professional advice. In his direction of the war there is nothing in what he did, as opposed to what he said, which reflects a serious lack of judgement.

When he was occasionally strategically weak, the problem proceeded from a failure to take on board changes in the nature of warfare. He did not recognise the reduced significance of the infantry: he continued to talk of 'sabres and bayonets'. His concept of 'fortresses' like Tobruk and Singapore was consequently flawed. He did not remember how fast modern armies could move: when he criticised the idea of American landings in the south of France, for instance, he talked of the length of their 'march' to the front. His ideas about warfare were drawn from earlier centuries and refined by what he had seen of the First World War, and the lessons of that war continued to dominate his thinking and his fears. The nature of the battles in North Africa did not dislodge from his mind the fear of a line of trenches across Europe, and even after D-Day he feared a return to the lines and the wire of 1915.

There were *idées fixes*, of which the appeal of northern Norway is probably the best example. There was a determination, after America's entry into the war, that Britain should do as much as her more powerful ally, not solely so that she had the right to an equal share in the direction of the war, but partly because it was demeaning to do less. As late as April 1945 he complained to Clementine, 'The only times I ever quarrel with the Americans are when they fail to give us a fair share of opportunities to win glory. Undoubtedly I feel much pain when I see our armies so much smaller than theirs. It has always been my wish to keep equal, but how can you do that against so mighty a nation and a population nearly three times your own?'[2] Similarly, strategy was sometimes evolved with an eye to the history books. At Casablanca ambitious, perhaps unrealistic, plans were promoted simply because it was unworthy of two great powers to do less.[3]

Brooke made the complaint, especially in the early stages of the war, about a lack of a joined-up vision. But Churchill's preference for feints and probes was not entirely born of a lack of alternative. Throughout the war he favoured seeking opportunities that could be exploited, rather than allowing logistics to dictate the prosecution and persistence of an unprofitable campaign. This was to be at the centre of the difference between him and America in relation to OVERLORD in June 1944.

In the early stages of the war, in any case, what else could he do? The linchpin of British planning had disappeared with France. There had been a steady process of disillusionment with America as an ally since 1919. When she turned her back on the League of Nations, she appeared to turn her back also on Europe and a strengthening anti-British feeling led to the conviction in the United Kingdom that

America would not be a reliable ally: a conviction that to an extent lay behind the argument for appeasement.

Having been expelled from the mainland of Europe, Britain had to conduct her offensive operations elsewhere. Despite Churchill's continuing fondness for Norway, the fact that there was a British presence in Egypt dictated that it would be in North Africa that Britain, and later America too, would concentrate her military activities in the first half of the war.

Despite the fact that a Mobile Force (Egypt), subsequently Armoured Division (Egypt), had been established in 1938, the British presence in Egypt was not substantial and was intended principally to protect the Suez Canal. But Churchill's ambitions for the Middle East were central to his strategic views at this stage. The crucial change of strategy of July 1940, the determination to hold the Middle East and the eastern Mediterranean for as long as possible, reversed the established policy of giving precedence to the Far East.

Mussolini played a part in events, planning to seize the Canal and extend his North African possessions. With the Italian declaration of war on Britain on 10 July 1940, Britain's Middle Eastern interests were at risk, and Mussolini can be added to the list of those responsible for the Mediterranean Strategy. In response to this threat Churchill bravely took 154 tanks away from defence of the homeland in August and sent them to Wavell in North Africa. On 13 September Graziani attacked from Cyrenaica in Libya, but after initial successes ran out of steam.

Wavell had not always been Churchill's favourite general, and he did not remain in favour for long. He had come to London to ask for increased resources in August 1940, but at a series of meetings between 8 and 15 August the relationship between the two men deteriorated badly. Neither really understood the other. Churchill became convinced that the general was pessimistic and excessively cautious. The Prime Minister constantly complained that not enough men were in the field: the tail was too long, the discrepancy between the ration strength and the fighting strength too great. Thus, early in the following year, after successes in the desert, he wrote to Wavell apologising for spoiling 'the hour of your victory by awkward matters of housekeeping . . . I beg you to convince me that you will continually comb, scrub and purge all rearward services in a hard unrelenting manner, as Kitchener did.'[4] Critics claimed that the PM did not understand the changes since Kitchener's day, but he did understand the caution that generals frequently and sometimes commendably display.

Wavell for his part certainly did not understand Churchill's confrontational, dialectic, debating-chamber approach. The process was bewildering for those who were not used to it. Ismay recalled a young brigadier from Middle East Headquarters who asked the Prime Minister if he might be quite frank. 'Of course', was the reply, 'We are not here to pay each other compliments.'

The Prime Minister would seize on the point he wished to make, overstate it and surround it with distorted half-truths and exaggerations.[5] He expected his interlocutor to respond in a similar style, and that out of the fury of the exchanges a consensus would emerge. That did not always happen. His antagonist often knew not whether to concentrate on the main point or try to correct the encircling errors. Brooke would doggedly fight the issue out, but others did not, and Wavell certainly could not cope with the browbeating violence. At their meetings in August he sat in almost complete silence. The CIGS, Sir John Dill, understood Churchill, though he was not impressive at managing him and called their meetings a 'daily circus'. He pleaded with Wavell, '*Talk* to him, Archie', but Wavell did not do so, and as early as 15 August 1940 Churchill and Eden were discussing the question of a successor for the Middle East Command.

The appointment with which Churchill toyed was a remarkable one: Major-General Bernard Freyberg, VC, a very junior officer, although a very brave one, and one without any of the political diplomatic and administrative skills needed for a command such as the Middle East.[6] In addition to his VC, Freyberg held no less than three DSOs and had been wounded on innumerable occasions. There is dispute about just how many wounds he had suffered: there may have been too many to count. Churchill, who had always courted danger in his military career, was fascinated by physical courage and admired gallantry. He himself had willingly sacrificed part of his pelt to patch up a wounded fellow-officer. When he met Freyberg between the wars he asked him to strip so that he could admire his wounds.

Dill wrote of the relationship between the PM and the Commander, Middle East, 'They are poles apart. Wavell is very reserved – "withdrawn" is perhaps a better word – whereas Winston even thinks aloud'. After the first of the difficult series of meetings, Churchill invited Wavell to Chequers for the weekend. Wavell told Dill that he had no intention of going to 'risk further treatment of the kind to which he had just been subjected'. Dill went to the heart of things: 'Archie, no one would deny that you have had unbearable provocation. But he is our

Prime Minister. He carries an almost incredible burden. It is true you can be replaced. He cannot. You must go to Chequers'.[7]

Wavell retained the command for the moment and got his tanks, but there were disputes about whether they should be convoyed straight through the Mediterranean, as Churchill wanted, or round the Cape, as Wavell wished. Churchill got his way, and at the end of the war, 'Gil' Winant, the American ambassador in London, referred to it as 'the bravest thing' the Prime Minister had done in the war.

When British Somaliland was evacuated on 17 August, despite the fact that British casualties were far fewer than Italian casualties, Churchill wanted the local commander, Major-General Godwin-Austen, removed at once. Wavell stood up to the demand with the reply that 'a heavy butcher's bill is not necessarily evidence of good tactics', a remarkably injudicious thing to say to Churchill. He was greatly infuriated. Dill said he had never seen him so angry. He flushed and glowered. Wavell had not made a judicious career move.

Wavell had planned his first offensive, COMPASS, against a background of very strict security, with only Generals Wilson and O'Connor and essential staff officers aware of what was to happen. With notorious espionage circles in Cairo, that was wise. It was not so wise to tell the Prime Minister himself as little as possible of his plans. It was more unfortunate still that a message from Wavell to Dill, 'Please do not encourage optimism', found its way to Churchill. It is difficult to imagine a less Churchillian sentiment. Churchill's own prodding messages could be infuriating. Admiral A.B. Cunningham said that they were often 'ungracious and hasty . . . Such messages to those who were doing their utmost with straitened resources were not an encouragement, merely an annoyance.'[8] Wavell had already formulated a foolish policy of ignoring a large part of Churchill's stream of instructions and enquiries; he should not have been surprised if as a result Churchill concluded that what he liked to call his Army of the Nile was doing nothing. It was only when Eden, as Secretary of State for War, arrived in Cairo that Wavell's plan for COMPASS became known.

Churchill reacted with delight when Wavell at last sent him his plan for offensive action in the Western Desert in November 1940. 'At long last', he told Ismay, 'we are going to throw off the intolerable shackle of the defensive.'[9] While the Italian forces awaited re-supply a much smaller British force under O'Connor counter-attacked in Operation COMPASS on 9 December.

O'Connor, a capable and attractive character who shared the general enthusiasm for casual dress in the Western Desert, favouring corduroy trousers, leather jerkin and tartan scarf, turned what Wavell had planned as a very limited, five-day operation, into a great success. When Sidi Barrani fell on 11 December 1940, Churchill did two things. He sent a splendid message to the King: 'My humble congratulations to you, Sir, on a great British victory – a great Imperial victory'. And then he sent for the two books that Wavell had written, in a further attempt to try to understand his commander in the Middle East.[10]

By 30 January O'Connor had taken more than 20,000 prisoners. He pushed forward to capture Bardia and Tobruk and by February 1941 the Italians had been comprehensively defeated. They were surrounded at Beda Fomm in February where 25,000 men were captured. What was left of the Italian force fell back to El Agheila by 9 February 1941. In three days O'Connor halted Graziani's advance and took 38,000 prisoners including four generals (the joke of the times was that the more Italian generals he captured, the greater O'Connor's service to the Italian war effort), at a cost of 624 casualties, and in two months he had advanced 350 miles, taken 130,000 prisoners, almost 400 tanks and 845 guns, at a cost of 500 killed, 1,373 wounded and 55 missing. O'Connor had eventually moved as far as El Agheila, overrunning the whole of Cyrenaica. Pretty well the whole Italian army had been captured.

Churchill had found an occasion to rise to: 'The Army of the Nile [a favourite designation with important Napoleonic echoes] has rendered glorious service to the Empire and our cause, and rewards are already being reaped by us in every quarter'. The victory would not have been won if Churchill had not pushed Wavell into COMPASS, and nagged him about the size of his tail.

Until this point, the North African campaign was an unqualified British success, and Italy was close to being knocked out of the war. But 'the great British victory' was soon overshadowed, and the next phase of the Desert War was a series of disastrous setbacks. Two things happened.

First, what had been a more or less independent adventure by Mussolini had to be supported by Germany if her Italian ally were not to be abandoned. Rommel was sent out with the Afrika Korps.

Secondly, the Axis attack on Greece was to put an end to O'Connor's romp through Cyrenaica. Britain moved air cover to Greece and by the beginning of January 1941 it was decided to provide maximum support to the Greeks. The policy was temporarily thwarted when General Metaxas, the Greek Prime Minister, declined British aid; but when he died on 29 January his successor requested assistance. Wavell was told that Greece was to take precedence over North Africa. This decision continues to excite controversy.

Rommell's brief initially was a defensive one, but the nature of his mission changed almost immediately when he realised that the British forces, stretched between North Africa and Greece, were extremely light. He won a victory at El Agheila on 24 March and then launched an offensive which put Britain right back to Sollum on 15 April, where Graziani had been on 17 September 1940. The whole of Libya was now in Axis hands except for Tobruk. O'Connor, along with General Neame, got lost, fell into enemy hands and remained in captivity until the Italian surrender – payback for capturing the Italian generals in COMPASS, but a disappointing fate for a good general who might have turned out to be a great desert general. Wavell was conscious of the loss and pressed for an exchange for an Italian general – at one for one a remarkably favourable ratio so far as Italian generals are concerned. Churchill vetoed the swap.

It was not only the end for O'Connor: Tobruk itself was under siege. Attempts to relieve it, operations BREVITY and BATTLEAXE, were unsuccessful, and for the moment the lines were stabilised. COMPASS was at an end.

O'Connor believed he could have gone on to take Tripoli. After the war Wavell said that was too ambitious a claim, but Rommel had disagreed. In any event O'Connor was not allowed the opportunity. How far did the decision to support Greece bring an end to early successes in North Africa? How far was Churchill responsible for that decision?

Greece

Churchill is often blamed for sabotaging COMPASS for the sake of a quixotic Greek adventure.[1] Wavell's supporters still think his efforts were undercut by his being forced to divert resources to Greece, but it is wrong to think that COMPASS was brought to a premature end because of a switch to Greece taken against his wishes.

The decision to enter Greece was not essentially Churchill's. Additionally, Wavell's forces were partly depleted for quite another reason. He had detached the 4th Indian Division so that it was available to attack the Italians in East Africa. That was not a bad decision. General Cunningham opened a campaign against Italian Somaliland from Kenya in February 1941, and by May 1941, Mussolini's East African empire had been effectively destroyed. Moreover, Wavell was not confident that Tripoli could be taken; on the other hand, he thought that operation LUSTRE – forward defence in Greece – was militarily feasible.

In the event Greece proved a disaster, but there was a political inevitability at the time about coming to the aid of a country which Britain had undertaken to defend in 1939. It was important to show that Britain honoured her obligations. There could not be a repeat of Munich.

Churchill was indeed initially averse to a diversion of forces, and faced Cabinet criticism on that count. Eden and Dill were sent out to Egypt to assess the situation, and Churchill only came to be supportive of the Greek campaign after they, the men on the spot, strongly pressed the case, supported by Wavell. Eden signalled that 'assistance to the Greeks, who are fighting and threatened, must have first call on our resources'.[2] As the League of Nations man who had resigned as Foreign Secretary in part over sanctions against Italy, he felt strongly that Britain must stand by its pledge to aid Greece. Wavell, for his part, had always been concerned about the threat from the north, rather than the west. He had agreed earlier with Weygand that Greece and Yugoslavia would be the front line. Even ahead of Eden's arrival at his head-quarters he had started moving experienced troops out of Cyrenaica. He greeted Eden with the words, 'As you were so long I felt I had to get started, and I have begun the concentration for the move of troops to Greece'.[3]

Churchill had certainly made vague romantic declarations – 'Let your first thoughts be of Greece' – but when it came to a considered judgement it was not he who argued for action. He cabled to Eden: 'Do not consider yourself obligated to a Greek enterprise if in your hearts you feel it will only be another Norwegian fiasco. If no good plan can be made, please say so. But of course you know how valuable success would be'.[4] There is no evidence that Churchill pushed for the Greek campaign in the face of opposition. There was none. Members of the Cabinet were asked for their views one by one and they were unanimously in favour. The politicians on the spot were also in favour. Wavell was for it, so was Pound and so were the Chiefs of Staff.[5]

The decision to enter Greece was made by the Cabinet on 7 March 1941. The decision was influenced and endorsed by the Australian Prime Minister, Robert Menzies, who arrived in Britain on 20 February and did not leave until 3 May, participating in War Cabinet meetings during his stay.

But there were certainly some generals against Greece at the time. A General Staff minute by Kennedy, Director of Military Operations, for example, said that, 'Nothing we can do can makes the Greek business a sound military proposition . . . In the Middle East we must not throw away our power of offensive action by adopting an unsound policy in Greece . . .'[6] Brooke said that he always considered Greece to be 'a definite strategic blunder. Our hands were more than full at the time in the Middle East . . .' Subsequently Churchill's critics have consistently tried to represent Greece as an adventure that sabotaged North Africa. Correlli Barnett argued that the thought of intervention in Greece 'was to grow until it dominated the Prime Minister's obstinate mind, was made fact against all initial advice by his formidable will; it led to two immediate military disasters; and prolonged the war in Africa by two years'.[7]

This view is simply not supported by the evidence. Indeed Churchill never bought entirely into Greece. His heart was for it, but intellectually he hesitated. He had been enthusiastic about a Greek campaign at a slightly earlier stage, before it became clear that the Greeks did not want

British assistance and before he knew about Wavell's offensive. And later he said that Wavell had 'spoiled his African show for the sake of a Greek adventure in which he believed and in which he was much pressed by Eden, with the consent of Dill, on general political grounds . . . His great mistake was allowing the desert flank to be broken in. I would never have gone to Greece if I had not thought the desert flank was secure.'[8]

Dill had initially been against Greece, but when he was sent out with Eden he changed his mind. Eden had been given extraordinarily wide powers: 'His principal object will be the sending of speedy succour to Greece. For this purpose he will initiate any action he may think necessary'. He was not to be 'deterred from acting upon his own authority if the urgency is too great to allow reference home'. Back in London, Kennedy was disconcerted to find that Dill and Wavell had changed their minds, and kept sending telegrams suggesting that there was a fair chance of success. He concluded that they had gone native, and were giving political as opposed to purely military advice, but he found he could not overturn the growing opinion in favour of the project.[9]

The campaign was also endorsed by Admiral Andrew Cunningham. He thought that there would be great dangers to troop and supply convoys, but he signalled, 'We are, I am convinced, pursuing right policy and risk must be faced up to'. *Later* he recorded in his diary that he 'was against it [Greece]' but acquiesced for the political reasons *put forward by Eden.*[10]

Some months later Churchill told Colville that Greece had been his government's only mistake in the war to date and in his history of the war he did say that he took 'full responsibility for the eventual decision' – but only 'because I am sure I could have stopped it all if I had been convinced'.[11] He also took pains to explain that his decision had been made on the advice of the men on the spot. Rather unfairly in view of the wide powers he had given to him, he told Eden, a week after the decision to go ahead with the campaign had been made, that 'no one but you can combine and concert the momentous policy which you have pressed upon us'.[12] Eden's position was an uncomfortable one and there is a distinct feeling that he was being set up to carry the can. Churchill further secured his position by ordering an inquiry into whether he had bypassed his professional advisers. That was found not to be the case. During that inquiry Wavell said too that he had 'never questioned the decision to support Greece . . . I am sure that our general strategy was correct in the circumstances.'[13] Some of the criticism of the Greek adventure, both at home and in Cairo, was of course made in ignorance of Enigma intelligence, and possible German moves against Greece were regarded as no more than bluff.

There were indeed arguments against assisting Greece, even if they are clearer in retrospect than they were at the time. The British Army in Libya could not really afford to shed resources, and the Greeks did not withdraw, as they had agreed to do, from Macedonia to the River Aliakmon, which Britain and Greece were supposed to defend together. Churchill was annoyed. On 13 April he sent a telegram to Wilson: 'It is impossible for me to understand why the Greek western army does not make sure of its retreat into Greece'.[14]

On 18 April, the Greek Prime Minister, Korysis, contemplating defeat, committed suicide. On the following day Wavell joined Wilson in Greece and decided on evacuation. They did not tell Churchill. He had already been complaining about lack of information from Wavell and he reiterated his concern about the lack of reports on 19 April. 'This is not the way the Government should be treated. It is also detrimental to the Service as many decisions have to be taken here . . .' He requested 'a short, daily report on what is happening on the Front of the British and Imperial Army'.[15] His position was entirely reasonable, but Wavell and Wilson (the latter not usually prickly) resented the criticism.

The Greek campaign was short and may have been misconceived – although it has been argued that without the 1941 action there would not have been moral authority for the decisive intervention in the Greek civil war in December 1944.[16] What is more likely is that the Greek campaign delayed the German onslaught on Russia by five or six weeks, and may have saved Moscow.[17] Britain also gained some points in America. She was defending a smaller country that was under attack, and Roosevelt approved.[18]

Evacuation of Wilson's forces from Greece began as early as 24 April, just eighteen days after Germany launched her attacks on Greece and Yugoslavia. Although Jumbo Wilson was in tactical control of LUSTRE, it was Wavell who held overall responsibility. He was not assisted by the quality of his staff in Cairo, and he failed to eliminate unsatisfactory officers. Wilson wrote to his wife on 1 May: 'So ended a military adventure which I hope I will not participate in again. The political considerations overrode the military ones and led us into a gamble based on the uncertain quality of Balkan allies.'[19] Some of the withdrawn troops were taken to Crete, a practical decision rather than a strategic one, but a decision that was to lead to yet another disaster.

Difficulties with Wavell

In the face of the offensive Rommel opened on 25 March 1941, Churchill consistently sought to reinforce Wavell, in particular in tanks. He was supported by Eden, but opposed by Dill and Kennedy, who pointed to the very great risk that the convoys would not get through the Mediterranean. Brooke, looking at his responsibilities for the defence of Britain, talked of 'raiding his orchard'. Churchill's decision was the right one, as Kennedy later acknowledged, but it was a brave one and a lonely one, which he made without military support.

Events were moving fast and horribly badly. On 25 April Rommel entered Egypt. Just a week earlier, as Greece surrendered, the Chiefs of Staff ruled that restoring the Libyan front should have priority over Greece, as Tobruk came under attack, and by the end of the month they had concluded that Crete rather than being a safe fallback position was now itself vulnerable and critically required urgent defence against a background of intelligence reports of imminent German attack from the air.

The principal ground commander in Crete, Major-General Sir Bernard Freyberg, VC, Churchill's unlikely suggestion as Wavell's successor in August of the previous year, did not handle the Battle of Crete perfectly, but Wavell, admittedly burdened by a huge range of responsibilities, had tended to overlook the defence of the island, despite that the fact that its importance had been urged on him since 1940. Churchill certainly thought there was a lack of grip in his handling of Crete and of Greece. He tried to impress both on Wavell and Freyberg the need for stout action. Churchill later said that there was no point in the war when they had such detailed intelligence about German movements. He appears to have passed it on in detail even to local commanders. Freyberg may have been told by Wavell of the existence of Ultra itself. What he was not told was that Hitler was committed to domination of the whole Mediterranean area. Accordingly, even with the information he was being given by Churchill, he could not conceive that a huge airborne attack would be launched on what he regarded as a secondary position.[1]

More importantly, Freyberg and Wavell had been told by the intelligence chief, Sir Stewart Menzies, 'C', that to avoid compromising Ultra, nothing could be done on the basis of information obtained only from that source. Accordingly, although Ultra indicated that Germany's plans depended on taking Malame aerodrome, Freyberg felt himself unable to reinforce it. 'The authorities in England', he said, 'would prefer to lose Crete rather than jeopardise Ultra'. Looking up from his breakfast at the parachuting Germans, he grunted, 'Well, they're on time'.[2]

Churchill did not know that 'C' had given these instructions, and never forgave Wavell and Freyberg for their inaction. But Freyberg does not deserve much sympathy. He acted on his instructions in an unimaginative and inflexible way. Defending the principal aerodrome on Crete would scarcely have compromised his intelligence. Wavell does not seem to have taken pains to clarify the issue.

Greece and Crete, together with Rommel's spectacular advance in North Africa, were massive blows to British morale. Evelyn Waugh vividly recorded the impact on the troops – and indeed how bitterly he himself was affected. It is difficult to see that Churchill was to blame. The fault lay in the quality of the commanders, and in a poor local command system.

There was a need for wholesale changes at a senior level; but the moves after Greece and Crete were limited. Sir Arthur Longmore, the Air Commander in the Middle East, had made clear his disapproval of intervention in Greece. He was sacked in May 1941. After Crete, Andrew Cunningham, Commander of the Mediterranean Fleet, was prepared to resign because he had not been given the air cover he had requested. His resignation was not accepted.

Churchill was dismayed by this dismal performance and his mood did not lift when he heard of preparations that Wavell had made for an evacuation of Egypt. Wavell had no immediate withdrawal from Cairo in mind, and on one view, the war could be continued quite effectively from positions further south. Indeed, it would have been negligent not to engage in forward planning. But as so often Wavell failed to keep Churchill advised of what he was really thinking, and to carry the Prime Minister with him. The existence of contingency plans for the evacuation of Egypt had emerged after a magnificent clash between Churchill

and General Kennedy, the Director of Military Operations, on 27
April. Churchill bellowed, 'Wavell has 400,000 men. If they lose Egypt,
blood will flow. I will have firing parties shoot the generals'. When the
shaken Kennedy responded by mentioning the evacuation plans, he
threw petrol on Churchill's smouldering rage: 'This comes as a flash of
lightning to me. War is a contest of wills. It is pure defeatism to speak as
you have done.' On the following day he ordered revocation of all plans
for the evacuation of Egypt which, he said, 'would be a disaster of the
first magnitude to Great Britain, second only to a successful invasion'.[3]

He would have been even more horrified if he had known, as indeed
he did discover a few weeks later, that Wavell had elaborated plans for
an even worse case: the conduct of the war from Africa following the
defeat not just of Egypt, but of the British Isles.

Kennedy's memoirs, *The Business of War*, were published in November
1957, just a few months after those of Brooke, now Lord Alanbrooke.
Both books attracted immense interest. Kennedy's book was serialised in
the *Evening Standard*, under the headline 'Churchill and the Generals –
Who knew best?' The critical response was divided in both cases, but
overall was very much in favour of Churchill. In the *Daily Mirror*, under
the headline 'Meet General Superman', Cassandra said that Alanbrooke
had jumped from nowhere to 'the highest literary military pedestal built
within living memory'. His editor, Bryant, had poured out on him 'a
sickening, sweetened slime of unending praise', whereas Churchill was
depicted as 'positively dangerous when it came to the major decisions of
the war'. If his story were true, said Alan Tomkins in the *Daily Mail*, it was
remarkable that Britain had won the war.[4]

In the same paper Henry Fairlie made a much more analytical
comment regarding the Kennedy book: Kennedy revealed that Churchill had been the goad of his executives, but more importantly the book
showed 'why the goad was needed'. Kennedy's book is petulant, self-
regarding and self-justifying, containing long extracts from generalised
and banal memoranda that contributed little to the prosecution of the
war. Churchill would have been surprised at the time to think that both
his Director of Military Operations and Chief of the Imperial General
Staff had the time and energy to compose lengthy diaries at the end of
their working days.

Kennedy was a man of his time and background. He was horrified at
a lunch at the Russian Embassy: 'The Russian officers were as usual a
crude lot . . . [They] ate caviar off their knives; my neighbour held his
bread with both hands as he tore pieces off with his teeth. I could not

help feeling they were odd allies.'[5] He starts from the usual position of a military professional with limited vision who resents the interference of an unqualified outsider; but as the days pass he gradually comes to recognise that it was often the amateur who got things right, and that even if Churchill was sometimes prepared to take a gamble, gambles, rather than dogged staff work, were often what was needed.

Lodged among the criticisms contained in his diaries are innumerable later admissions that it was not the War Office, or Hankey or Menzies, or the other conventional observers who were right, but the unconventional Prime Minister – in regard to reinforcing the Middle East, for example,[6] or in his attitude to Wavell towards the end of the latter's command.[7] The observation that 'we sometimes longed for a leader with more balance and less brilliance'[8] reveals less about the PM's shortcomings than those of his military advisers. Kennedy tries to square the circle by an apologetic disclaimer. '[Despite] all the butterflies released by [Churchill's] limitless fancy . . . the massive figure of the Prime Minister towers above . . . all . . . His glory remains.'[9] Alanbrooke backtracked similarly. But they cannot have it both ways. If their final qualifications mean what they appear to, the petty criticisms that precede them, interesting though they are, tend to paint a picture that is inaccurate, misleading and lacking in perspective.

There never was any real affinity between the Churchill and the silent Wavell. Despite the Prime Minister's own enthusiasm for the verses of the popular Victorian anthologies and his love of the written and spoken word, he could never feel that it was appropriate for a warrior to profess a love of poetry. After the war Wavell was President of the Royal Society of Literature and of the Kipling, Browning, Poetry and Virgil Societies and of the Edinburgh Sir Walter Scott Club: pretty remarkable. Churchill said, 'It may be my fault, but I always feel as if in the presence of the Chairman of a Golf Club'.[10]

Wavell must have seen that in the days of total war, waged by democracies, the political leaders are the true military leaders, and indeed often have access to intelligence which makes them the best military leaders. But he clung to the notion that war was the business of the soldiers, and did not to be discussed with the politicians. The idea of a separation between the political command and the professional soldiers died hard, but those who recognised that it had died survived longer in Churchill's circle. Wavell's responsibilities as a theatre commander have been emphasised by his supporters. They may have been onerous, but Churchill's were infinitely greater.

The Prime Minister had to contemplate not only the performance of the generals in North Africa, but also matters at home. Although the threat of invasion of the British Isles had lifted to a degree in the summer of 1940, it had not gone away. General 'Hap' Arnold, head of the American Army Air Corps, visited London in April 1941 and found real concern at high levels in London about the chance of a German landing on the south coast. 'Dill, Beaverbrook, Freeman and Sinclair all believe it can be done and will be tried.'[11] As early as 15 February Churchill had been worried about invasion and minuted that a 'reduction in population in coastal areas should begin now'.[12] On 6 May 1941, Dill sent the Prime Minister a formal memo, arguing against further movement of troops to the Middle East. By June it was known that Germany was to launch BARBAROSSA on the Soviet Union, but the CIGS expected that Russia would be defeated within six weeks at most. Churchill took a different view: 'I bet you a monkey [£500] to a mousetrap [a guinea] that the Russians are still fighting, and fighting victoriously, two years from now.' No one else thought so.

Dill's memo of 6 May, 'The relation of the Middle East to the security of the United Kingdom', was a lengthy document prompted by Churchill's declarations regarding the importance of Egypt to the war effort. Churchill's position may have been partly emotional, but it was severely practical too: an evacuation of Cairo would have been disastrous for morale and for British standing in America. And the Axis forces could not be defeated in the Far East. It was Dill, and not Churchill, who was adhering blindly to traditional doctrine. In his paper, in what was the most fundamental of many clashes between him and the Prime Minister, Dill argued that

> [The] loss of Egypt would be a calamity which I do not regard as likely and one which we should not accept without a most desperate fight; but it would not end the war. A successful invasion alone spells our final defeat. It is the United Kingdom . . . and not Egypt that is vital, and the defence of the United Kingdom must take first place. Egypt is not even second in our order of priority for it has been an accepted principle in our strategy that in the last resort the security of Singapore comes before that of Egypt . . .[13]

The 'accepted principle' to which Dill referred had been rejected in the reinforcement of the Middle East, which had already taken place in August 1940, but the difference between Dill and Churchill was more profound than that. Churchill was according to Ismay 'shaken to the core' and according to his own account 'astonished' to receive the memo. He replied a week later

> I gather you would be prepared to face the loss of Egypt and the Nile Valley, together with the surrender or ruin of the army of half of million we have concentrated there, rather than lose Singapore. I do not take that view, nor do I think the alternative is likely to present itself . . .[14]

Churchill was wrong about 'the alternative'. In his history of the war he said that his response to Dill put an end to the matter. It did not. Dill responded by saying that, 'I am sure that you, better than anyone else, must realise how difficult it is for a soldier to advise against a bold and offensive plan . . . It takes a lot of moral courage not to be afraid of being thought afraid'. Indeed Dill threatened to resign and to appeal to the War Cabinet if his resignation were not accepted.[15]

But the minute of 6 May 1941 *was* flawed, and represented an unthinking adherence to conservative strategy. Dill continued to think that if his views had been accepted, and if he had been supported by the Secretary of State for War of the time, Margesson, things might have gone differently in Singapore.[16]

Dill was never as robust in confronting Churchill as Alanbrooke would be, but he was not a pushover. He understood Churchill and respected him, but he could never accept the violence of Churchill's style of constructive confrontation. Churchill expected the fury and temper of these exchanges to be forgotten as soon as they were over, as they would be after a clash in the House of Commons. Dill could not react in this way, and he was particularly touchy when his professional loyalties were attacked. In 1940, when he returned to the War Office after a long meeting, his Director of Military Operations 'saw that he was agitated. He said: "I cannot tell you how angry the Prime Minister has made me. What he said about the army tonight I can never forgive . . . He asked me to wait and have a drink with him after the meeting, but I refused and left Anthony [Eden] there by himself" '.[17] To be fair to Dill, what he had to deal with at the time was WORKSHOP, a rather wild plan of Sir Roger Keyes which greatly appealed to the Prime Minister for the occupation of the island of Pantellaria, between Sicily and Libya.

At this point in the war Churchill felt that his role had been critical in staving off defeat in 1940 and that equally *he* had to continue to take the initiative and override the negativism of his professional advisers. On WORKSHOP he and Keyes were more or less alone, and he was prepared to bulldoze the project through the Defence Committee in the face of opposition from all concerned. Even Eden was against it. Fortunately for Churchill WORKSHOP was postponed, first temporarily as a result of a false report about a German attack on Spain, and then permanently, when Germany attacked Greece.[18]

Press and Parliament were rarely docile at any stage in the war and the defeats in Greece and Crete stirred up criticism of the government. There was a two-day debate in the Commons, on Crete more than Greece, which culminated in a vote on 7 May: a comfortable win for Churchill, 447 votes for him, and just 3 against. The figures, as in all such votes during the war, overstate support for the government. There were powerful, critical speeches from Lloyd George, Hore-Belisha and others. A considerable victory was pretty inevitable but there was muttering in the background. Churchill tried to lower expectations:

> I have never promised anything or offered anything but blood, tears, toil and sweat, to which I will now add our fair share of mistakes, shortcomings and disappointments, and also that this may go on for a very long time, at the end of which I firmly believe – though it is not a promise or guarantee, only a profession of faith – that there will be complete, absolute and final victory.[19]

Ismay thought it impossible to run a war when so much time had to be devoted to justifying one's actions in the House of Commons, and Churchill, who did not consider that there had been any errors or miscalculations from London, had to spend much time in preparing for the debate. He spoke for a full hour and a half, and permitted himself to point out that the House did not have the right to information on tactical matters, and to complain that Hitler did not call on the Reichstag to explain the loss of the *Bismarck* and that Mussolini did not have to apologise for his reverses in Africa.[20]

As late as 10 June, Harold Nicolson and Duff Cooper were frustrated by Churchill's belief, which they considered erroneous, that anxiety about the war was confined to the House of Commons.[21] The idea of a country united behind the Prime Minister was a retrospective myth, except at one or two key moments.

Wavell made another mistake. In May 1941 there was revolt in Iraq, a British client state, and the Prime Minister, Rashid Ali, attempted to defect to Germany. Iraq was within Wavell's sphere of command. He took the view that he had insufficient resources with which to intervene, and urged negotiation. Churchill overruled the man on the spot and the revolt was indeed speedily crushed.

Wavell's uncooperative stance ('I have consistently warned you that no assistance could be given to Iraq from Palestine . . . My forces are stretched to the limit everywhere . . . I do not see how I can possibly accept military responsibility') contrasted badly with the offer from Auchinleck, the commander in India, of five infantry brigades for Basra. This received Churchillian approval: 'Your bold and generous offer greatly appreciated'. In the following month, the same sort of situation arose in Vichy French Syria. Churchill's insistence on action proved sound. Syria was subdued and the result of the two operations, Churchill claimed, was to put an end to German threats to the Persian Gulf and India.

The damage Wavell did himself in Churchill's eyes was immense and lasting. Wavell told Churchill that 'Your message [about Iraq] takes little account of realities'. Churchill's response, unsurprisingly, was to consider dismissing Wavell immediately for insubordination; but he decided to await the outcome of the next offensive in the desert, BATTLEAXE. Churchill's directive to Wavell that he should proceed with EXPORTER, the invasion of Syria and Lebanon which began on 8 June, was marvellous: 'And should you feel yourself unwilling to give effect to it, arrangements will be made to meet any wish you may express to be relieved of your command.'[22]

The bravura of the instruction to Wavell to get on with things or go shows how shaky the Commander's position had become. But it also gives an exaggerated impression of Churchill's strength and of his freedom of movement. At one stage, for instance, Dill and Eden went to the length of threatening simultaneous resignation in support of Wavell. Those who complained, like Hankey, that Churchill exercised dictatorial powers, knew nothing of the battles he had to fight to get his way.

De Gaulle Flexes his Muscles

Relations with de Gaulle as 1941 began were still reasonably good. There were of course always countless events which would cause him offence. He had, for instance, been irritated by British attempts to detach Weygand from Vichy and encourage him to take up arms in North Africa. But the essentially cordial relationship with the general was emphasised in January when both parties weathered the storm that followed from the arrest by Britain of Vice-Admiral Muselier on the suspicion, which turned out to be based on false evidence, that he was pro-German. (Muselier was a serial source of embarrassment, sometimes to de Gaulle as well as to the British: there were no less than three 'Affaires Museliers'.)

By May de Gaulle had, however, become increasingly angry as it became evident that Britain would neither intervene herself nor assist Free French forces to intervene in Syria, a country within France's sphere of influence, where Germany was using airfields. It was worse than that: throughout the Levant, Britain tended to treat the Vichy officials with courtesy – and indeed with a good deal more affection than they had for the Free French.

General Louis Spears, who had been Churchill's personal representative to Paul Reynaud, the French Prime Minister in 1940, and who was appointed on 28 June that year as head of the 'Spears Mission', with the role of liaising with de Gaulle, had as much as anyone to do with the general's position as leader of the Free French. In the dying days of the Battle of France he had not been impressed by Reynaud and he saw de Gaulle as the man who could sustain French resistance to Hitler – and this despite de Gaulle's lowly military rank and the fact that he was not in government at the time. Spears had no idea how de Gaulle would be received in England, but he organised a theatrical exit from France for him. De Gaulle went to the airport ostensibly just to see Spears off, but at the very last moment he was pulled aboard the aircraft to join him.

Spears was now in the Middle East as Churchill's representative. He shared the general's contempt for Vichy and tended to support his stance on the Levant. In his memorandum, *The Free French, Vichy and Ourselves,* Spears wrote 'Our painstaking attempts to propitiate the Vichy government might, conceivably, make a dispassionate observer conjure up the picture of a well-meaning person bent on feeding a lettuce to a rabbit while it is being chased around its cage by a stoat'. Spears was an old friend of Churchill and was allowed a large degree of critical freedom.

Churchill was himself increasingly coming to the conclusion that further parley with Vichy was a waste of time. He accelerated in this direction when Syria came to be seen in a different light after the eruption of rebellion in Iraq. Churchill saw that, whatever Vichy's sensibilities, Syria was a jumping-off ground for air domination of Iraq and Persia and could not be allowed to remain unchallenged.

Despite what de Gaulle owed to Spears – or probably because of it – the relationship between the two men was a difficult one. De Gaulle did not see himself simply as part of Britain's paraphernalia for defeating Hitler. He saw himself as the representative of a world power. He had grave suspicions that Britain would take advantage of the war to extend her sphere of influence in the French Empire in the Middle East. Britain had indeed made certain promises of independence, in order to fuel anti-Vichy sentiments, but Churchill had no intention of trying to acquire bits of the French Empire.

By the spring of 1941, Spears had come to the conclusion that de Gaulle was more interested in the narrow question of the Free French in Syria and Lebanon than in the allied cause as a whole, and thereafter he was overtly hostile to de Gaulle. He concluded that de Gaulle should be replaced and possibly even imprisoned. In view of the fact that the Vichy authorities in Syria had allowed German planes to refuel there on their way to Iraq, he was much in favour of the invasion of Syria and the Lebanon, EXPORTER.

EXPORTER, in which the Free French were the larger partner, began on 8 June 1941. Churchill loftily told de Gaulle that '[A]t this hour when Vichy touches fresh depths of ignominy, the loyalty and courage of the Free French save the glory of France'. De Gaulle replied in a no less elevated tone, 'Whatever happens the Free French are decided to fight and conquer at your side as faithful and resolute allies'. That was a high-water mark of fraternal amity. Almost immediately, de Gaulle's paranoid antennae began to twitch at suggestions of a lack of reference by the British to their Free French comrades, leniency towards Vichy and above all a fear of the transfer of the Lebanon and Syria to Britain. His suspicions of British imperial ambitions were a persistent part of his mindset, which took no cognisance of the fact that Britain was more than fully occupied in fighting for her life.

The outcome of EXPORTER was an armistice with Syria signed by Jumbo Wilson on 14 July 1941, which de Gaulle said, 'amounted to a pure and simple transference of Syria and Lebanon to the British'. De Gaulle blamed Spears for British policy in the area in its entirety. He was less than fair; even Spears thought the terms of the armistice went too far. De Gaulle was hugely overreacting to what was a very minor matter in the context of holding together the only alliance that could restore liberty to France. He wanted the French soldiers who surrendered in the Middle East to have the chance of joining him or of being imprisoned, but Britain had not abandoned the idea of working with Vichy, which they still saw as the legitimate government of France, and allowed the Frenchmen the alternative, to which they were legally entitled, of being repatriated to France. As usual the vote for Free France was disappointing: 37,500 of them chose to go home, as against a mere 6,000 who wished to fight alongside the Free French.

What de Gaulle did now, which was so often to be part of his tactics, was to launch the most violent of attacks on the hapless British representative on the spot, in this case the Minister of State in Cairo, Oliver Lyttelton. Lyttelton recorded, 'There was nothing for it but what women call "a scene", and a scene we certainly had'.[1] De Gaulle handed Lyttelton a paper 'which could only be read as terminating alliance between Free French and Great Britain'. It is hardly surprising that Spears wanted him locked up.[2]

So the first great Anglo-de Gaulle confrontation broke out. Spears was present at the interview: he was wholly taken aback by what he saw and for the rest of the war de Gaulle's loyalest British ally became his most outspoken critic. In no time at all Jumbo Wilson, the local British Commander, was threatening to impose martial law; and de Gaulle, for his part, was threatening to break the alliance with Britain.

If the negotiations between Britain and Vichy caused de Gaulle problems, they were nothing compared with the problems he himself caused by his so-called 'Brazzaville Manifesto' on 16 June, which set up the French Empire Defence Council, which amounted pretty well to a declaration of war on Vichy. Britain, it will be recalled, was not at war with Vichy. De Gaulle violently denounced the armistice with Vichy, which had settled the conflict in Syria. The Foreign Office asked the British press not to make mention of the manifesto, but de Gaulle went more public still and sent a note to Roosevelt via the United States Consul in Leopoldville.

At the end of August he returned to Brazzaville and gave an interview to George Weller of the *Chicago Daily News*. He made various proposals to the Americans about dealing with French colonies and offering the United States air and naval bases. The Foreign Office was furious and was well aware that de Gaulle had kept them in the dark precisely to emphasise the independence of his Empire Defence Council. Why, he asked, did Britain not break with Vichy and recognise his government? 'What, in effect, England is doing is carrying on a war-time deal with Hitler, in which Vichy acts as a go-between'. Britain was happy to see Vichy remain in power as that kept the French fleet away from Hitler. 'What happens, in effect, is an exchange of advantages between hostile powers which keeps the Vichy government alive as along as both Britain and Germany are agreed that it should exist'.[3]

Britain was horrified by the interview and by an enormous volume of reports that came back to Churchill of de Gaulle's hostile statements and Anglophobic remarks in Brazzaville and in Syria. Churchill himself was more tolerant of de Gaulle at this stage and understood that 'he had to be rude to the British to prove to French eyes that he was not a British puppet. He certainly carried out this policy with perseverance'.[4]

All the same, Churchill agreed with the Foreign Office that an attempt should be made to rein de Gaulle in, and on 10 November wrote to him asking him to come back from Africa to London. On this occasion de Gaulle complied. That was not to be his usual response to such requests.

Churchill's patience was increasingly eroded by the diplomatic chaos that flowed in the general's wake. Part of the trouble was that de Gaulle, without political experience, was increasingly playing a political role; but that does not go very far towards excusing his conduct. Churchill wondered whether the general had gone off his head. Eden, who had moved to the Foreign Office and entered the War Cabinet in December 1940, when Halifax was shunted off to Washington, was trying to avoid a complete breach of relations, but even he had his doubts. He conceded that 'it may well be that we shall find that de Gaulle is crazy; if so, he'll have to be dealt with accordingly. If, however, he shows indications of repentance, I hope you will not under-estimate your power to complete the cure'.[5] When de Gaulle reached London, he received a cold welcome letter from Churchill: 'Until I am in possession of any explanation you may do me the honour to offer, I am unable to judge whether any interview between us would serve a useful purpose'.

De Gaulle and his Free French continued to be a pain in Britain's neck. Harold Nicolson, profoundly Francophile and later referred to as the Member for Paris because of his unofficial but accepted role in representing French interests in the Commons, was in 1941 at the Ministry of Information. He gives a good description of de Gaulle at this stage. He lunched with him at the Savoy.

> He has the taut manner of a man who is becoming stout and is conscious that only the exercise of continuous muscle power can keep his figure in shape. I do not like him. He accuses my Ministry of being 'Pétainiste'. '*Mais non!*' I say, '*Monsieur le Général.*' '*Enfin, Pétainisant.*' '*Nous travaillons,*' I said, '*pour la France entière.*' '*La France entière,*' he shouted, '*C'est la France libre. C'est MOI!!!*'[6]

A month later Nicolson was again at lunch with de Gaulle. 'I sit bang opposite to de Gaulle and had much talk with him. I dislike him less than I did at first. He has tired, ruminating but not unkindly eyes. He has curiously effeminate hands (not feminine hands but effeminated hands without arteries or muscles)'.[7]

De Gaulle, three-quarters statesman and one-quarter figure of fun, as Roy Jenkins described him (some would say the proportions were generous), was at this stage in the war only one of a number of minor French players on the periphery of the main arena of events. By the end of the war he had come to be synonymous with the image of the France that had resisted the Germans. That was a role for which he was always avid, but for the moment there were other and more likely contenders. Churchill claimed in his history to have identified de Gaulle, even before the fall of France, as *l'homme du destin*, but in the course of the war he certainly described him in other ways, once as a female llama surprised in her bath. After Cadogan met de Gaulle for the first time at 10 Downing Street, he reported to his Foreign Office colleagues that 'I can't tell you anything about de Gaulle except that he's got a head like a pineapple and hips like a woman'.[8] He was a great French patriot, but with a flawed sense of how France's interests could best be served. His efforts may not actually have delayed the liberation of his country, but they certainly did not accelerate it. He had more affection for France than for his fellow Frenchmen.

Until October 1942, when the Germans occupied the nominally independent part of France, Vichy was technically a legitimate regime and a neutral country. Britain more or less respected this convention. America accepted it much more wholeheartedly. Partly for this reason and partly because Roosevelt simply did not like the man, the United States was hostile to de Gaulle and to British-backed Free French operations. Churchill overestimated French hostility to the occupying Germans, just as he overestimated German hostility to Hitler. Thus he excoriated the French regime that had surrendered, and sought to stimulate resistance to it. During his excursion to Canada in the course of the Washington visit at Christmas 1941, he spoke to the Canadian House of Commons, referring to Pétain and Lavalle as having ' fawned' over Hitler and as now lying 'prostrate at the foot of the conqueror'. Some Frenchmen, however, 'would not bow their knees, and under de Gaulle, continued to fight at the side of the allies'. The Gaullists enjoyed 'increasing respect by nine Frenchmen out of every ten throughout the once happy, smiling land of France'. These sentiments, voiced at the time when the Free French were occupying the Vichy islands of St Pierre and Miquelon, contrasted sharply with US Secretary of State Cordell Hull's pedantic indignation about the attack on the islands.

The wooing of de Gaulle was a rough business; the seduction of America was much more important and proceeded at a much more decorous pace.

The End of Wavell. Auchinleck

In North Africa during the early summer of 1941 Wavell appeared to an increasingly frustrated Prime Minister to be doing very little and saying nothing about what he *was* doing. Eventually, under pressure and earlier than he or Dill would have wished, Wavell began BATTLEAXE on 15 June. Material assistance including 238 tanks and 43 fighters had arrived in Egypt in the TIGER convoy on 12 May, and were probably not fully operational. TIGER had been rushed through the Mediterranean at Churchill's insistence following Rommel's advance, and now he wanted the weapons used without delay, ignoring the need to modify them for desert warfare and to train troops on how to use them.

The Prime Minister recalled Foch's resolution in 1918, and tried to put heart into his own generals with a lengthy Directive of 28 May. He sought to imbue them with his own determination. He referred to a potential loss of Egypt and the Middle East as

a disaster of the first magnitude to Great Britain, second only to successful invasion and final conquest . . . It is to be impressed on all ranks, especially the highest, that the life and honour of Great Britain depends upon the successful defence of Egypt. It is not to be expected that the British forces of the land, sea and air in the Mediterranean would wish to survive so vast and shameful defeat as would be entailed by our expulsion from Egypt, having regard to the difficulties of the enemy and his comparatively small numbers . . .

All plans for evacuation of Egypt or for closing or destroying the Suez Canal are to be called in and kept under the strict personal control of headquarters. No whisper of such plans is to be allowed. No surrenders by officers or men will be considered tolerable unless at least 50 per cent casualties are sustained by the unit or force in question. According to Napoleon's maxim, 'when a man is caught alone or unarmed, a surrender may be made'. But Generals and Staff

Officers surprised by the enemy are to use their pistols in self-defence. The honour of a wounded man is safe . . .

One can feel the sense of frustration. He was convinced that the Germans were fighting with more courage and skill and under better generalship than the British. He believed that the higher levels of command were of poor quality as a result of the losses of the Great War, and permeated by a mood of caution and defeatism. He was requiring no one do to more than he himself would have done. But the reaction of the Director of Military Operations was to take the time and trouble to draft a Note on the Directive, criticising it petulantly and complaining about interference in military etiquette. Of Paragraph 4 of the Directive, for example, which started, 'The Army of the Nile is to fight with no thought of retreat or withdrawal', he felt it worth saying, 'The first sentence is all right as a directive to the troops. But it is not all right as a directive to the Commander-in-Chief.' No wonder the Prime Minister lost his temper with his military advisers.[1]

Wavell was pressed to move too soon and he gave in to the pressure. His communication skills failed again. He managed to combine the worst of two worlds: he fought before he should have done without appearing to have the will to fight. His troops lacked training for desert warfare and his resources were inadequate. Rommel said that Wavell had planned BATTLEAXE well and was distinguished from other British Army Commanders by his preparedness to deploy his forces without concern for the moves that his opponent might make. But he cannot be relieved of responsibility for the failure of BATTLEAXE. Ultimately it was his decision whether or not he was ready to launch the operation. And if it had not been for Churchill, the Chiefs of Staff would have diverted much of such material as he had to the Far East, for Malaya and Singapore. At any rate, it was clear that Wavell's days were at an end.

Dill, who had consistently backed Wavell, and urged Churchill to do the same, finally tended to the view that he had not been badly treated by London. In an important letter, which tried to explain what Middle East commanders stubbornly failed to understand, he wrote to Wavell's successor:

From Whitehall, great pressure was applied to Wavell to induce him to act rapidly . . . the fact is that the Commander in the Field will always be subject to great and often undue pressure from his Government. Wellington suffered from it: Haig suffered from it:

Wavell suffered from it. Nothing will stop it. In fact, pressure from those who alone see the picture as a whole and carry the main responsibility may be necessary. It was, I think, right to press Wavell against his will to send a force to Baghdad, but in other directions he was, I feel, over-pressed.

You may be quite sure that I will back your military opinion in local problems, but here the pressure often comes from very broad political considerations; these are sometimes so powerful as to make it necessary to take risks, which, from a purely military point of view, may be seen as inadvisable. The main point is that *you* should make it quite clear what risks are involved if a course of action is forced upon you which, from a military point of view, is undesirable. You may even find it necessary, in the extreme case, to dissociate yourself from the consequences.[2]

Wavell never behaved as if he understood this, and his successor was only a little better. He took his dismissal well. The signal arrived while he was shaving, and it was read out to him. He said, 'I think the Prime Minister is quite right: this theatre wants a new eye and a new hand', and he went on shaving.[3]

Was Wavell's dismissal merited? On the one hand he had built up a viable command from nothing in the course of two years, had conquered the whole of Italian East Africa, seized Cyrenaica and taken 400,000 prisoners. On the other hand, his victories were generally against poor opponents, and he went on to lose Cyrenaica, Greece and Crete. While he had a splendid three months at the beginning of 1941, little went right for him thereafter. The reason that he was dismissed, and should indeed have been dismissed, was simply that his conduct, and his concept of how a professional soldier should behave towards the politicians, was not in tune with the realities of a total war fought by a government elected by universal suffrage in a modern democracy. Beyond that, like many soldiers in the Second World War, he deluded himself by imagining that matters of strategy, and even of grand tactics, were too complicated for civilians, and quite failed to understand that civilians might handle them as well as, or sometimes even better than, the soldiers.

In the aftermath of his dismissal, Churchill came to realise something of Wavell's heavy burdens: 'It was only after the disasters had occurred in Cyrenaica, in Crete, and in the Desert that I realised how over-loaded and under-sustained General Wavell's organisation was. Wavell tried his best; but the handling machine at his disposal was too weak to enable him to cope with the vast mass of business which four or five simultaneous campaigns imposed on him.'[4] Oliver Lyttelton and General Haining were now appointed to stiffen the administrative machinery in the Middle East, the former with political responsibilities and the latter to look after rearward administration and supply. The fact that the Prime Minister made these comments and these appointments after the dismissal simply point up Wavell's woeful failure to communicate properly with London.

Dill warned Churchill that Wavell might say that he was being blamed for the government's mistakes. It seemed best, then, to swap Wavell with his successor, Auchinleck, the Commander-in-Chief in India, and not to allow him home leave. The swap was made against the wishes of Amery, the Secretary of State for India and Burma, who wanted to keep Auchinleck, rather than the 'failed' Wavell. Dill was also against the swap. When it went ahead he warned Auchinleck that Churchill would want results and want them quickly.

The Auk was a slightly unlikely choice as Wavell's replacement. Churchill had come across him during the Norwegian campaign and had not liked his caution. Auchinleck recalled meeting Churchill in the War Office at the start of the campaign, when he was greeted unenthusiastically: 'I thought you were on your way General!' Churchill had been impressed at the time of Basra by his readiness to move troops from his command to the Middle East, but Auchinleck's experience was of India and the Indian Army. He did not know many senior British officers well. As a result he made some appointments that proved unwise, such as that of Lieutenant-General Sir Alan Cunningham as Commander of the Eighth Army. Cunningham had almost no experience with tanks and had difficulty in adapting to the scale of the operations he had to deal with. Cunningham was obliged to learn entirely new skills in a period of just two months. He could not operate a radio-telephone, much less command rapidly moving armoured warfare. His health suffered under the strain.

Churchill had pressed strongly for Wilson rather than Cunningham, but Auchinleck flatly refused. In *The Second World War*, Churchill recorded his regret that his advice, 'subsequently repeated' was not taken.[5]

Such examples of his wishes rebutted are a salutary reminder that Churchill was far from an all-powerful warlord. He said to Eden in July 1941, 'Remember that on my breast are the medals of the Dardanelles,

Antwerp, Dakar and Greece'. He never overruled the Chiefs of Staff on any major issue. He remembered Fisher's resignation in 1915 too well.

Churchill described Auchinleck as 'a lively fish', in contrast to Wavell, 'a tired one'. Or, in a changed metaphor, 'it might be said that we had ridden the willing horse to a standstill'. Wavell did not look tired to Auchinleck: 'Wavell showed no signs of tiredness at all. He was always the same. I think he was first class; in spite of his silences, he made a tremendous impact on his troops. I have a very great admiration for him . . . but he was given impossible tasks.'[6]

From the start things did not go well with Auchinleck. He incurred criticism for sending quality troops to Cyprus, in defiance of Churchill's arguments. Very soon after his appointment on 21 June 1941, his caution started to disappoint the Prime Minister. He stubbornly refused to have recourse to common-sense diplomacy. He ended an exchange of signals with the blunt statement that 'I must repeat that to launch an offensive with the inadequate means at present at our disposal is not, in my opinion, a justifiable operation of war'. He knew that the Prime Minister thought himself pretty knowledgeable about operations of war, and he could easily have been more tactful, but like Wavell he stuck to the principle that it was for him, the soldier, and not Churchill, the civilian, to run a military campaign. That could no longer be the case.

Churchill contemplated sacking Auchinleck even before the month of July was out.[7] But he could not go through the generals quite as fast as that. So Auchinleck was summoned to London where he convinced the Chiefs of Staff, if not Churchill, that the forthcoming offensive, CRUSADER, should be delayed until November.

There is much testy correspondence on both sides regarding the speed of tank turnaround and availability of aircrew, but on the whole Auchinleck tended to be irritated in silence by Churchill's interventions. He ignored advice from Ismay to write 'long personal chatty letters occasionally. I know normally you would recoil in your modesty from doing so'. Dill, too, tried to make Auchinleck understand that he had a diplomatic function as well as a military one, and that he must take Churchill with him. But the Auk, like his predecessor, failed to understand the nature of total war. When, for instance, Churchill wrote to ask why a particular division had been sent to Cyprus, he haughtily replied, 'If you wish I can send you detailed reasons which actuated me and which appeared to me incontestable. I hope you will leave me complete discretion concerning dispositions of this kind.' One understands his irritation, but this was no way to address an embattled Prime Minister whose responsibilities were infinitely greater than his. He saw the conduct of the war as a matter for military men in which his political masters should intervene only to give the broadest of directions. Although he and Wavell were aware of Enigma, they were necessarily supplied only with the information that was directly relevant to what they were doing. They did not allow that they were unaware of a larger picture, on the basis of which many of the government's instructions were based.

Paradoxically, much of the Ultra decrypts emanating at this time from North Africa consisted of complaints from Rommel about inadequate resources, both in terms of materiel and personnel. Churchill and the War Cabinet believed what Rommel was saying; German High Command did not, and they were right. Rommel was simply complaining to his government, as commanders tend to do.

Auchinleck's appraisal of his own forces was more accurate. He could see that his troops were exhausted and their morale low. His guns could not destroy the German panzer tanks, to which his own tanks were hugely inferior. He was horrified by the decadence of the idle staff set-up in Cairo. Egypt was not at war, and the extravagance and luxury of life in Cairo is well described in many novels of the period.[8] The changes he attempted to impose on his officers made him unpopular. His austerity and the desire to share the privations of his men may have made him popular with the rank and file, but was not appreciated by some officers: 'Any fool can be uncomfortable.' Even his decision to leave his wife behind in India so that he could devote himself wholeheartedly to his responsibilities was misunderstood, and alas contributed to the marital break-up which caused him so much pain.

In summary, what happened next in the desert was that Auchinleck began his offensive, CRUSADER, on 18 November 1941. Just as Churchill pushed Auchinleck, Auchinleck in turn pushed the army commander, Cunningham, to move earlier than he wanted. Cunningham's nerve had broken by 23 November, and he invited Auchinleck forward for consultation. The Auk found that Cunningham had lost the confidence of his subordinate commanders, and on 26 November replaced him with Major-General Neil Ritchie. But it was Auchinleck's own intervention in CRUSADER that turned the course of the battle. He sensed – it was a brilliant, intuitive conclusion – that Rommel had run out of steam and that instead of breaking off the offensive, as Cunningham had wanted, it was worth risking continuation.

Auchinleck's action was critical and his assessment of what CRUSADER could do was both bold and accurate. He needed a strong nerve; fortunately he had that. Rommel performed an audacious counter-stroke, not as expected against the head of the British force, but in a swing round it, to attack the units in rear that communicated with Egypt. What General Norrie called 'the Matruh Stakes' began, as units scampered back to adapt to the new shape of the battle. There was flap everywhere except around the Auk himself. He was convinced that Rommel was making a desperate last effort, with few tanks and no supplies. As Cunningham left to enter hospital, suffering from severe strain, the war correspondent Eve Curie, coming across the Auk by chance, was struck by his quiet and assured demeanour.[9]

At the end of the year CRUSADER was over. It was a success to the extent that the Germans had again abandoned Cyrenaica. There were some setbacks, but all the same the Afrika Korps had retreated and lost all the territory gained by Rommel, apart from two garrisons. The siege of Tobruk was ended. By the last day of 1941 the British frontline returned to El Agheila, where it had been in February. But British casualties were higher than those of the Axis forces, and there was an unacceptably high loss of tanks. Morale had been very greatly damaged and would take much time to recover. Eighth Army was seriously weakened.

Auchinleck's troops did not have a chance to settle in to their new positions. He seriously misread the situation after Pearl Harbor and withdrew experienced formations to serve in Syria, Palestine and the Delta. He overestimated Axis losses and in two cables of 12 January 1942 told Churchill that the enemy were numerically weak, tired and disorganised.[10] In reality, Rommel had shortened his lines of commu-nication and received important supplies of new panzers, armoured cars and aircraft. He was ready to renew his offensive and did so just nine days after Auchinleck's two cables. When Rommel began his second offensive on 21 January 1942 he was able to push the inexperienced British 1st Armoured Division back across Cyrenaica, seizing Agedaba and Benghazi on the way. He did all this despite the fact that Churchill broke his golden rule and allowed Auchinleck full texts of relevant Ultra material.[11]

The first Benghazi Handicap had been under O'Connor in April 1941; now the second Benghazi Handicap opened and Benghazi soon fell. Brooke was increasingly critical of Auchinleck, while Dill, possibly unfairly, blamed the Director of Military Intelligence, Shearer. Shearer

was sacked and Auchinleck replaced him with Freddie de Guingand –
only a lieutenant colonel and with no intelligence experience. The front
settled down on a line between Gazala and Bir Hakeim, while both sides
prepared for an offensive.

The End of Another Desert General

Churchill was appalled to find that his second desert general was doing no better than his first. On 26 February 1942 the PM cabled, with menacing courtesy, 'I have not troubled you much in these difficult days, but I must now ask you what are your intentions. According to our figures you have substantial superiority in the air, in armour, and in other forces over the enemy . . . pray let me hear from you'. Auchinleck's reply ran to seven pages, but it failed to reassure an increasingly angry Prime Minister. His long, negative response crossed with a message from the Chiefs of Staff telling him to recapture air bases without delay in order to allow a convoy to get through to Malta, which was under great pressure.

Churchill was increasingly infuriated by the lack of action. An unsent telegram said 'Soldiers were meant to fight'. The Auk was reminded that a larger picture was visible in London and told by the Chiefs that he must either attack or face 'the loss of Malta and the precarious defensive'. Auchinleck's reply of 4 March was far from diplomatic: 'I find it hard to believe in view of your telegram of 17 February that [the message] COS 241 had your approval as it seems to fail so signally either to appreciate facts as presented from here or to realise that we are fully aware of the situation as regards Malta in particular or the Middle East in general. We are here trying to face realities and to present to you the situation as it appears to us, not as you would like it to be'.[1]

The exchange went on for some time in this way, and it was clear that there were substantial discrepancies between the number of tanks which London and the Middle East respectively regarded as being on Auchinleck's strength. In the circumstances, Churchill asked him to come home to discuss the whole situation and in particular to resolve the question of the tank numbers. Auchinleck not only declined, but did so very abruptly. On 9 March Brooke pressed him again to return and Auchinleck again refused, suggesting that Brooke came out to see *him*.

There were now good reasons for sacking him for insubordination, and Churchill was very tempted to do so. Cripps was sent out to see him and Ismay attempted to broker a reconciliation. He took the time to write a long, kind and understanding letter:

> The outstanding point is that although the PM is *at present* at cross-purposes – and even at loggerheads – with you this is a purely temporary phase of a relationship which is marked by mutual esteem and, I might almost say, affection.
>
> You cannot judge the PM by ordinary standards, he is not in the least like anyone you and I have ever met. He is a mass of contradictions. He is either on the crest of a wave, or in the trough; either highly laudatory or bitterly condemnatory; either in an angelic temper, or a hell of a rage; when he isn't fast asleep he's a volcano. There are no half measures in his make-up – he apparently sees no difference between harsh words spoken to a friend and forgotten within the hour under the influence of friendly argument, and the same harsh words telegraphed to a friend thousands of miles away – with no opportunity for 'making it up' . . .
>
> You must do what you did with such happy results last time. YOU MUST COME HOME. I know how hard it is for you to leave your command at this juncture, but nothing matters so much as the removal of the wall of misunderstanding which has grown up between you two. I know that at heart the PM thinks the world of you, but he will never confess this, even to himself, until you have got together again and had the whole thing out.[2]

Ismay's letter is a perceptive one and a wise one. Auchinleck should have complied or resigned. He did neither and continued to irritate and delay. He faced a further threat of dismissal when he said that he would not be able to resume the offensive until June or July. Churchill said it was to be June or resignation.

Churchill's messages to Auchinleck were toned down again and again by Brooke, now CIGS. Phrases like 'Armies are not intended to stand around doing nothing!' were removed. Only unanimous opposition from the Chiefs of Staff prevented Auchinleck's immediate dismissal and replacement with Gort, now Governor of Malta – a strange choice. But the Chiefs themselves were little more enthusiastic about the C-in-C, whom they regarded as excessively cautious. Like Wavell, Auchinleck was more concerned about an attack from the north on Persia than what went on in the wastes of the Western Desert. It was because of these larger concerns that Auchinleck infuriated Churchill by refusing to come to London to confer; but his greatest concern should have been for concerting his plans with those of the Prime Minister and Minister of Defence. '[W]e can't settle this by writing letters', snarled the Prime Minister.

Brooke went on too long in defending a general in whom even he was losing confidence. The Chiefs of Staff, as well as Churchill, were not impressed by the way Auchinleck conducted his long discussions with the Prime Minister and by some of his telegrams, such as his reply of 10 May to an order from the Cabinet to open his offensive at their risk, in which he asserted that the loss of Malta would not affect the position in the Middle East.[3]

What Auchinleck was doing in the long gap that so annoyed Churchill after Rommel's advance of January 1942 was preparing for a counter-offensive, which he planned for June. It was unfortunate that Rommel got off first. There was a grim battle, 'the Cauldron', when he defeated the British at Gazala. It was only when Auchinleck removed Ritchie and took personal command of Eighth Army that he was able to halt Rommel just short of Alexandria at First El Alamein. Ritchie had been appointed only to a temporary command of Eighth Army when he replaced Cunningham in the middle of CRUSADER. He had performed well enough then, with Auchinleck in attendance, but leaving him in position was as serious a mistake as appointing Cunningham had been. Churchill had suggested a month earlier that Auchinleck should take personal command of Eighth Army in the coming battle: the Commander-in-Chief felt that his wider responsibilities made this impossible. Churchill's judgement had been sound.

Churchill did not appreciate Auchinleck's skill and success in bringing Rommel to a halt at First El Alamein. Rommel did: 'I could weep' he said. But now, instead of fighting to the last man, as Churchill had wanted, Auchinleck fell back in a fighting withdrawal, which involved losing Mersah Matruh. Mersah Matruh is only 170 miles east of the Egyptian frontier and is halfway to Alexandria.

Auchinleck always failed to convince Churchill that the new troops with which he was supplied were simply not ready for fighting, supply and maintenance. He failed to get his point across, just as he failed to emphasise adequately that both his tanks and his anti-tank guns were inadequate. The British standard anti-tank gun, the two pounder, was too small. At over 600 yards, the shots simply bounced off German tanks.

Tobruk had great significance for Churchill. He always referred to Tobruk as a fortress and probably overestimated its importance, seeing it as a defensive position in terms of a static war, which war in the desert was not. On the other hand, Auchinleck, while minimising its importance, did recognise that the fact that it remained in British hands had contributed to the success of CRUSADER. Indeed it is difficult to know precisely what Auchinleck's intentions for Tobruk were.

Earlier – in January 1942 – he had told the War Office that he did not intend to hold Tobruk, or anywhere else, as a fortress under siege. His views were shared by Admiral Cunningham for the navy and Air Chief Marshal Tedder for the air force. But it all became very confused. London appears to have overlooked what the Commander-in-Chief had said in January. In any case, the fairly clear terms of his January Operation Instruction, No. 110, were eroded by the partially contradictory terms of that of 11 February. At any rate, no doubt partly for reasons of morale at home, Churchill now gave very specific orders that Tobruk was to be held at all costs. Auchinleck appeared to fall in line, confirmed that Tobruk would be held, and gave Ritchie explicit instructions.[4]

But by now the defences of Tobruk were in ruins and the place could really only be defended as part of a Tobruk–Gazala line. Ritchie knew the line would not hold, and indeed it soon dissolved into 'the Gazala Gallop' as allied troops tried to escape from Rommel's advance. At one stage Ritchie flatly refused to accept the Auk's orders; at other times he gave responses that were evasive and open to different constructions. If Auchinleck was simply resting on his January 1942 Operation Instruction to the War Office he avoided facing up to a confrontation with Churchill by saying so. He failed to secure Ritchie's compliance with his own orders and he failed to repair the deficiencies in Tobruk's defences or to communicate them to Churchill. Tobruk fell.

The Prime Minister said later, 'We did not . . . know the conditions prevailing in Tobruk. Considering that Auchinleck's plan had been to await an attack, and remembering all the months that had passed, it was inconceivable that the already well-proved fortifications of Tobruk should not have been maintained in the highest efficiency, and indeed strengthened.'[5]

In the event the loss of Tobruk was a very serious blow to national morale, as Churchill had known and Auchinleck had not understood. In military terms it was also a disastrous enough loss: 35,000 British and Empire troops were lost as casualties or prisoners, together with much materiel. Churchill had accurately understood the effect the fall of the town would have in Britain. As a result of the long siege of 1941, Tobruk had come to have an iconic significance for the public, and the mood after its fall was one of despondency. In Cairo the stock exchange plummeted, and the Gazala Gallop prompted the habitués of Groppi's Café and the Shepheard Hotel – 'Groppi's Horse' and 'Shepheard's Short Range Desert Group' – to retire to Jerusalem. The Royal Navy abandoned Alexandria. The Cabinet was obliged to order an Inquiry, and in the Commons a Motion of No Confidence was tabled by a backbench Conservative member. For all this, and despite his many excellent, soldierly qualities, Auchinleck was to blame.

His supporters argue still that Tobruk should not have been defended, but abandoned as he had originally planned. They overlook the significance of the place: the parliamentary debate was an uncomfortable one for Churchill. The debate was on a vote of censure, and the backbencher who moved it, Sir John Wardlaw-Milne, was not insignificant: he was Chairman of the all-party Finance Committee. Bevan contrasted the defence of Sebastopol for months with the fall of Tobruk in twenty-six hours. There was much reference to the fact that Churchill had said the British weapons in the desert were the equal of German weapons, which was evidently not the case. The Liberal, Clement Davies, talked of impeachment. Ismay referred in his memoirs to the severe criticism that Parliament visited on the Prime Minister's conduct of the war from time to time when things went badly. '[T]here is always a tendency to attribute to faulty direction the blame for failures which are due to very different causes. The House of Commons was not at its best in these debates.'[6] The best feature of the debate for Churchill was when Wardlaw-Milne, who had started well enough, lost all credibility by making an impromptu suggestion that the new defence supremo should be the particularly incompetent royal prince, the Duke of Gloucester. Wardlaw-Milne had intended a purely ceremonial role for the Duke, but the damage was done. Churchill's supporters hooted with derision and Channon recorded that 'the House roared with disrespectful laughter, and I saw Winston's face light up, as if a lamp had been lit within him and he smiled genially. He knew now that he was saved, and poor Wardlaw-Milne never quite regained the hearing of the House'.[7]

Outside Parliament criticism was echoed in the quality press and in a report for the Cabinet from Stafford Cripps in his capacity as Leader of the House. Cripps said the recent loss of Maldon in a by-election 'shows the profound disquiet and lack of confidence of the electors' and that there was 'a general feeling that something is wrong and should be put right without delay'.[8]

Auchinleck realised what had happened. On 23 June he wrote to the CIGS offering his resignation if it were wished. Significantly, his letter referred to 'the disastrous fall' of Tobruk. He suggested Alexander as his successor. On the following day he wrote a fine letter to Churchill: 'I thank you personally and most sincerely for all your help and support during the last month, and deeply regret the failures and setbacks for the past month, for which I accept the fullest responsibility'. Churchill's response was equally up to the level of events, and in an immediate telegram he conveyed his complete confidence. In reality he genuinely liked the Auk, as opposed to Wavell, and to the end he remained basically well disposed.[9]

Auchinleck had no illusions about the indifferent quality of the Eighth Army at this stage of the war, and he was frustrated by the fact that lack of a real reserve and of fresh troops made it impossible to do more than halt the enemy. But he *had* halted them, and German observers, such as Rommel's Chief of Staff, General Bayerlein, acknowledged his achievement: 'if Rommel had not been beaten then, he would have advanced deep into Egypt'.[10]

But Auchinleck's conception of his role was not Churchill's. The general considered that his duty was to protect the Middle East. That was his command and his responsibility. Thus he saw it as proper to envisage fighting a retreating battle if necessary, so that his army was kept intact and capable of protecting the Persian oil fields, which were ultimately important as Egypt was not – or so it was thought: in fact Hitler never showed any interest in the Middle East oil.[11] Auchinleck's analysis was logical enough, but it was not a concept that would win the war. Montgomery's approach was quite different, and much more in tune with the Prime Minister's.

Dilly-Dally and Brookie

Dill had a tough time as CIGS. His wife had suffered a serious stroke not long before his appointment, and he could no longer communicate with her or she with him. When he escaped the stress of working with his demanding chief, it was not to relax in domesticity but to agonise over his wife's attempts to speak to him and watch the pain in her eyes as she failed. The strain of his two burdens must have been almost unsupportable. Churchill, who could sometimes be touchingly sympathetic, was not specially understanding. When Dill remarried after Lady Dill's death he asked for three days' holiday as a honeymoon. Churchill refused. Eventually he had one day off.

Churchill's relationship with him was neither as turbulent nor, ultimately, as fruitful as with Brooke. In fact Dill understood Churchill well, and acted as an effective gear between him and the generals. The very lack of turbulence was uncongenial for the Prime Minister.

Dill had been appointed CIGS in May 1940, in succession to Ironside, but Churchill was criticising him to Eden as early as July of the same year, talking of what a disappointment the new CIGS was, and claiming that he was unduly alarmed by Germany's strength. Thereafter Dill was 'Dilly-Dally' or, quite unfairly, 'the dead hand of inanition'. The second appellation was applied to him in front of the Cabinet.

Churchill started to think of getting rid of Dill as early as May 1941 as a result of his support for the Far East against Egypt.[1] In the event, he was reprieved till the end of the year, when he was eased out of office by the use of a rule which Churchill is usually said to have invented, and which required the CIGS to retire at the age of sixty, which he attained on Christmas Day 1941. In fact it was Dill himself who devised the rule that was his own undoing. He said to Kennedy as early as 20 August 1941 that he thought he should go at the age of sixty, and intended to submit his offer to go in writing. It is not quite clear, then, why he was so surprised to be taken at his word in November: 'The world is upside down for me. I am to go. The Prime Minister told me last night.' Everyone liked him and was sorry to see him go, but no one thought he should stay.

Even Kennedy, always inclined to support soldiers against politicians, thought Dill was tired. He had told him in August that he was right to submit his resignation, and he still felt the same way in November.[2] Hollis noticed the strain telling more on Dill than on the other Chiefs to the extent that he could no longer concentrate and at Chiefs of Staff meetings would sit asking questions that were quite irrelevant to the matters under discussion.[3]

'Dilly-Dally' and 'the dead hand of inanition' are powerful examples of how damaging and persistent in their effect critical sobriquets can be. A close examination of Dill's record reveals none of the weakness that the nicknames suggested. The chemistry between the CIGS and Churchill was unproductive and Dill was too easily bullied. If he had responded more forcefully to Churchill's sometimes grotesque comments, accusations of cowardice against the generals and indeed the whole military Establishment, as Brooke was to do, he might have lasted longer. As it was, his responses were too slow, and were usually put on paper. That was not how Churchill operated. But Dill did oppose Churchill when he thought it necessary, did understand him, and did give good and perceptive advice to men such as Wavell on how Churchill should be handled.[4]

Sir Alan Brooke succeeded Dill. In his diary on 20 October 1941 Brooke had written:

> Winston had never been fond of Dill. They were entirely different types of character and types that could never have worked harmoniously together. Dill was the essence of straightforwardness, blessed with the highest principles and an unassailable integrity of character. I do not believe that any of these characteristics appeal to Winston. On the contrary, I think he disliked them as they accentuated his own shortcomings in this respect.

The changeover was not made at the last minute, and Brooke and Dill worked together in the last month or two of the latter's time as CIGS. The original idea for Dill's retirement activity was to be Governor of Bombay, 'followed', as Churchill said, 'by a bodyguard with lances'. In the event, because he accompanied Churchill to

Washington for the Christmas visit of 1941, Dill had a very different kind of retirement: he played a key role in liaising between Churchill and the American Chiefs. It is difficult to overstate how much he contributed to the working of the combined military machine. It operated much less smoothly after his death. Brooke was not able to persuade Churchill to recommend a peerage for Dill, but he was promoted field marshal, and he was appointed to his crucial role in Washington.

Although Churchill cut him out of the loop on occasions, Dill and General George Marshall, the American Chief of Staff, got on extremely well. The two men met for the first time at the Placentia Bay Conference off Newfoundland in August 1941, and they hit it off from the first, corresponding from that time onwards. Marshall told Dill that he had so many battles to fight that 'I am never quite sure whether I'm fighting you, or the President or the Navy!' After Dill's appointment to Washington, he and Marshall were in touch on an almost daily basis and lunched weekly, often only with their wives present. Even if he did get tired from time to time of 'begging from the Americans', his commitment to making the Anglo-American military alliance work was total, and reciprocated by Marshall.

To the end, Churchill's attitude to Dill was both unfair and ungenerous. The Joint Chiefs in Washington sent their commiserations to Churchill when Dill died. Churchill's response was inadequate and prompted this reaction from Marshall: 'To be very frank and personal, I doubt if you or your Cabinet associates fully realise the loss you have suffered'.[5] Three months after Dill's death Marshall told Major Reginald Winn, Dill's Personal Assistant, that he still felt completely lost without him; he had never met another man of such character, integrity, breadth of vision and selflessness. He thought Brooke was good, but Dill was irreplaceable.[6] Anglo-American relations deteriorated steadily after his death.

Brooke was a pretty inevitable successor to Dill. Churchill had not been excited about the prospect, hence his preposterous toying with reappointing Gort. Beaverbrook had urged the appointment of General Nye, on the presentational grounds that he had risen from the ranks, but Nye himself said that Brooke would be the better man. It was then that Churchill famously responded by forecasting the nature of their relationship: 'When I thump the table and push my face towards him, what does he do? Thumps the table harder and glares back at me – I know these Brookes – stiff-necked Ulstermen and there's no-one worse to deal with than that!'[7]

Brooke was to prove, however, not only a very great CIGS, 'the greatest . . . ever produced by the British Army' according to his biographer, Sir David Fraser, but also, in wonderful coincidence, the only soldier of his generation who could work productively with the greatest War Prime Minister that Britain has ever produced.

In his history of the war, Churchill makes scant reference to Brooke when he first appears on the scene. What was almost worse was the warmth of the very lengthy footnote in which he wrote with admiration and fondness of Brooke's two older brothers with whom had soldiered in his youth. Subsequently he continued to minimise the contribution of the Chiefs of Staff in general and the Chief of the Imperial General Staff in particular. Part of the reason was simply thoughtlessness. Although he could rise to the very zenith of magnanimity and be moved by a profound sense of humanity towards individuals as well as towards countless masses, Churchill could also be appallingly self-centred.

Part of the reason for downplaying Brooke's role was to elevate Churchill's. There was no room in his account for a second energising brain. The great man view of history required that one man inspired the direction of the war, with minimal assistance and without opposition. The reality would be too prosaic. The Chiefs are intended to appear to have played a minor part in the war compared to, say, Alex and Monty. Brooke himself is credited with 'services of the highest order' in his role as Chairman of the Chiefs of Staff Committee, but not a lot else.

In August 1942 Brooke selflessly declined command of the Middle East in succession to Auchinleck, because he felt it his duty to stay on as CIGS and support Churchill. But on several occasions he had been promised command of OVERLORD. Supreme Command of the Allied forces in the conclusion of the strategic policies which he had nurtured would have been a wonderful finish to Brooke's professional career. The promise, first made on 15 June 1943, gave Brooke 'one of my greatest thrills during the war . . . I felt it would be the perfect climax to all my struggles to guide the strategy of the war . . . to find myself ultimately in command of the Allied Forces.' The promise was confirmed on 7 July: 'I was too excited to sleep when I returned home'. Until now Brooke had been sworn to secrecy, but a week later Churchill confirmed the promise in the presence of Brooke's wife, asking her how she felt about her husband's being the Supreme Commander on the return to France.

Then, almost on an impulse as it seemed, he decided in Quebec in August 1943 that the OVERLORD commander was to be American. Brooke said, 'Not for one moment did he realise what this meant to me. He offered no sympathy, no regrets at having to change his mind, and dealt with the matter as if it were one of minor importance.' The acknowledgement that Brooke 'bore the great disappointment with soldierly dignity' was only stuck in to the Memoirs as an afterthought, at the instigation of Churchill's advisers.[8]

His shabby treatment in the War Memoirs prompted Viscount Alanbrooke, as he had become, to reverse what had been his very firm decision not to publish the diary he had kept since 28 September 1939, and which had been marked in capitals 'ON NO ACCOUNT MUST THE CONTENTS OF THIS BOOK BE PUBLISHED'. In impoverished circumstances, and living in his former gardener's cottage, Alanbrooke handed his papers to the historian, Sir Arthur Bryant. Quite how Bryant was able, very easily, to persuade Alanbrooke that the diaries *should* be published is not clear. He had been commissioned by the Royal Regiment of Artillery to write a posthumous official biography of the field marshal, but when he saw the diary and Alanbrooke's annotations he knew at once the immediate appeal that even an edited version would have. Alanbrooke's earlier reticence disappeared. He certainly felt that the role of the Chiefs of Staff Committee, as well as his own, throughout the war had been ignored by Churchill, and he may well have been motivated in part by financial necessity. He was a poor man, and his gratuity was £311; Haig got £100,000.

In any event, he strangely did not appear to realise how offensive some of the diary entries would be to Churchill. 'If Winston should take offence in anything you have written,' he wrote to Bryant, 'he would certainly fall in my estimation, but I feel such a contingency is most unlikely'.[9] That was a widely unrealistic apprehension, but Brooke was not good at human relations. Although he could be kind and considerate to younger people, he was grudging and prickly to his coevals. In the War Office his nickname was 'Colonel Shrapnel'. In argument he was bleak and uncompromising; his response to unwelcome proposals was negative and frequent: 'I flatly disagree'. He was tactless, distant and unclubbable, and avoided social contact with the other Chiefs. As the war went on his resilience grew less and the enormous strain of his huge responsibilities took their toll. He felt close to breaking at one point.

It is important to remember that Churchill was not alone in irritating him. He had a pretty poor opinion of many of the actors in the drama, and he could be excessive in his criticism of them. He could be very rude about Alexander, Marshall and Eisenhower, for example. Marshall's 'strategic ability was of the poorest. A great man, a great gentleman and a great organizer, but definitely not a strategist . . . [H]is stunted strategic outlook made it very difficult to discuss strategic plans with him . . .'[10] Eisenhower was dismissed as having 'absolutely no strategical outlook'. His regard for Monty was uniquely positive.

He had a high opinion of his own strategic abilities, and he was arrogant and always ready to write off others. His diaries contain innumerable dismissals of his contemporaries on both sides of the Atlantic, and very little admiration or respect for those he worked with. He was negative in outlook and cautious to a fault. Like so many of his contemporaries, he would not accept the need to subordinate the military to the political, as Clausewitz said must always be the rule. Wars are fought for political ends, and it is no use looking for the military ideal, a set-piece battle which cannot be lost. When he was in command of the south coast Brooke had feared invasion and argued that it was inevitable. He could not see the need for diversion of resources to the Middle East if the war were to be won.[11] 'Always', said Hollis, who was present at most meetings of the Chiefs of Staff, 'it was Churchill who pushed; it was Brooke who admonished and urged caution'.[12] Caution is all very well, but it would not win the war these men were fighting. In his evaluation of the relative merits of Brooke and Churchill, Hollis concluded that '[t]he true defence of Churchill is that he always knew when to attack. He was not only the architect of victory, he was also its accountant; he knew which attack would bring the best dividend with the least risk of catastrophe'.[13]

Churchill was very often infuriating in argument with Brooke, but Brooke did not trouble to exercise any skills of advocacy. His 'I flatly disagree' was not calculated to win his opponent over, and he spoke far too fast, 'like a Gatling gun', according to Hollis, whose editor describes the exchanges beautifully:

Mr Churchill, who had heard his reply perfectly well, would then turn to General Ismay and cup a hand to his ear.

'I cannot hear what he says', he would observe, as though General Brooke were not even present. Ismay would then repeat Brooke's comments more slowly and in a louder voice. Churchill would nod, as if the words were just reaching him for the first time. Then, if he did not wish to enter into an immediate argument, he would suddenly change the subject completely and discuss other matters. Otherwise, he would still affect not to hear the opposing point of view, and it had to be repeated in an even louder voice for a second time.

'Oh', Churchill would say disconcertingly, '*Oh!* So *that's* what he says. *Oh!* I see'.

Finally, at the end of the meeting, General Hollis recalls, 'As the other members of the War Cabinet or Staff began to gather up their papers to leave, Mr Churchill would unexpectedly return to the point with which General Brooke had disagreed, presenting his view from a different angle, and by surprise and determination would often carry the day'.[14]

Bryant had been an appeaser, and although he edited out some criticism of Churchill in the edition of the Alanbrooke diaries which appeared in 1957, the 'unexpurgated' version which appeared in 2001[15] showed that the eliminations were minimal. It also showed that Bryant's work was fairly sloppy: he worked not from the original diaries, but from typescript notes which Brooke had prepared. He copied and added to discrepancies contained in the originals.[16]

The diaries were the repository for the stress and anxiety borne by the CIGS, this lonely and introverted figure, during the years in which he bore burdens that were almost intolerable. They were not history. At the outset they contained the declaration, 'The thoughts I express may contradict themselves as I wish to give full scope to free expression and do not care if I am found to change my mind by events'. Along with most tender remarks to his wife, to whom he was devoted, are references to military matters, statesmen and his beloved ornithology. Coming from accounts of meetings with Molotov and Stalin to the fact that he has spent a day photographing a 'Marsh Tit', one assumes that his subject was Marshal Tito.

Brooke's style was bleak and one does not warm to the man. But he had some human qualities. As well as a love of birds and fishing (he once caught 100 salmon in a season) and wildlife, he was immensely devoted to his family. He also had an endearing fondness for the science fiction comic strip, *Flash Gordon*. It appeared in the *Daily Mirror*, and when Brooke was a guest at Sandringham, where that paper was not viewed with approval, it was smuggled in to him with his early-morning tea.

He faced up daily to Churchill's confrontational attacks. These attacks were not *simply* the technique of the debating-chamber:

Churchill was frequently boorish, offensive and unreasoning. The generals and the chiefs were often accused of cowardice. Brooke had to deal with this without the breaks and relief afforded by Churchill's routine of afternoon rests and baths and evening dinners and film shows. He did not have Churchill's capacity for convivial relaxation.

Indeed, Brooke's recurrent complaint is to do with the hours that Churchill kept, and that he had to share. But in fact he adapted very early to the afternoon rest that Churchill had adopted in his subaltern days in India, and while his master was asleep the CIGS would disappear for three hours, browsing in bookshops for books on birds, or in camera shops for gadgets to help him film them.[17] If he too had spent some of the time in bed he might not have found the Midnight Follies so wearing.

But he did find them wearing and the evening outpouring in his diary must be understood as having a therapeutic rather than historical function. Ismay was certainly thinking of Brooke's diaries when he wrote, 'Perhaps if I had kept a diary the entries on these unproductive nights [when Churchill was too exhausted to work effectively] would have been querulous and critical. And how sorry I would have felt when I read them the next day!'[18] Brooke's entries were never intended as history, and the account they contain is a distorted one. Churchill's own story should be read against the diaries. Both have elements of the truth, but Churchill's picture is the more complete.

Brooke could say, as he did of Churchill at a meeting on 6 July 1944 (which started at 10 p.m. and ended at 2 a.m.), that the Prime Minister (who had just made a major speech in the Commons on the flying bomb threat) had 'tried to recuperate himself with drink. As a result he was in a maudlin, bad tempered, drunken mood, ready to take offence at anything, suspicious of everybody, and in a highly vindictive mood against the Americans. In fact, so vindictive that his whole outlook on strategy was warped. I began by having a bad row with him. He began to abuse Monty because operations were not going faster, and apparently Eisenhower had said that he was over vigilant. I flared up and asked him if he could not trust his generals for 5 minutes instead of continually abusing them and belittling them.'[19] And so on.

But after returning to the War Office, muttering 'That man, that man . . .', he would add 'but *what* would we do without him?'[20] And just a month before the 6 July incident, and a couple of days after 'another of Winston's awful meetings' Brooke had been charmed at Chequers when the Prime Minister 'said some very nice things about the excellent opinions that the whole Defence Committee and War Cabinet had of me and that they had said we could not have a better CIGS.' Later he annotated that entry: 'He was an astounding mixture, could drive you to complete desperation and the brink of despair for weeks on end, and then would ask you to spend a couple of hours alone with him . . . and you left him with the feeling that you would do anything within your power to help him carry the stupendous burden he had shouldered.'[21]

In his final notes on Churchill, Brooke confessed to surprise that in their differences the Prime Minister had never replaced him. Churchill told Moran that he had never even thought of doing so.[22] Brooke concluded by saying that

> On reading these diaries I have repeatedly felt ashamed of the abuse I had poured on [Churchill], especially during the latter years. It must, however, be remembered that my diary was the safety valve and only outlet for my pent up feelings . . . I shall always look back on the years I worked with him as some of the most difficult and trying ones of my life. For all that I thank God that I was given an opportunity of working alongside of such a man, and of having my eyes opened to the fact that occasionally such supermen exist on this earth.[23]

When he qualifies his criticisms to this extent – and Kennedy does the same – one has to wonder whether the criticisms remain worth noting.

There were others who had to bear the brunt of daily exposure to Churchill's exigent requirements. Most, despite occasional irritation, came to love him for his peculiarities. Ismay, for instance, had to work far more closely than Brooke with his demanding master. After the war he wrote of his appointment as Churchill's principal staff officer: 'Many of my friends said at the time, and others have written in their memoirs, that they would not have had my job for all the world. I can only say, in all sincerity, that I would not have changed places with any of them for a king's ransom.'[24] He was on hand day and night, dealing particularly with relationships that were fraught, and sensitivities that were bruised, but he scarcely ever complained, and then only for tactical purposes. Brooke on the other hand complained frequently – and not only about Churchill.

When the diaries were reviewed by Milton Shulman for the *Evening Standard*, he spoke of the picture of a 'dedicated, all-seeing Field-Marshal doing his best to win the war almost single-handed at the conference table while constantly being hampered and harassed by the childish petulance of Winston Churchill and the strategic ignorance of his American colleagues, Marshall and Eisenhower'.[25] For G.M. Trevelyan the diaries were the final proof not of Churchill's failings, but of his greatness, because they showed that he asked for advice and was prepared to take it, even when it was contrary to his own instincts. Whether he was considerate in summoning advisers at two in the morning was beside the point. 'This habit of taking counsel, combined with his own personal qualities, is what won the war.' Sir Martin Gilbert has said that no other writings have given 'a more distorted picture of Churchill's war leadership.'[26] So they do, if they are regarded as an historical record.

The diaries are however accurate in what they purport to be, the *reaction* of the Chairman of the Chiefs of Staff Committee to the way in which the Prime Minister conducted business. They are written by a soldier of outstanding ability who was a great administrator and a great chairman. Brooke was one of the three or four men who contributed most to the outcome of the war, and in the process he drove himself relentlessly and selflessly. His mind was focused and his nervous energy concentrated, even if his reactions to Churchill's difficult ways were less tolerant than those of others who had to cope with them. He was a strategist of considerable ability, but he lacked the strategic vision of his Chief. It was a great fortune for Britain that Churchill had Brooke, but the war would probably not have been won without Churchill; it could have been won without Brooke.

Britain's contribution to the strategy that won the war for the allies was disproportionately large and it was the product of these two men. Churchill used to murmur, 'Dear Brookie, how I love him', but not to Brookie. On the other hand, and on another occasion, he told Ismay that 'Brookie hated him and would have to be sacked'. When Ismay told Brooke, he replied, 'I don't hate him, I love him; but when the day comes that I tell him he is right when I believe him to be wrong, it will be time for him to get rid of me'.[27] It may seem a pity that the mutual respect and admiration was not more openly avowed: but on that basis the relationship would not have worked.

After the horrors of the First World War, there had been a thoroughgoing reappraisal of the methods of warfare in Britain. Many commentators believed that the First World War had been an anomalous and mistaken abandonment of Britain's tradition of fighting wars by using her economic and naval strength while staying out of major military clashes. In the eighteenth and nineteenth centuries, for instance, she had mounted naval raids on the periphery of her enemies' territories, and generally employed mercenary armies or allies to do the fighting for her. In the interwar years, Liddell Hart had referred to this method of fighting as 'the British way of warfare'; General J.F.C. Fuller used the more cynical phrase 'strategy of evasion'. This philosophy was broadly accepted by the Chiefs of Staff as the Second World War opened. The idea of huge advances in line had been rejected in favour of the concept of a narrow, concentrated thrust to finish off what had been achieved by bombing, blockade and economic attrition. All of this was the antithesis of the alternative, a Clausewitzian concentration of strength, which was the basis of American military philosophy. Churchill, the historian, was truer than Brooke to the British way of war.

So the new CIGS did not have to wait long before facing the Churchillian proposals that so infuriated him. In his first two weeks Brooke had to deal with suggestions for assaults on Trondheim and Sicily and the suggestion that two divisions be sent to Russia. Similarly, in the autumn of 1941 Dill had had to deal with plans for action in Norway, Sicily, Italy, France and North Africa. These Churchillian interventions can seem wayward and capricious, but they are, rather, the products of a fecund imagination and of a conscious philosophy of opportunism. In October 1941, Churchill said, 'He is an unwise man who thinks that there is any certain method of winning this war. The only plan is to persevere.'

Part II

'There is only one thing worse than fighting with allies.'
(Churchill to Sir Alan Brooke, 1 April 1945)

Westward, Look!

In a broadcast speech on 27 April 1941, Churchill spoke movingly of his identification with the people he met at 'the front', by which he meant 'the streets and wharves of London or Liverpool, Manchester, Cardiff, Swansea or Bristol [and the people he met there] . . . Of their kindness to me I cannot speak, because I have never sought it or dreamed of it, and can never deserve it . . . You can imagine how deeply I feel my own responsibility to all these people; my responsibility to bear my part in bringing them safely out of this long, stern, scowling valley through which we are marching, and not to demand from them the sacrifices and exertions in vain.' He dealt frankly with Greece, which Britain had been bound to assist, the reverses in Libya, 'this whipped jackal, Mussolini, who to save his skin has made all Italy a vassal state of Hitler's Empire, frisking up at the side of the German tiger with yelpings not only of appetite . . . but even of triumph'. He did not minimise what lay ahead. But he ended by referring to America, and quoting two verses of one of his favourite poems, Arthur Hugh Clough's, 'Say not the struggle naught availeth':

> For while the tired waves, vainly breaking,
> > Seem here no painful inch to gain,
> For back, through creeks and inlets making,
> > Comes silent, flooding in, the main.
>
> And not by eastern windows only,
> > When daylight comes, comes in the light;
> In front the sun climbs slow, how slowly
> > But westward, look, the land is bright.

The metaphor was very obvious, and his listeners knew what he meant. They understood as well as he did that Britain might hold her own, but that she could never hope to defeat Germany without American aid. But even as late as April 1941 Churchill had to look hard to discern much brightness in the west. In the end the United Kingdom and the United States fought the war together, and, as far as Churchill's memoirs revealed, as the closest of cousinly allies. But in 1939 or indeed 1941 the relationship was distant and reserved. It was indeed almost hostile.

Ever since the end of the First War the transatlantic connection had been strained and cool, weakened by differences in three key areas: trade, naval rivalries and war debts.

In 1922 Lloyd George proposed an all-round cancellation of the debts that had arisen out of the First World War. At the beginning of that war, America had been a net debtor nation, but by the end of the war she was net creditor of $3.7 billion, precisely the reverse of her debt in 1914.[1] Britain owed the United States $4,000 million but was owed $7,000 million by her European allies. America however refused the proposed debt cancellation and insisted that Britain pay her debts in full. That left Britain with no alternative but to seek payment from her other allies and to require payment of German reparations. The consequences had much to do with the origins of the Second World War. Britain's response to America pointed out to the world where generosity was not to be found: the Balfour Note of 1922 publicly stated that Britain would only seek from her wartime allies and from Germany such sums as she needed to enable her to pay her debt to America.

It is worth noting that Churchill's attitude to foreign debts was typically generous. As Chancellor of the Exchequer, he presented very moderate terms to the French. 'We have not sought', he explained at a party dinner in Birmingham, 'to be judged on this question by our ability to extract the uttermost farthing. We think it our duty to consider not only the capacity of our debtors to pay, but the circumstances under which these debts were incurred.'[2] How far short of his policy was that of America.

Eventually, as the Depression bit, Britain effectively defaulted on her war debts to America and the Lausanne Conference of 1932 linked the reduction of German reparations to a corresponding reduction in war debt payments. The reaction in America was bitter, and in 1934 the Johnson Act forbade loans to any government that had not repaid its First World War debts. This Act was still in force at the outbreak of the Second World War and had to be revoked before Lend-Lease could be enacted. Much of the hostility to Lend-Lease stemmed from recollection of what had happened in 1932.

Differences with America continued, principally in relation to trade and Far Eastern interests, tensions which crystallised into a strong naval rivalry. In 1927 when America intervened in Nicaragua, Sir Robert Vansittart, then in charge of the American Department at the Foreign Office, proposed despatching a British warship to the area. A class of British warships was planned specifically for use against America.

American naval expansionism was reflected in the Washington Naval Treaty of 1922, which allowed America parity with Britain in terms of numbers of capital ships. At that time Churchill was prepared to accept parity at this level, providing Britain retained superiority overall, taking into account warships such as cruisers. At the 1927 Disarmament Conference in Geneva, America tried to go further and sought overall parity. Churchill was very resistant to this: 'There can be no parity between a power whose navy is its life and the power whose navy is only for prestige . . . It always seems to be assumed that it is our duty to humour the United States and minister to their vanity. They do nothing for us in return but exact their last pound of flesh.'[3] He was instrumental in bringing the Cabinet to reject the concessions which the Americans sought. On 20 July 1927 he went further:

> We do not wish to put ourselves in the power of the United States. We cannot tell what they might do if at some future date they were in a position to give us orders about our policy, say, in India, or Egypt, or Canada, or on any other great matter behind which their electioneering forces were marshalled. Moreover, tonnage parity means that Britain can be starved into obedience to any American decree. I would neither trust America to command, nor indeed to submit. Evidently on the basis of American naval superiority speciously disguised as parity immense dangers overhang the future of the world.[4]

This strand in Churchill's thinking is reflected by various remarks in these years. He was recorded as saying that the Americans were 'arrogant, fundamentally hostile to us, and that they wished to dominate world politics'. In a memorandum of November 1928 he wrote: 'Whatever may have been done at enormous cost and sacrifice to keep up friendship is apparently swept away by the smallest little tiff or misunderstanding, and you have to start again and placate the Americans by another batch of substantial or even vital concessions.'[5]

As late as 1916, and not long before America entered the First War alongside Britain, the General Board of the [US] Navy considered how it would use airships in a war against the United Kingdom.[6] It was an axiom of American naval planning between the wars that the rivalries of Britain and the United States made a conflict not unlikely. Equally, speakers at the US Army and Navy War Colleges, many of them with experience of fighting alongside the British armies in 1917 and 1918 emphasised, first, the differences that had existed between the allies as Britain sought to control American troops and, secondly, that alliance between Britain and America was an unnatural state of affairs.

American war games in the 1920s and 1930s involved wars against Red. Red was Britain. 'Every senior American officer who attended one of the two service war colleges in the interwar years was educated to be wary of Great Britain, if not to distrust her'.[7]

These games and lectures had a profound effect in conditioning American officers to an attitude of suspicion and even hostility towards Britain. They were told that the Americans alone had entered the First World War for altruistic reasons, and that America could not fulfil her role as a first-class power unless she developed fleets of the same size as Britain's. The first three questions from the audience put to Herbert Gibbons, lecturing to the Army War College in 1928, began with the words, 'In the event of our becoming involved in a war with England . . .'

It is interesting that Admiral Ernest J. King, the Chief of the Navy when America entered the war as Britain's ally, not only had a generalised hatred of the British, but had distilled it in his Naval War College thesis on the subject of the Royal Navy as a potential enemy in the context of trade, shipping and naval disputes. It is said that when King opened the first meeting of the Combined Chiefs of Staff he said that he had served under Britain in the last war and would never serve under her again or allow any of his ships to serve under her if he could help it.[8] In these years, if Britain had a special relationship it was not with America but with France, the strongest military power in Europe.

In 1917 Woodrow Wilson said to Colonel House, 'England and France have not the same views with regard to peace that we have by any means. When the war is over we can force them to our way of thinking because by that time they will, among other things, be financially in our hands.'[9] After the war, America did indeed preserve the economic lien, but the *political* link of the war years dissolved when she failed to join the League of Nations. Her financial harshness to her former allies contrasted with her generosity to her former enemy, when she granted a huge loan which allowed Germany to reform and modernise her industry.

There was in fact little talk of anything like a 'special relationship' in these days. It was not a concept which America readily invoked. In the famous speech at West Point on 5 December 1962 when the former Secretary of State, Dean Rusk, spoke of Britain's having lost an empire and having not yet found a role, he spoke about *the chimerical and illusory concepts* to which Britain attached herself, and specifically to 'a role based on a "special relationship" with the United States'.

America and Europe

In the years, then, that ran up to the Second World War, the relationship between Britain and the United States was about as cool as it ever was in times of peace between the two countries. America's naval ambitions had been awakened by the First World War and there were real and worrying tensions in this area between America and Britain, still the paramount naval power in the world. But overall America's reaction to the First World War was an inward-looking one, reinforced by the Neutrality Acts passed from 1935 onwards. The war had been an anomaly in American policy: being drawn in to the disputes of the decadent imperial powers had been a mistake.

While the interwar years were generally a period of isolationism for the United States, in the second part of the 1930s Roosevelt attempted to modify that isolationism by removing artificial trade barriers and by seeking a diplomatic solution to the tensions on the European continent. So far as military preparations were concerned, the President did not wish any involvement in Europe, but rather the creation of a powerful American rim from which a defensive air force could operate. Beyond that rim, he preferred to let others fight for America: at the time of Munich he summoned the British ambassador, and told him that dismembering Czechoslovakia would be 'the most terrible, remorseless sacrifice that has ever been demanded of a state'.

America's lack of interest in substantial military operations is reflected in the fact that in 1940 she was twentieth in the world in terms of military power. She had only five army divisions, a one-ocean Pacific navy and 160 pursuit planes with 52 heavy bombers.[1] When war broke out the British Chiefs of Staff thought the most useful help they would be likely to receive from America would be in the realm of financial and economic support.

They were not alone in viewing America without any great enthusiasm. Chamberlain had considerable reservations about America, and as late as January 1940 recorded that, 'I don't want the Americans to fight for us – we should have to pay too dearly for that if they had a right to be in on the peace terms'.[2] It was indeed only after Hitler's attack on Czechoslovakia that Chamberlain saw America as having any place at all in Britain's foreign policy. Thus, what had been planned as a royal visit to Canada was extended into a visit to America, and the Canadian element became insignificant. The British ambassador had noted that despite extensive isolationism in the United States, '[I]n the event of a very grave crisis [this visit] might have decisive results'.[3]

The ambassador in question was Sir Robert Lindsay: his appointment had been extended to allow him to manage the royal visit, but he was shortly succeeded by Lord Lothian. Lothian's background had been as an appeaser, but his mission to strengthen Anglo-American relations was important and fairly successful. Partly as a result of lobbying between 12 and 21 September 1939 Roosevelt persuaded Congress to perform a turn-around on the Neutrality Acts and allow exports to belligerents on a cash-and-carry basis. Obstacles were put in the way of significant purchases by Germany and Russia.

Chamberlain's scepticism was part of a long tradition. In 1927 Lord Hankey, a particularly cold-blooded spokesman for the interwar establishment, enunciated it: 'Time after time we have been told that, if we made this concession or that concession, we should secure the goodwill in [*sic*] America. We gave up the Anglo-Japanese alliance. We agreed to pay our [war] debts . . . I have never seen any permanent result follow from a policy of concessions. I believe we are less popular and more abused in America than ever because they think us weak.'[4]

Churchill was ready to apply flattery to the United States and her President with his bricklayer's trowel, and from time to time he was genuinely carried away by romantic notions of links between the English-speaking peoples. But there were plenty of occasions when he recognised the cold self-interest of the American administration for what it was. In November 1937 he wrote to Lord Linlithgow about the 'increasingly grim' situation in Europe. He referred to the fact that the United States 'signals encouragement to us', but significantly added, 'for what that is worth'. His realistic appreciation is reflected in the 'Theme' of the second volume of his history of the war: 'How the British people held the fort alone till those who hitherto had been half-blind were half-ready.'

The encouragement which the United States signalled, to which he referred, was the product of a slight change in Roosevelt's position.

When he first became President in 1933 he was not greatly interested in Hitler and regarded Germany as a problem for Britain and France, but after the Spanish Civil War in 1936 and Japanese attacks on China in 1937 he became more involved. In October 1937 he spoke of the need to 'quarantine' aggressor states.

In January 1938 the President offered to convene an international conference to try to devise a general peace settlement. Chamberlain requested that it be delayed so that he could deal directly with Germany and Italy. Under pressure from Eden, whose resignation was in part precipitated by this issue, he ultimately asked Roosevelt to go ahead. Chamberlain had said a year earlier that it was 'always best and safest to count on nothing from the Americans except words' and his view was justified in this instance: the talks never took place.

By the end of 1938 Roosevelt was talking of the need for more planes, and there was a steady increase in the production of armaments in the United States from 1940, but he continued to see responsibility for facing up to Hitler as resting with Britain and France. If they accepted the burden they would be acting as what he called 'America's front line of defence'.

'What the British need today' he said as late at February 1939, 'is a good stiff grog, inducing not only the desire to save civilisation but the continued belief that they can do it. In such an event they will have a lot more support from their American cousins'.[5] It was convenient that civilisation should be saved by someone else, on a front line of defence that was 3,000 miles away from Washington.

On 10 June 1940, following the dire events in France, he delivered a speech at Charlottesville, Virginia, which must have encouraged Churchill. But just four days later he wrote to Churchill saying that 'while our efforts will be exerted towards making available an ever increasing amount of materials and supplies[,] a certain amount of time must pass before our efforts in this sense can be successful to the extent desired'.[6]

There was then a period of two months when the President did not communicate with Churchill at all, although in the same period Churchill wrote to Roosevelt no less than four times. No one knows what was going on in the President's mind during these eight weeks. Of this period Harold Ickes, Secretary of the Interior, said, 'I do know that in every direction I find a growing discontent with the President's lack of leadership. He still has the country if he will take it and lead it. But he won't have it very much longer unless he does something. It won't be sufficient for him to make another speech and then go into a state of innocuous desuetude again. People are beginning to say: "I am tired of words; I want action."[7]

Every positive initiative the President took was followed by qualifications and retractions. James MacGregor Burns, not a hostile biographer, memorably described Roosevelt in 1941:

Once again Roosevelt was caught between divided administration counsels, between the conflicting demands of isolationists and interventionists. Once again there was a period of veering and drifting in the White House; once again Roosevelt's advisers – Stimson, Ickes, and others – lamented the President's failure to lead. And once again Roosevelt responded to the situation by improvisation and subterfuge. He publicly ordered naval patrolling in the now enlarged security zones; he privately ordered a policy of seeking out German ships and planes and notifying British units of their location. On May 27, while pickets trudged dourly back and forth in front of the White House with their anti-war signs, Roosevelt announced his issuance of a proclamation of 'unlimited national emergency'. The next day, however, he took much of the sting out of his move by disclaiming any positive plans along new lines.

The President, said Hopkins, 'would rather follow public opinion than lead it'. Indeed, as Roosevelt anxiously examined public opinion polls in 1941, he once again was failing to supply the crucial factor of his own leadership in the equation of public opinion. His approach was in sharp contrast to that of his great world partner. 'Nothing is more dangerous in wartime', Churchill said later in the year, 'than to live in the temperamental atmosphere of a Gallup poll, always feeling one's pulse and taking one's temperature. There is only one duty, only one safe course, and that is to try to be right and not to fear to do or say what you believe to be right.'[8]

Roosevelt may simply have felt that he could not move too far ahead of opinion, or it may be that he was simply enjoying a period of the tranquillity which his capacity for a philosophic detachment from day to day worries frequently allowed him. Some events during this period suggest that his mind was slowly moving towards giving some sort of support to Britain. For instance he brought the Anglophile Stimson into the Cabinet as Secretary for War, and the Republican Frank Knox became Secretary of the Navy. But Roosevelt was far from being the most enthusiastic supporter of Britain in her fight against fascism. Ickes and the Secretary of the Treasury, Morgenthau, were more anti-fascist than he: they attributed the President's caution to Hull, the Secretary of State.[9] As the Presidential election approached, it was his opponent, Wendell Willkie, rather than Roosevelt, who campaigned for increased assistance to Britain.

When the President broke his silence, his first message to Churchill proposed the Destroyers for Bases deal. Churchill's reaction to the very substantial strings attached to the Destroyers deal, and later to Lend-Lease, was realistic: '[We] cannot afford to risk the major issue in order to maintain our pride and to preserve the dignity of a few small islands.'[10] But some Cabinet members took a different view. Leo Amery, Secretary of State for India, saw the strings attached to Lend-Lease as tugging at the sinews of the Empire. Beaverbrook said, 'They have taken our bases without valuable consideration. They have taken our gold. They have been given our secrets and offered us a thoroughly inadequate service in return.'[11]

Churchill could see that the invidious nature of the deal was not something that should be unduly publicised, and in a letter to Roosevelt of 22 August 1940 he pressed that the two parts of the transaction should not be linked in a formal exchange of letters. 'I had not contemplated anything in the nature of a contract, bargain or a sale between us. It is the fact that we had decided in Cabinet to offer you naval and air facilities off the Atlantic coast quite independently of destroyers or any other aid.'[12]

After the war, Churchill spoke affectionately of Roosevelt, partly because of the picture he wanted to leave for posterity and in part simply because his emotional nature often put extravagant language into his mouth; but there *were* times when he genuinely warmed to FDR's vitality and enthusiasm. Within the multiplicity of unresolved and sometimes contradictory sentiments that filled the President's mind, there was indeed in the early part of the war a weakness for the British and French cause. Indeed, after the war, Truman objected to publication of any correspondence between the President and the Prime Minister on the grounds that it would encourage the Congress to press for publication of that correspondence in its entirety; it was thought that publication in full might reveal a bias on the part of FDR towards Britain during the time that America remained neutral.[13] But there was not a great number of exchanges between Roosevelt and Churchill during the Phoney War.

Behind the scenes, British Intelligence worked on American public opinion, with hundreds of agents operating in America as British Security Co-ordination. Three floors in the Rockefeller Center were filled with these people, manipulating moods, planting stories and trying to effect a change in the climate of opinion. They had to work on an amalgam of views in America some of which were positively hostile to assisting Britain, some indifferent. Even at the top of the Democrat political Establishment, there was huge ambivalence about the British cause. Irish and Italian Americans were key elements of the FDR coalition. His ambassador in London, Joseph Kennedy, wanted Germany to win. His Secretary of State, Cordell Hull, was anxious to see the British fleet moved to America. In the event, the steps that nudged America towards support for Britain were closely tied to recognition of her self-interest. The Destroyers for Bases deal and to an extent Lend-Lease appealed to her desire to strengthen her peripheral defences and enhance her capacity to strike.

Destroyers for Bases

Roosevelt's true sentiments are difficult to ascertain. It was he who inaugurated correspondence with Churchill at the beginning of the war, while the latter was still at the Admiralty, but he had little affection for him. He thought Churchill had snubbed him at a formal dinner in London during the First World War when he was a lowly Assistant Secretary of the US Navy. FDR told Joseph Kennedy in December 1939 that at the dinner Churchill had 'acted like a stinker . . . lording it all over us'. Ten years after that meeting, when Churchill was out of office and on a visit to America, Roosevelt, then Governor of New York, declined to see him.[1]

Roosevelt's ambivalence towards Britain was pervasive. While he was hostile to many aspects of what he considered Britain stood for, he certainly had some sympathy with her in the war that she was now fighting alone. Isolationist pressures, evident since his first victory in 1933, and American neutrality statutorily enshrined in successive Neutrality Acts, made it inevitable that America would not enter the war at the outset. The question was whether, and if so when, she might join in. If Pearl Harbor had not taken place the question might have had a different answer; it is impossible to say for certain that FDR would otherwise have exercised sufficient leadership to enter the war.

Roosevelt's policy before the war had been based on a desire to strengthen France and Britain against Germany with promises of material aid. They would be America's front line. He sought to establish closer links with British political leaders. He had got on well with Ramsay MacDonald, but not with his successors. Chamberlain, not well disposed towards America, declined an invitation to visit the United States. Roosevelt encouraged and promoted the visit by the King and Queen in 1939 and made reassuring noises to the King about what might happen if Britain were bombed. He told them that he would sink any U-boats he saw. He expressed fears about German naval activity in South America and said he would wish to establish a western hemisphere naval patrol, using British bases in the West Indies. He raised this again formally with the British government some weeks later and it was eventually to form part of the Destroyers for Bases deal of September 1940.

The King was much reassured, as was Mackenzie King who acted as a sort of minister-in-attendance throughout the visit. But as always, Roosevelt was telling people what they wanted to hear: when in the event war broke out and he clearly proclaimed neutrality, Mackenzie King felt 'really ashamed'.

The fact is that Roosevelt's thoughts on foreign policy were shallow and immature, and his pronouncements often spontaneous and meaningless. He told Canada's Governor General, Lord Tweedsmuir, that if war broke out in Europe the United States 'would be in the next day'. Duff Cooper, as First Lord of the Admiralty, was told that America would be with him 'within three weeks'. On the other hand he was not against appeasement: when Chamberlain went to Munich to meet Hitler, Roosevelt sent a personal telegram: 'Good man'.[2] He thought that he knew Germany better than any career diplomat. He had indeed visited the country many times before the First World War and even went to school there for six weeks. Later he honeymooned there. He met the Kaiser and from the imperial yacht stole a pencil that bore the Kaiser's tooth marks. Despite all this, he had no affection whatsoever for Germany; and yet he supported Boer relief during the South African War.

His failure to wake up to the reality of Soviet expansionism towards the end of the war was rooted in a firm view formed before the war that Russia had given up militant communism in favour of a benevolent state socialism. This flawed vision survived the show trials and murders of the 1930s. On the whole he saw Russia moving in a social democrat direction, rather as the United States was doing under his leadership. On the other hand, the empires, particularly the British Empire, were institutions of the past, whose policies had largely been responsible for the outbreak of the First World War, and for the eastern dimensions of the Second. He had a collection of no less than 1.2 million postage stamps. Churchill spent an exciting evening at Washington watching him sticking them into his albums. The collection accompanied the President to Casablanca and Teheran. Anthony Eden said that Roosevelt had learned his geography from his stamps. His appreciation of world politics was of about that level.

Churchill's appeal for destroyers was made in a desperate telegram, his first communication with the President after becoming Prime Minister, sent on 15 May 1940, when the Battle of France was at its height. A bad day, 'an awful day' said Cadogan, 'Don't know where this will end'. The telegram began, 'Although I have changed my office, I am sure you would not wish me to discontinue our private, intimate correspondence . . . The small countries are simply smashed up, one by one, like matchwood.'[3] The crux of the message lay in the words,

> I trust you realise, Mr. President, that the voice and force of the United States may count for nothing if they are withheld too long. You may have a completely subjugated, Nazified Europe, established with astonishing swiftness, and the weight may be more than we can bear. All I ask now is that you should proclaim non-belligerency, which would mean that you would help us with everything short of actually engaging armed forces. Immediate needs are, first of all, the loan of 40 or 50 of your older destroyers to bridge the gap between what we have now and the large new construction that we put in hand at the beginning of the war . . . We want several hundred of the latest types of aircraft . . .[,] anti-aircraft equipment and ammunition . . .

Roosevelt replied speedily enough but essentially negatively. He offered no tangible help. Lending destroyers would require the approval of Congress, which he did not want to seek at that time.[4] His reply ended with a limp dismissal: 'The best of luck to you. Franklin D. Roosevelt'.[5]

Churchill was more realistic than the Foreign Office, which was inclined to offer concessions to the United States in the vague hope that this would redound ultimately to Britain's advantage. Churchill wanted only to make concessions for value. Despite what he said to the President about a lack of linkage, he refused to allow the Americans to build bases on British islands except in exchange for destroyers and munitions. He fought the Foreign Office, seeking to minimise the number of leases offered: 'It doesn't do to give way like this to the Americans. One must strike a balance with them.'[6] He refused to allow information about Asdic and Radar to be given gratuitously to the Americans. He wrote on 17 July 1940, 'I am not in a hurry to give our secrets until the United States is much nearer war than she is now'.[7] The secrets eventually went to America in

August 1940 in a box which found its way into the wine cellar of the British Embassy in Washington.

The Destroyers for Bases deal is very frequently represented as a unilateral act of generosity on the part of the Americans. It was far from that. The deal was opposed by a number of senior officials, notably Ambassador Kennedy and Admiral Stark. Roosevelt eventually decided that opposition to the deal would be so great in Congress that he resorted to executive action to implement it. He only did so after repeated demands from Churchill, culminating on 31 July 1940 with a message which enumerated eleven British destroyers that had been sunk or put out of action within the last ten days: 'Mr. President, with great respect I must tell you that in the long history of the world, this is the thing to do now'.[8] This message seems to have done the trick: only a few days earlier, Roosevelt had told the Secretary for the Navy Knox that Congress would veto a *sale* of destroyers, and had suggested that Knox might think '*at a little later date* of trying to get Congressional action to allow the sale of these destroyers to Canada on condition that they be used solely in American hemisphere defence' (my emphasis). Roosevelt knew that the Caribbean islands were 'of the utmost importance to our national defence as naval and air operations bases', while the destroyers were 'the same type of ship which we have from time to time been striking from the naval list and selling for scrap for, I think, $4,000 or $5,000 per destroyer'.

In the event of course there was not a sale but a deal: it was a deal which the British ambassador, Lord Lothian, 'who had been almost tearful in his pleas for help and help quickly', had first suggested to Churchill on 24 May. At that time Churchill dismissed it out of hand. Now he had to accept the ignominious terms.

There were weeks of difficult negotiation before the agreement was signed on 2 September. As Roosevelt had privately acknowledged, the fifty destroyers Britain received were elderly relics of the previous war, and of limited value. By the end of the year only nine of them were in service with the Royal Navy. They were notoriously poor sea boats, which required extensive modification before they could be used. Their British crews hated them. By October 1943 the Admiralty wanted to scrap these ancient vessels, which needed constant refits. On 31 December 1940 Churchill allowed himself to hint to FDR that his destroyers would be more useful if they were in better order. He annexed to his telegram a list of defects, 'in case you want to work up any of the destroyers lying in your yards'.[9] In return America received long leases of no less than eight British islands in the Caribbean and Western Atlantic, where they could build naval and air bases.

In 1939 one fairly typical poll found that 62 per cent of Americans were in favour of neutrality and only 2 per cent wanted to go to war. The reasons for this lack of enthusiasm were diverse. Irish- and German-Americans would obviously be against war, but there was also a large constituency that was simply disillusioned with the failure of the First World War to end wars: 126,000 Americans had died in that war. There was no enthusiasm for war in 1939: there was indeed positive opposition, reflected in movements such as America First. This body was highly organised and by spring 1941 consisted of 700 chapters with a total membership of 1,000,000. It was supported by many high-profile figures such as Charles Lindbergh who said just before Pearl Harbor that only three groups wanted war: 'the British, the Jews and the Roosevelt Administration'.

America First was not quite balanced by its adversary, the Committee to Defend America by Aiding the Allies, which had about 600 chapters. The Committee was supported by some interesting political heavy-weights such as Secretary of War Henry L. Stimson, Congressman J.W. Fulbright and Dean Acheson. It also had its scattering of showbiz personalities: if America First had Lillian Gish, the Committee to Defend America had Gene Tunney.

The various anti-fascist groups – there was a number, including the Century Group and the White Committee – must not be thought of as sentimentally pro-British. Indeed the democratic idealism which ani-mated some of them made them very critical of a Britain that they tended to regard as unattractively reactionary. They were first and foremost pro-America. It was the Century Group which produced the idea of exchanging the old destroyers in return for bases and assurances about the British fleet. White said that many of his Committee

> had no great love for the British ruling classes. We have not relented in our general theory that George III was a stupid old fuddy duddy with instincts of a tyrant and a brain corroded and cheesy with the arrogance and ignorance which go with the exercise of tyranny. Yet I think I am safe in saying that our whole group felt . . . that if Great Britain were inhabited by a group of Red Indians under the command of Sitting Bull, Crazy Horse and Geronimo, so long as Great Britain had command of the British fleet, we should try to arm her and keep that fleet afloat.[10]

The fact that there could be such large unofficial bodies arguing for and against involvement in the war is a reflection in part of the lack of leadership offered by the President.

Roosevelt certainly saw Churchill as the representative of an outmoded, aristocratic regime of which he disapproved, though he was far richer than Churchill and much more at the centre of the Establishment. Churchill's views about Roosevelt, and about America in general, are complicated but easier to understand. He was proud of the fact that he was not only half-American, but also descended from a native American, as he would not have referred to her. He was mesmerised by the brash vitality of America and her economy. He found a romantic appeal in the coming together of the two English-speaking nations. He declared frankly that 'no lover ever studied every whim of his mistress as I did those of President Roosevelt' But while his emotions affected him and informed his wooing of Roosevelt, their union was a marriage of convenience, and his motives were mercenary rather than romantic.

Roosevelt could indeed be positively flirtatious. When Wendell Willkie was sent to London in 1941 he took with him the celebrated handwritten note that included the verse from Longfellow:

> Sail on, Oh ship of state!
> Sail on Oh Union strong and great.
> Humanity with all its fears,
> With all the hope of future years
> Is hanging breathless on thy fate.

What was Churchill to make of this? He referred to the letter and the verse it contained soon afterwards in his broadcast to America of 9 February 1941, the broadcast which contained the famous words 'Give us the tools, and we will finish the job.' Roosevelt's message had obviously meant much to him. But in the event it was to be very many months, and only after Pearl Harbor, that Roosevelt's practical encouragement was translated into an alliance in war. Roosevelt's interlocutors tended to come away from him convinced that he had made promises at which he had done no more than hint. Churchill as much as anyone else was frequently misled in this way.

Where the Prime Minister had initially looked for America's support purely for its moral value, he came increasingly to need it also for material reasons. He was still, however, not looking to America for manpower. An overlooked passage in the 'Tools' speech contains the words 'It seems now to be certain that the government and people of the United States intend to supply us with all that is necessary for victory. In the last war the United States sent two million men across the Atlantic. But this is not a war of vast armies, firing immense masses of shells at one another. We do not need the gallant armies which are forming throughout the American Union. We do not need them this year, nor next year; nor any year that I can foresee.'

He was convinced that America would not stand by if they knew that British cities were being bombed. De Gaulle described him in the garden at Chequers 'raising his fist towards the sky as he cried: "So they won't come!"' De Gaulle asked him why he wanted to see the bombers and Churchill replied that the bombing of Oxford, Coventry and Canterbury would cause such a wave of indignation that the United States could not stand apart. On other occasions he felt that invasion itself might have the same beneficial effect. He came however to accept that America would not enter the war before the Presidential election on 5 November 1940. By 1 November he was convinced that Roosevelt was going to win by a large majority and that he would then lose no time in bringing America into the war. In the event, of course, the result of the election no more resulted in an American declaration of war than the bombing of Britain had done.

Churchill sent an elaborate telegram of congratulations to Roosevelt following his victory in the Presidential election and was very concerned that he had received no reply. He tried to chase matters up through the British Embassy and eventually an unconvincing story came back about the message's being lost.

In February 1941 FDR sent Wendell Willkie, his Republican opponent in the 1940 Presidential election, to Europe to assess the situation. Willkie was anxious to see whether a peace could even then be negotiated, and Roosevelt was by no means committed to joining in the war against the Axis powers. He was still anxious to know exactly what Hitler and Mussolini were after. He was certainly not bending all his efforts to preparing America for entry into the war.

Before the 1940 Presidential election Churchill had been very critical of America's detachment from Britain's desperate plight. On 27 May 1940 he said that the United States 'had given us practically no help in the war, and now that they saw how great was the danger, their attitude was that they wanted to keep everything which would help us for their own defence'.[11] A month later he told his American friend, Bernard Baruch, 'I'm sure we shall be all right here but your people are not doing much'.[12] It was bitterly disappointing to find that things appeared to have changed very little after the election.

It is very difficult to be clear about Roosevelt's deepest beliefs. He may have had few. He was essentially a political and pragmatic creature, reactive in instinct, seeking to achieve practical ends. Douglas Macarthur was typical of some of his critics when he described the President as 'A man who never told the truth when a lie would serve him just as well'. But his reputation for unreliability largely flowed from his desire to avoid making enemies unnecessarily. In May 1942 Roosevelt famously told Morgenthau, 'You know I am a juggler, and I never let my right hand know what my left hand does . . . I may have one policy for Europe and one diametrically opposite for North and South America. I may be entirely inconsistent, and furthermore I am perfectly willing to mislead and tell untruths if it will help win the war.'[13]

Despite the obscurity of his convictions, exacerbated by his practice of committing little to paper and rarely dictating records of his conversations, he certainly entertained some prejudices that informed his relations with Britain and with Churchill. He, and the Democratic Establishment generally, had a distaste for the institution of empire – except in its American form – so great that they conceived themselves as charged with the responsibility for dismantling it wherever they could. In Britain, Roosevelt said, there was 'too much Eton and Oxford'. Quite why a political party in one country should have seen it as their duty to alter the culture of another is not easy to understand today, but Roosevelt's circle was gratified by signs of the erosion of the traditional class structure in Britain under the influence of the stresses of the early months of the war. They saw Bevin, Laski and others as instruments of change.

Both Roosevelt and Churchill were warm and convivial men. They wanted to get on well and they often did. The picture which Churchill was concerned to paint in his history and in his public pronouncements was of a close and trusting relationship. In reality, there was no great measure of trust on either side. Both parties entered the alliance for the benefit of their own national interests. Both were frequently angered, and expressed their anger, when differences emerged. Churchill was particularly upset by what he regarded as instances of a mean-minded failure to look at the interests of the alliance as a whole. He referred to the President's pet dog when he expostulated in 1944: 'What do you want me to do – stand up and beg like Fala?' There were many similar outbursts in a relationship that was far from the romantic union as it was later portrayed.

Lend-Lease

On 7 December 1940 Churchill appealed to Roosevelt in a letter on which he had worked for no less than two weeks and extensively revised, and which was patently addressed to America's self-interest.[1] It had originally been drafted by Lothian and was greatly redrafted for circulation to the Cabinet. Churchill then worked up a third version, which was the one that went to Roosevelt. It has been described as perhaps 'the most carefully drafted and redrafted message in the whole Churchill–Roosevelt Correspondence'.[2]

His communications, like his speeches, did not consist simply of magnificent and memorable phrases. The bravura climaxes followed on detailed, supremely well-argued and logical forensic analyses. The Secret Session speeches are particularly worth studying. They are almost completely free from oratorical flourishes, but rather consist of the logical deployment of substantial data, skilfully set out in a persuasive argument of which a distinguished member of the Bar would be proud.

So the letter began with a painstaking explanation of the circumstances by which Britain was surrounded. Churchill set out precisely her dangers and weaknesses. He then put forward arguments that were directed towards America's own welfare:

> The moment approaches when we shall no longer be able to pay cash for shipping and other supplies. While we will do our utmost, and shrink from no proper sacrifice to make payments across the Exchange, I believe you will agree that it would be wrong in principle and mutually disadvantageous in effect if at the height of this struggle Great Britain were to be divested of all saleable assets, so that after the victory was won with our blood, civilisation saved, and the time gained for the United States to be fully armed against all eventualities, we should stand stripped to the bone . . . We here should be unable, after the war, to purchase the large balance of imports from the

United States over and above the volume of our exports which is agreeable to your tariffs and industrial economy. Not only should we in Great Britain suffer cruel privations, but widespread unemployment in the United States would follow the curtailment of American exporting power.[3]

His arguments were well chosen. America's reaction to the war, and to the fall of France, was concern for her own safety. Roosevelt feared the loss of the British fleet to Germany. He used Mackenzie King, the Canadian Premier, as an intermediary in an attempt to obtain a promise from Churchill that Britain's navy would be sent to America rather than fall into German hands.

Lend-Lease was distinct from the Destroyers for Bases deal. The difference between the situations of Churchill and Roosevelt at this point in the war is neatly reflected in the fact that Churchill's letter setting out Britain's urgent need for military supplies was read by Roosevelt as he lay back in a deck chair on the US warship *Tuscaloosa* cruising in the Caribbean sun.[4] Churchill's message, at over 4,000 words, was the longest he had sent to Roosevelt.

The message did the trick. It was at the press conference at the end of the cruise that the burning house and the metaphor of the hosepipe made their appearance. Roosevelt pinched the metaphor from Secretary of the Interior, Harold L. Ickes. Ickes was distinctly pro-intervention and had written to Roosevelt on 2 August 1940, in favour of the Destroyers for Bases deal and going on to say that 'It seems to me, we Americans are like the householder who refuses to lend or sell his fire extinguishers to help put out the fire in the house that is right next door although that house is all ablaze and the wind is blowing from that direction'.

British public opinion liked the metaphor; American public opinion noted that the policy proceeded 'on the general theory that the best defence of Great Britain is the best defence of the United States'. Churchill's description of the deal as involving the British Empire and the United States being 'somewhat mixed up together in some of their affairs for mutual and general advantage' was a euphemistic gloss. The deal was very much a practical one to the advantage of the United States, and it even had to incorporate a pledge that the British fleet would never be surrendered to the Germans but would, if the worst came to the worst, be moved to the Empire.

That last point was of significance. Churchill was aware of America's concern about the fate of the British fleet, and frequently used it to blackmail Roosevelt. America's fleet was designed for use only in the Pacific, leaving her Atlantic coast vulnerable to a victorious Germany. In his important message to Roosevelt on 20 May 1940 Churchill had been at pains to say that if his government fell as a result of invasion, its successor might be required to surrender, as he would never do.[5] 'Excuse me, Mr President', he wrote 'putting this nightmare bluntly . . . Evidently I could not answer for my successors who in utter despair and helplessness might have to accommodate themselves to the German will.'

He pressed home this point in successive telegrams. Roosevelt did not answer the 20 May message. His next letter – of 30 May – is in jolly terms that fail to echo Churchill's anguish: 'My dear Churchill:- Ever so many thanks for that remarkably interesting story [of 7 May] of the Battle of the River Plate – a grand job by your three cruisers.'[6]

It was hardly surprising that at the end of 1940 Churchill complained that he had found American attitudes chilling. He considered that America had given Britain nothing that had not been paid for and nothing that was essential to Britain's resistance. But he became much more sanguine in the course of January 1941. There were two reasons for this. One was Roosevelt's submission of the Lend-Lease bill to Congress, and the other was Harry Hopkins's mission. Hopkins was a close friend and confidant of Roosevelt – indeed he had his own apartment in the White House. He was not an obvious Churchillian. He was committed to the New Deal and shared Roosevelt's suspicion of aristocratic decadence. For all of the war years Hopkins was in very poor health, his life in the balance on many occasions. But he took no account of his frailty and committed himself to the service of his country at war without regard for the cost. He travelled ceaselessly, not only within the United States: he made repeated and frequently very uncomfortable journeys back and forth across the Atlantic. He was present at all the great conferences. At times Roosevelt relied on him and his judgement more than any other person.

The influence of this frail Rasputin whose powers rested on no legitimate constitutional basis was greatly resented – not least by those on the right who remembered Hopkins's career in the Civil Works Administration and the Works Progress Administration, and feared that as America increasingly exerted influence on the shape of post-war Europe he and his President were bound together on a mission to impose a socialist character on the liberated Continent.

The extent of Hopkins's influence is all the more remarkable in view of the fact that this former welfare administrator had no wide vision or sense of history. He prided himself on being a 'doer' rather than a 'talker', and rather enjoyed his popular image as a playboy. But he came to be a friend and confidant of Churchill almost as much as of Roosevelt, and he was certainly liked more by Clementine Churchill than by Eleanor Roosevelt. His great ability was to cut through the talk and diplomacy that surrounded complicated issues and insist on a no-nonsense approach to the practical question that lay at their heart. It was for this reason that Churchill proposed elevating him to the peerage with the title 'Lord Root of the Matter'. When Truman conferred the Distinguished Service Medal on Hopkins, the citation referred to his attacks on the problems of the war by means of 'piercing understanding'.

Not long before his own death, Dill wrote a moving letter of condolence on the death of Hopkins's son in the Pacific. He said, 'Harry, this war has hit you very hard. I know of no one who has done more by wise and courageous advice to advance our common cause. And who knows it? Some day it must be known.'[7] Long before the end of the war Churchill's trust in the man was such that he treated him almost as his ambassador to the President.

He referred to his first meeting with Hopkins in his history of the war and to 'that extraordinary man, who played, and was to play, a sometimes decisive part in the whole movement of the war. His was a soul that flamed out of a frail and failing body. He was a crumbling lighthouse from which there shone the beams that led great fleets to harbour.'[8]

Hopkins's formal letter of authorisation from the President was couched in the ornate style of an earlier age:

Reposing special faith and confidence in you, I am asking you to proceed at your early convenience to Great Britain, there to act as my personal representative. I am also asking you to convey a communication in this sense to His Majesty King George VI.

You will, of course, communicate to this Government any matters which may come to your attention in the performance of your mission which you may feel will serve the best interests of the United States.

With all best wishes for the success of your mission,

I am

Very sincerely yours,

Franklin D. Roosevelt.

Hopkins arrived in Britain with the peculiar prejudice that Churchill was hostile to America in general and to Roosevelt in particular. He himself certainly had had a personal prejudice against Britain, which had only recently been dispelled when he had been charmed by the Queen's kindness to his infant daughter during the Royal visit of 1939.[9]

Churchill rolled out every available red carpet, and Hopkins was with him for three of his four weeks in Britain, and on the most intimate basis, seeing him at the closest of quarters, watching him at work throughout the day and at play when partially off-duty in the long evening sessions at Chequers. Hopkins was indeed, as Bracken said, 'the most important American visitor to this country we have ever had'.[10] Unknown to Hopkins or to Churchill, the FBI kept a watch on Hopkins's activities, and J. Edgar Hoover reported to Roosevelt on how the trip was going.[11] They were also keeping a file on Churchill.

Hopkins was met at Poole by Brendan Bracken (whom he described rather quaintly in his report as 'Churchill's Man Friday') and was then taken in some state to the capital. No effort was spared to make him feel welcome. All the trouble that was lavished on Hopkins was worthwhile. Even before he returned to the United States, he reported favourably to his boss:

Dear Mr. President:

These notes are sent by Col. Lee, who is returning with Halifax. Will you save them for me until I get back, when I shall try to put them into readable form.

The people here are amazing from Churchill down, and if courage alone can win – the result will be inevitable. But they need our help desperately, and I am sure you will permit nothing to stand in the way. Some of the ministers and underlings are a bit trying, but no more than some I have seen.

Churchill is the gov't. in every sense of the word – he controls the ground strategy and often the details – labour trusts him – the army, navy, air force are behind him to a man. The politicians and upper crust pretend to like him. I cannot emphasise too strongly that he is the one and only person over here with whom you need to have a full meeting of minds.

Churchill wants to see you – the sooner the better – but I have told him of your problem until the [Lend-Lease] bill is passed. I am convinced this meeting between you and Churchill is essential – and soon – for the battering continues and Hitler does not wait for Congress.

The perceptive comment about the 'politicians and upper crust' is instructive.

At the first meeting over dinner at Number 10, Hopkins asked Churchill if there were anything that the USA could do for Britain. Churchill said, 'I should like a million rifles. I don't like telling the British army to fight the Germans with dummy rifles made of wood.' Hopkins said he was not sure that they had a million rifles; perhaps they could find 500,000. Soon he left the room, returning to say that he had spoken to the President, and that the first consignment of a million rifles would be shipped on the following day. Churchill dissolved into tears. This anecdote was told by Bracken (who was at the dinner) to Lascelles. It is almost certainly a true account of what happened at the dinner, though it is not known whether the shipment was ever made. Hopkins understood the magic of moments such as this, and what they meant to Churchill – and to an extent to Roosevelt. Such alchemy could impart a romantic and emotional dimension from time to time into a relationship that was otherwise cold, calculating and often unappealing.[12]

Colville's diary records one of the Chequers weekends:

> When the women had gone to bed, I listened in the Great Hall to as interesting a discussion as I ever hope to hear. We sat in a circle, Portal, Hopkins, Jack Churchill and myself and the Prof. [Cherwell], while the P.M. stood with his back against the mantelpiece, a cigar between his teeth, his hands in the armpits of his waistcoat. Every few seconds he would start forward, trip over the marble grate, walk four or five paces, turn abruptly and resume his position against the mantelpiece. All the while a torrent of eloquence flowed from his lips, and he would fix one or other of us with his eye while he drove home some point. He talked of the past, the present and the future . . .[13]

During his final weekend at Chequers, Hopkins produced a box of gramophone records with an Anglo-American theme. 'We had these until well after midnight, the PM walking about, sometimes dancing a *pas seul*, in time with the music. We all got a bit sentimental & Anglo-American, under the influence of the good dinner & the music. The PM kept on stopping in his walk & commenting on the situation – what a remarkable thing that the two nations should be drawing so much together at this critical time, how much we had in common etc.'[14] Churchill enjoyed these *pas seuls*, and was inclined to say that although he danced indifferently with a partner, he danced beautifully on his own.

However beautifully he danced, it was bold of him to allow Hopkins such a privileged sight. But Hopkins was won over, and he told Roosevelt that the story about anti-American prejudice could be disregarded. He saw no evidence, equally, that Churchill's capacities were ever impaired by alcohol: in February 1940, Sumner Welles reported that he had visited Churchill at the Admiralty to find him drunk at 5 p.m. When Churchill became Prime Minister, Roosevelt said that he 'supposed Churchill was the best man England had, even if he was drunk half the time'.[15]

The Hopkins visit concluded with a very moving small dinner party in the Central Hotel, Glasgow, before he went aboard ship to return to the States. Everyone wanted to know what the burden of Hopkins's report to Roosevelt would be. When he rose to his feet he said that he was going back to Roosevelt to 'quote a verse to him from the Book of Ruth, which the President would know well: "Whither thou goest, I will go; and where thou lodgest, I will lodge: thy people shall be my people, and thy God my God."' In a whisper he added four words of his own: 'even to the end'. Churchill was again in tears.

Hopkins returned to America seized of an admiration and respect for Britain – and for Churchill in particular – that was all the more important for being so new to him. He remained an American first and foremost, and indeed towards the end of the war could, with some regret, differ from Churchill on aspects of policy. But overwhelmingly his role was that of a broker between the two English-speaking countries, and his influence on Roosevelt undoubtedly made the President a better friend to Britain that he would otherwise have been.

In the course of his visit, Hopkins concluded two important agreements with Britain. One provided that American aircraft carriers would transport aircraft to Britain 'in case of urgent need'. The other provided for the pooling of British and American intelligence in enemy-occupied countries. On the same day that these agreements were signed, a staff conference opened in Washington to discuss unity of field command in joint operations between Britain and America, in the event of America declaring war. A critical conclusion of the conference was that *even if war broke out in the Pacific,* the European theatre would take precedence. That was a crucially important decision, though taken well below the level of heads of government.

At about the same time, America provided Britain with a 'Purple' machine, the Japanese equivalent of Enigma. It went to Bletchley Park, accompanied by two American signals experts. When the American crypto-analysts arrived at Bletchley Park with Purple, they were shown the deciphering machine and how the Enigma Code had been broken. Although at that stage Ultra, the intelligence product itself, was not shared, one of the American experts acknowledged when he returned home that they had been saved years of labour.[16] Without any overt political decision, the practical foundations of integrated command were being laid.

While Purple was shared with Britain, the crucial Japanese ciphers, 'Magics', which the Americans had discovered prior to Pearl Harbor were not yet communicated to the British. Churchill was furious to discover after the war that in the run-up to Pearl Harbor he was only being advised selectively, and late, about shift in Japanese positions. It is often forgotten that it was the Poles who courageously provided Britain with the Enigma machine, which was eventually to allow access to first Luftwaffe signals, then those of the German navy, and by 1942 those of the army. Equally it should be remembered that the process of prising these secrets from the machine was achieved with the help of a team of French cryptologists, who worked alongside the British until the fall of France, and thereafter never disclosed their secret to Vichy. De Gaulle and the Free French, with their appalling lack of security, never knew about Enigma.

But even if a rapprochement was taking place, it was discreet and largely unobserved by the American public or politicians. Measures that had to be taken visibly and in the political arena were taken more grudgingly. Churchill described Lend-Lease for propaganda purposes (in his obituary tribute to FDR in the House) as 'the most unsordid act in the history of any nation'. But Lend-Lease was no altruistic gesture. Even so the legislation only got through Congress after two months of hard fighting.

And Roosevelt had not rushed into Lend-Lease. After his 1940 election victory he had a quick look at the US Treasury estimates of Britain's resources – 'Well they aren't bust – there's lots of money there' – and went off on his cruise.[17] It was only later that he admitted to one of his Cabinet members, 'We have been milking the British financial cow, which had plenty of milk at one time but which has now about become dry'.[18]

The Lend-Lease Act of March 1941, formally House Bill 1776, a significant collection of digits, grew out of the press conference after the post-election cruise. It was developed at a US Cabinet meeting in December 1940. At that meeting, the President and Henry Morgenthau, Junior, the Secretary of the Treasury, required as a precondition for assistance that Britain should liquidate all its American holdings, worth some two billion dollars. In return for that the Act would provide just $7 billion of aid. Senator Taft said that returning the garden hose after the fire was out was like asking someone to return used chewing gum. Taft did not think Britain's survival was essential to the welfare of the United States; fortunately Roosevelt did.

Morgenthau was instructed that Britain's assets in America and throughout the world were to be taken from her. Roosevelt requires 'a couple of billion . . . as collateral'. Morgenthau wanted 'a hundred cents on the dollar' for every item that was provided. There was little of 'lending' in the transaction. Indeed Roosevelt's original intention was to deal with Britain's inability to pay cash by taking over British possessions, especially in the western hemisphere in exchange for cash or credit. Morgenthau supported Britain by pointing out that this scheme was unfair and would not work.[19]

Much of this had to be done to get the measures through the Congress, and the negotiations were not attractive. The US Treasury required full details of Britain's financial position; Britain's assets in the United States were to be sold; and South African gold was pledged to cover any shortfall. A ship was sent to collect $120 million of gold bullion: Churchill's reaction was that it was like a 'sheriff collecting the last assets of a helpless debtor'. This least mercenary of men had been appalled earlier by America's insistence on payment in cash at a time when France was collapsing and Britain threatened to go with her. Now he drafted one of his bitterest telegrams to Roosevelt, a telegram which in the event was not sent:

> I am much puzzled and even perturbed by the proposal now made to send the United States battleship to collect whatever gold there may be in Cape Town . . . It is not fitting that any nation should put itself in the hands of another, least of all a nation which is fighting under increasingly severe conditions for what is proclaimed to be a cause of general concern . . . I should not be discharging my responsibilities to the people of the British Empire if, without the slightest indication of how our fate was to be settled in Washington, I were to part with this last reserve, for which alone we might buy a few months' food.[20]

This unsent telegram stressed the fact that Britain was being asked to hand over her gold without knowing what if anything the United States was planning to do.

To understand the nature and background of Lend-Lease it is necessary to remember that there was as much opposition in America to this measure as to anything that Roosevelt had pushed through to date. But that was partly because Roosevelt wanted to achieve a degree of consensus and did not use his considerable legislative majorities to bulldoze the legislation through. Rather, he accepted innumerable amendments and watched the Bill create as much controversy as his Supreme Court measures. American public opinion, quite apart from feelings within Congress, was far from overwhelmingly in favour of Britain. Even after Pearl Harbor, polls in 1942 showed that 30 per cent of Americans wanted a compromise peace with Germany.

Quite how Roosevelt saw Lend-Lease is far from clear. It seems unlikely that he thought it through in detail. But in the event the deal had little to do with hosepipes. Lend-Lease, for one thing, dealt only with the future. Morgenthau insisted that orders already placed should be paid for, even though it meant selling British investments overseas and writing off gold reserves. Keynes complained that America was treating Britain 'worse than we have ever ourselves thought it proper to treat the humblest and least responsible Balkan country'.[21] At the time Britain's concerns were far too great to allow the luxury of looking the gift-horse in the mouth. Most of Churchill's countrymen took the gesture at face value as an example of American open-handed generosity which would end in a writing-off of debts, but Keynes said that with the arrival of Lend-Lease Britain 'threw good housekeeping to the winds'; and the story certainly did not end in debts being forgotten.[22]

Churchill was much less than complimentary in private when America's niggardly approach was discussed. In August 1940 the government contemplated requisitioning gold, including wedding rings, to shame America.[23]

The idea of Lend-Lease was sold to the American public not as something that would accompany American participation in the war, but as something that would make participation unnecessary: Britain was being paid to do America's fighting for her. The Bill's title was 'An Act to Promote the Defense of the United States'. America's role was limited to being 'the great arsenal of democracy'. And a price was to be paid for what was provided. The terms were at the President's discretion, which was why there was always the prospect in British minds that the debt might be written off against the 'moral debt' which Churchill reasonably enough felt the world owed Britain. Truman ended Lend-Lease extraordinarily precipitately immediately after Japan surrendered in 1945, and while goods were actually in transit to Britain, and there was no writing-off.

While the Lend-Lease legislation did not in itself deal with the concept of repayment, discussion of payment, of what was called 'the Consideration', followed very swiftly. Both the State Department under Cordell Hull and the US Treasury saw Lend-Lease as part of America's foreign and economic policy, and not simply in terms of self-interested defence, which was Roosevelt's approach.[24] In November 1944, for instance, the Treasury threatened to end Lend-Lease unless she received Civil Aviation advantages. The ambassador in London, Gil Winant, was ashamed, and this was one of those occasions when Churchill's belief in an ultimate American altruism was badly shaken.[25]

The State Department saw the measure as a means of advancing the cause of economic liberalism and the Treasury saw it as a means of effecting a shift in world financial power to the United States. There is of course no reason why any country should not use its policy to advance its own interests: that is what governments are meant to do. What is singular is the extent to which America proclaimed itself to be following a path of altruism, and the extent to which the world took her to be doing so.

Churchill imagined that when America became a belligerent the penny-counting days of Lend-Lease would be over. He told Halifax on 10 January 1942, 'Lend-Lease is practically superseded now'.[26] He was very wrong. As Cherwell put it, 'the fruits of victory which Roosevelt offers seem to be safety for America and virtual starvation for us'.[27] The negotiations over the Consideration were so fiercely conducted that even Dean Acheson, the Assistant Under Secretary on the American side, accused the American Treasury of 'envisaging a victory where both enemies and allies were prostrate – enemies by military action, allies by bankruptcy'.[28]

The legislative basis of the Consideration was contained in the Master Lend-Lease Agreement. The Lend-Lease Act itself was passed on 11 March 1941 and the associated Appropriations Act on 27 March (both only after Britain had been obliged to conclude some humiliating sales of American assets such as the American Viscose Corporation, a subsidiary of Courtaulds, at knock-down prices), but it was almost a year before the Master Lend-Lease Agreement was signed. The part of the Agreement which rankled most with Britain was Article VII, which prohibited discrimination in either country against a product originating from the other. It thus attacked Imperial Preference and the Sterling Area. There were long and difficult negotiations before a softening form of words was adopted to which the British Cabinet could agree.

The practical implementation of Lend-Lease was no broad-brush affair, but was associated with careful accounting and precise financial scrutiny. In practice, America got the use of some British assets: it was by no means a one-way trade. The concept of 'Pooling' or 'Reverse Lend-Lease' took account of this fact and was not insignificant. America provided Lend-Lease aid to Britain in the sum of about $27 million; in the reverse direction the total was about $6 million.[29]

It is worth stepping aside for a moment from the march of events to look at the implication for Britain of paying for the war. The US Treasury, to further its policy of achieving international financial domination, sought to emasculate post-war Britain by using control of Lend-Lease to diminish, virtually to extinguish, British reserves. It is a remarkable and unedifying fact that while Britain struggled to fight a war for survival alongside the United States, its principal ally was prepared to leave her bankrupt when the war ended. At the first Quebec Conference in the autumn of 1943, Churchill had to fight the battle of the reserves with Roosevelt and Hopkins, but Treasury Secretary Morgenthau was unmoved. Hull began to take the point that a bankrupt Britain would not be able to assist post-war America either as an economic partner or as a political one and the State Department became an ally of Britain in the fight against the Treasury. Finally Morgenthau himself, after a visit to Britain in August 1944, saw that Britain was now pretty well bankrupt: in any event, the Bretton Woods Agreement had established the post-war international monetary system which he wanted. When he returned to America Roosevelt's reaction was 'very interesting. I had no idea that England was broke'. He compounded his ignorance by making a joke: 'I will go over there and make a couple of talks and take over the British Empire'.

The Bretton Woods Agreement was the outcome of the monetary talks that took place in the Mount Washington Hotel in Bretton Woods, New Hampshire in July 1944. These historic talks addressed more than the question of Lend-Lease. They established monetary arrangements that regulated international finance in the second half of the twentieth century, and that still do in many respects. The World Bank and the International Monetary Fund were its progeny, and so far as Britain was concerned the arrangements in respect of her debts were to last beyond the end of the century. The terms were onerous.

Far from writing off the loan, or indeed making a further gift to help Britain out of her dire post-war financial straits, Keynes and Halifax, Britain's negotiators, found that America required payment in full. Worse still, interest would be payable on the loan.

Keynes told the House of Lords, 'I shall not, as long as I live, cease to regret that this is not an interest-free loan'. The rate of interest was 2 per cent; by later standards that may sound low, but it was not: it was quite simply the current Federal Reserve Prime Loan Rate. No concessions to sentiment were made.

While the war brought Britain to bankruptcy, it brought huge prosperity to America. Although the National Debt had risen from $37 billion to $269 billion, Gross National Product was up from $90.5 billion to $211.5 billion, personal savings had risen from $6.85 billion to $36.41 billion, steel production had increased from 53 million tons to 80 million tons and agricultural output had risen by 15 per cent.[30] After Britain's efforts in the common cause of the war, her economy did not return to pre-war strength until the 1980s.

Assessing the cost of war is inevitably a callous exercise. Recourse to war is a negation of our ability to regulate our affairs by the exercise of reason and humanity, and one life lost in war is one too many. A table of relative losses is a crude way of assessing who 'won' a war, but perhaps a necessary measure.

America suffered 418,500 deaths, 11,200 of them civilian. Total deaths were 0.32 per cent of her population. She entered the war not to defeat the Axis Powers but to defend herself, and she was able to do so without any fighting within her own borders. She emerged as the richest and most powerful nation on the globe, with a world role in both economic and diplomatic terms. Truman did not exaggerate when he said, shortly after taking office, 'We have emerged from this war the most powerful nation in the world – the most powerful nation, perhaps, in all history'. Sellars and Yeatman had written in 1930 that with the end of the First War 'America was thus clearly top nation'. As always their perception was particularly sharp, but by 1945 their judgement was shared by the whole world.

The Soviet Union had become the other dominant power, but at a frightful cost in terms of lives. No one will ever know how many of her citizens died in a war that was won essentially by her alone. It is estimated that 23.5 million died, 1 million of them Holocaust deaths, and 10.7 million civilians: in all 13.39 per cent of her population. Can a country that suffers losses on that scale be said to have won a war? Communist theory, which saw history as a determinist pattern in which the individual counted for nothing, would say so.

Germany started the war and she paid for it. Some 7.5 million Germans died, including 160,000 Holocaust deaths and 1.84 million civilians, 10.77 per cent of her population. After the war her victors defended her frontiers and gave her the financial aid that fuelled the post-war economic miracle.

Poland, the immediate *casus belli,* lost 5 million citizens, 3 million in the Holocaust. Proportionally she suffered more than any other country, losing 18.51 per cent of her population in a war which was fought to defend her territorial integrity. She ended with Communist annexation instead of Nazi rule.

France made peace and her deaths were 1.35 per cent of her population. Total deaths were 562,000, including 83,000 holocaust victims and 267,000 civilians. Her allies restored her frontiers, and reinvestment fuelled by American aid stimulated the golden economic recovery of the de Gaulle years. But her self-respect was dealt a severe blow. The dark memories and confused loyalties of the Vichy years still have social resonance.

Britain lost 450,400 lives, 67,800 of them civilians, the total being 0.94 per cent of her population. Her dominions and Empire also sacrificed their lives in a struggle with which some of them were only remotely connected. The war hastened the end of Empire for Britain and her decline from a position of world pre-eminence. The route to economic recovery was a long and difficult one. She avoided invasion and defeat.

The Bretton Woods agreement provoked very strong resentment in Britain, in the press and in Parliament, which only reluctantly accepted the terms that were dictated to it. In America there was also resentment in the legislature, but it was resentment of the generosity of the deal. 'Just what kind of saps do they think we are?' asked one Congressman. Others referred to 'Britain's rotten imperialism', and to a country that was 'as covetous as a sponge'. As opposition to the terms hardened in the Congress, Truman carefully distanced himself, and it was largely to try to swing American opinion that Churchill went to make his famous speech at Fulton, Missouri. While the 'Iron Curtain' remark stuck in popular memory, his main purpose was to remind America of the alliance with Britain, and reassure her that the present government, though socialists, were patriotic men and his former colleagues.

And so what had started off in a kindly metaphor about lending your hosepipe, without thought of reward, to the neighbour whose house was on fire resulted in a series of payments to America over the next sixty-one years. The *Economist* wrote in December 1945, 'Our reward for losing a quarter of our national wealth in the common cause is to pay tribute for half a century to those who have been enriched by the war'. As well as paying interest, Britain had to make over intellectual property in connection, amongst other things, with research and jet planes, radar, antibiotics and nuclear issues. The final payment of interest, $83 million, was made on 31 December 2006.

Placentia Bay

Before sending Hopkins to see Churchill, Roosevelt had reflected that a face-to-face meeting with the British leader would be the best way forward. That meeting eventually took place at Placentia Bay, off Newfoundland, on 9 August 1941 when Churchill, on board the *Prince of Wales*, escorted for the last part of his voyage from Scapa Flow by two American destroyers, dropped anchor close to the USS *Augusta*, flagship of the American Atlantic Fleet. The *Augusta* carried the President of the United States together with Admirals Ernest King and Harold Stark and Generals George Marshall and Hap Arnold, the commander of the army in the air. Churchill sent a self-consciously historic telegram to the King: 'With humble duty, I have arrived safely, and am visiting the President this morning'.

The secrecy of the arrangements on the American side point up the sensitivity in America about any visible contact with Britain. It had been announced that the President was going on a fishing trip off New England on the Presidential yacht, the *Potomac*. The real nature of the voyage was kept secret even from Roosevelt's family as well as his White House staff and the Secret Service. The *Potomac* made her way to Point Judith, Rhode Island, and then to Martha's Vineyard Sound, where it met a flotilla of American warships. After Roosevelt transferred to the *Augusta*, the *Potomac* returned through Cape Cod Canal, so that those watching could see an FBI look-a-like, wearing white ducks and smoking a cigarette in a long holder.

Churchill had boarded the *Prince of Wales* to set off for Placentia Bay on 4 August 1941, the anniversary of the outbreak of the First World War. He telegraphed to Roosevelt, 'It is twenty-seven years ago today that the Huns began their last war. We must make a good job of it this time.' When he reached Placentia Bay, he joined Roosevelt on the *Augusta*. He was uncharacteristically nervous: 'I wonder if he will like me', he mused to Averell Harriman.[1]

Thus began the first wartime meeting between Churchill and Roosevelt. They would have nine meetings in the course of the war, spending a total of 120 days together. On the following day, Roosevelt transferred to the *Prince of Wales* for the famous, heavily charged service at which Churchill had chosen the hymns, including Roosevelt's favourite, 'Eternal Father, Strong to Save'. Later in the day Churchill had a romp ashore and collected a posy of wild flowers. Jacob noted, 'We clambered over some rocks, the PM like a schoolboy, getting a great kick out of rolling boulders down a cliff'.[2]

It is not clear what Roosevelt expected from Placentia Bay. A meeting with Churchill had been talked of for some time and the immediate catalyst appears to have been the German invasion of Russia. This jolted the President out of a state of exhaustion induced in Hopkins's view by long battles with the isolationists. He was now concerned that Britain should be pinned down to precise war aims before America entered into extravagant arrangements with Russia. If, ultimately, America were to fight alongside Britain, Roosevelt wanted to be doing so on the basis of something like Wilson's Fourteen Points, rather than appearing to be simply baling out a bankrupt imperial power.

Churchill was quite frank in his entreaties of the President. He made no attempt to suggest that he was not there to beg for aid. '*You* know that *we* know that without America the Empire won't stand'.[3] He might have been better to substitute 'Britain' for 'Empire', but the avowal was well judged, as part of Roosevelt's purpose in attending the conference was to assess just how desperate Britain's position was, and whether she could continue the defence of the West without America.

At a technical level at least, Britain could hold her own at the conference. The British delegation was bigger and better prepared than their opposite numbers. Hap Arnold did not even have an assistant to take notes for him. The British came with a better understanding of twentieth-century war: they had been fighting since 1939, and more of them had experience in the First World War.

The imbalance of representation pointed up the difference in expectations. Roosevelt simply did not attach to the conference the historic importance that Churchill accorded it. Cordell Hull, the Secretary of State, did not attend – indeed he did not even know the conference was taking place.

On the second day of the conference, 11 August, three series of separate talks began, one among the diplomats, one between the Chiefs of Staff, and one between the President and Prime Minister. Churchill had great if imprecise expectations of what the meetings might lead to. He had told the Queen before he left, 'I do not think our friend would have asked me to go so far for what must be a meeting of world-wide importance, unless he had in mind some further forward step'.[4] He expected more than the limited results that the conference delivered. He failed to take account of Roosevelt's caution and his capacity for tentative advance. At a personal level, Churchill unfortunately failed to recall his earlier 1918 dinner encounter with Roosevelt. The circumstances of that meeting had been bad enough, but Roosevelt was now miffed that he had made so little impression on Churchill.

Because Roosevelt did not commit his thoughts to paper, there are only glimpses of the impression Churchill made on him at Placentia Bay. According to his son, Elliott, Roosevelt described Churchill after the conference as, 'A real old Tory, of the old school', with 'eighteenth-century methods' of running the Empire.[5] While Elliot Roosevelt's statements have to be read with caution, that description does sound like an authentically superficial FDR appraisal.

At most of the war conferences Churchill was accompanied by one of his daughters, and similarly Roosevelt liked to have a member of his family with him. His third child, Elliot, was his ADC at most of the great meetings. At Placentia Bay, Franklin, Junior, was present too, and at Potsdam Anna was there in his place. Elliot was very different from his parents, and from time to time he was to some extent estranged from them. He settled neither in his marriages, of which he had five, nor in his careers, of which he had rather more. He volunteered to join the air force at the outset of war but failed a medical for active service and was given a desk job. There were suggestions that he had used his family connection to avoid danger, and to obtain promotion. This was not the case, but FDR faced some embarrassing heckling from students – 'Poppa, I wanna be a captain!' He managed to secure a move into aerial photo-reconnaissance, where he faced considerable danger with some distinction. He ended by being promoted brigadier general, certainly not on his father's initiative, but again facing criticism for favouritism as the rank was normally only awarded to pilots.

In 1946 he published *As He Saw It*, which consisted mostly of his memories of the great war conferences that he had attended. The book was intended to make a humanitarian point that the world need not face the dangers of confrontation between the West and the USSR. He portrayed Russia in an idealised form, and attributed a similar view to his father. His vocabulary is limited, his observations banal, and the book is astonishingly naïve and superficial. His targets are in part the State Department, of which FDR thought little, and Churchill, who is portrayed as an antique relic from earlier centuries whose devotion to the perpetuation of the British Empire obstructed the President from redrawing the world in accordance with what is repeatedly referred to as 'the twentieth century' – a world order in which colonial peoples have been given their freedoms. FDR seems to have felt himself at one with Stalin in wanting an end to territorial acquisitiveness.

When they saw the book in draft, Elliot Roosevelt's publishers told him that it needed spicing up. Perhaps as a result there are aspects that are unconvincing. There are suspiciously large chunks of *verba ipsissima* dialogue that just do not ring true, any more than the conversation which Elliot Roosevelt claims to have had at Chartwell, with Churchill emerging naked from his bath, with a cigar in his mouth. More importantly, were FDR's criticisms of Churchill as the representative of empire, or his views of the benefits of decolonialisation, quite as simplistic as they are made to appear? Eleanor Roosevelt is said to have disagreed with some of the contents of the book. Churchill's response to it was moderate and pretty restrained: Elliot Roosevelt was 'not much of a fellow'.

But Eleanor Roosevelt was not at the conferences as Elliot was. And she did not disavow the book: on the contrary she wrote the foreword, which ended with the words, 'This book gives one observer's firsthand account of what went on at the major conferences and will furnish future historians with some of the material which will constitute the final evaluation of history.' The book cannot be relied on in any individual detail, but it is written by someone who was on the periphery of great events and at the centre of the President's family circle, and it hangs together convincingly as a record of the prejudices, assumptions and culture which informed FDR's direction of the war.

The most important strands that emerge, apart from the insistence on the evils of empire and benefits of self-determination, are a desire to open up trade, particularly to America, a belief that Britain is always trying to play America off against Russia, and hence a desire to convince Stalin that Britain and America are only closely linked for the purpose of defeating Germany. Elliot Roosevelt reveals that as the war went on the conviction strengthened that Churchill had devious wishes that must be circumvented, perhaps notably a desire to postpone indefinitely the cross-Channel landings. If the book is broadly an accurate record of Roosevelt's views, he regarded Churchill with a generally tolerant amusement, as an anachronistic survival with a quaint enthusiasm for wearing uniforms whenever he could.

At a human level, there is a certain poignancy in the photographs of the meetings on board the two great battleships. Roosevelt stands erect and apparently unaided, but in reality only with great effort, and with leg braces hidden in his trousers. In other photographs, Elliott Roosevelt supports his father with a firm grip on the elbow. Churchill, although the older man and the petitioner, is grinning, a swashbuckling buccaneer in his Trinity House uniform. Who was truly in command, Roosevelt, with all the power of twentieth-century America, or Churchill, with his enthusiasm and the confidence of an eighteenth-century grandee? After the war, Halifax, who had been British ambassador to the United States throughout most of the war years, recalled 'I am sure [Roosevelt] was jealous [of Churchill]. Marshall told me that the President would not look forward to Winston's visits. He knew too much about military matters; besides, he kept such shocking hours'.[6]

The outcome of the meetings was sadly far less than Churchill had hoped for. As usual the President said as much and did as little as he could. He told Churchill that he 'would wage war, but not declare it'. According to an early draft of Churchill's history Roosevelt 'made clear that he would look for an "incident" which would justify him in the opening hostilities'.[7] What he meant by such statements, which he had made before, remains obscure.

All that publicly emerged was the declaration of war aims, the 'Atlantic Charter'. It had been prefigured a month or so earlier, when Roosevelt sent Churchill a telegram saying that there was disquiet in the United States about reports that Britain had set up 'trades and deals' with some of the occupied countries. There was a 'stupid story' that Yugoslavia would be set up again in its old shape, or that Trieste would be given to Yugoslavia. These rumours antagonised groups in America.[8] The Charter was not an innocent and idealistic statement of common intent: it was a severely political document, designed to limit potential actions by the British government, reassure American critics and spell an end to the British Empire. Article 1 disclaimed territorial ambitions. Articles 2 and 3 said that territorial changes were to be in accord with 'the freely expressed wishes of the people concerned', and Article 4 defended the 'right of all peoples to choose the form of government under which they live'.

Subsequent articles attacked imperial preference. It was a strange document to present for signature by a country which was struggling for its very survival, particularly as nothing tangible was received in return. Roosevelt had managed to attach checks and balances to the powers of a decadent imperialist nation. All that Churchill could hope for was that somehow, imperceptibly and subtly, America was closer to the British camp than it had been.

Churchill's reaction to what Keynes called the 'lunatic proposals' of Article 4 was that America was 'trying to do away with the British Empire'. He handled the matter well. He pointed out that the agreement could not be disposed of without the concurrence of all the separate Dominions and added to the draft proffered by Welles the bland formula 'with due regard for their existing obligations', which effectively made the Article meaningless. But just eight days after signing the Charter, Churchill was having misgivings. He wrote to Amery, the India Secretary, saying that Article 3 was presumably only intended to apply when there was a transfer of power: it could not be intended 'that the natives of Nigeria or of East Africa could by a majority vote choose the form of Government under which they live, or the Arabs by such a vote expel the Jews from Palestine.'[9]

Churchill had not wished to commit himself to something akin to a statement of war aims at this stage in the war. He told Eden in 1941, 'I am very doubtful about the utility of attempts to plan the peace before we have won the war.'[10] He had already been pressed by British Cabinet members for a statement of war aims, but had managed to resist until the meeting with the President. This tying of hands ran contrary to his philosophy of opportunism.

America undertook to give very substantial aid to Russia in coordination with Britain, to provide more merchant ships to take war materials to Britain, to augment the British Atlantic convoys with five American destroyers, and to carry out patrol duties as far east as Iceland. This was important; but there were disappointments too. Japan was asked to stop further expansion in the south-west Pacific; but while Roosevelt undertook, at Churchill's urging, to threaten war if Japan did not comply with this request, he withdrew from that undertaking on his return to Washington. Secondly, the supply of heavy bombers to Britain was to be reduced because of shortages in America. Finally, Jacob recorded that not one American army officer showed any wish to be involved in the war on Britain's side; the American navy may have been a little more enthusiastic.[11] The British Chiefs of Staff reported to Churchill that the results of their conversations were not startling: 'The American Chiefs of Staff . . . have so far not formulated any joint strategy for the defeat of Germany in the event of their entry into the war'.[12]

The differences that emerged at Placentia Bay were perfectly evident to the British. There had been divergent views about freedom of trade. Over dinner in the Officers' Ward Room in the *Prince of Wales*, where the menu, which was headed with Churchill's personal crest (hardly a touch to appeal to the progressive President), showed little evidence of the privations of wartime Britain – smoked salmon and caviar, roasted grouse, champagne, fine wines and brandy – Roosevelt told the Prime Minister that trade was not to be encumbered by artificial barriers. The reference was to the Ottawa Agreements and the favoured status for intra-imperial trade. Churchill, only half-jokingly, told the Americans that Britain had adhered to free trade for eighty years in the face of ever-increasing American tariffs.

Under-Secretary of State Sumner Welles negotiated with Cadogan on the Agreements. He was under instructions from the Secretary of State, Cordell Hull, to ensure that Lend-Lease would be conditional on revocation of the Agreements. This issue had already been discussed between Hopkins and Churchill in London, when the Prime Minister had been resistant to any move that would undermine Britain's imperial role. Cordell Hull was adamant that at the end of the war America should not be left waiting for an insolvent Britain to repay its debts. For no more generous a reason than this, the Treasury Secretary, Morgenthau, was instructed to say at Placentia Bay that if Britain returned undamaged material at the end of the war, the balance due by her would be written off – but only provided the Ottawa agreements were brought to an end. For himself Churchill was an out-and-out free trader, but he knew that the Conservative Party would never back down on Imperial Preference. The negotiations at Placentia Bay resulted in a meaningless agreement in which 'free markets' replaced 'free trade', and 'due respect for existing obligations' qualified its terms.

Harold Macmillan as Minister Resident at Allied Headquarters in North-West Africa met Hull on 13 October 1943 and his diary contains a good description of the Secretary of State, both of his physical appearance and of his character: 'I don't know why American Statesmen are always so old. Secretary Stimson (Secretary for War) who came through here is over 80. Hull is 74. He is exactly like the portraits of all Americans of the Civil War period – a fine southern gentleman. His views on internal politics are reactionary and on foreign politics based on the sort of vague Liberalism of the 'eighties' tinctured with personal prejudice'.[13]

Superficially at least a warm and convivial relationship was established at Placentia Bay between President and Prime Minister. The meeting on the final day had been the most productive from that point of view. There had been no business to transact and Roosevelt entertained Churchill, Beaverbrook and Hopkins to lunch. Beaverbrook was not only one of Churchill's oldest friends but also an old friend of the President, and Hopkins deliberately worked as a catalyst or marriage broker to try to demonstrate to the two leaders that they could be at ease with each other.[14] The relationship between Churchill and Roosevelt is a difficult one to analyse. There *was* a large degree of conviviality and joshing at their early meetings, and each man had a real respect for the other. Although in public they addressed each other with formality, using the title of their offices rather than Christian names, in private informality tended to rule. But the friendship did not go deep. Each man knew what his job was, and, despite protestations to the contrary, always put the interests of his own country first. When they were apart, Churchill, the romantic, very rarely spoke critically of the President; Roosevelt, the colder, more Machiavellian politician, was much more detached and could refer to Churchill with dry amusement or, at times, with irritation.

As Churchill sailed back from Placentia Bay, watching on the way the Laurel and Hardy comedy, *Saps at Sea*,[15] he took with him the clear sense that America would be coming to Britain's assistance, that the President was his friend, and that the Atlantic Charter would produce practical results before long.

But at Placentia Bay the President's utterances had been typically Rooseveltian: genial and sympathetic, but finally no more than vague adumbrations, nebulous and without commitment. Post-Placentia Bay, Roosevelt responded to challenges from the isolationists by saying repeatedly that the Atlantic Charter had brought the United States 'no closer to war', that there were no 'secret commitments' and that the conference had amounted to no more than 'an exchange of views'. The British Cabinet and public opinion were equally disappointed to find that the expectations aroused by the conference had proved to be false. Churchill made the best of things, reporting to the Cabinet that he had 'established warm and deep personal relations with our great friend'. But he exaggerated the warmth of these relations – or he may simply have been attempting to put heart into the War Cabinet. As early as 28

August 1941 he reported a 'wave of depression' within that Cabinet in a telegram to the White House and asked Roosevelt, via Hopkins, whether 'you could give me any sort of hope'. He spelled out what was happening to British shipping: 'I don't know what will happen if England is fighting alone when 1942 comes.' Could there be any hope for the future? Hopkins did not reply.[16]

Pearl Harbor

Until the end of 1941 the outlook for Britain was as perilous as it had ever been. Churchill was in a small minority in being reasonably confident that Russia would remain in the war for any appreciable time. Within the War Cabinet there was a very real fear that Moscow would not survive for another year. And despite a few friendly noises from Roosevelt at Placentia Bay, America seemed as far away as ever from coming in. If Russia were out and America stood on the sidelines, Britain would be back to the darkest days of 1940, and almost bankrupt.

Two things happened to transform the picture. The first was receipt of Enigma decrypts in the course of September indicating that imminent Russian collapse was not to be expected. The second was the attack on Pearl Harbor on 7 December 1941. The story of how the news came to Churchill is well known. He was at Chequers that evening, where his guests were Averell Harriman and Gil Winant, the American ambassador. The butler brought in a portable radio on which they heard the evening news on the BBC Home Service. Churchill leapt to his feet, saying that he must declare war on Japan. His guests prevailed upon him not to do so on the basis of a radio broadcast. Churchill phoned Roosevelt: 'Mr. President, what's this about Japan?' 'It's quite true. They have attacked us at Pearl Harbor. We're all in the same boat now.'

Churchill's reaction to Pearl Harbor was straightforward and understandable: 'No American will think it wrong of me if I proclaim that to have the United States at our side was to me the greatest joy. We had won the war. England would live; Britain would live; the Commonwealth of Nations and the Empire would live.'

Churchill's reaction to the news of Pearl Harbor is sometimes contrasted with the laconic response in Brooke's diary. Brooke wrote: 'After dinner listened to wireless to discover that Japan had attacked

America!! All of our work of last 48 hours wasted! The Japs themselves have now ensured that the USA are in the war.' He made a telephone call to see if there was to be another Chiefs of Staff meeting that night. 'Luckily not! So off to bed for some sleep before another hard day's work.'[1]

That was all. In an exchange with the author, which in some ways was the seed of this book, the late Lord Jenkins of Hillhead used the contrast between the two reactions to distinguish the respective contributions of the two men to the military winning of the war. To be fair to Brooke, his response is that of the staff officer that he was. To be fair to Churchill, Brooke's response was no more than that of a staff officer.

It is interesting that at the very time that, unknown to him, the Japanese fleet had been preparing for its attack on Pearl Harbor, Churchill was writing to Roosevelt, imploring him to declare what would be the consequences of Japanese aggression. 'I beg you to consider whether, at the moment which you judge right, which may be very near, you should not say that "any further Japanese aggression would compel you to place the gravest issues before Congress", or words to that effect.'[2] Britain would make a parallel commitment. Roosevelt made no such declaration.

Well before Pearl Harbor, in February 1941, Churchill reviewed an apprehensive Royal Naval appreciation of risks from the Japanese in the Pacific. He dissented strongly from the views he read. Less than accurately he asserted that 'We think it unlikely that Japan will enter the war against Great Britain and the USA. It is still more unlikely that they would attempt any serious land operations in Malaya entailing movements of a large army and the maintenance of its communications while a US fleet of adequate strength remains at Hawaii.'[3] Part of the reason for this disastrously flawed stance arose from a desire to do nothing that might dismay the Americans. The United States was wedded to a Pacific view, and it would have been a mistake to interfere in that theatre. Britain should 'loyally accept the US Navy's dispositions for the Pacific'.

Later in the year his views changed, and by October 1941, American naval activity in the Atlantic had allowed Britain to send ships for the defence of Singapore. Churchill was behind this initiative as much as anyone else. In August 1941 he had minuted the Admiralty requiring 'a deterrent squadron in the Indian Ocean'. Pound was against releasing modern battleships of the King George V class, preferring to retain them in home waters in case the *Tirpitz* broke out. Churchill thought, wrongly, that a show of force could deter Japanese expansionism and insisted on the despatch of the *Prince of Wales* and the *Repulse*, plus four destroyers and the aircraft carrier *Indomitable.* He must take a large degree of blame for the loss of the ships. The concept of a deterrent force was very much his, and it was also very much his idea that Japan was not to be taken too seriously as a naval power. From the example of the *Tirpitz*, hidden in the fjords, and interdicting British shipping operations, he concluded that the *Prince of Wales* could do something similar in the East. It was he who persuaded the Defence Committee, in the face of arguments from Pound and Admiral Phillips, that the ships should go. The Admiralty recorded its dissent.

The *Indomitable*, which was to provide the essential air cover for this vulnerable fleet, was temporarily out of action, and the two capital ships went ahead – but only after many battles between Churchill on the one hand, supported by Eden and Atlee, and Pound on the other, and ultimately only on condition that the matter was to be reviewed when the *Prince of Wales* reached Cape Town.

By the time the *Prince of Wales*, commanded by Admiral Tom Phillips (who had been a favourite of Churchill's until he quarrelled with him over the diversion of troops and ships to Greece in 1941), had reached Cape Town, it was clear that the *Indomitable* could not join her and for some unexplained reason the promised review of the position never took place. Later Churchill tended to blame Phillips for the disaster. Phillips always underestimated the threat to ships from the air. 'Bomber' Harris said to him once, 'Tom, there is no reasoning with you. One day you will be on the bridge of your ship and you will be hit by bombs and torpedoes dropped from the air. And as you sink you will swear it was a mine.' The news of the loss of the *Prince of Wales* and the *Repulse* caused Churchill great pain. 'I put the telephone down. I was thankful to be alone. In all the war I never received a more direct shock!' The responsibility was his more than anyone else's.

After meeting Phillips in Cape Town, Smuts had sent a telegram to Churchill, warning him about the vulnerability of the British ships: 'If Japanese are really nippy, there is here opening for a first-class disaster'. In the aftermath of Pearl Harbor, Churchill had given some thought to having the ships lose themselves at sea or join the remnants of the American navy, but as he worked in bed on 10 December and received the terrible news no decision had been taken. Indeed the previous evening it had been decided to 'sleep on the problem'. Sleeping on problems is not always a good policy in wartime.

Even in the aftermath of the loss of the ships, Churchill misread the situation and told the Chiefs of Staff that Singapore could withstand attack for a further six months. In the event, it fell just two months later.

On 22 December, immediately after the loss of the ships he made a Statement to the House. There was some criticism of the fact that there was not an opportunity for backbenchers to comment and express disagreement. Churchill affected to miss the point, and said that if the House did not want him to make statements, he would be happy not to; he was only trying to be respectful to the House. The Commons were able to return to the subject later in the month in Secret Session. By then Churchill was in America. The government faced a good deal of criticism in relation not only to sending the ships out, but also to defence of aerodromes, general unpreparedness in the Far East and the vulnerability of India. Lord Winterton attacked Churchill's role, and A.V. Alexander, the First Lord, was heckled by a group of Conservatives. The government had to abandon a motion to adjourn for a month in the face of a counter-motion from Shinwell, rather than face an embarrassing vote.[4]

Immediately after the Japanese attack on Pearl Harbor Hitler made that strange mistake that guaranteed German defeat: he declared war on the United States and 'the lout Roosevelt'. A disastrous and unnecessary move. The Treaty obligation between Germany and Japan amounted to no more than that if either country were attacked, the other would consult to see what help could be given. At this stage, Japan had not been attacked, and even if she had been, Germany was under no obligation to come to her aid.

He had ignored Ribbentrop, who had warned Hitler not to do it. If he had not done so, America could have confined her war to the Pacific. It is unlikely that she would have done so, but not impossible. There were many Americans, particularly in the navy, who thought that America's Pacific interests should come first; and without Hitler's initiative a declaration of war on Germany would constitutionally have required the approval of Congress. It was a fatal mistake. Hitler's unnecessary intervention completed Churchill's work. America was at Britain's side. Hitler was doomed.

What would have happened if Japan had not attacked Pearl Harbor is much more difficult to say. Hindsight suggests that America was inexorably and inevitably coming towards war alongside Britain, but the evidence is far from compelling. Roosevelt was always ready to point to his difficulties with Congress, and indeed since the Supreme Court crisis of 1937 he faced an increasingly hostile legislature, which, from January 1939, was an effective cross-party conservative coalition.[5]

But as Chamberlain, not usually a literary type, pointed out, Congress was often Roosevelt's Mr Jorkins, and more often an excuse than a cause of inaction. As Churchill said in a letter to Randolph in August 1941, 'The President, for all his warm heart and good intentions, is thought by many of his admirers to move with public opinion rather than to lead and inspire it'.[6] Roosevelt had displayed little leadership when the Neutrality Act was to be revised. Chamberlain said of Congress over the Neutrality Act, 'Their behaviour . . . is enough to make one weep, but I have not been disappointed for I never expected any better behaviour from these pig-headed and self-righteous nobodies'. Even Butler was jolted out of his usual urbanity. He minuted the American Department of the Foreign Office, 'I cannot tell you what a deplorable impression it makes on my mind. In my political life I have always been convinced that we can no more count on America than on Brazil, but I had led myself to hope that this legislation might at least be passed.'[7] Stimson once said that discussing policy with the President was 'very much like chasing a vagrant beam of sunshine around a vacant room'.[8]

Roosevelt was aware of the significance of the Tripartite Pact between Germany, Italy and Japan, and one of his reasons for not wanting to declare war on Germany had been that he was convinced that doing so would bring in Japan. He made this point to Mackenzie King as late as November 1941.[9] But his reluctance to go to war was more rooted in his nature than that. Even after news was coming in about the attacks on Pearl Harbor he talked about his 'earnest desire to complete his administration without war' which had now been frustrated by the Japanese.[10] There are many records of his hatred of war, and it is an irony that, like Woodrow Wilson and Lyndon B. Johnson, he should, as a pacific politician without great interest in foreign affairs, be remembered in large part for his involvement in overseas belligerence.

After the fall of France FDR talked of 'full speed ahead'. He rearmed and he gave material assistance to 'the opponents of force', but by the time of Pearl Harbor he had not even reached the stage of waging an undeclared war. What would have happened without Japanese aggression will never be known, and the question is a sterile one. In the absence of other evidence, it is probably fair to assume that the President was an honest man who meant what he said.

In the run-up to the 1940 election, for example, he said on four successive days: 'I have said this before, but I shall say it again and again and again: Your boys are not going to be sent into any foreign wars' (Boston, 30 October); 'I am fighting to keep our people out of foreign wars. And I will keep on fighting' (Brooklyn, 1 November); 'Your national government . . . is . . . a government of peace – a government that intends to retain peace for the American people' (Rochester, 2 November); and 'The first purpose of our foreign policy is to keep our country out of war' (Cleveland, 3 November).

ARCADIA

As soon as he heard the news of Pearl Harbor, the PM resolved to go to America to see Roosevelt. Roosevelt was none too ready to see him. He was worried about the Prime Minister's safety, but he was much more concerned that public opinion did not yet want America aligned closely with Britain in a war against Germany. Churchill could now afford to be much more confident in his dealings with the President. It was pointed out that he was insisting on a meeting in much more assertive terms than he would formerly have used. 'Oh, that is the way we talked to her while we were wooing her; now that she is in the harem we talk to her quite differently'.

There was a variety of motives for his anxiety to meet Roosevelt again, including a boyish desire to be on the scene as history was being made. But his main practical concern was to ensure that America did not divert her resources from the European theatre to the Pacific. Although the staff talks earlier in the year had involved an acceptance of the priority of the European war, in the aftermath of the shock of Pearl Harbor, as Churchill confided to Gil Winant, things could be different.[1]

American entry in the war was about the only good news at this time. Churchill received the news of the loss of the *Repulse* and of the *Prince of Wales* (on which he had travelled to Placentia Bay just a few months earlier) when he boarded the *Duke of York* for the ARCADIA conference in Washington; and as he travelled across the Atlantic, Hong Kong was attacked by the Japanese. All the same, the atmosphere on the voyage to Washington was very different from that on the way home from Newfoundland. There was now the prospect – the certainty – of ultimate victory, of working in partnership, albeit as a junior partner, with the most powerful industrial nation in the world. There was no apprehension of the humiliations he would suffer when he was increasingly denied any real share of direction of the joint enterprise.

But even at this stage, Churchill had to accommodate himself to the President's requirements. When he had told Roosevelt of his plan for an immediate visit, he was advised that the President would be unable to see him for at least a month: they eventually met on 22 December.

During ten days on board the *Duke of York*, Churchill and the British mission did very substantial preparatory work, which stood them in good stead when they met their American opposite numbers. The discussion was not entirely harmonious. Churchill faced a battle from the Chiefs of Staff (Pound, Portal and Dill – whose successor, Brooke was holding the fort in London). He was reminded that after Pearl Harbor and the loss of the *Prince of Wales* and the *Repulse* air superiority was a total prerequisite which limited naval operations. Equally, he was distressed that the Chiefs were prepared to countenance the idea of the Japanese 'running wild in the western Pacific' while the European war was fought out.

But despite their cavils, he presented them with a series of masterly appreciations of the post-Pearl Harbor situation in the course of the voyage. They have been described as 'some of the most influential and prescient state papers of the war'.[2] The papers consisted of 'The Atlantic Front' which set out more or less what was in the event to happen: Anglo-American landings in Vichy North Africa meeting British forces from the east; 'The Pacific Front', flawed by over-optimism as the fall of Singapore was to show just seven weeks later; and 'The Campaign of 1943', which envisaged a Continental landing to be greeted with enthusiasm and assisted by those liberated from Nazi rule. On board the *Duke of York*, he was deeply conscious that he had to impress the Americans with an optimistic assessment of the type of war he wished to wage. He had warned the King before his departure that following Pearl Harbor it was to be feared and expected that America would reduce her material support to Britain. The papers were intended to energise and shock-start the American war effort.

Together they outline the grand strategy which in the west at least was to be the basis of what actually happened, and which won the war; they were designed also to stimulate the Chiefs of Staff into a more ambitious frame of attitude than they usually adopted and to overcome what Churchill saw as a narrow, pedestrian and over-cautious frame of mind.

He was not alone in that view. On 22 July 1941 Colville recorded in his diary that 'The more I see of the Chiefs of Staff's conclusions, the more depressed I am by the negative attitude they adopt. They seem convinced their function is to find reasons against every offensive proposal put forward and to suggest some anodyne, ineffective alternative. Their excuse may be shortage of equipment, shipping and manpower; but they show no disposition to improvise or take risks.'[3] There is a good deal of his master's voice in this; but professionals in committee are inclined to excessive caution.

Three years after making that observation about the Chiefs, Colville returned to the subject with a more analytical and very perceptive reflection: 'Whatever the P.M.'s shortcomings may be, there is no doubt that he does provide guidance for the Chiefs of Staff and the F.O. on matters which, without him, would often be lost in the maze of inter-departmentalism or frittered away by caution or compromise. Moreover, he has two qualities, imagination and resolution, which are conspicuously lacking among other Ministers and among the Chiefs of Staff.'[4] On the day after he wrote that, looking at the sheer volume of paper that the war generated, Colville said something no less perceptive: 'I pity the lot of the future historian'.

Realistic logistic assessments had still to be made, and it was a mistake to imagine, as Churchill did, that the British navy could make much of an impression in the Pacific; but caution alone will not win wars, and it was necessary to inspire the Chiefs of Staff to think ambitiously. Brooke was to be a very great CIGS, a very great planner, but he was not imaginative or original: his skill was in what he called 'prevision, preplanning and provision'. Even his generally approving biographer, Sir David Fraser, acknowledges that Churchill's 'conceptual reach, at best, far surpassed that of his professional advisers; including Brooke'.[5] Again, 'He could and often did impressively surpass his supporters in his imaginative span. He was capable of seeing the war as a whole and envisaging how it might be won.'[6]

Eventually Churchill and Roosevelt met as allies for the first time on 22 December 1941. The welcome Churchill received from FDR was warmer than that extended by Eleanor, who remained distant from the representative of Empire. When the two sides met formally in the ARCADIA talks, the Americans, including the President, were generally impressed by the plans that were presented to them. Essentially the American Joint Chiefs accepted that the western theatre was decisive, confirming the Staff Conversations of February 1941 when Germany had been designated 'the key to victory'.

Churchill had arranged that his papers and draft agenda were radioed ahead via the embassy in Washington so that no time was lost when conversations began. Many Americans felt that they had been bulldozed at Placentia Bay: this time they wanted none of that, and Roosevelt instructed his advisers to study the British agenda and prepare their own. There were differences among the President's senior advisers. Admiral ('Ernie') King succeeded Admiral Harold R. ('Betty') Stark as Chief of US Naval Operations after Pearl Harbor. Stark had opposed war aid to Europe, but King was even more negative. He was always regarded as one of the more extreme examples of Anglophobes among the American Chiefs. He 'was vindictive, irascible, overbearing, hated and feared . . . drank too much, seduced his fellow officers' wives, was a poor support'.[7] He did not trust Churchill and particularly detested Brooke. On the other hand, he liked Pound and Portal and had plenty of distaste for his own countrymen. He thought Marshall stupid, Hap Arnold a 'yes' man and Admiral Leahy, on whom Roosevelt particularly depended, a fixer.

One of the potentially sticky moments at Washington occurred when the Prime Minister thought it as well to disclose to the President at a late-night session that he had been reading deciphered State Department intelligence. He had stopped the practice after Pearl Harbor.[8] Roosevelt does not seem to have been greatly concerned. He was presumably told about Ultra, but had limited interest in ciphers and codes.[9]

At this first conference as allies Churchill and Roosevelt got on pretty well at a personal level. There was the warmth of a house party, and Churchill was treated as a welcome guest. The President took pleasure in personally mixing cocktails for the company before dinner. But among the professional entourages there was no such camaraderie. It was disappointing for the British to find that their new colleagues were suspicious, prickly and far from part of one united team.

Dill found the Americans hopelessly disorganised. Portal annoyed them by suggesting that they put their air forces at Britain's disposal. Marshall and many of his colleagues were none too happy about the British 'indirect' strategy. For Marshall there would have to be another Great War with a huge land offensive, and what he called 'Fabian strategy' was irrelevant. Given his distance from the British position he was all the more astounded to be hugged by Dill in the course of the talks. The spirit of some of these meetings is conveyed in a description by General Stilwell of a meeting at Cairo later in the war, in 1943: 'Brooke got nasty and King got good and sore. King almost climbed over the table at Brooke'.[10]

There were differences over a Joint Declaration of Allied War Aims based on the Atlantic Charter and to be signed on New Year's Day 1942. Churchill was irritated that Roosevelt and Hopkins had proposed that India should be a separate signatory. Roosevelt's views on India were to take up a lot of Churchill's time at various stages in the war, but for the moment the Americans dropped the matter.

North Africa was an important topic, negotiated directly between the two top men. Churchill raised it with FDR before the top level conferences even began. He was concerned that Algeria was in the hands of the Vichy authorities and by the fact that the French battleships *Jean Bart* and *Richelieu* were stationed there. He wanted action in the area. Roosevelt agreed, and repeated his agreement on the following day: 'He considered it very important to morale to give this country a feeling that they are in a war, to give the Germans the reverse effect, to have American troops somewhere in active fighting across the Atlantic'. On the other hand, he thought that major operations in Europe itself might have to wait until 1944, as opposed to two years earlier, as Churchill wanted.

From the start and for a long time thereafter the President's advisers tried to row back from what had been agreed about North Africa: as far as even limited operations were concerned, by 26 December the Americans were saying that shipping shortages meant that they could not cope with North Africa as well as relieving British forces in Ireland and Iceland. Roosevelt supported the American change of position. The time 'was not right at present' for North Africa. Churchill was angry, 'reluctant to take No for an answer because of shipping'; during the First World War, the Americans had brought 2 million soldiers to France in five months. The matter was not resolved.

This sort of exchange and stalemate was repeated in innumerable separate meetings where the implications of grand strategy were thrashed out. Though there are no official American records of ARCADIA, it is clear that feelings ran high. Hopkins noticed that because the British came much better prepared than the Americans their opposite numbers could do little more than be flatly negative. He asked Halifax to tell British staff officers that 'negative replies from [the] US Staff . . . should not, repeat not, be taken too seriously'.[11]

Apart from anything else, while Churchill continuously worked very closely with the Chiefs of Staff, the same was not true on the American side. By now the British command, civil and military, knew each other very well and, despite frequent, furious outbursts, understood each other. On the way over on the *Duke of York,* Churchill had emphasised to the Chiefs of Staff that the important thing was that they should present a united front. The result overwhelmed the Americans. Later, Marshall recalled that in this period there 'was too much anti-British feeling on our side: more than we should have had. Our people were always ready to find Albion perfidious.' After the conference, Stilwell excoriated the British who had 'completely hypnotised' Roosevelt and sold him 'a bill of goods'.

One ally was not present at ARCADIA, but de Gaulle managed to remind everyone of his existence. On 24 December Admiral Muselier, now de Gaulle's Minister of the Marine, seized the Atlantic island group of St Pierre and Miquelon, which were controlled by Vichy France. Britain had hitherto refrained from any action against the islands because America did not want the Vichy regime alienated. Now de Gaulle ordered Muselier to act despite the fact that he had undertaken not to do so without British agreement. Indeed he ordered that no warning was to be given to 'the foreigners' – Britain, the United States and Canada. The move annoyed everyone, except the islanders. The Canadian government was considerably embarrassed. Germany considered action against Vichy North Africa for allowing it to happen. The Vichy naval commander at Martinique, with a powerful fleet at his disposal, demanded the eviction of the Free French. Above all, America, squarely for Vichy and hostile to de Gaulle, was far from happy.

Secretary of State Cordell Hull, in particular, was furious. He took the narrow, legalistic view that 'the so-called Free French' had no right to do what they had done. Hull was no friend of the Free French: he did not want them for instance to sign the Declaration of War Aims. But his views were not those of all Americans. Individual Americans were not displeased to see the Axis forces or their friends being given a kick, and the *New York Herald Tribune* preferred Churchill's approving response to the raid. 'The Prime Minister has certainly blown all question of St. Pierre-Miquelon and Washington's "so-called Free French" through the dusty windows of the State Department. For Mr. Churchill there is nothing "so-called" about the Free French "who would not bow their knees" and "whose names are being held in increasing respect by nine Frenchmen out of ten" . . . [Few] Americans after this can do otherwise than criticize the befuddlement and want of courage in the manner of [the State Department's] utterances.' It was in fact hardly open to Churchill to be too censorious about de Gaulle's frolic, as he had authorised Ismay on 13 December to allow 'a Free French descent upon

Miquelon and St Pierre' ahead of an Anglo-America ultimatum: '[I]f you feel it better to unmuzzle Muselier now, I am prepared to consent'.[12]

Churchill felt that Hull cut 'a rather pathetic figure' in a matter which 'did not enter at all into our main discussions'.[13] Hull rumbled on for quite some time, even complaining to an outsider, Mackenzie King of Canada, that 'he thought both the President and Mr. Churchill had yesterday been headed in the wrong direction . . . [T]hey had not realised what it would mean if the American government lost touch with Vichy, and if the South American republics got the idea that the US was countenancing force in any way.'[14]

The Americans unfairly regarded de Gaulle for most of the war as a closet fascist and, on the other hand, they did not find Vichy particularly distasteful. Hence Churchill: 'You're being nice to Vichy; we're being nice to de Gaulle'. Hull went on and on. America threatened naval action against the islands. There was much diplomacy, proposal and counter-proposal, before a face-saving communiqué was issued – after which the Free French remained in place.

Pushing a jammed window open to get some air one night at Washington Churchill suffered a slight heart attack. His doctor, Charles Wilson, later Lord Moran, did not burden him with a diagnosis. He decided that the Prime Minister could not receive the conventional treatment of rest and convalescence, and the conference continued. Churchill found time, despite still feeling under the weather, to travel to Ottawa and make his speech to the Canadian Parliament ('Some chicken! Some neck!'). He had already spoken to both Houses of Congress and told them that if his father had been American and his mother British, he might have got there on his own. Congress always enjoyed his addresses ('We only hear about the war when Churchill talks to us', he was delighted to hear), and he revelled in the occasions. Roosevelt was not pleased.[15]

ARCADIA Resumed

The visit to Canada was followed by a short trip to Florida, where Churchill spent some days splashing in the sea as he loved to do. He returned to Washington for the end of the conference on 12 January.

In the absence of the principals, the discussions had gone on. Despite the agreement on Europe first, the strategic implications of the policy left plenty of room for dissension. There was a critical shortage of sealift for Europe, and Marshall argued that the problem was not that of finding troops. There were plenty of troops for both theatres. The problem was finding the shipping. It was proposed that the troops destined for Iceland and Northern Ireland be cut from 8,000 and 16,000 men to 2,500 and 4,000 men respectively, allowing 21,800 to be sent to the Far East. There were ramifications implied in any such decision. Marshall himself was concerned that the diversion of shipping to the Pacific would cut Lend-Lease to the Soviet Union by 30 per cent. Stilwell observed the discussions: 'All agreed on being disgusted with the British hogging *all* the material: quite willing to divide ours with us, but never any question of putting *theirs* in the pot.'[1]

When these staff proposals were brought back to Roosevelt and Churchill, the Prime Minister was alarmed, particularly by the impact on the Russians. There was not, at this stage, a lot to separate the PM and the President on Russia: both were fairly well disposed towards Stalin. Roosevelt consistently dismissed the idea that Russia wanted to dominate Europe. Like Churchill, he took the view that the Soviet leader was not unconstrained: they both thought that their Russian opposite number was controlled by others more extreme than he. Sometimes Molotov was thought to be this powerful influence, at other times 'a council of commissars' or simply, as Churchill described them, 'the Soviet Leaders, whoever they are'.[2] At a less personal level, Roosevelt thought that Russia had to be drawn into a closer relationship with the West, so that she could be one of the world's policemen.

Roosevelt's views were broadly those of his entourage. The Secretary of State, Cordell Hull, identified a distinction between America's 'sane and practical liberalism' and Churchill's 'conservatism'.[3]

Before the principals came to adjudicate on the shipping issue, Roosevelt returned to the North African offensive. He embarrassed Churchill by forcing an admission that Auchinleck's battle against Rommel was not going well. At an informal meeting over dinner on the evening of 12 January, when FDR was absent, it was clear that neither Stimson nor Marshall was in favour of immediate action in North Africa.

The discussions did finally turn to shipping. The meeting closed with Roosevelt's confirmation of the figures that Marshall had proposed, but with Beaverbrook and Hopkins told to find more ships for Russia. At dinner at the British Embassy that night there was a degree of discord. The high point was reached when the Secretary of State, Cordell Hull, turned to the matter of Imperial Preferences and the Ottawa Accords of 1932. He proposed that an 'Agreement to discard the Empire tariff and trade program' be included in the Lend-Lease contract. Churchill was not amused and refused even to consider the proposal. Roosevelt denied that Lend-Lease was being used as a lever to overturn Imperial Preference, but he was not remotely credible. Churchill relished American slang, which he could deploy to good effect. He must have been tempted on occasions to echo Roosevelt's famous remark of 1928, when he was told that he could stand as Governor of New York while continuing with therapy for his legs: 'Don't hand me that baloney'.

The remaining meetings of the conference were disturbed by strong undercurrents. Many Americans felt that American war production was being developed to protect Britain and her Empire, rather than to safeguard America's own Pacific interests. The Anglophobic Stilwell complained about the consensus around an invasion of North Africa. The Limeys 'shot off their faces as if they were our delegates and not theirs'.[4] He did not approve of the idea that British troops in Northern Ireland were to be replaced by Americans. It would then be 'home to jolly old England, thank you'.

On the British side Dill wrote to Wavell, 'As for war, my own belief is that [the Americans] don't know the first thing about it. And yet as you know only too well, they are great critics. How they have the nerve to criticise anyone beats me. However they do. At present our relations with the Americans could not be better, but we are in the honeymoon phase. When we settle down to married life things will, I fear, be very different.'[5]

The most difficult discussions were on supply and the structure of command. On supply, Churchill proposed two 'Combined Allocation Committees', one in London and one in Washington, 'each caring for the needs of the allies for whom [the host nation] has accepted responsibility'. Marshall was greatly angered by what appeared to him to attack the concept of the single Combined Chiefs of Staff sitting in Washington.

The concept of the Combined Chiefs of Staff originated from a proposal by Pound. He may have had in mind a body to control the Far Eastern theatre, rather than the war as a whole. In the event, the former was established in the shape of ABDA, an American, British, Dutch and Australian joint body, commanded by Wavell.

Churchill had envisaged Wavell, shipped off to India, 'sitting under a pagoda tree' in the Indian sun, but the Americans insisted that he be appointed to the command. Churchill had not wanted him and Roosevelt had preferred an American, ideally Macarthur. He said that the commander should be an American because 'An American would be accepted more readily by the Australians and the Dutch than any Britisher'. It was Marshall who demanded Wavell, on the basis that it had to be a British commander in view of British and Commonwealth dominance in the theatre and of the fact that Wavell was much the most experienced among the British commanders in the area. Churchill, in Washington at the time, wired to London: 'You will be as much astonished as I was to learn that the man the President has in mind is General Wavell'.[6] Apart from the choice of Wavell, the British were also against the concept of unity of command in the Far East, because of the distances involved. America got her way, and ABDA came into existence in January 1942. It did very little. Churchill's assessment of Wavell's suitability for running an Allied Command was in the event more or less vindicated.

Brooke, left behind in London during ARCADIA, was characteristically critical of ABDA: 'The whole scheme [is] wild and half-baked and only catering for one area of action, namely Western Pacific, one enemy, Japan, and no central control.'

The more significant joint command, the Combined Chiefs, would include the heads of the British Joint Staff Mission in Washington, representing their respective service chiefs. The Americans had to reform their command structure to provide their component in the

CCS Committee. To do so they established the Joint Chiefs of Staff (JCS), which included the Army Chief of Staff, Marshall, and the Commander-in-Chief of the US Fleet, King. The American Air Force had not been represented in the former Joint Board, but to match the numbers of the British, Marshall included on the JCS General Arnold, Commanding General of the US Army Air Forces, despite the fact that there was technically no such thing as an American Air Force.

Churchill regarded the establishment of the Combined Chiefs of Staff as the most important result of ARCADIA. Unlike ABDA the Combined Chiefs worked well. The Committee was very much the personal achievement of Churchill and Roosevelt, although a fairly informal one. Indeed Churchill never did give any formal approval to their functions, and Roosevelt's endorsement was a scribbled note, 'OK, FDR'. The service chiefs on both sides were fairly unenthusiastic. The chief American naval planner, for instance, Admiral Richmond Kelly Turner, complained about 'large unwieldy bodies . . . in which British officials would be given half the total authority for matters now solely under American control'. When the British delegation returned to London and Brooke learned what had happened, he said that his colleagues had 'sold our birthright for a plate of porridge'. He continued to resist any combined element in areas that he regarded as primarily British responsibilities, such as Burma.[7]

Brooke's special complaint was that the CCS should be based in the United States. In fact, after the secret American–British Conversations of early 1941, there had been a clutch of British officers permanently based in Washington, nominally military advisers to the British Supply Council. They met with a corresponding American component.

The British all had nicknames, Admiral Sir Charles 'Tiny' Little, General Sir Colville 'Chicken' Wemyss and Air-Marshall Arthur 'Bomber' Harris. The addiction to nicknames seems to have persisted once these secret contacts were replaced by the CCS. Its staff officers were Brigadier Vivien 'Dumbie' Dykes and the American Brigadier-General Walter Bedell 'Beetle' Smith. 'Dumbie' Dykes had further nicknames for the Combined Chiefs themselves. General Marshall was Tom Mix, Admiral King was Captain Kettle, Admiral Stark was Tugboat Annie, Brooke was Colonel Shrapnel and Admiral Pound was the Whale. By this time the British Joint Staff mission was a huge organisation with almost 3,000 people working for it.

It was also a very efficient organisation, which was able to deliver highly professional results in terms of presentational and negotiating skills. By contrast, Dykes, for example, found his American opposite numbers '*completely* dumb and appallingly slow'.[8] From the President down, Americans felt they always lost their arguments with the British. Roosevelt might say more or less sardonically that he always got 20 per cent of what he wanted, and his allies 80, but others took their defeats less philosophically. Many resented the superiority of their junior partner. A Senate report of 1943 talked of 'smart, hard-headed Britons . . . daily outwitting, ousting and frustrating the naïve and inexperienced American officials'.[9] For the British it was for the moment all very gratifying, but resentments were being built up for which they would pay.

Churchill also proposed that Dill remained in Washington as his representative and with access at the highest levels in America. Marshall saw this as an opportunity for Churchill to interfere in the chain of command, which was to be directed from Washington. Churchill's objective was indeed to ensure that he himself had access to the President, without having to go through the Chiefs of Staff – or indeed the British Military Mission in Washington. Dill wrote to Wavell: 'It is odd that Winston should want me to represent him here when he clearly was glad of an excuse to get me out of the CIGS job. We disagreed too often . . .'[10] Marshall had no reservations about Dill at a personal level, but told the President that as a matter of principle he did not want an 'additional level of authority' interposed between the Combined Chiefs and their political masters. The American team wanted the Combined Chiefs to be the ultimate and sole source of military advice.

The nature of Dill's appointment in Washington was the subject of considerable negotiation between the two countries. Eventually he fulfilled two roles, the first openly and the second, in theory at least, secretly. The first was as Head of the British Joint Staff Commission in Washington, in which capacity he represented the views of the British Chiefs to the Combined Chiefs in America. In the second capacity he was a direct and personal link between Churchill and Roosevelt and Hopkins. The constitutional intricacies of his relationship with the Chiefs of Staff collectively and the Heads of the Joint Staff Commission in Washington individually were potentially Byzantine, but in practice Dill facilitated communications enormously and helped to avoid innumerable conflicts.

As so often in these conferences, a decision was deferred and ultimately fudged. The eventual draft, an American one, made no reference to Dill at all, either as Churchill's representative or as one of the Combined Chiefs. It was only after ARCADIA that the device was arrived at of settling Dill's position as Churchill's representative in a document separate from that appointing him to the Chiefs of Staff Committee.

In Washington Dill enjoyed an Indian summer, at least as effective as he had been in Whitehall, working closely with the American service chiefs and senior members of the administration. When he died in November 1944 he was buried in Arlington Cemetery with great pomp and ceremony. He was the only foreigner to have received such an honour. The pall-bearers were the United States Chiefs of Staff. One observer said, 'I have never seen so many men so visibly shaken by sadness'.

The contribution that Dill made to the effective prosecution of the war was enormous. His days in America were very different from what Churchill had planned for him as Governor of Bombay, with his bodyguard of lancers.

Reconciling the status of the Combined Allocation Committees with the principle of the supremacy of the Combined Chiefs was finally achieved to Marshall's satisfaction: both Committees were subordinate to the Combined Chiefs. There had to be unity of command.[11] Agreement was not however achieved without great heat at the second-last staff conference of ARCADIA on 13 January. The Americans had been briefed that British proposals 'will probably have been drawn up with chief regard for support of the British Commonwealth. Never absent from British minds are their post-war interests, commercial and military. We should likewise safeguard our own eventual interests.'[12]

The most difficult part of the negotiations was left to last. One outstanding supply issue remained. The mechanics for the sharing of war materials had proved to be extraordinarily difficult and was not dealt with until the final full session of the conference at 5.30 p.m. on 14 January. It was common ground that a Raw Materials Board would report directly to President and Prime Minister. Alongside it there was to be the Munitions Assignment Board (or Munitions Allocation Committee). Originally it was to be divided into two equal parts, one in Washington under Hopkins and one in London under Beaverbrook. The Board was to be at the same level as the Combined Chiefs. At five o'clock, half an hour before the final session was to begin, Marshall told Roosevelt that he would resign rather than try to plan operations if a body over which he had no control could refuse to furnish material. Hopkins, who had strangely not been consulted, supported Marshall, and said that he would not chair the Washington committee if Marshall's argument were not accepted. FDR could not oppose their combined position, and at 5.30 p.m. he told Churchill that there was to be 'a common pool' for war materials and that it would be controlled by the Combined Chiefs.

The war was to be run from Washington, and running it, amongst other things, meant controlling the material of war. Roosevelt softened the blow by proposing that war resources be controlled by a board operating under the Combined Chiefs of Staff Committee 'in a manner similar to the arrangement for unity of command in the south-west Pacific area'. It was a loose form of words and it did not appeal to Churchill. It did not leave him in control of British munitions allocation. He finally agreed that it 'be tried out for a month'. Then if necessary there could be a redraft. Roosevelt was delighted to have found a way of avoiding a decision: 'We will call it a preliminary agreement and try it out that way'.

Even before ARCADIA concluded, Moran wrote in his diary that the Prime Minister had 'wanted to show the President how to run the war. It had not worked out quite like that'. George Marshall had dominated the proceedings 'in his quiet, unprovocative way'. Hopkins, who might have been expected to be on side after his long exposure to the Churchillian phenomenon, had tended to support Marshall and American interests in general. The conference took so much out of him that he collapsed at the end of it and had to spend two weeks in the Navy Hospital.

Before that Hopkins was able to send a letter to Clementine: 'You would have been quite proud of your husband on this trip': he had been 'ever so good natured', had not taken 'anybody's head off,' and had eaten and drunk 'with his customary vigor'.[13]

Roosevelt's valediction to Churchill was encouraging: 'Trust me to the bitter end'. Churchill had obtained from ARCADIA one of his objectives: all-out American commitment. The Prime Minister also returned without having had the fact of American superiority in the alliance rubbed in his face. It would be a year before Roosevelt clearly emerged as the leader of the alliance, after the Casablanca Conference. The reality of American power was however clear enough. Churchill had wanted a commitment to Germany First, but he had that before the conference even opened, thanks to Hitler's gratuitous declaration of war. He also had to establish a truly unified war effort. That was achieved, but not with him at the centre and not in London.

As early as March 1942 he was reminded that he was not the pivotal figure he had been, when the Combined Chiefs postponed the immediate activity in North Africa which Churchill had sought at ARCADIA. The Combined Chiefs of Staff system took much control away from him and though he would subsequently try direct lobbying of the President, and indeed of others, including Eisenhower and Marshall, the principle of the CCS Committee, as it had been established at ARCADIA, remained in place throughout the war. Combined air operations or combined war at sea in the Atlantic appealed to Churchill: they would have been more within his geographical sphere of influence. He did not get them.

Despite the fact that Europe was to be first, immediately after Pearl Harbor America transferred large numbers of her escort vessels to the Pacific. Between December 1941 and August 1942, Dönitz's 'grey sharks' made 184 patrols and sank 609 ships with a gross tonnage of 3.1 million tonnes in American waters, losing only 22 U-boats. The United States did not bring full naval and air power to bear on the war in the Atlantic until March 1943.

After a final dinner (English lamb pie) on Wednesday 14 January, Churchill returned to Britain by flying boat after an absence of thirty-six days. As they approached home, the Boeing clipper was briefly lost in fog. In the War Memoirs, Churchill recorded that the aircraft was mistaken for a hostile bomber and that six Hurricanes had been sent up to shoot it down. It was a good story, but not part of the official flight record. In little matters as well as great, truth could be adjusted for the sake of the story he wanted to tell.

Part III

'Beneath these triumphs lie poisonous politics and deadly international rivalries. . . . The misery of the whole world appals me.'

(Churchill to Clementine, 1945)

Political Weakness in 1942

If the heart attack that resulted from the tussle with a stiff window in Washington had been a fatal one or if a scrambled fighter had brought down his seaplane when he came back from America, Churchill would still have been rated as a very great Prime Minister. He had stifled pressure for a humiliating negotiated peace. He had kept Britain in the war, alone until America had thrown her strength into the struggle. He had ensured that the United States gave priority to the European war which was Britain's principal concern. Even if he had died after just nineteen months in office, it is certain that Britain would still have been safe.

All that was evident at the time. What was not certain in the spring of 1942 was Churchill's own safety and security at a political level. While it was inconceivable that the Allies could be defeated, how victory was to be won was far from clear, and how long the war might continue was equally wrapped in gloomy doubt. In the desert, as Roosevelt had pointed out to Churchill at ARCADIA, Rommel was doing better than Auchinleck. The war at sea was going disastrously badly for Britain, and Germany was romping across mainland Europe.

On 15 February Singapore surrendered in the most humiliating of circumstances: 130,000 British and Commonwealth troops went into captivity and Britain's prestige in the Far East never recovered. Churchill had learned just weeks earlier that Singapore had no substantial landward defences. 'I ought to have known. My advisers ought to have known and I ought to have been told, and I ought to have asked.'[1] When he did come to appreciate the state of Singapore's defences, he queried with the Chiefs of Staff whether the imminent loss of Singapore should be accepted, and troops moved to defend Burma. Curtin, the Australian Prime Minister, heard of this and said that evacuation of Singapore would be regarded as 'an inexcusable betrayal'.

Curtin had already been a nuisance, writing in the newspapers on 27 December 1941 that 'Australia looks to America, free of any pangs as to our traditional links with the United Kingdom'. His intervention in January was decisive; and contrary to what Churchill said 'a purely military decision should have been', the 18th British Division went to Singapore (not, it transpired, to save it but to surrender). Churchill was to blame his concentration on the North African theatre for allowing himself to take his eye off Singapore.

In truth, what happened flowed directly from the conscious switch in Britain's priorities from the Far East to the Middle East a year before. Dill had sought to continue the traditional emphasis on the former ('In the last resort the security of Singapore comes before that of Egypt'). In doing so, according to Ismay, he shook Churchill to the core. Dill lost the battle, though he now consoled himself with the reflection that history would have been different if his views had prevailed. But the loss of Singapore did not affect the outcome of the war. If, on the other hand, Britain had been thrown out of North Africa and the Middle East in 1941, the Allies would have had great difficulty in fighting a European war.

That point did not register with the public or Parliament. In December 1941 the Conservatives had already been worried about the possibility of the fall of Singapore, and Nicolson reported that they were 'angry with Winston'.[2] In January 1942 Macmillan recorded that the House of Commons was in the sort of mood it had been in before the Norway debate. On 16 February 1942 Nicolson detected a shift against the government: 'I fear a slump in public opinion which will deprive Winston of his legend'. A statement in a Sydney newspaper was repeated in the London papers: 'If Singapore falls, Churchill will fall with it'. Churchill was tired, disheartened and suffering from a cold; he told Eden 'the bulk of the Tories hated him, that he had done all he could and would only be too happy to yield to another'.[3] Brooke found him depressed by the mood in the House, and the King said that the Prime Minister was angry and felt that he 'was hunting the tiger with angry wasps around him'.[4] A far cry from the picture of a country united round its leader.

Amery, at the India Office, and at odds with Churchill because of his refusal to make concessions to nationalism, told the Chief Whip, James Stuart, that it was 'his duty to be really frank with Winston' about the 'discontent in the Party'.[5] Stuart was not keen to be the bearer of unwelcome news, and Churchill was in any event well aware of the lack of enthusiasm in the Conservative Party. It was all particularly painful as he saw himself returning from a triumphant and historic meeting with Roosevelt in Washington.

He felt compelled to strengthen his position by demanding a vote of confidence in the House of Commons on 29 January. He made one of his most impressive speeches and won the House over with a majority of 464 to 1. He worked on his speech until the very last minute – indeed he was five minutes late in setting off for the House – and in it he elaborated on the constitutional position he had created for himself, working with the Chiefs and submitting the policies he arrived at on their advice for the approval of the War Cabinet. It was an arrangement that provided him with substantial protection. Opposition to Churchill was split in that while some wanted his powers diminished, others, notably Sir Roger Keyes, argued that the Prime Minister was hamstrung because he insisted on taking the advice of the Chiefs of Staff. The contradiction did not go unnoticed. 'Chips' Channon described the debate as 'One of the great days in parliamentary history'.[6] The debate put an end to proposals that Churchill's influence over the Chiefs of Staff should be reduced by the appointment of a separate Minister of Defence.

But although there was for the moment no more talk of a defence supremo or the alternative, a Combined General Staff with an independent Chairman, Churchill's standing was damaged all the same. Critical speeches in the Lords by Hankey and particularly Chatfield, a former Minister of Defence, were telling: there was criticism of the Defence Committee, the extent of Churchill's authority and his working habits. There had to be a new direction of the war effort, 'instead of the burden resting on a single pair of shoulders, however broad, however able, whatever confidence we may have in these shoulders . . . I can assure your Lordships that I have had representations made to me by those that work in Whitehall that the hours they have to work are perfectly intolerable. It does not lead to efficiency. Nobody is at his best in the Middle Watch . . .'[7]

Churchill was well aware that the outcome of the vote did not secure his future and his position remained precarious. 'I am like a bomber pilot', he said. I go out night after night and I know that one night I will not return.'[8] Cripps and others advocated a War Planning Directorate, operating independently of the Chiefs of Staff and taking pressure off them. Churchill would have none of that. He was 'resolved to keep my full power of war-direction . . . I should not of course have remained Prime Minister for an hour if I had been deprived of the office of Minister of Defence'.[9] The austere, unbending Cripps had in fact, and rather strangely, emerged as Churchill's main rival. By June 1942 he told Tory malcontents, and there was never any shortage of them, that he foresaw 'a joint government consisting of Oliver Lyttelton, Anthony Eden and himself. He implied that in due course Churchill would be pushed aside, because he did not understand the home front. He did not deny that Churchill was the best for the strategic war period.'[10]

A long, sad letter to Roosevelt of 5 March 1942 dealing with the shortage of shipping begins, 'When I reflect how I have longed and prayed for the entry of the United States into the war, I find it difficult to realize how gravely our British affairs have deteriorated by what has happened since December seven [*sic*]. We have suffered the greatest disaster in our history at Singapore, and other disasters will come thick and fast upon us.'[11]

Brooke reflected the mood of these months in his diary entry for 31 March 1942: 'The last day of the first quarter of 1942, fateful year in which we have already lost a large proportion of the British Empire, and are on the high road to lose a great deal more of it!'[12] In his Secret Session speech on 23 April, Churchill gave a remarkably full and candid account of the circumstances surrounding the fall of Singapore. '[O]ur affairs', he said, 'are not conducted entirely by simpletons and dunderheads as the comic papers try to depict . . .' He refused the Royal Commission which some were demanding.[13]

Parliamentary attacks were not generated by Singapore alone. The Prime Minister's conciliatory approach to Russia also caused disaffection. Acquiescence in an extension of Russia's frontiers attracted opposition from both anti-appeasers, generally on the left, and anti-Soviets, generally on the right. The whole issue generated tensions between Churchill and Eden, who differed in their general approach towards Russia, following the same fault-line in the Conservative Party.[14]

Harold Nicolson had been sacked by Churchill in July 1941, but held no grudges. In his diary of 22 April 1942 he recorded that Malcolm MacDonald, who had been lunching with Churchill and reported the 'bomber pilot' remark, had been appalled by the slump in the Prime Minister's popularity. 'A year ago he would have put his stock at 108, and today, in his opinion, it is as low as 65. He admits that a success will enable it to recover. But the old enthusiasm is dead forever. How foul is public life and popular ingratitude!' On the following day, with the House in Secret Session, Nicolson recorded that Cripps, who had just returned from India, was received with more acclaim than Churchill.

Even if Churchill personally would survive, there was still a great measure of unhappiness with the performance of the government as a whole. In the Confidence debate, Emmanuel Shinwell said that he wished there could be two votes of confidence, one in the Prime Minister and the other in the government. There was a feeling that too many members of the government were doing nothing to justify their continued presence. When Stafford Cripps returned from his subsequent mission to Russia (Churchill had not wanted him back: he was 'a lunatic in a country of lunatics' and it would be a pity to move him[15]), he made his joining the government contingent on the removal of some of the 'old gang'.

Churchill could not simply ignore all this and concentrate on the conduct of the war. When he complained to Captain Pim, who was in charge of the Map Room, that he was seriously thinking of resigning, Pim had given the opinion that most of the noise was being made by those who hoped to benefit from a reshuffle.[16] A limited reshuffle had indeed been made on 4 February 1942; but after the fall of Singapore he had to go further. He was obliged to sacrifice the Secretary of State for War, Margesson, who had not really done anything wrong, and to bring Cripps into the Cabinet as Lord Privy Seal and Leader of the House, the latter appointment in particular recognising his popularity. In doing so he was acknowledging the need to be seen to do something to address domestic issues. At long last, he was also able to take the opportunity of getting rid of numbers of the Men of Munich – not as an act of vindictiveness, but rather because they had continued to be disloyal and to make themselves troublesome. Kingsley Wood was demoted, replaced by Oliver Lyttelton. James Grigg came in as Secretary of State for War in place of Margesson. Attlee received the title of Deputy Prime Minister.

And so the January Vote of Confidence, which was forced by discontent on the Tory right, resulted in a Cabinet move to the left. Rab Butler thought the new Cabinet was far too short of Conservatives. Under pressure Churchill was obliged to set up an 'India Committee', but behind the scenes he intrigued to sabotage Cripps' Indian Mission, by convening one of the very rare meetings of the full Cabinet, which was dominated by the Conservative Party, and by communications to the Viceroy, Lord Linlithgow. Linlithgow was no fan of Cripps, whom he referred to as 'Sir Stifford Craps'. (That was deliberate. It was a genuine slip of the tongue that caused Indira Gandhi, handing round nibbles at her wedding, to invite Sir Stafford to help himself to some potato cripps.[17]) On 12 April 1942 Roosevelt made an early incursion into British imperial policies and wrote privately to Churchill, proposing that Cripps stay in India until a Nationalist government had been set up. Churchill was greatly angered and proposed to keep the correspondence from the Cabinet. 'Anything like a serious difference between you and me would break my heart . . .'[18]

For the moment Beaverbrook remained in the Cabinet, although when he had been appointed, Clementine Churchill, in Mary Soames's words, 'blew up'. But he continued his incessant threats of resignation, and shortly carried them out in order to campaign for a Second Front. He had been superb as Minister of Aircraft Production, but he could still be a frightful nuisance.

In the House of Commons Churchill faced savage attacks from Bevan's stinging oratory, and in *Tribune* from Frank Owen under the pseudonym of 'Thomas Rainsborough'.

His vulnerability had been hinted at a full year earlier when the Australian Prime Minister, Robert Menzies, visited London. He attended a Cabinet Meeting, after which he asked Eden 'Has no one in this Cabinet a mind of his own?' He was unimpressed by Churchill's conduct of the war, partly because Australians had been sent to Greece against his advice, and there was intrigue among Menzies, Hankey, Lord Simon and Lloyd George. They wanted a stronger War Cabinet, with more effective men in it, and the Prime Minister's wings clipped so that he could no longer dominate the Chiefs of Staff.

On 29 April 1941, during Menzies's prolonged stay in England, Churchill faced critical questions in the House of Commons from some of the usual enemies. He was asked by Geoffrey Mander whether he would consider appointing a small Supreme War Cabinet consisting of non-Departmental Ministers and whether he would consider inviting statesmen 'of the calibre of Mr Menzies' to sit in it. His answer was commendably uncompromising: 'No, Sir'.[19] There was never any real possibility of Menzies, an Australian, replacing Churchill (although the possibility of Smuts' appointment in the event of Churchill's death had been canvassed in 1940 and approved by the King[20]), but the dissatisfaction that was expressed by influential figures near the centre of power shows that Churchill's continued tenure of 10 Downing Street was not taken for granted. And all that had taken place in 1941: the degree of criticism and dissatisfaction of 1942 was very much greater.

Strategy on the Sea and in the Air

Things were not going well on the oceans. The toll on the Arctic convoys continued, and Admiral Tovey, who was in charge of the Home Fleet, argued strongly against their continuation. His stock had been high after the sinking of the *Bismarck*, but this stand angered the Prime Minister, and matters did not improve. He not only misread the enemy's intentions when the *Scharnhorst, Gneisenau* and *Prinz Eugen* broke out of Brest, but also wanted more ships to deal with the breakout than Churchill (wrongly) thought he needed. Tovey had already crossed swords with Churchill when he demanded more long-range aircraft for the Battle of the Atlantic, and it was hardly surprising that the Prime Minister felt it was time to replace him.

There were few admirals for whom Churchill had much regard, and this is reflected in the fact that his choice as a replacement was Andrew Cunningham, not a man with whom the PM was comfortable. The appointment did not go ahead. It was indeed a reflection of ABC's sturdy independence that he responded to the offer of the job by saying that he would only take it if Tovey fell dead on his bridge.[1]

Churchill did not give up. He proposed that the shift should go ahead as part of a larger reshuffle, but it was flatly blocked by Pound, who said that Tovey's displacement would affect the navy's confidence in the Admiralty. After some further kerfuffles there was a game of musical chairs at a slightly lower level.

Pound thought that his role in the matter had come close to ending his career. When Cunningham called on him in April 1942 he found the First Sea Lord 'in great distress . . . Winston was thinking of getting rid of him and putting Mountbatten in as 1st Sea Lord'.[2] Cunningham said that he told Pound 'to glue himself to his chair' and that he did just that, but the whole story is suspect. Churchill respected Pound, and talked of him as the best sailor in the navy; he genuinely liked him and regarded him as a friend and not just an adviser. Although for various reasons he had an exaggerated view of Mountbatten's abilities, the latter would have been quite unacceptable to the service – and probably in the last resort to Churchill too. Charming though Mountbatten might be, his rank of vice-admiral was an acting one only, to allow him to operate as Director of Combined Operations. His substantive rank was only that of post captain, and his very limited experience did not begin to qualify him for appointment as First Sea Lord.

The navy attributed a large part of the losses in the Battle of the Atlantic to the fact that they did not receive the degree of cover from the RAF that they needed. Pound and A.V. Alexander, the First Lord, were not a strong team, and could not prevail over Churchill or over the strategic bombers, led by Harris and Cherwell. Some of the faults were those of the navy itself: when Cripps proposed a 'super C-in-C' to take control of the battle in its entirety, Pound opposed the idea with the familiar service argument that it would conflict with the whole principle of naval control. Again the navy was wrong to press for heavy bombing of the pretty well indestructible U-Boat bases in France, and probably also in their insistence on air patrols over the Bay of Biscay which would have been better used out in the Atlantic. But the net effect of the conduct of the battle was that by the end of 1942 U-Boats were being built faster than they were being sunk.

It is argued that the battle would have been shorter and its effects less costly if Churchill had responded more favourably to requests for, for instance, escort ships and aircraft fitted with centimetric radar, and had listened to the plea of the Minister of War Transport, Lord Leathers, that the security of Britain's sea communications should be given the highest priority for allocation of men and materials. The problem with arguments of this sort is that they are so often *ex parte*. Churchill's responsibility was to adjudicate between competing claims. Thus he had to listen to America's need for escort vessels, which Pound came to recognise was 70 per cent greater than Britain's. The Prime Minister concluded that Bomber Command's requirement for new radar allocation was greater than the navy's. There are two views – at least – on the offensive policy of strategic bombing, but it simplifies issues crudely to suggest that Churchill imperilled the safety of Britain's sea communications by allowing himself to be persuaded by Cherwell and Harris that the use of aircraft to drop bombs on Germany should have priority over protecting the convoys.

Churchill was more aware of the critical importance of the Battle of the Atlantic than anyone else. He ceaselessly monitored the statistics.

He was always aware the war could be lost on the sea. In October 1942 Churchill told FDR, 'First of all I put the U-Boat menace. This, I am sure, is our worst danger.' And just as he apprehended the menace of the U-boats, so he had considerable reservations about the efficacy of strategic bombing. The man responsible for the concept of the strategy was Lord Trenchard, who pressed it on Churchill relentlessly. The Prime Minister noted on one of his papers that he could not 'entirely neglect the needs of the Navy and of the Army as Lord Trenchard seems to suggest'. On another occasion he told Harris that Trenchard 'flogs a good horse to death'.[3] He also disliked the bombing policy on humanitarian grounds.

One of the most moving vignettes of Churchill in the war is when he emerged from watching a film of bombing raids on German towns in June 1943. He might have felt some satisfaction in seeing the terror and destruction that had been visited on British cities being returned to Germany, but as the lights came up the tears were running down his face: 'Are we beasts? Are we taking this too far?'

Churchill found nothing appealing about destroying civilians' homes and killing non-combatants, but apart from the purely military considerations there had to be a recognition of the public desire to see that Britain was doing to German towns what Germany had done to British ones. In the heat of war there were very few who complained about what was happening to Hamburg, Cologne, Frankfurt, Munich or Stuttgart. Most people thought instead about London, Coventry, Bristol, Plymouth, Birmingham, Liverpool, Glasgow, Swansea and Belfast.

Of course, on many occasions Churchill stated that the 'dehousing' of the German civilian population, with its expected effect on morale, was official policy. It was the only offensive operation on which Britain could embark at the time: Churchill's insistence on an offensive policy was not some sort of character defect. In a letter to Beaverbrook, then Minister of Aircraft Production, in July 1940, Churchill reviewed all that Hitler could do and all that Britain could not do: 'But there is one thing that will bring him back and bring him down, and that is an absolutely devastating, exterminating attack by very heavy bombers from this country on the Nazi homeland'.[4] He had to demonstrate that Britain was fighting an offensive war – partly to convince America that her prospective ally was not moribund and defeated. But much more importantly, Stalin had to be shown that Britain was contributing significantly to a war which otherwise Russia would have been fighting alone. It is highly significant that after his 1942 meeting with Stalin Churchill reported to FDR: 'We then passed to the ruthless bombing of Germany, which gave general satisfaction . . . I made it clear that this was one of our leading military objectives.'[5]

There were battles between Churchill and the Chiefs over the bombing issue in July and August 1942. Attlee was opposed to the strategy of strategic bombing, and Wavell, Auchinleck and others also criticised the emphasis on using bombers in Germany as opposed to other theatres. They could certainly point to weaknesses in bombing tactics: a committee of inquiry in May 1942 found that less than a quarter of bombs fell within five miles of their targets, and only 30 per cent even managed to find built-up areas.[6] Indeed, in 1941 Bomber Command casualties exceeded German casualties in bombing raids.[7] The Americans' strategic bombing was much more precise, making use of the Norden bombsight which they refused to pass on to the United Kingdom. The concept of area bombing of German towns originated with Portal, Chief of the Air Staff, and Sir Arthur Harris, Commander-in-Chief of Bomber Command from February 1942. They were supported by Cherwell, whose paper of March 1942 suggested that bombing could make a third of the German population homeless, thus destroying her will to fight. But Churchill was a reluctant bomber, and not a doctrinaire one. He was not as convinced as Cherwell of the merits of bombing. He did it because there was not yet any other obvious way to strike at Germany.

Furthermore Churchill was readier than others to change his views. On 31 July 1941 the Chiefs of Staff accorded top priority to production of explosives for offensive bombing action, but just two months later Churchill was telling Portal that experience during the war had showed that strategic bombing was no more than 'a heavy and I trust seriously increasing annoyance'. It would not win the war.[8]

The RAF was not subjected to much interference. Indeed Churchill was rather in awe of the gallantry and dash of what he called the cavalry of the twentieth century. Harris, who chose not to pay much attention to the Chiefs of Staff (or indeed the Air Ministry), enjoyed Prime Ministerial respect for his unshakeable determination. Dowding was also particularly admired.

When James McGregor Burns says that Churchill 'lacked the steadiness of direction, the comprehensiveness of outlook, the sense of proportion and relevance that mark the grand strategist',[9] he may be technically right – if there has ever been a grand strategist who had the luxury of operating in a conflict in which he had unlimited resources, entirely compliant allies and a population that did not require to be inspired and urged forward. That was not Churchill's position and the argument, from a purely naval standpoint, that if aircraft had supported shipping instead of bombing Germany the Battle of the Atlantic could have been shortened by at least six months[10] is theoretical and irrelevant.

The navy's truest grievance is perhaps that it did not have a strong advocate for its interests in its First Lord, Alexander, who did not fight his corner as other departmental chiefs sometimes did. But he was unlucky to have a Chief who had himself been First Lord – and not once, but twice.

Meanwhile reverses in the Pacific continued to occur. On 3 May Rangoon was abandoned and Churchill wrote to Roosevelt that Britain's position was now worse than at the time of Pearl Harbor. He strengthened the direction of the war by appointing Brooke as Chairman of the Chiefs of Staff Committee in place of Pound, who remained on the Committee as First Sea Lord. Mountbatten succeeded Sir Roger Keyes as Chief of Combined Operations – both examples of men of vigour and charm appointed above their abilities. Churchill had made attempts before to move Pound from the chair of the Chiefs of Staff Committee. He had started to fall asleep during Chiefs of Staff meetings. Brooke described him in his diary of 3 February 1942 as looking 'like an old parrot asleep on his perch!' Another officer described Pound in the Chair at a meeting in June 1940; 'After a not very long time, I noticed that Pound was drooling down the stem of his pipe – not just a drop, for I was at least five yards away. He may not have been asleep, but he was quite "out for the count". It was noticeable that Power [the Assistant Chief of the Naval Staff (Home) who was sitting on Pound's right] was aware of this, for he continued the meeting as if his Chief was no longer present.'[11]

To be fair to poor old Pound, his frequent naps were the involuntary consequence of severe osteoarthritis, which kept him awake through long nights when he should have been asleep. He also started work every day before dawn, rather earlier than the Prime Minister. He may already have been suffering from the brain tumour which was to kill him in 1943.

While Pound was happy enough to give up the Chairmanship, he was very much opposed to Churchill's promotion of Mountbatten to be a full member of the Chiefs of Staff Committee now that he was in charge of Combined Operations. Churchill intended that Mountbatten should have commensurate rank in each of the three Services. Pound referred to 'a very widespread belief, not only in the Services but also in the country, that you do override the opinion of your professional advisers'. He denied that *his* advice had been overridden in any material respect – even in regard to the despatch of the *Prince of Wales*, but he was prepared to resign if the Mountbatten plan were executed. He said that Mountbatten's promotion by three steps in rank from that of 'a junior Captain <u>in a shore appointment</u>' would be attributed simply to his royal blood. Churchill went ahead and Pound did not resign, but the choice of Mountbatten was a strange one.

The Alliance's Teething Problems

From the start there was an essential difference between the allies about what Germany First really meant in terms of strategy. The Americans always thought in terms of a body blow against the Germans on mainland Europe: the Civil War way of fighting. The British were more inclined to peripheral strategy, which the Americans disparaged as 'scatterization'.

It was a feature of the early conferences that they ended with some questions unanswered. Other questions were answered, but no one was quite sure what the answer had been. It was usually Marshall and Hopkins who were sent to work out what had been agreed. They were sent to London in April 1942 to attempt to crystallise the inconclusive discussions of ARCADIA in a form acceptable to the American military. Roosevelt was worried about an imminent Soviet collapse (a fear that continued to concern the western leaders, though Churchill was always the more sanguine), and favoured SLEDGEHAMMER, a desperate scheme for a limited Continental landing as early as the autumn of that very year, as a way of keeping Russia in the war. Marshall in fact was even more in favour of ROUNDUP, a huge single invasion in the spring of 1943, preceded by an American logistical build-up in Britain: BOLERO.

There was an important and unrecognised lack of consensus in the discussions: Ismay later recorded that 'Our American friends went happily homewards under the mistaken impression that we had committed ourselves to both ROUNDUP and SLEDGEHAMMER', whereas the British were in fact quite clear that SLEDGEHAMMER was out of the question. Was this just one of those misunderstandings and differences of emphasis that occur in the course of wide-ranging discussions, or was it something more sinister? The Americans certainly thought the British had deliberately broken their word,[1] and some still do.[2]

Ismay explained pretty convincingly how the misunderstanding arose. The British Defence Committee listened to Marshall and Hopkins carefully and accepted their proposals, in principle only. The British assumed that it was understood that the proposals still had to be assessed in detail, and that their reservations about ROUNDUP and even greater doubts about SLEDGEHAMMER were equally taken for granted. But on the surface 'in fact everyone appeared to agree with the American proposals in their entirety. No doubts were expressed; no discordant note struck. It is easy to be wise after the event, but perhaps it would have obviated future misunderstandings if the British had expressed their views more frankly.'[3] There is no evidence that the British were doing anything other than moving the proposals through the stages of consideration, but later it appeared to the Americans that there had been a breach of faith. The episode had lasting effects on relations between the allies, and contributed to a sense of frustration. In the short term the atmosphere at the upcoming Second Washington Conference was poisoned.

Brooke said at a Defence Committee attended by Hopkins and Marshall on 14 April that the British accepted the American 'proposals for offensive action in Europe in 1942 *perhaps* and 1943 *for certain*' (my emphases). In his later annotations he said that Marshall's 'Castles in the Air' could not be taken too seriously: 'It must be remembered that at that time we were literally hanging on by our eye-lids!' Later he spent two hours with Marshall discussing the British position in detail. He was horrified to discover that Marshall had not thought through the implications of a landing, or in particular what you did when you were on the Continent facing experienced troops that were being reinforced at twice the rate of your own.[4]

Churchill is sometimes said to have admitted in the war memoirs that he had been less than candid with Marshall and Hopkins. In fact all he said was that he had been doubtful about the viability of the plan, but

> I was very ready to give SLEDGEHAMMER . . . a fair run with other suggestions before the Planning Committees. I was almost certain the more it was looked at the less it would be liked. If it had been in my power to give orders I would have settled on TORCH and JUPITER [a Norwegian jaunt], properly synchronised for the autumn, and would have let SLEDGEHAMMER leak out as a feint through rumour and ostentatious preparation. But I had to work by influence and diplomacy in order to secure agreed and harmonious action with our cherished Ally, without whose aid nothing but ruin faced the world. I did not therefore open any of these alternatives at our meeting on the 14th [April, with Hopkins and Marshall].[5]

It is difficult to see anything dishonourable about that. Roosevelt was certainly less candid with Molotov a month later when the Russian Foreign Minister visited the President in Washington and asked for an Anglo-American landing on a scale that would draw forty divisions away from the Eastern Front. SLEDGEHAMMER, as Roosevelt knew, postulated no more than six to ten divisions, but he equivocated and responded ambiguously. Molotov correctly dismissed his response as insincere; but Roosevelt had ostensibly promised him a Second Front in 1942. Churchill was much franker with Molotov, and told him that a 1942 landing 'was doomed to failure' and 'would do nothing to help the Russians'.

Later it was Churchill above anyone else who sought to delay a Continental landing until the circumstances were evidently propitious, but at this stage it was Brooke who persuaded Churchill that invasion in 1942 and indeed 1943 was premature. Churchill accepted his arguments and Mountbatten was despatched to Washington to expatiate to the President on 'the difficulties of 1942' and to pull away from what had been agreed with Marshall and Hopkins.

Churchill's personal fear had always been that SLEDGEHAMMER in 1942 might prejudice the much more important ROUNDUP in 1943. His position was finally reflected in the Chiefs of Staff Committee decision of 6 July 1942, endorsed by the War Cabinet on 7 July; a 1942 invasion was 'out of the question' and might put back ROUNDUP by two or three months. This awkward decision had to be shared with the Americans.

Before the conference proper began, Churchill had joined Roosevelt at his home at Hyde Park to tell him that there could be no mainland landing in September 1942 and that therefore the war zones should be the Atlantic and Africa. Roosevelt had been nobbled in advance, seduced by Mountbatten's charm. In any event he was aware that that there was a shortage of landing craft. He agreed that SLEDGEHAMMER was off, but he was clear that *something* had to be done before ROUNDUP eventually took place. He always had a weakness for North Africa. He had been in favour of the idea at ARCADIA, and now he was again 'very struck' by Churchill's plans for a landing there, GYMNAST (later TORCH). He did not appreciate, any more than Churchill, that GYMNAST in 1942 would make ROUNDUP in 1943 impossible. The two men were thus already agreed on North Africa when they moved from Hyde Park to meet their advisers at Washington for the Second Washington Conference (the first had been ARCADIA).

Until the Quebec Conference of 1943 Anglo-American strategy was largely British strategy. At Washington in July 1942 the American planners had little success in getting their own way. Marshall and Stimson were angered to find the President again siding with the British – or at least with Churchill: Brooke and the British Chiefs of Staff, alarmed by events in the Western Desert, were hesitant about any sort of operation in 1942. Relations between the two sets of Chiefs suffered because the Americans could not believe that Churchill's views were frequently arrived at independently of what his advisers were saying. This contributed to an appearance of deviousness and reinforced the impression that the British Chiefs were not being frank with them.

Stimson's comment on the dispute over North Africa as against a major Continental landing was that they had 'a fatigued and defeatist government blocking the help of a young and vigorous nation'. Part of the problem was that Roosevelt tended to intervene and frequently supported what Churchill and the British Chiefs wanted. In fact Brooke as much as the American Chiefs worried about what their bosses might agree at Hyde Park before the conference proper began. Roosevelt personally was more favourably disposed to the 'peripheral' approach than the US professional preference, a direct single thrust of enormous power.

Churchill had arrived in Washington on 20 June and on the following day was told of the fall of Tobruk with the loss of 25,000 British soldiers as prisoners. In fact the loss turned out to be higher: 33,000. Churchill telegraphed to Auchinleck: 'Whatever views I may have had about how the battle was fought, or whether it should have been fought a good deal earlier, you have my entire confidence, and I share your responsibilities . . . You are in the same kind of situation as we should be in England if we were invaded, and the same intense drastic spirit should reign'. If Auchinleck had been capable of responding at the same level and in a genuine spirit of openness his relationship with the Prime Minister would have been a productive one.

But the fact was that the Allied strategy was not going well. At the earlier Washington Conference at Christmas 1941 a coordination of a British drive westward from El Alamein and an Anglo-American drive eastward from French North Africa had been agreed. For the moment, the British component in this joint operation was going in the wrong direction.

It was embarrassing that the Tobruk news broke in Washington. The gravity of the situation in North Africa is reflected in a telegram

Roosevelt sent to Marshall on 30 June. He asked Marshall if there was anything that could be done to improve the situation in the Middle East and he put detailed and specific questions on what would happen 'on the assumption that [Nile] Delta will be evacuated within ten days and the Canal blocked'. Marshall replied saying that there was nothing the United States could do to affect matters and that different army estimates said that Rommel could be in Cairo within one to two weeks. He did note that Rommel was greatly extended and could be checked by destruction of his supply bases and lines. Shortly afterwards Marshall sent a message to Hopkins, stressing the disaster which the fall of Cairo would represent, and recommending that the President emphasise the unity of the Allies ahead of such a possible eventuality.[6]

At this Washington Conference Churchill agreed with Roosevelt, although not in writing, that there would be a free exchange of information between Britain and America in regard to research on the atomic bomb, which had begun in Britain in August 1941, the project code-named 'Tube Alloys'. In the event the Americans very soon failed to honour the agreement and the matter had to be addressed again at the meeting in Quebec in August 1943. There is plaintive correspondence from Churchill to Hopkins on the subject. In the secret Quebec Agreement it was formally accepted that there was to be a free exchange of information between the two powers, although no information was to be passed to any other country. In reality the prospect of an independent British bomb disappeared when the United States secured the entire Canadian output of uranium and heavy water for a period of nine years from May 1943. For what it was worth, neither Britain or America would use an atomic bomb without the consent of the other; Churchill's consent was indeed obtained to the use of the bombs at Hiroshima and Nagasaki, although in the event they were dropped after he had left office. But in the following year Congress unilaterally cancelled the Quebec agreement and passed the McMahon Act. The position was confirmed in agreements of 1948 and 1955. Britain had almost no entitlement to share America's nuclear secrets.

The atmosphere at Washington was strained by divergent views over empires in general and the Indian Empire in particular. America's preoccupation with imperialism is difficult to understand, and not free from ambivalence, even hypocrisy. Cordell Hull said that the United States' relationship with the Philippines was 'a perfect example of how a nation should treat a colony or dependency'. America had experience of more direct overseas rule during the Spanish American War, and although American expansion, which went ahead apace during the war, was generally achieved in an informal way, there was not a great difference in practice between America and Britain. The Atlantic Charter, with its references to self-determination, both expressed and reinforced America's anti-colonial position, and Roosevelt went so far as to talk about placing all colonies under international trusteeship. His mission to see the end of colonies, particularly if they were British or French, is all the stranger in view of his admiration for the colonial exploits of his kinsman, Theodore Roosevelt.

The State Department felt it their right and responsibility to request strict timetables from Britain for independence for its colonies. Pressure of this sort became very strong in the course of 1942 and 1943. Thereafter things were slightly easier, not least because America found herself extending her own territorial possessions, particularly in the Pacific. There were also embarrassing questions about Puerto Rico and the Virgin Islands. At the end of the war United Nations trusteeship was only applied to League of Nations mandates which already existed and to captured enemy territory.

That however was in the future. For the present, Churchill had to face personal pressure from Roosevelt; and indeed in April 1942 he sent the President via Hopkins a palpably insincere threat of resignation on the colonial issue: 'I should personally make no objection at all to retiring into private life'; but his view, he said, would be supported by the Cabinet and by Parliament'.[7]

On 10 March 1942, the day before Churchill announced the Cripps mission to India, he had to put up with a long cable from Roosevelt on the Indian problem. The President took it upon himself to analyse some of the constitutional arrangements that had been established in America during the War of Independence, including the temporary government formed under the Articles of Confederation. He put forward complex proposals for arrangements in India based on the experience of the emergent United States in the eighteenth century. He said that all of this was 'none of his business', and he was of course entirely right. The first draft of Roosevelt's message contained the revealing phrase that what he was writing was no more than 'a purely personal thought based on very little first-hand knowledge on my part'. Harry Hopkins said that nothing that Roosevelt had done during the war had annoyed Churchill so much as making his various proposals regarding a problem which was, as he said, none of his business, and certainly had nothing to do with the war that was being fought.

Even Republicans like Henry Luce saw the twentieth century as 'the American Century', in which the United States had 'our duty and our opportunity as the most powerful and vital nation in the world'.[8] Luce was strongly against the New Deal, and he did not want positive intervention abroad: America's influence would be passive, not active. But New Dealers were interventionists and went further and saw America's domestic reforms as a model for the world, a world in which Britain was not regarded as truly democratic. Reg Tugwell, for instance, said in April 1941, 'This war will never be won by force. It can only be won as a by-product of carrying the New Deal to the world . . . This is the Democratic revolution we must preach and practise everywhere'.[9]

It is easy to understand that this exporting of the New Deal caused disquiet among those Americans who saw their President as a closet socialist or worse, now exporting his quasi-communist views. Roosevelt's global interference was resented at home as well as abroad. Robert Taft saw that exporting American values might appeal both 'to the nationalistic sentiment of those Americans who picture America dominating the alliance and the world', and to 'the do-gooders who regard it as the manifest destiny of America to confer the benefits of the New Deal' on other nations and other races. But he also recognised the new American policy for what it was, one example of imperialism replacing another: 'It is based on the theory that we know better what is good for the world than the world itself. It assumes that we are always right and that anyone who disagrees with us is wrong . . . Other people simply do not like to be dominated, and we would be in the same position of suppressing rebellions by force in which the British found themselves during the nineteenth century'.[10]

London, July 1942.
Where to Attack and When

The Second Washington Conference had the same aftermath as the First: Marshall and Hopkins together with King came back to London in July 1942, this time to try to unpick the agreement on North Africa. The two military men at least were unhappy with what had been agreed at Washington. Roosevelt was also concerned that delay in tackling Hitler carried a risk of a switch to a Pacific policy. The Americans came to press for ROUNDUP in 1943, and failing that for SLEDGEHAMMER in 1942. A choice between the two was an easy one for Churchill: dropping SLEDGEHAMMER on the one hand meant the abandonment of a wildly premature landing and on the other relief for the embattled British army in Egypt.

So SLEDGEHAMMER was subjected to close examination in the course of the Americans' visit. Brooke bluntly pointed up the fact that America lacked the six trained divisions that the operation required, that there were not the necessary landing craft, or logistical backup, that the weather would be unsuitable and that the German resistance would be formidable. He was clear that there could be no landings in 1942, and even 1943 was doubtful, depending on what happened to Russia. He found Marshall difficult to deal with, intent on a rigid strategy which would not alter with events.[1] After four days Marshall gave way. SLEDGEHAMMER was abandoned. Instead there would be an Anglo-American landing in North Africa, TORCH, commanded by Eisenhower, with Alexander as Deputy Commander and Montgomery in charge of the British element. As TORCH was only agreed in July, it would transpire later, but was not evident then, that ROUNDUP could not take place in 1942 or 1943 and would be subsumed in OVERLORD in 1944.

Churchill was delighted. TORCH was what he wanted, and the operation would preponderantly be a British one. If the adoption of

TORCH was a success, however, JUPITER, a Churchillian projected landing in Norway, was a failure. Brooke complained that Churchill could not pass a map of Norway without suggesting a landing there. But not everyone was so dismissive of Norwegian adventures: when Churchill suggested a raid on Norway to take the pressure off Russia and the Chiefs vetoed it, he was supported by Eden, whose private secretary, Oliver Harvey's comment was, 'The slowness and lack of imagination of the Chiefs of Staff are enough to frighten one'.[2] Churchill wanted to roll 'the map of Hitler's Europe down from the top'. His real wish was for the vetoed JUPITER plus TORCH in 1942. He was never to have JUPITER.

The outcome of the visit, acceptance of the TORCH concept, was a triumph for Churchill's diplomacy and his decision to let the Americans see for themselves the practical impossibility of implementing SLEDGE-HAMMER. It was not however an outcome that Marshall and the American chiefs accepted easily. Hollis found that neither Marshall nor King had a grasp of strategy. Their gift was in procurement. 'Their plan therefore seemed childlike in its simplicity.'[3] They could not resist the appeal of the short crossing of the Straits of Dover; what could be done when they landed with an American contribution of only two and a half divisions, minimal air cover and no suitable landing craft did not concern them; nor did the tidal discrepancies along the French coast. They resisted the displacement of SLEDGEHAMMER by TORCH to the last. A.B. Cunningham noted the American Chiefs' lack of enthusiasm. He told the First Sea Lord in August that King was dead against TORCH.[4] At one point Roosevelt had asked the Chiefs what they would substitute for North Africa. 'The Pacific' was the reply. 'Very well', said Roosevelt, 'Send me your plan to Hyde Park'. There was of course no plan.[5]

With SLEDGEHAMMER abandoned, ROUNDUP was to be a full-scale invasion with about forty divisions, taking place in 1943. Churchill's ideas about ROUNDUP are contained in a paper of 15 June 1942 where, as so often, he argues for a series of feints and probes. 'At least six heavy disembarkations' were envisaged along the north and west of Europe, from Denmark and Holland in the north, to the Pas de Calais and on to Brest and Bordeaux. These were the views which he communicated to Marshall and to Stalin, but his plans were thrown out in their entirety by the Chiefs of Staff, who insisted on a maximum of four thrusts, concentrated on the Pas de Calais and Le Havre. The Chiefs of Staff dissented from Churchill on the value of any contribution by the liberated peoples. Contrary to what was later said, Churchill was entirely committed to a 1943 Second Front, although a very different type from that on which the Chiefs of Staff insisted and more different still from OVERLORD as it was to evolve.

Brooke was cautious and uncertain on many of these issues. He was favourably disposed to ROUNDUP and Churchill only won him over with great difficulty to TORCH, which was to prove a crucial allied operation and, incidentally, the one which opened the way to the 'Mediterranean Strategy' of which Brooke was to be so proud.

Lascelles, from his privileged viewpoint as the King's Private Secretary, got it right in his diary for 13 May 1943: 'Winston is so essentially the father of the North African baby that he deserves any recognition, royal or otherwise, that can be given to him. It was his imagination (stimulated perhaps by Smuts to some extent) that first saw the prime importance of this theatre of war; and it was his unflinching courage that built up the 8th Army into the wonderful fighting machine that it has become. He has himself publicly given the credit for TORCH to Roosevelt, but I have little doubt that W. was really its only begetter.'[6]

Churchill and the British had largely got what they wanted, but by 10 July 1942 the American Chiefs had become so exasperated by delays in establishing a Second Front that they proposed shifting from Europe First to a major offensive against Japan. King always tended to argue for Pacific priority, but even Marshall, who was generally committed to the European theatre, was concerned that TORCH did nothing for Russia, diverted troops away from any French landing, and required a new line of sea communications. More generally, there was a growing feeling that the British were simply not doing enough to engage the Germans. Dill had much work to do to reassure his American contacts, and to argue that TORCH had a logical place in the advance on the European mainland.

Roosevelt, however, having been told that no responsible British general, admiral or air marshal could recommend SLEDGEHAMMER, resisted his advisers. He said to Hopkins, 'I do not believe that we can wait until 1943 to strike at Germany. If we cannot strike at SLEDGE-HAMMER, then we must take the second best – and that is not the Pacific.'[7]

The blame for the delay in a mainland European landing lay in part with America herself. Despite what had been said about Germany First, America was tending to Pacific First for 1942. Admiral King and even the European-minded Marshall diverted troops and landing craft that had been earmarked for Britain to Guadalcanal. The pre-invasion

American build-up in Britain, BOLERO, stalled. By mid 1942 there were almost 400,000 US soldiers in the Pacific: only 60,000 in Europe. By October of that year just one and a half American divisions had reached Europe. Between that and the lack of landing craft that persisted throughout the war, Marshall was not in a strong position to push even for a 1943 Continental landing. The importance of landing craft was realised late and it never proved possible to produce adequate supplies. In the spring of 1943 most of America's were in the Pacific. In the Atlantic theatre she had just eight converted merchantmen; Britain had eighteen.

Another consequence of the backtracking on Germany First was that, largely because of the diversion of shipping to the Far East, the American Chiefs told Eisenhower out of the blue on 25 August that the TORCH landings would be confined to Casablanca and, possibly, Oran. Nothing would be attempted further into the Mediterranean. This was a bombshell to American planners, and precipitated what Ike called 'the Great Transatlantic Essay Competition' as they sought to change Washington's mind.

From the British perspective it was even more unwelcome. Part of the justification of TORCH for Britain was that it would secure entry to the Mediterranean, and in doing so would save something like a million tons of Allied shipping a year. America ignored this consideration.

ALL BEHIND YOU, WINSTON

Low's vision of a country united behind Churchill, 14 May 1940. The image was misleading. Popular opinion and the Labour Party were largely with him, but not the Establishment, the Crown or many Conservatives. The Tories do not feature prominently in the illustration.
Solo Syndication/Associated Newspapers Ltd

WINTERTON'S NIGHTMARE

In May 1942 an attempt was made in the Commons to limit Churchill's powers. He admitted later that he was surprised that he was not dismissed during 'this bleak lull'. But the general public, like Low, was reassured by his vigour. *Solo Syndication/Associated Newspapers Ltd*

FDR and WSC attending the Service on the *Prince of Wales* in August 1941. Their meeting at Placentia Bay was a crucial encounter. 'I wonder if he will like me'. *Imperial War Museum*

Still wondering. The President sails off in the *Augusta*. For all his geniality it was far from clear that FDR would take America into the war. *Imperial War Museum*

Low's drawing of 3 September 1941 reflected frustration over Roosevelt's lack of commitment. Isolationism in the United States had revived. *Solo Syndication/Associated Newspapers Ltd*

The White House Rose Garden, 1942. America is in the war and WSC skips with joy. The official caption says that he is demonstrating 'for photographers and ciné-camera operators the freedom of movement allowed by his siren suit'. *Imperial War Museum*

Above. The allied Chiefs meet. A lunch given by Brooke for Marshall in 1942. Left to right: Mountbatten, Marshall, US Rear Admiral Ghormley, unidentified US officer and Brooke. *Getty Images*

Right. The burdens the Prime Minister bore. Emmwood's drawing of 2 November 1959 was prompted by publication of Brooke's diaries. *Solo Syndication/Associated Newspapers Ltd*

Left. Stafford Cripps was Churchill's most serious rival through the vulnerable years, 1940–late 1942. In the circumstances it was not a bad idea to send him on extended missions to India (here he is with Pandit Nehru in New Delhi in March 1942) and Russia. Of the latter mission Churchill said that Cripps was 'a lunatic in a country of lunatics' and it would be a pity to bring him back. *Getty Images*

Below. Vichy France and friends, December 1941. From left Darlan, Pétain, Goering. The interpreter, Schmidt, promotes understanding between the regimes. *Getty Images*

At Casablanca, January 1943, the bride (de Gaulle, third from left) and the groom (Giraud, first from left) were forcibly united. The union was not a happy one. *Imperial War Museum*

Left. De Gaulle saw himself as the embodiment of the Free French. Britain tended to do so too, but not necessarily his fellow Frenchmen and certainly not America, which preferred Giraud. *Author's Collection*

Below. Harry Hopkins and General Marshall in London in 1942 on one of their trips to find out what they had agreed to at the last conference in the United States. *Getty Images*

Desert generals. O'Connor, left, and Wavell. *Imperial War Museum*

Teheran Conference, December 1943. Whatever FDR said to Brooke has produced an interesting reaction among the British. Behind Roosevelt and on his right Vorishilov. Extreme right US Admiral William D. Leahy. *Imperial War Museum*

Carthage, Christmas Day, 1943. After his serious illness WSC was well enough to entertain the five Commanders-in-Chief to lunch, wearing his famous red dragon dressing-gown. From left, Eisenhower, Alexander, WSC. *Imperial War Museum*

Above. WSC back on mainland Europe, visiting French troops on 12 June 1944, just six days after D-day. Montgomery acts as beach-master as WSC descends from a DUKW. *Imperial War Museum*

Left. 'The Naughty Document'. The script is WSC's; the tick is Stalin's. This copy is displayed in Romania, a copy of a scrap of paper which determined that country's destiny for half a century. *Author's Collection*

Athens, December 1944. WSC in the middle of a shooting war – where he always liked to be.
Imperial War Museum

British tanks in Athens. *Imperial War Museum*

The Citadel, Jülich, Germany, 6 March 1945. WSC and Brooke have drinks with two American Generals. The abstemious Monty sits apart, working on notes. *Getty Images*

WSC with the US 9th Army on the Siegfried Line. From left Brooke, Monty, WSC and US General Simpson. Cameras were banned when WSC urinated on the Line. *Getty Images*

Victory photograph of the Chiefs of Staff Committee in the garden of 10 Downing Street. From left: front row, Portal, Brooke, WSC, A.B. Cunningham. Back row, Hollis, Ismay. *Imperial War Museum*

Above. VE Day. WSC on his engagingly informal way to the House of Commons. *Getty Images*

Right. Potsdam, July 1945. *Auld Lang Syne.* A moment of remarkable hilarity at a pretty grim Conference. WSC, Truman, Stalin. *Getty Images*

An Indian Interlude

Cripps, at least, gradually became less of a threat. His mission, with proposals for a greater degree of Indian self-government, failed, the failure due more to a lack of cooperation from the Indian political parties than to Cripps himself. But Cripps's goose was pretty well cooked by then, anyway. He did himself more harm than good in India, and as far back as 29 September 1942 Churchill had told the King that he was thinking of disposing of him for good.[1] That he could now contemplate something that would have caused such a hoo-ha just a year earlier reflects a remarkable fall in Cripps's stock. Cripps resigned from the War Cabinet in November.

The Cripps mission had given Roosevelt the opportunity to give lots of gratuitous advice: a greater degree of independence was 'in line with the world changes of the past half-century and with the democratic processes of all who are fighting Nazism'. When the talks failed, he asserted that American opinion put the blame almost entirely on Britain. Churchill, in his history, referred to Roosevelt's interfering as 'idealism at other people's expense and without regard to the consequences of ruin and slaughter . . . The President's mind was back at the War of Independence, and he thought of the Indian problems in terms of the thirteen colonies fighting George III'. Churchill was against independence moves not only because of his underlying prejudices, but also because he thought that premature self-government would lay India open to Japanese expansion. His reference to not having 'become the King's First Minister in order to preside over the liquidation of the British Empire' in his Mansion House speech in November 1942 was a swipe at Roosevelt's interference.

It was not as if Roosevelt's America was a model of interracial harmony. Throughout the 1930s lynchings and other racially moti-vated murders took place at about the rate of thirty a year in the United States. With FDR's first victory, those who sought to outlaw the practice looked to him for help, but he chose not to support the Costigan-Warner Bill and in the process lose support in the southern states. In 1939 he did go so far as to create the Civil Rights Section of the Justice Department to address the evil, but it was 1946 before anyone was successfully prosecuted for lynching. The perpetrator, a police official, was fined $1,000 and sentenced to one year in prison.

In different circumstances and in an age when American imperialism is commonplace, it is difficult to see why the Roosevelt administration felt obliged to interfere with other countries' colonial possessions. Roosevelt thought that the fact that America was fighting the Japanese was excuse enough. He said on one occasion that the only reason that American boys were being killed in the Pacific was because of land grabs by Britain, France and Holland. The historical analysis was peculiar, but the interference went on.

William Phillips was sent to India as American High Commissioner, with the rank of ambassador, towards the end of 1942. He was authorised personally by Roosevelt to investigate India. He criss-crossed the subcontinent and interviewed officials, nationalists and journalists. He met Dr Muhammad Ali Jinnah, the head of the Muslim League, but not Gandhi who was on hunger strike at the time. He had two meetings with Churchill. In the second, a very unsympathetic Churchill told him, 'My answer to you is: take India if that is what you want! Take it by all means! But I warn you that if I open the door a crack there will be the greatest blood bath in all history; yes, blood bath in all history. Mark my words, I prophesied the present war and I prophesy the blood bath.'[2] The prophecy was, sadly, all too accurate. The cost of the end of imperialism in India was 15 million displaced persons, 12 million of them left homeless, and at least half a million deaths.[3]

Phillips concocted a high-handed recommendation that America should try to bring the Indian politicians together in order to push forward an agreed programme for independence. Throughout 1943 Churchill had to spend a lot of time and effort in resisting the Declaration on Colonial Policy which the State Department tried to impose. The Viceroy had complained to the War Cabinet in January that there was little prospect of disposing of American 'ill feeling, misunderstanding and prejudice' because 'the element in that country which has any real understanding of . . . major colonial problems is very small'.[4]

Churchill did not point out the discrepancy between FDR's racial liberalism in other people's countries and his attitude at home, where he made no great efforts to resist southern Democrats who were opposed to racial integration. It was Roosevelt who had insisted that the work forces in the Works Progress Administration and the Civilian Conservation Corps, for example, be segregated by race. Of course the WPA and the CCC would not have been supported by Congress in desegregated form, but the fact remains that FDR did not find it difficult to compromise on what might have been thought to be a major issue of principle.

Indians who came to Britain could vote there, but only a tiny minority of blacks in America had effective voting rights. Registration was almost impossible, and even by 1964 only 6 per cent and 19 per cent of voting-age blacks in Mississippi and Alabama respectively were on the rolls.[5] President Johnson attempted to address the problem with the National Voting Rights Act of 1965, which outlawed various devices that had been used to deny blacks the vote and gave the Federal government powers to ensure that registration took place. Parts of the Act are however only temporary, and it has been necessary to renew them on each occasion when they were due to expire. The last renewal, effective until July 2031, took place in July 2006. The renewal bill passed through the Senate unanimously, but was not unopposed in the House of Representatives.

After the Quebec Conference in 1943, a guest at a lunch which Roosevelt gave for Churchill was Mrs Helen Ogden Mills Reid, the Vice President of the *New York Herald Tribune* and a hostile critic of British India. After lunch she raised the matter of India with Churchill. He replied, 'before we proceed any further, let us get one thing clear. Are we talking about the brown Indians of India, who have multiplied alarmingly under benevolent British rule? Or are we speaking of the red Indians in America, who, I understand, are almost extinct?' There was no further discussion of India.[6]

At Placentia Bay Churchill had been bounced into the Atlantic Charter, and Britain had failed to realise the full significance of the Charter's reference to 'oppressed peoples'. Preoccupied with strategy, Churchill tended to isolate himself from the day-to-day impact of such presumption, although Amery, as Secretary of State for India, found himself obliged to bite his tongue and tolerate much of it, rather than offend Britain's paymasters. Eden was unimpressed by the vague, ill-connected liberalism of the American administration. There was little contact between the President and Secretary of State Hull; for Eden it was 'a mad house'. He was concerned by FDR's 'cheerful fecklessness' in 'disposing of the fate of many lives'. He was 'a conjuror, skilfully juggling with balls of dynamite, whose nature he failed to understand'.[7]

One has a certain amount of sympathy with Eden. He was a man of good, liberal principles, but he remained sceptical about the efficacy of doctrinaire idealism as a means of regulating world affairs. As Foreign Secretary he wanted to have a foreign policy, not just because that is what Foreign Secretaries do, but also because he saw a real risk that when the war ended, the post-war situation would be a dangerous one, in which Britain would be able to exercise little influence, and in which Europe would be dominated by America, a resurgent Germany or by Russia. For most of the war Churchill was too absorbed in winning it to feel that time could be taken to fight with allies over what was to happen afterwards, and as an able, sensitive and intelligent diplomat, Eden's relationship with the Prime Minister was frustrating.

'This Bleak Lull'

On 1 July 1942 Churchill faced a debate on a further motion of confidence. The debate lasted two days. Of course he won the debate – by 475 votes to 25 – but the opposition he faced was real, and greater than the figures suggest.

In his history, Churchill acknowledged his political weakness: 'I had now been twenty-eight months at the head of affairs, during which we had sustained an almost unbroken series of military defeats, galling links in a chain of misfortune and frustration to which no parallel could be found in our history. It is indeed remarkable that I was not in this bleak lull dismissed from power, or confronted with demands for changes in my methods, which it was known I should never accept'. A remarkable admission in the aftermath of victory.

But the admission did not reveal to what an extent he was confronted by demands for changes in his methods. In Parliament, in the July Confidence debate, Bevan alleged that Churchill was filtering the advice of the Chiefs of Staff, choosing what the War Cabinet should know and what they should not. Churchill denied that, but Harold Nicolson described Bevan's performance as 'a brilliant offensive, pointing his figure in accusation, twisting and bowing'.[1] 'The Prime Minister', Bevan said, 'wins debate after debate and loses battle after battle. The country is beginning to say that he fights debates like a war and the war like a debate'. Nicolson said that despite the vote at the end of the debate, 'the impression left is one of dissatisfaction and anxiety, and I do not think it will end there'. A few weeks later he spoke approvingly of Cripps and his attitude, 'probably wholly disinterested and sincere'.[2] A more informed and more accurate take on the interplay of the War Cabinet and the Chiefs came on another occasion from Ernest Bevin. He told Churchill that he 'shouldn't come asking the Cabinet for its opinion on matters about which they knew nothing and which were too serious to be settled by amateur strategists'.[3]

Immediately after the debate, prompted by Julian Amery, just back from the Western Desert, the embattled Prime Minister decided to go out to Cairo. Bevin tried to dissuade him, saying that he would be in the way. Churchill: 'You mean like a great blue-bottle buzzing over a huge cowpat?' As he made his plans to leave, an Arctic convoy reached Russia arriving with only eleven of its merchant men left out of thirty-four. Five hundred of the six hundred tanks it carried were lost. In a single week in the Arctic and the Atlantic nearly 400,000 tonnes of shipping had been lost, a figure unmatched at any time in Britain's history. Losses on this scale could not continue. Bracken told Moran that the Prime Minister had to 'win his battle in the desert or get out'.[4]

On his return to London from the second Washington Conference, Churchill returned also to the subject of war in the Western Desert. By now, but not hitherto, Ultra material was providing Auchinleck with good *detailed* information. Until then Rommel had enjoyed a better tactical intelligence.

In these days Rommel enjoyed a status that modern military historians would not allow him and it did not help the desert generals that their opponent was regarded as exceptionally able as well as unusually gallant. Churchill referred to him in the Commons in more generous terms than he would use of one of his own commanders: 'We have a very daring and skilful opponent, and may I say across the havoc of war, a great general'.

If Rommel's advance had been unchecked, a coordinated campaign in North Africa would have been impossible, and Allied landings on mainland Europe would have been delayed until perhaps Stalin had control of the whole of the western continental land mass. But the defensive positions that Auchinleck and his Chief of Staff, Major-General Gorman-Smith, established held, and Rommel's offensive stalled.

That was far from evident at the time: what was clear to Auchinleck was that his army was exhausted and demoralised and he had insufficient reserves to allow him to advance.

The main purpose in going to the Middle East was to see Auchinleck, the general who could not find time to come home to see the Prime Minister and Minister of Defence. It is all very well to portray Auchinleck as the ultimate, uncompromising professional. In this war, generals needed to be something more than that. They had to work with politicians; they had to an extent *be* politicians. Auchinleck's successor, Montgomery, knew that: he understood what Churchill wanted, and he kept him informed. He gave very great attention to political and public relations matters. Before he was carried away by notions of grandeur, he knew exactly how to work on Churchill. So, in a much more gentlemanly way, did Alexander. Auchinleck and Wavell did not understand the need to do so.

Of course, Auchinleck's delays were based on sound and humane considerations, and on succeeding him, Montgomery also delayed action; but what mattered was that the Auk failed adequately to explain his reasons for delay or to give any indication that he was actively preparing for a time when he would set the desert aflame. If he failed to tell Churchill what he was doing, he could not really be surprised that he was ultimately disposed of. Dill, Ismay and Brooke all told him to be conciliatory but he remained infuriatingly unresponsive, close to the edge of insubordination. Later, in his interviews with David Dimbleby he made much of the lack of training his troops had received, but he did not adequately explain this to Churchill.[5] He could even be evasive about the materiel at his disposal.

At a time when Churchill was, remarkably patiently, sending repeated requests to Auchinleck for information to which he was reasonably entitled, the general sent his staff officers a copy of a letter from the Duke of Wellington to the Secretary of State for War:

My Lord
     If I attempt to answer the mass of futile correspondence that surrounds me I should be debarred from the serious business of campaigning.
     I must remind your Lordship – for the last time – that so long as I retain an independent position I shall see that no officer under my Command is debarred by the futile drivelling of men quill-driving in your Lordship's Office from attending to his first duty which is, and always has been, so to train the private men under his Command that they may, without question, beat any force opposed to them in the field.
     I am, my Lord,
     Your Obedient Servant
     Wellington

Auchinleck added: 'I know this does not apply to you, but please see to it that it can never be applied to you or to anyone working under you.'[6] He had no notion of just how anachronistic these self-important views were. Wellington's circumstances were very different.

In the Dimbleby interviews Auchinleck said that he simply had to disregard Churchill's interventions, which were 'a disturbing influence on a chap like myself who the whole day and night was concentrating on one thing and determined to get the best of out of it . . . I didn't want any encouragement to put everything I had into beating the Germans.'[7]

When Churchill travelled to Cairo, he was clear that something needed to be done about the nature of the Middle East command. In the aftermath of the fall of Tobruk, 'I was politically at my weakest', and wanted a dramatic victory. He himself had not yet decided on dismissing the Commander-in-Chief. But Brooke thought he should be moved, and the Prime Minister was certainly coming round to that view.

Churchill was not alone in being unhappy about the army's performance. In the War Office it was felt that Auchinleck's days had been numbered ever since he announced on 21 June that he would not stand at Sollum. Kennedy, the Director of Military Operations, was so ashamed of the army's performance that he stopped lunching at his usual club. Parliament was also dissatisfied, and Brooke too said, 'It was quite clear that something was radically wrong.'

Churchill's intention, rather than to sack Auchinleck, was to confine him to his duties as Commander-in-Chief, putting another general in charge of Eighth Army.[8] Brooke's preferred choice for the role, not a wise one, was Ritchie, who had been his Chief of Staff in France. Ritchie might have been a good Chief of Staff, but was not a good commander. If not Ritchie he wanted another favourite. Brooke had always had a high opinion of Montgomery – higher than of Gott, whom he thought exhausted. Brooke and Montgomery had been fellow instructors at Camberley and it had been Brooke who secured Montgomery's immediate appointment as Commander of 3rd Division when it went to France as part of Gort's field force.

Churchill's preference was Gott –'They don't call him "Strafer" for nothing'. He flew out to see Gott at El Alamein, and was reassured by the experience. Alexander also appealed to Churchill, but Brooke regarded Alex's best role as providing a barrier between Churchill and the Army Commander.

Once in Cairo, Churchill became convinced that Auchinleck could not simply be moved sideways. He had to be moved from the theatre. The dismissal was badly handled. Brooke allowed Churchill to effect it, while constitutionally it was his responsibility. When the dismissal came it was not even done face-to-face, but by letter. Churchill said later, rather unconvincingly, 'Having learned from past experience that that kind of unpleasant thing is better done by writing than orally [better for whom?], I sent Colonel Jacob with . . . the letter'. Jacob said that he felt 'as if I were just going to murder an unsuspecting friend'. Auchinleck 'opened the letter and read it through two or three times in silence. He did not move a muscle and remained outwardly calm and in complete control of himself . . . I could not have admired more the way in which General Auchinleck received me and his attitude throughout. A great man and a fighter.'[9] But one who was not prepared to use political skills. If he had gone to meet Churchill in Cairo, rather than requiring the elderly Prime Minister to visit him in the spartan surroundings of his desert headquarters he might have retained his position.

Moran saw Auchinleck shortly afterwards. 'Auchinleck sat with his forearms resting on his thighs, his hands hanging down between his knees, his head drooping forward like a flower on a broken stalk. His long, lean limbs were relaxed; the whole attitude expressed grief; the man was completely undone.'[10] Along with Auchinleck out went Generals Corbett, Dorman-Smith and Norrie. The extent of the purge at the highest levels was remarkable.

Churchill now offered Auchinleck's command to Brooke. Poor Brooke agonised over the tempting offer and, to his very great credit, declined it for two very unselfish reasons. First, he felt that he could work with Churchill better than anyone else was likely to and, secondly, he did not want to appear to have come out to Cairo to engineer Auchinleck's removal and grab his job. By the time Churchill came to write his memoirs he had forgotten about the offer to Brooke, which must have been hurtful.[11] Alexander was given the Middle East command. Brooke, true to form, was not impressed by Alex's intellect. At Staff College Alex had not been regarded as particularly bright, but he had a good First War when he attracted considerable admiration, and later he acquitted himself extremely well at Dunkirk. He was polished, debonair, brave and diplomatic. As Commander-in-Chief, Middle East, he performed adequately, and proved very diplomatic in his relations with the Americans. His performance in Italy was slow, but he never faced dismissal because, unlike Wavell and Auchinleck, he kept his Prime Minister very fully briefed.

Churchill's first choice of army commander for Eighth Army, Gott, was frustrated just a day later, when Gott was shot down as he flew back to Cairo. He escaped from the plane but when he courageously went back to rescue his companions he was killed in the explosion. Churchill then accepted Brooke's recommendation of his protégé, Montgomery. Brooke was happy to think that Alex would let Monty have his head. He did.

Churchill did not underestimate Auchinleck's abilities. Later he told Harold Nicolson about his decision to remove Auchinleck. It was a terrible thing to have to do. 'He took it like a gentleman but it was a terrible thing. It is difficult to remove a bad general at the height of a campaign: it is atrocious to remove a good general.'[12] He wanted to retain Auchinleck with the Middle East command split in two, Alexander in Egypt, Palestine and Syria, and Auchinleck in Persia and Iraq.

His plans for Auchinleck's redeployment were however frustrated by a remarkable revolt from the normally docile members of the War Cabinet. They objected to the division of Middle East command. They met twice on 7 August to discuss Churchill's proposals and to rebuff them on both occasions. They did not want to create the impression that a command had been established just to let Auchinleck down lightly. They wanted someone to blame. That was understandable, but even Churchill, probably Auchinleck's biggest critic, knew that was unfair and simplistic. Auchinleck's principal fault was simply that he never adjusted to what Brooke described in his diary as 'a regular disease that [Churchill] suffers from, this frightful impatience to get an attack launched'.

But the War Cabinet's worries were academic: they thought the offer to Auchinleck too generous: but he thought it too mean and indicated that he would not accept it, even if Churchill had been able to make it. Perhaps his failure to continue to serve his country emphasises his disdain for political control.

A Llama and a Crocodile

In the midst of the more pressing issues with which Churchill had to deal at Cairo, he required to spend time with de Gaulle, who seized repeatedly on instances of 'flagrant violations of French sovereignty', 'insults to France', and 'new Fashodas'. In May 1942 there had been problems over IRONCLAD, an attempt to seize Vichy-occupied Mada-gascar. Because of memories of Dakar – and the general impossibility of working with him – the general was kept in the dark and was predictably furious. As usual, the unfortunate Anthony Eden had the job of trying to repair the damage with de Gaulle, who now threatened to withdraw his base to the Soviet Union. As always, he saw any movement against a French colony as part of a British plan for imperial expansion.

Now he was on the spot in Cairo. After a fairly brief meeting with Churchill on 7 August, de Gaulle went off to negotiate with Casey, who had replaced Oliver Lyttelton as Minister of State, and to survey the problems arising from Syria. All that poor Casey wanted was to have elections in Syria, scarcely evidence of imperialist designs, but he received such savage treatment from de Gaulle that Churchill, who had decided to replace Spears with someone more acceptable to the Free French, now changed his mind. De Gaulle threatened to go to war with Britain and, not for the first time, to withdraw the Free French to Africa. His own account of the meetings with Churchill reveals some of the fury of the occasion. Churchill: 'You claim to be France! You are not France! I do not recognise you as France!'[1] Even the sanitised official record of the conversations show how bad things had become:

The Prime Minister said that they seemed still to be very far apart. There seemed little use to proceed further with the conversation. The General had been unsuccessful in winning the confidence of the Americans, who had also had hopes of working with him. He could not understand why the General did not try to make things go well. (The Foreign Secretary interjected that other allies did not find us so difficult to deal with.) General de Gaulle was his own worst enemy. The Prime Minister had hoped to work with him. Gradually, bit by bit, that hope had been destroyed. We carried a pretty heavy load on account of France. Things could not go on as they were.

By the end of the interview, despite his incandescent rage, Churchill told Eden that he was just 'sorry for the man, he was such a fool'. Eden later said that 'he had never seen anything like it in the way of rudeness since Ribbentrop'.[2]

De Gaulle never realised how close he came on occasions to being dropped. He was not indispensable, and America would have been delighted to see him go. Churchill felt attached to him, but that attachment could wear thin. British public opinion helped de Gaulle. So repeatedly did Eden. So did the War Cabinet: in May 1943 in Washington Churchill was ready to let the Frenchman go, and it was only a rebellion by the War Cabinet that saved him.[3]

Yet again, it was Churchill who took the trouble to repair the breach: at the end of October he sent Desmond Morton to de Gaulle's headquarters at Carlton Gardens with emollient messages which did the trick nicely: the government soon learned that de Gaulle 'had been very *ému* by what Major Morton had said to him' and ' was delighted at the Prime Minister having made this gesture and felt that the situation had improved remarkably'.[4]

But de Gaulle apart, Churchill's morale had improved. After all the disappointments and dismissals in the Middle East, he had at last assembled a team that would remain in place for the rest of the war. He splashed in the Mediterranean surf before flying on to Teheran and then to Moscow.

The August visit to Moscow had been contemplated and discussed by Churchill and Roosevelt for some time. But behind the Prime Minister's back the President had his own plans. He was already trying to cut Churchill out of his negotiations with the Russian leader, as he would do increasingly in the course of the war. He told Churchill in March 1942, 'I think I can personally handle Stalin better than either your Foreign Office or my State Department. Stalin hates the guts of all your top people. He thinks he likes me better, and I hope he will continue to do so.'[5] Later he was to say 'Three's a crowd. We can arrange for the Big Three to get together thereafter. Churchill will understand. I will take care of that.'

But Roosevelt's heart was never in travels. It was Churchill who went east. His flight to Moscow involved a journey of 20,000 miles, not above cloud level, with no beds, only 'shelves'. The aircraft was unheated and vibrated under the impulses of its piston engines. The 67-year-old Prime Minister's discomfort was only slightly alleviated by a modified oxygen mask, which allowed him to smoke a cigar. General Macarthur said of it, 'a flight of 20,000 through hostile and foreign skies may be the duty of young pilots, but for a Statesman burdened with the world's cares it is an act of inspiring gallantry and valour'. Macarthur was no admirer of Churchill. This journey was merely part of many long, dangerous and exhausting travels that Churchill made in the course of the war, amounting in all to some 107,000 miles.

He had the unpleasant task of confirming to Stalin, face to face in Moscow, what the Russian leader had already been told by telegram: the 1942 second front had been cancelled, and he would have to wait until 1943. After a hot bath he was driven to the Kremlin to draw a picture of a crocodile for Stalin, so that he could point out its soft underbelly. Throughout 1942 Russia was going to have to continue to bear the main burden of fighting the Germans. Between June 1941 and June 1944 93 per cent of German combat losses were inflicted by Russia. The account of the meeting that Churchill gave in his history was a prime example of his sanitisation of the record. It was a very difficult meeting indeed, and came very close to disaster.[6]

The atmosphere only relaxed a little when Churchill promised bombing of German cities on a vast scale.[7] Bombing was to be Britain's Second Front: as Churchill put it, bombing was paying Britain's way. All the same, Stalin's mood changed from day to day and he remained capable of accusing Britain of cowardice. Churchill responded, 'I pardon that remark only on account of the bravery of the Russian troops'. He told Stalin that the 1942 Second Front would be in North Africa and that there would also be 'a reconnaissance in force' across the Channel that summer.

At this stage the full implications of TORCH were not fully appreciated. But military planners, American and British, both saw that TORCH would mean that there could not be a quick follow-up on the Atlantic coast on a significant scale. Churchill is usually thought to have been pro-TORCH at the expense of Atlantic landings, but he actually aired, though not with the Americans, the idea of closing down the Mediterranean operations at the end of June 1943 to allow for ROUNDUP in August.[8]

Conversely, although conventionally America is regarded as having been lukewarm about the Mediterranean, and impatient for a Second Front, as early as 11 November 1942, just days after the TORCH landings started, Roosevelt suggested 'forward movements directed against Sardinia, Sicily, Italy, Greece and other Balkan areas'.[9] Who was the Mediterranean strategist? In the event the North African campaign took much longer to complete than planned. It took six months to capture the Tunisian ports, and only four months were then left before the winter gales of 1943.

The Moscow visit followed a pattern which would be repeated in the course of the war: apparent rages on Stalin's part, followed by conciliation; enormous consumption of food and alcohol; great bonhomie, which could be succeeded the following day by chilling coldness. Churchill sometimes erroneously attributed these changes of mood to instructions that Stalin had received from mysterious party bosses who, he thought, limited his freedom of movement. While Churchill was dictating replies to telegrams in his dacha on 13 August he was warned that the room was probably bugged. He broke off from his dictation to bellow some comments for the benefit of the hidden microphones and for transmission to Stalin: 'The Russians, I am told, are not human beings at all. They are lower in the scale of nature than the orang-utan. Now then let them take that down and translate it into Russian'.[10] Some of his remarks were particularly ill chosen. He referred to Stalin as a peasant, and said he would not leave until he was in his pocket. Tedder warned him by scribbling a note, '*Méfiez-vous*'. Wise advice: at Teheran Stalin took great interest each morning in the previous evening's transcripts[11] and in October 1944 no less than sixteen microphones were found in the British villa in Moscow. What Stalin thought of it all is not known, except that he was astounded by the British lack of security. But the indiscretions may have contributed to the problems of what was in reality a very difficult series of meetings, which at one point looked liked ending very badly. Churchill came close to threatening to leave prematurely.

He returned to Cairo on 17 August and on the following day he, Brooke and Alex went to Monty's headquarters in the desert. Although Monty was not subjected to the same degree of harassment as Wavell and Auchinleck had been, and was insulated by the suave Alex, he was not immune from pressure. There was to be more pressure in the course of September, which Churchill later excised from his record of events, as also the serious setbacks at the outset of Alamein itself.[12]

On the following day, 19 August, the Dieppe raid, the 'reconnaissance in force' that Churchill had mentioned to Stalin, resulted in the loss by death, wounding or capture of 68 per cent of the largely Canadian forces involved. The raid had first been planned, as RUTTER, in early July. These plans were abandoned because security had been compromised and the weather was bad. They were subsequently revived by Mountbatten, possibly without top-level authorisation, and certainly without any very full discussion or any records being taken. Churchill's concern was evident in a minute of 21 December in which he said 'It would appear to a layman very much out of accord with the accepted principles of war to attack the strongly fortified town front without first securing the cliffs on either side, and to use our tanks in frontal assault off the beaches'.[13]

On 30 August, Rommel unleashed an attack on Montgomery, but did not break through the British defences at Alam Halfa Ridge, 15 miles south of east El Alamein. The battle of Alam Halfa was unequivocally a victory, but a defensive one from which Montgomery turned to plan the offensive which would open at Second Alamein in October. Poor Brooke had taken a brief holiday – the only one that year – and was peremptorily called to the telephone by Churchill to discuss Alexander's latest signal. ' "You have not seen it! Do you mean to say you are out of touch with the strategic situation?" I replied, "I told you I was going grouse shooting today, and I've not yet solved how I am to remain in touch with the strategic situation whilst on a grouse butt." ' That was not good enough for Churchill and a contact officer rode through the night by motorcycle from Whitehall to Darlington with a copy of the signal.[14]

Montgomery opened his offensive from El Alamein on 23 October 1942. By now, Alexander had the benefit of the full text of the Enigma decrypts, which helped the British to know when to follow through. For all that, the outcome of the battle was very far from a foregone conclusion. There is some doubt whether the church bells rang out two days later to celebrate the victory of Second El Alamein, or were delayed on Brooke's advice and against Churchill's wishes until after the fall of Tunis;[15] either way there was hard fighting before Tobruk fell on 13 November.

Second Alamein and TORCH

Later Churchill was to say, 'It may almost be said, "before Alamein we never had a victory. After Alamein we never had a defeat"', but at the time the possibility of further defeats seemed very real – and not only on land: Britain still could not read the German submarine signals. On 24 November 1942, a month in which the highest tonnage of Allied shipping in any month in the war was lost, Churchill telegraphed to Stalin, 'You who have so much land, may find it hard to realise that we can only live and fight in proportion to our sea communications'.

Montgomery's critics have pointed out that the plans for Second Alamein were largely those that Auchinleck and Dorman-Smith had prepared, and that he delayed the start of the offensive for a month more than poor Auchinleck had proposed. The criticism is facile and misses the point: Montgomery had a great deal of organisation to put in place, changes to make, a new esprit to build up; and the army he used at Second Alamein was very different from the army with which the Auk had fought at First Alamein.

From Churchill's perspective, however, the delay before the start of Second Alamein was exactly the sort of delay that Wavell and Auchinleck had insisted on, and he was as annoyed by it as he had been in the past. But he could not afford to dismiss another desert general, and when Monty hinted at resignation if he were not allowed an adequate gap between Alam Halfa and Second Alamein he admitted he was indulging in pure blackmail.[1]

That does not mean that he went out of his way to irritate Churchill – at least not until he was much more certain of his security of tenure. On the contrary, he took great pains to humour and cosset him. When the PM had visited Auchinleck in the desert because the Auk could not take time to come up to Cairo, he had endured considerable discomfort in the C-in-C's fly-ridden wire cage, an unnecessary ordeal for a man of his years and distinction from which he escaped with relief to the amenities thoughtfully provided by the RAF. They had arranged to have an epicurean repast brought out into the desert from Shepheard's Hotel.

Montgomery's personal regime was even more abstemious that Auchinleck's, but when Churchill visited him in the desert after Alam Halfa, the occasion was celebrated with the provision of every luxury that could mitigate the privations of war. Monty's own caravan was handed over and placed close to the sea, to accommodate his guest's well-known love of bathing. Wine and brandy flowed in the mess. The Prime Minister was indulged and spoiled. He enjoyed being 'the man on the spot', sharing in the making of history and the planning of victories. It was all very different from, say, the days of Wavell when the plans for O'Connor's offensive were only disclosed to the War Cabinet when Eden happened to visit the Commander-in-Chief.

While they were in Cairo Sir Charles Wilson, as Moran still was, fell mildly ill with the local stomach bug. The medical tables were turned, and Churchill loved it, telling everyone, 'Sir Charles has been a terrible anxiety to us the whole time, but I hope we'll get him through'.[2]

Monty had used his delay for constructive purposes and even if very much of the planning was taken over from his predecessors without acknowledgement, perhaps even denied, the kind of war the Eighth Army fought was never the same again. Monty was arrogant, cocksure, untruthful, ruthlessly ambitious and unpleasant in his dealings with senior fellow-officers, but he loved his vulgar showmanship, and it worked very well with most, if not all, of those on whom it was deployed. He put new heart and confidence into junior commanders and other ranks. Morale was transformed and a very tired and dispirited army was persuaded both that it was an effective fighting force and that lives would not be wasted. When Brooke revisited the Eighth Army he was astounded by the change he found.

At the same time Montgomery recognised the continuing limitations of his army, and took care not to demand too much of it. He sought, not with complete success, to address the persisting problem of integrating armour and infantry, and he curbed the proliferation of special units, insisting that divisions fought as divisions.

When all that is said, however, Second El Alamein was not immediately or self-evidently the turning point that it turned out to be, and Alex took a chance when he reported to Churchill on 6 November 1942: 'General Alexander to Prime Minister. Ring out the bells! Prisoners estimated now at 20,000, tanks 350, guns 400, M.T. several thousand. Our advanced mobile forces are south of Mersa Matruh. Eighth Army is advancing.'

That was the stuff to give the PM, but Brooke was nearer the mark when he said of the battle, 'It may be the turning-point of the War . . . or it may mean nothing'. While the fighting continued, the outcome seemed very much in doubt. It did not go in accordance with Montgomery's Master Plan (though that was not acknowledged) and the breakout was postponed from day ten to day twelve. Churchill had been acutely concerned. 'Haven't we got a single general who can win even one battle?' he shouted at Brooke, who thought he was going to be hit.

And all this was despite the fact that at Alamein as at Alam Halfa, Montgomery fought with a huge numerical superiority, particularly in tanks, and that Rommel was very far from well. At Alam Halfa, suffering from a swollen liver and an infection of his nose he could not even leave his truck.

But the appearance and presentation of events in warfare is often more potent than reality. Monty knew that, and so did Churchill. Although he wrote of Alamein as marking a turning point between a series of defeats and a series of victories, he omitted to mention that before Alamein Britain fought alone; after Alamein America fought alongside her. TORCH was launched on 8 November, and as Rommel said, 'This spelled the end of the Army in Africa'.[3]

But the importance of Second Alamein did not only appear in retrospect. Even at the time, it was recognised as significant. The nature of the Desert War had changed. Hitherto, lack of supplies had been responsible for the nature of warfare as well as for the victories and defeats. Movement between the Italian base at Benghazi and the British base of Alexandria could only be made along a narrow coastal strip. In Graziani's original advance, an impressive thrust of about a thousand miles right up to the Egyptian border, Italian success was finally checked by lack of supply. The equally impressive British drive well into Libya failed for the same reason. Germany reinforced the Axis effort, and yet ultimately suffered in the same way. But in the course of 1942 the Italians had been expelled from the Mediterranean, which was now dominated by the Royal Navy, while the Royal Air Force, operating from Malta, largely controlled the air. Consequently, when Montgomery broke out at Second Alamein, although the quality of his armaments was inferior to Rommel's, supply and support were infinitely better.

Just three days after the Alamein breakout, TORCH brought American and British troops on to the North African coast, to the west of the Germans. The full implications of TORCH were not clear in 1942, but there now existed the possibility of trapping Rommel between the Allied forces in French West Africa and the largely British forces in the Western Desert. For the moment, Rommel continued to fight an impressive series of rearguard actions, but Montgomery was able to continue westwards, capturing Sidi Barrani on 9 November and taking Benghazi on 20 November.

TORCH proceeded on the assumption that the Vichy authorities in French North Africa would welcome the Allies with open arms. In the event the Frenchmen on the spot showed as usual no great desire to be freed from the shackles of Vichy. There was fierce resistance in Oran and Morocco, in which the French navy played an enthusiastic part. In Algiers, on the other hand, the Resistance seized power and the Vichy commanders were handed over to the Allies on their arrival.

The fighting was finally brought to an end when the American general, Mark Clark, persuaded the Vichy commander, Darlan, to order an end to hostilities in Oran and Morocco, in return for which Darlan would head the Free French. It simplified things greatly that Germany now decided to occupy Vichy Metropolitan France. Darlan's position had been very ambivalent until then, and there was even a fear that he might arrest his liberators. Indeed, when it looked as if Vichy might be able to safeguard the fleet he contemplated revoking his ceasefire. Clark stopped that and Darlan remained under house arrest until he concluded that Pétain was no longer a free agent. He 'invited' the Commander-in-Chief at Toulon to sail for North Africa. In the event the Toulon fleet scuttled. Godfroy's fleet, holed up in Alexandria, had some difficulties in withdrawing from the amenities to which they had now become accustomed, and took six months to enter the war. The Vichy Army in North Africa was rather quicker in joining the Allies.

This was a huge relief: Churchill had said to Clark that, 'If I could meet Darlan, much as I hate him, I would cheerfully crawl on my hands and knees for a mile if by so doing I could get him to bring that fleet of his into the circle of the Allied Forces'.[4] The fleet was not in the circle, but at least it was now denied to Germany, and Churchill was saved an uncomfortable indignity.

Churchill's vision, the idea of linking up Allied troops in French North Africa with Commonwealth troops in the Western Desert, proved the key to victory in the Mediterranean. Brooke and the British

Chiefs had initially been at one with the Americans in regarding TORCH as impracticable, and the credit for ensuring that it went ahead in the face of their opposition goes to Churchill, and his skill in pressing the idea on FDR.[5] Brooke's supporters make much of his 'Mediterranean Strategy'. He certainly believed the concept was his, and Churchill's failure to say as much may have contributed to the CIGS's decision to allow the publication of his diaries. In his annotations to the diary entries he certainly is at pains to suggest that from the start as CIGS he saw a logical progress through North Africa to the Mediterranean and Italy, and only then and only if Russia were still in the war, to the Atlantic coast.

But Brooke had opposed TORCH, and there could have been no Mediterranean Strategy if he had succeeded in killing the operation off. In reality, the Mediterranean Strategy was born when Churchill made the enormously courageous decision (which Brooke deplored) to send half of Britain's armoured forces to the Middle East at the very time when the Battle of Britain was at its height. Even afterwards, the adoption of the strategy had more to do with Churchill's preference for attack from the south rather than a confrontation on the Atlantic seaboard. Furthermore Brooke abandoned commitment to the Mediterranean before Churchill did: last in and first out.

The outcome of TORCH was critical to Churchill's political future, and he was well aware of it. There continued to be significant machinations among potential successors. Eden was irritated by many aspects of Churchill's thoughts on foreign policy and sometimes toyed with the idea of resignation. He was encouraged by his friends to declare clearly his claim to the succession, but he remained totally loyal. He felt ready to be Prime Minister, but would do nothing unless Churchill fell. Churchill was under no misapprehensions. He said that 'If TORCH fails then I am done for and must hand over to one of you'.[6]

Realism was however always tempered by buoyancy and optimism, and the day after TORCH was launched, and long before there was any certainty about its outcome, Churchill opportunistically told the Chiefs of Staff that rather than limit a follow-up to the impending operations in Sicily and Sardinia, there should be an offensive on the mainland of Mediterranean Europe. He had the support of Eden, but not of the Chiefs.

He was being too optimistic. At a staff conference on 16 December 1942 the COS submitted a paper arguing that the slow rate of American build-up in Britain, BOLERO, because of the diversion of American resources to the Pacific, had made a cross-Channel landing in 1943 impossible. There was reference also to the fact that German rail routes would allow them to bring superior forces to the Atlantic front. The recommendation was to hold forty German divisions on that front by the *threat* of invasion, while eliminating Italy and possibly entering the Balkans.

Churchill and the Chiefs learned that the Americans had gone back on their undertakings and were putting what were known to be good engines in their own landing craft and what were known to be poor engines in the British landing craft. Eden and Churchill accepted the Chiefs' recommendations. They made it clear that they accepted them with reluctance, and would have preferred a 1943 landing, and indeed Churchill asked the COS to look again at their figures. But the fact that Churchill did accept the recommendations meant the end of Britain's commitment to ROUNDUP and the formal adoption of the Mediterranean Strategy.

Cancellation of a 1943 Continental landing was desperately disappointing to Churchill, who was trying hard to instil an offensive spirit into the Chiefs, arguing against too much 'perfection' or paralysis. But events were moving so slowly that it became obvious that there would be no cross-Channel attack in 1943. Tunis had not been captured before winter weather got in the way. Things might have been different if the Americans had been prepared to land more forces east of Gibraltar, but they did not do so because of the danger that Hitler might enter Spain and attack them from there; Britain did land troops to the east of the Pillars of Hercules. Vichy, still not at war with Britain, allowed the Germans to use their airfields in Tunisia. Reluctantly Churchill abandoned plans for a 35-division invasion of France in 1943.

Simultaneously he had anxious negotiations with his American allies about the shipping problem. He told the Cabinet that Britain needed 'a solemn compact, almost a treaty, with the United States about the share of their new building we are to get in 1943 and 1944'. By the end of November he received the sort of assurance he needed from Roosevelt, although the undertaking was only implemented after delays and difficulties.

It was his additional complaint that British troops were being 'misemployed' in Burma in order to protect America's air route to 'their very over-rated China'. Churchill saw Burma as a country to reconquer. For America that smacked of imperialism: for them Burma was largely there to provide bases for the supply of their Chinese ally. Churchill was also upset to learn that at the first wave of TORCH landings at Algiers, a critical part of the war material brought ashore was a large number of dentists' chairs.

The French Dimension

As 1942 drew to a close the French dimension took up more and more of Churchill's time. Although America's embracing of Darlan in Algiers had brought resistance in Vichy North Africa to an end, his chance recruitment opened up a long and difficult passage in Anglo-American relations in regard to the leadership of non-Vichy France. The tensions that were created contributed to the growing distance between the two allies.

Darlan had been Pétain's deputy and his degree of his collaboration with the Germans made him distasteful to the British and unacceptable to the Gaullists. His name was almost synonymous with collaboration. In a broadcast speech on 24 August 1941 Churchill had addressed the French people: 'Lift up your heads, gallant Frenchmen: not all the infamies of Darlan and Laval shall stand between you and the restoration of your birthright'.[1] America was much less fastidious about Vichy collaborators. Darlan's background presented no problem to the State Department, even if American public opinion found him pretty unappealing.

The installation of Darlan had been extraordinarily badly handled by the Americans. He was endorsed by Eisenhower pretty much on the basis that he happened to be there when the general arrived. Eisenhower justified the choice in a long cable to Roosevelt on 14 November, which displayed a considerable degree of naïvety. Roosevelt had some difficulty in extracting his general from the position in which he had placed himself, but gave him his support, while saying that Darlan's appointment could be regarded only as 'a temporary expediency'.

Roosevelt was not really in a position to be too hard on Eisenhower. Darlan's accession to the Allies was not as adventitious as it appeared. The Americans had been courting him in preference to de Gaulle, and brought him out of occupied France. The reason that Darlan was in Algiers when the Americans arrived was that he was visiting his son who was in hospital suffering from polio. When Roosevelt, another polio victim, heard of the boy's illness, he wrote a kind letter of support to Darlan and later invited his widow to bring the boy to the therapy centre that he had established at Warm Springs in Georgia.

America's ideal Frenchman was Giraud. His credentials were impeccable, as he had only recently escaped from a German prisoner of war camp. America wanted him, and Britain would have been delighted if their man, de Gaulle, could have worked with him. But de Gaulle's egocentric concept of patriotism did not lead him to accept Giraud as his leader and he emphatically refused to subordinate himself to him.

Roosevelt was no more impressed by de Gaulle now than he had been at the time of the *Affaire St. Pierre et Miquelon*; indeed his prejudices were reinforced not only by Sumner Welles, but also by Admiral Leahy, who had recently come back from Vichy France, and by Alexis Léger, Washington's principal French expert and a fierce opponent of de Gaulle from before the war.

Churchill had not discouraged contact between the United States and Vichy France – indeed in May 1941 he had told Roosevelt that Britain was 'more than willing' that the United States should take the lead in this area. But America's relationship with Vichy was unrealistic. Britain's position was that the fact that France was under duress was no justification for assisting Germany. Hull seems to have failed to see what 'collaboration' implied.

No one knew what de Gaulle's response would be to TORCH, the invasion of what was after all a *Département Outre-mer* of metropolitan France. Left to himself, Churchill would have liked to tell the general what was afoot well ahead of the North African landings, but Roosevelt vetoed the suggestion and all Churchill could do was to give the general the Trusteeship of Madagascar as a consolation prize. It was not until 6 November Eden told de Gaulle what was happening and invited him to Chequers for 8 November, the start of TORCH. In a message of 11 November 1942, Roosevelt wrote to Churchill, deleting from his draft the words in brackets, 'In regard to de Gaulle [it is my considered opinion that any association by him with the TORCH operation at the time would add serious difficulties to our efforts in that area.] I have hitherto enjoyed a quiet satisfaction in leaving him in your hands – apparently I have now acquired a similar problem in brother Giraud. [I trust it will not come to a meeting at thirty paces on the Field of Honour, each provided with a rifle.]'[2]

De Gaulle took the news of TORCH surprisingly well and his subsequent broadcast contained words that – from him – were remarkable: 'Ignore the traitors who try to persuade you that the Allies want to take our Empire for themselves'. But the fact that he had not been taken into the confidence of his allies from the outset did sow seeds of future discord all the same.

What was very much more serious was the Darlan issue. Darlan, designated 'High Commissioner for North Africa in the name of the Marshal [Pétain]' with Giraud as Commander-in-Chief, could not have been more unacceptable to de Gaulle and the Free French. They could not believe what had happened. Prime Minister and Foreign Secretary sought to reassure de Gaulle that Roosevelt had said that Darlan's position was entirely temporary, but bit by bit the temporary expedient began to look fairly permanent. Towards the end of November Churchill was beginning to warm to the man he had recently wanted shot. He told Eden that 'Darlan has done more for us than de Gaulle'.

But Darlan's continued place at the head of affairs in French West Africa became increasingly unacceptable in Britain. Press and Parliament were very unhappy about the connection. In the face of complaints, Churchill made an important Secret Session speech to the House of Commons in early December. He spoke of his own love for France and of his support for de Gaulle:

> We have most scrupulously kept our engagements with him and have done everything in our power to help him. We finance his movement. We have helped his operations. But they have never recognised him as representing France . . . I cannot feel that de Gaulle is France, still less that Darlan and Vichy are France.
>
> [Y]ou must not be led to believe that General de Gaulle is an unfaltering friend of Britain. On the contrary, I think he is one of those good Frenchmen who have a traditional antagonism ingrained in French hearts by centuries of war against the English.

He continued by referring to the mischief de Gaulle had brought in Syria and French central and West Africa. He referred to the *Chicago Daily News* interview and recommended the House not to build all their hopes and confidence on him. Like Roosevelt, they should try to base themselves 'on the will of the entire French nation rather than any sectional manifestations, even the most worthy'. The critical references to de Gaulle were bravely made to a House which did not wish to hear such an appraisal of someone who had become a British icon, and they were excised from the text of the Secret Session speeches published in 1946. He tried to set the events in North Africa in a historical perspective: 'I must say I think he is a poor creature with a jaundiced outlook and disorganized loyalties who in all this tremendous African episode, west and east alike, can find no point to excite his interests except the arrangements between General Eisenhower and Admiral Darlan'.[3] Churchill regarded this speech as having changed the mood of the House more than any other he had given.

Eisenhower's recognition of the admiral had been much resented in Britain not just because of what Darlan had stood for, but also because de Gaulle himself was the idol of the popular press and public opinion. While Churchill was able to check this mood and minimise the significance of what Eisenhower had done in regard to Darlan by putting it in the context of the great and crucial events that were taking place in North Africa, his warnings about de Gaulle were less well received.

Fortunately, as far as is known, de Gaulle never heard of this speech. In any event the situation soon changed dramatically. On 24 December Darlan was assassinated. The circumstances of his assassination remain unclear. It has been suggested but never proved that the assassin, Fernand Bonnier de la Chapelle, was a Gaullist, possibly aided by Britain. At the time care was taken not to examine Britain's role, if any. Bonnier was tried *in camera* and executed in less than forty-eight hours. Whoever was responsible for the assassination, it made life much easier for the Allies. SOE's Controller for Western Europe and the Free French Navy's Chief of Intelligence celebrated with a bottle of champagne.[4]

Darlan's replacement was America's favourite, Giraud. When Giraud had emerged as one of the key players in the new North African arrangements, de Gaulle had spoken of him as being a good general, but there was now increasing tension between them. Giraud had been appointed by Vichy Imperial Council (under intense background pressure from America) but he had an impeccable record and de Gaulle was quite happy that he should command the Free French troops. On this occasion it was not de Gaulle who was to blame for the breakdown of the relationship. It was Giraud who repulsed de Gaulle's overtures.

The consequent feud soon came out into the open. De Gaulle went public and was supported by a wave of indignation in the British press. A corresponding but contrary wave started to roll in the United States and Cordell Hull crested it with statements on 5 and 7 January 1943 to the British Foreign Office complaining that British press and government officials were stirring up propaganda with the direct aim of arousing bitterness against the United States. Eden responded by saying fairly frankly that Hull did not know what he was talking about. 'I have no idea what Mr. Hull meant when he spoke of persons in the British government who are associated with de Gaulle publicity. No such person existed. Indeed most of our time was spent in trying to damp down de Gaulle's activities and his publicity'.[5]

While these political manoeuvres took place, the fighting continued. In hindsight, the flow from TORCH to the surrender of Axis troops in Tunisia seems obvious and inevitable; at the time that was not the case. Unlike Libya, Tunisia was eminently defensible. There are limited passes through the Atlas mountains, and in the plain between the Atlas range and the Matmata Hills there was a substantial defensive work which the French had already built, known as the Mareth Line. Moreover, Rommel had ports at Tunis and Bizerta, which could be supplied at night from accessible Italian bases on Sicily. Hitler imagined that Tunisia would hold out for a very long time and put paid to any early Second Front.

There was indeed a huge increase of German forces in Tunisia, which contributed to the threat to the 1943 cross-Channel landings. The Prime Minister told Alexander that it might be a good idea to give a friendly hint to Monty that he was unwise to make too many confident noises before a decisive battle with Rommel had been fought. He warned that Montgomery might seem 'foolish' if Rommel slipped away, rather than submitting to a confrontation at Agheila.

During the last weeks of 1942, it looked as if Hitler might well be correct about the impregnability of Tunisia. Despite a significant numerical superiority, the Allies faced repeated reverses and by 26 December 1942 were no further forward than they had been two weeks earlier. In 1943 the untried American troops did not perform well. At the Battle of the Kasserine Pass, at the cost of few casualties, Rommel was able to inflict serious losses on the Americans – 6,000 men and two-thirds of their tanks. The Americans had to be strengthened by British troops withdrawn from fighting the Germans at Sbiba.

George VI reacted to the news of the Battle of the Kasserine Pass by saying it looked as if the British 'would have to do all the fighting'. Churchill replied that 'The enemy made a great mistake if they think that all the troops we have there are in the same green state as our United States friends'.[6]

Needless to say, the Americans saw their contribution in a different light. The American press attributed victories in North Africa, and later in Italy, to their own boys, and quite soon there was a feeling that, as so often in the past, straightforward and innocent Americans were being taken advantage of by the wily and self-interested British. Senators reported that the Administration had been 'out-manoeuvred at every point [in relation to Lend-Lease] by the selfish but efficient agents of Britain'. Britain was criticised for not conducting operations in the east and for taking over territory won by Americans; Britain was not using her oil reserves in the Middle East, but making use of free American resources; Britain was putting her own labels on goods that were being sent to Russia.[7]

But British troops were still the largest element by far in the Allied forces. By 23 January 1943 Eighth Army had entered Tripoli. It was Eighth Army that reached the Mareth Line causing Rommel to pull off the offensive that had been fought at the Kasserine Pass, and it was Montgomery who broke the Mareth Line in PUGILIST on 19/20 March 1943. Brian Horrocks's X Corps swung round the Matmata Hills, and the Mareth Line was no longer a defensive feature. Rommel flew to Germany to try to persuade Hitler to abandon Tunisia. His request was denied and he was placed on sick leave; but even after his departure the Tunisian campaign was no walkover. On 30 April, for instance, the battle was called off temporarily because of the strength of the German resistance. The Battle of Tunisia proved harder to win than had been expected, but its eventual outcome was not really in doubt. The last Germans surrendered on 13 May 1943.

Casablanca

Nineteen forty-three opened with Churchill in a much more secure position politically and militarily than he had been a year earlier. He had delivered victories in the Western Desert, and American commitment to the joint enterprise could be seen in the Allied landings in French North Africa. It was very much his achievement that the next great Allied conference could be held on soil recovered from the Axis.

The drawback about allies is that they have to be consulted, and the drawback about very powerful allies is that what they think tends to prevail. Averell Harriman noticed that by the time of the Casablanca meeting, on many issues 'Roosevelt and Churchill did not march to the same drumbeat' and the theme of the first half of 1943 for Churchill was often one of frustration in his attempts to bend the Americans to his will. In the end he was usually able to ensure that his arguments were accepted, or at least received serious consideration, albeit at the cost of much effort. But Casablanca was a turning point, and at none of the subsequent conferences did Britain play the same role as she had at Placentia Bay, ARCADIA and the Second Washington Conference.

Despite family fears, which they did not communicate to him, that long-distance flying might precipitate a heart attack, Churchill set off at the beginning of January for the meeting with Roosevelt. He took the Chiefs of Staff plus Mountbatten and the Joint Planners. The American Joint Chiefs of Staff accompanied Roosevelt. Harold Macmillan gave a good account in his diary of the domestic arrangements for the conference:

> The Emperor of the East's villa [the PM's] was guarded by a guard of Marines, but otherwise things were fairly simple. His curious routine of spending the great part of the day in bed and all the night up made it a little trying for his staff. I have never seen him in better form. He ate and drank enormously all the time, settled huge problems, played

bagatelle and bezique by the hour, and generally enjoyed himself. The only other member of the government present was [Lord] Leathers, and the PM had nobody except his secretaries and so on.

The Emperor of the West's villa [the President's] was difficult of access. If you approached it by night, searchlights were thrown upon you and the hoard of what I believe are called G-men . . . drew revolvers and covered you. With difficulty you could get access, and then everything was easy. The Court favourites, Averell Harriman and Harry Hopkins, were in attendance as well as the two sons who act as aides and, tragic as it seems, almost as male nurses to this extraordinary figure.[1]

Again the British outnumbered the Americans. At one meeting of the Combined Chiefs there were nine British to five Americans and when HUSKY, the invasion of Sicily, was discussed there were seven to four.

Roosevelt came to Casablanca more determined than ever to improve the lot of the downtrodden subject races. He made some facile points about the conditions of the native inhabitants of Bathurst in the British colony of Gambia, where he had broken his journey to the conference. His regard for the Churchill family was not increased when Randolph arrived. Elliot Roosevelt had already met Churchill's son in England and had been overwhelmed by him, but it was the first time that the President had met his bombastic self-confidence. His reaction was mainly one of quiet amusement and he was kinder than he might have been: 'It must be wonderful to have so few misgivings'.[2]

As at Placentia Bay, the British came with their positions and arguments thoroughly rehearsed. It was a polished and professional affair. Brooke and his fellow Chiefs worked as a team and knew their briefs and they were supported by a 6,000-ton headquarters and communications ship moored nearby, filled with staff who could re-run figures and make adjustments in the light of developments in the discussions. All this tended, as it was meant to, to ensure that British arguments prevailed. It was impressive, but it also fed the suspicions of those such as the American Secretary for War, Stimson, who were ready to see guileless and innocent Yanks being outmanoeuvred by devious and selfish Limeys. One US planner said, 'All of us in keeping score counted Casablanca as lost.'[3] The British paid later for these victories.

But even now the Americans were getting their act together – Marshall and King, not natural allies, came to realise that they must cooperate to avoid being outmanoeuvred by the British. And the

Combined Chiefs as a whole realised that they had to assert themselves against the two political bosses. At meetings prior to and including Casablanca, they had been obliged to acquiesce in what they considered to be the meddling of President and Prime Minister. At Casablanca they achieved some successes, largely by fixing matters behind their chiefs' backs – something Churchill would accuse Brooke of, and which Brooke would hotly deny. The negotiations that had led to the abandonment of ROUNDUP and the adoption of TORCH, for instance, were largely effected by Churchill and Roosevelt with intermediary activity by Hopkins.

The great debate at the conference was on whether there should be a continuing Mediterranean Strategy, as Brooke argued, or an immediate switch to invasion, as the Americans wanted. In view of the suggestion that Churchill was always delaying the Second Front in defiance of the view of the Chiefs of Staff, it is interesting that at Casablanca quite the opposite was true.[4] Churchill tended to side with the Americans and argue for closing down TORCH and pressing on with ROUNDUP, ignoring arguments for pushing on to Italy and Turkey from Brooke, who was in the middle of his Mediterranean period; even by end of December 1942 he had become determined that operations should be continued in the Mediterranean theatre throughout 1943, undisturbed by a landing in France unless there were signs that Germany was breaking up. His innate conservatism contrasted with Churchill's impatience, reflected in a Directive that he had issued to the Chiefs, ordering a halt in the Mediterranean in June, and a switch to preparation for invasion. Brooke and the War Office retorted that the PM would ruin everything by premature invasion, that there was neither enough shipping nor enough landing craft and that anyway the Germans were too strong in France. He even argued for capitalising on the opportunities in the Balkans, as Churchill would do a year later.

But for the moment (and it was a fairly brief moment) Churchill was for invasion. He was unconvinced by the suspicious multiplicity of arguments that were directed against his position. Montgomery was also coming to the conclusion that it might be worth facing up to the cost of invasion. The Prime Minister was thwarted by a neat manoeuvre by the Chiefs, who won tacit acceptance of the Mediterranean Strategy by playing on the internal fault-line in the American position, and making concessions regarding the Pacific. A paper drawn up by Air Marshals Portal and Slessor and accepted by the Americans authorised continuation of operations in the Pacific and Far East, but only provided that in the opinion of the Combined Chiefs these operations did not imperil the chances of defeating Germany in 1943. This renewed pledge of Germany First implied continuation in the Mediterranean theatre in 1943 as there was now no time to mount a major offensive elsewhere. This satisfied both King and Marshall. At Dill's insistence, the document did not go to Prime Minister or President: 'You know as well as I do what a mess they would make of it'.

A series of further crucial decisions was made. Tunisia would be succeeded by an attack on Sicily. Although shipping constraints made it impossible to bring sufficient fresh troops from America to support a major cross-Channel landing, there would be a limited raid on the Cherbourg Peninsula, with a possibility of establishing a bridgehead if all went well. Germany was to be convinced that the assault on Fortress Europe was going to take place in 1943: to that end there would be landings on Brittany, Norway and the Pas-de-Calais, all of which would also take pressure off Russia.

The Combined Chiefs had come into their own, but their great days did not last long and from mid 1944 the organisation was more or less moribund, its meetings sporadic. Even now, and with a Mediterranean Strategy accepted in return for the Pacific deal, there were strong disagreements about its implementation. The Americans soon wanted to abandon the attack on Sicily, in favour of one on Sardinia, for example; and Sicily, if Sicily it was to be, should be the end of the Mediterranean operations in Marshall's view; Brooke wanted to spring on from Sicily to Italy.

De Gaulle at Casablanca

The Casablanca Conference had to deal with many major issues. A minor objective, though still important, was to effect a reconciliation between Giraud and de Gaulle and to establish some sort of working relationship between them. De Gaulle was slow to appear on the scene and Churchill professed not to know why. The Americans found it very amusing that the British were unable to bring the bride to the wedding, and they enjoyed the joke quite openly.[1] Secretly they were quite certain that de Gaulle was entirely under the control of Churchill, who was holding him back simply to enhance his importance.

In reality Churchill had no such control over the British protégé. When he met the American fiancé at Casablanca, the Prime Minister asked Giraud if he had heard from de Gaulle. Giraud said he had not. Churchill replied, 'Neither have I. It's astonishing. He ought to be here. I gave him all the means to come. He is being pig-headed, naturally. A tough customer, your friend de Gaulle'.[2]

Roosevelt was unsympathetic about de Gaulle's absence: 'Who pays for de Gaulle's food?' Churchill: 'Well, the British do'. Roosevelt: 'Why don't you stop his food and maybe he will come?'[3] The President's enquiry was not entirely flippant: he could not understand the licence the British gave to one very dispensable Frenchmen among many, and de Gaulle's demeanour at Casablanca reinforced him in a prejudice that was never dispelled.

Eventually, after a fairly stiff telegram from Churchill and much diplomacy by Eden, the general sulkily agreed to go to Morocco – because Roosevelt had asked him. He would not, he said, have gone for Churchill alone. At Casablanca de Gaulle continued to sulk and it was only after Harold Macmillan called on him that he agreed to go and visit Churchill in his nearby villa. The general was fuming. He took exception to the fact that, on what he regarded as French soil, he was surrounded by American bayonets. Churchill had no time for this nonsense. It was on this occasion that he told de Gaulle, *'Si vous m'obstaclerez, je vous liquiderai!'* [or in a good but inaccurate alternative version: *'Si vous m'opposerez, je vous getriderai!'*]. De Gaulle was equally rude. He told Churchill that it was not appropriate that they should be seriously discussing proposals that could only seem acceptable to American sergeant majors.

It was bad enough for de Gaulle to find himself escorted around what he regarded as his own country by American troops: it was as well that he did not know that when he met Roosevelt at his villa the gallery above the room in which they met was filled by a secret service detail with tommy guns: they even stood behind the curtains in the room itself.[4]

De Gaulle's final interview was in Churchill's recollection 'the roughest of all our wartime encounters'. Prime Minister and President were desperate that an amicable communiqué should be signed by de Gaulle and Giraud, and Churchill threatened that if de Gaulle did not sign it he would be denounced 'in the Commons and on the radio'. There was no agreement and no communiqué, but there were two handshakes for the press photographers between Giraud and de Gaulle, and this had to satisfy Roosevelt and Churchill. Neither then nor later did de Gaulle understand the importance of pragmatic compromise. He remained always unrealistic, pedantic and uncooperative. He saw himself not as a person, but as the representative of France. When Clementine Churchill told him, 'General, you must not hate your friends more than your enemies', de Gaulle replied, 'France has no friends – only interests'. The amenities and decencies of personal relationships and friendships that normally oil diplomatic relations were absent. Nations did not have friendships; France did not make jokes.

Bob Murphy, Eisenhower's political adviser and FDR's personal representative, acted as the best man and Harold Macmillan as the bridesmaid. They had more or less to push the respective spouses on to the terrace where Roosevelt and Churchill gave their press conference at the end of Casablanca.

Murphy, like Hull and Roosevelt's friend Admiral Leahy, was overtly anti-de Gaulle, and briefed the President accordingly. He was much impressed by Giraud and advised his boss that Giraud would make an ideal administrator. The advice was acceptable to the President who had for some reason formed the view that de Gaulle would never surrender the French colonies and indeed aimed at one-man rule in France. On balance, and more reasonably, the British thought de Gaulle preferable to Giraud. When Roosevelt actually met Giraud he liked the man, but disagreed with Murphy's assessment of his ability.

De Gaulle remained Britain's protégé and Giraud America's but Giraud was possibly more America's protégé than de Gaulle was Britain's. Britain never really knew what to make of Giraud. As a clerihew in the Daily Mail in May 1942 put it,

> I used to think General Giraud
> Was something of a hero.
> Now he's gone to Vichy
> It all looks a bit fishy.

America had taken even more trouble to get their man out of Vichy France than Britain had: he was extracted on a British submarine, but one flying an American flag, to the extent that a submarine flies a flag, and the extraction was made at Eisenhower's request. Hopkins took quite a detailed note of the impression that Giraud made on him at Casablanca, and his views carried weight with the President. He was aware that the Frenchman was a Royalist and 'probably a right winger in all his economic views' but he thought that he had confidence, vigour and the will to fight. More importantly, Hopkins '[h]ad a feeling that he had made up his mind that he was going to do whatever the President wanted in Africa'.[5] That was certainly something that no one would say of de Gaulle. Between the two principals de Gaulle became known as Churchill's 'problem child' and later just 'D'; Giraud was Roosevelt's 'problem child' or 'G'.

The extent of the State Department's infatuation with Vichy is shown by the draft letter which was given to Roosevelt to sign ahead of TORCH (the words in italics were deleted in the final version):

My Dear Old Friend:

I am sending this message to you *not only* as the Chef d'État of the United States to the Chef d'État of the Republic of France, *but also as one of your friends and comrades of the great days of 1918. May we both live to see France victorious again against the ancient enemy.*

When your government concluded, *of necessity*, the Armistice Convention in 1940, it was impossible for any of us to foresee the programme of systematic plunder which the German Reich would inflict on the French people.[6]

As Minister Resident, Harold Macmillan had the unenviable responsibility of seeing that the marriage was consummated. Part of the difficulty between the two generals was ideological. De Gaulle, more than Giraud, wanted an elimination of anyone tainted by contact with Vichy. He was also strongly critical of Giraud's slowness in repealing anti-Semitic laws in French North Africa. But there were personal conflicts too. Giraud rather stood on his rank as a five-star general, as opposed to the two-star de Gaulle. He did not want to be Foch to de Gaulle's Clemenceau. When the French Committee for National Liberation, the FCNL, was formed, de Gaulle insisted that he be the Commissioner for Defence, with the Chiefs of Staff reporting to him – a flattering imitation of the Churchillian model. Giraud, as Commander-in-Chief, wanted no such limitation of his powers, and in the controversy which followed, de Gaulle tendered his resignation as co-President and also as a member of the Committee. Giraud had started to write a letter accepting the resignation when Macmillan discovered what had happened, and convinced him that it would be a disaster if de Gaulle were to go at such an early stage in the history of the FCNL. He could see in it the danger of a complete break-up of the representation of the French Empire. Fortunately for the sake of unity, his views were accepted.[7]

After Casablanca, when he was ill and running a temperature of 102 degrees, Churchill wrote to the King saying that he 'put far more confidence in Giraud than in [de Gaulle] . . . The insolence with which [de Gaulle] refused the President's invitation (and mine) to come and make a friendly settlement at Casablanca may be founded on stupidity rather than malice. Whatever the motive, the result has been the same . . .'[8]

There is an intriguing picture of de Gaulle a day or two after these events. He went with Macmillan (less buttoned-up than usual on this occasion) on a trip to the seaside. 'I bathed naked in the sea at the far end of the Roman city; de Gaulle sat in a dignified manner on a rock, with his military cap, his uniform and belt. Then we had a nice little supper at the inn with the excited *patron*.'[9]

Soon afterwards Giraud's influence on the Committee began to wane. He made the mistake of going to America for a lengthy holiday. Macmillan's attempts to keep the FCNL working well for the benefit of the allies were made much more difficult by America's insistent interference in details of its work and in its composition. In his very moderate and sanitised account, Macmillan allowed himself to speak of 'the folly of the President in basing his policy towards France on the support of individuals rather than principles.'[10]

The problem about de Gaulle was that his behaviour was founded on imagined insults, an exaggeration of slights and a failure to rise to see what was important and what was not. His fear that France would not return to honourable independence – if the Allies won – was quite unrealistic. The US State Department may have had, briefly, an idea of post-war Europe in which France would be just one of a number of insignificant players, but for Churchill and the Foreign Office it was essential that France would resume a crucial and powerful role in post-war Europe.

It was at Casablanca that Roosevelt made the historic declaration that the Allies would accept nothing less than unconditional surrender from Germany. He appears to have done so without much discussion and without really understanding the implications of what he was doing. It was of course the opposite of what Churchill had stood for until now. The Prime Minister had always been ready to consider a negotiated peace with any element of German society that could deliver it. The declaration was bound to stiffen German resistance and to cut away at any prospect of a coup against Hitler. Victory as a result of war from the air was now impossible, and the Allies were committed to a full-scale land conflict.

Roosevelt's declaration was made at a press conference. The myth that it was a totally unscripted, unilateral declaration by America became part of British folklore, supported by Bevin in the Commons on 21 July 1949, when he said that the War Cabinet had never been consulted, and by Churchill, who confirmed that the first he had heard of unconditional surrender was at the press conference. But Churchill later apologised to the Commons. He had been at error. The declaration had been discussed by him and Roosevelt in advance of the press conference, Churchill had obtained the War Cabinet's approval, and they indeed sought to include in it all three Axis powers (rather than leaving Italy out to encourage her defection). Bevin's recollection had been as wrong as Churchill's.[11] But it is likely that Ismay was correct in holding that neither the President nor the Prime Minister appreciated the significance of the form of words on which they agreed.[12] In the final communiqué there was not even a mention of unconditional surrender.

De Gaulle, still uncomfortably harnessed to Giraud, continued to cause Churchill immense difficulties. Although Churchill could still think of him fondly when he remembered the dark days of 1940, by now he was more inclined to describe his protégé as 'the monster of Hampstead' (de Gaulle was aware of the appellation and on one occasion referred to 'the monster of Downing Street'). Things were now so bad that Churchill instructed Eden to prepare a document called 'Guidance for the Press and the BBC in the event of a break with General de Gaulle' – an extensive *curriculum vitae*, detailing all the general's anti-British history.

It was bad enough that de Gaulle was anti-British, but at a press conference in Washington on 9 February in which he criticised Allied policy in North Africa he stirred up much hostility in America too. Roosevelt was now complaining that Churchill was not keeping his puppet under control.[13]

In March 1943 de Gaulle decided to go to Cairo. Britain was very apprehensive that he would take the opportunity to stir up trouble. At length Churchill agreed to see de Gaulle on 2 April. The prickly general said that he was a prisoner and would soon be sent to the Isle of Man. Churchill reassured him: such a distinguished soldier would certainly be sent to the Tower of London. The interview ended a little more warmly, with de Gaulle making great efforts to melt the ice, and conveniently for Churchill, a message soon appeared from Eisenhower asking that de Gaulle should delay his visit to Egypt. Unfortunately a day or two later de Gaulle was persuaded that Eisenhower's message had been written at the inspiration of the British, and relations sank to their previous depths, with de Gaulle denied permission to go anywhere where he could cause problems as he certainly would have done.

But while de Gaulle's stock with the British and American governments was very low, it continued to rise in the bourse of public opinion. For that reason, and having been told by Eden to be nice to him, Churchill met de Gaulle again on 30 April and positively encouraged him to go to Algiers. He was ready to back any agreement that gave de Gaulle and Giraud equal powers. Just five days later Churchill sailed to the United States for the Third Washington Conference and received a memorandum of complaint from the President: 'I am sorry, but it seems to me the conduct of the Bride continues to be more and more aggravated. His course and attitude is well nigh intolerable . . . I do not know what to do with de Gaulle. Possibly you would like to make him Governor of Madagascar!'

This was followed by a meeting with Hull in which, in the context of an otherwise civilised exchange, the Secretary of State urged the British to stop building up de Gaulle and the Prime Minister urged the Americans to stop building up Giraud. In the face of all the American pressure, Churchill inclined to break with de Gaulle and reported so by telegram to the War Cabinet in London. Eden noted, 'Everyone against and very brave about it in his absence'.[14]

Churchill left America with no progress made in the de Gaulle *vs* Giraud battle. The situation was one of stalemate, and on 17 June Roosevelt wrote to Churchill in much the same terms as those of the memo which Churchill had received in Washington: 'I am fed up with de Gaulle and . . . there is no possibility of our working with de Gaulle . . . I am absolutely convinced that he has been and is now injuring our war effort and that he is a very dangerous threat to us. I agree with you that he likes neither the British nor the Americans and that he would double-cross both of us at the first opportunity . . . We must divorce ourselves from de Gaulle . . .'[15]

Churchill's response was more imaginative. The Conseil National de la Résistance had recently been set up at a meeting in the Rue du Four in Paris, as a result of the efforts of Jean Moulin. Moulin said there could be no question of subordination to Giraud: de Gaulle must be the sole leader. Churchill saw in this organisation the opportunity to do what he had wanted for some time and 'put de Gaulle into commission': neutralise him by making him simply *primus inter pares* – or, perhaps, not even *primus*.

In no time at all Churchill's manoeuvre backfired. Soon Giraud was extracted from the co-presidency of the Conseil and not long afterwards ceased to be Commander-in-Chief. By the end of 1943 it was clear that de Gaulle had certainly not been put 'in commission'. He remained unconstrained, free to roam and free to continue to make enormous mischief.

These ongoing Gallic problems were in the future. As the Casablanca Conference ended, the Eighth Army entered Tripoli. On the following day Churchill took Roosevelt to Marrakech, to show him the sun setting on the Atlas Mountains: 'the loveliest spot in the world' for Churchill. Roosevelt left on the following day and Churchill stayed on to paint the mountains, the only painting he executed in the course of the war. From Marrakech he flew to Cairo, where he decided on a British mission to Tito's communist partisans in Yugoslavia. He then flew on to Turkey for talks with President Inönü, but failed to persuade him to end his neutrality. On his return to Cairo, where he heard that the Germans had surrendered at Stalingrad, he quarrelled at dinner with

Randolph and then embarked on a long disquisition about Omdurman. The next day, on to Tripoli, where he told the Eighth Army, 'When history is written and all the facts are known, your feats will gleam and glow and will be a source of song and story long after we who are gathered here have passed away'. On 4 February he took the salute at a march past with the 51st (Highland) Division and other units. The tears ran down his cheeks as the pipes played and the men, fresh from battle, marched past.

Even the austere and vinegary Brooke came close to being moved as he too watched the Highland Division pass by, and compared them with what he had seen before Alam Halfa: 'Then they were still pink and white; now they are bronzed warriors of many battles and of a victorious advance. I have seldom seen a finer body of men or one that looked prouder of being soldiers . . . The whole division was most beautifully turned out, and might have been in barracks for the last three months instead of having marched over 1,200 miles.'

It was scarcely surprising that after all these travels and a four week absence from Britain Churchill succumbed on his return to pneumonia; 'Of course, I work wherever I am and however I am. That is what does me good'.

The Strains Intensify

In North West Africa Britain had three times as many men and four times as many ships as America but served under an American commander. This surprised Marshall, amongst others, but Churchill was quite frank in saying that it was a price worth paying for the adoption of his Mediterranean Strategy. In any event, he knew that in reality it was Alexander and not Eisenhower who was directing the battle.

There are telegrams in which the Allied Supreme Commander poignantly asks Alexander for 'the essentials of your broad tactical plan' and Churchill pointed to the nature of their relationship when he talked of asking Alex to go 'through the ceremonial processes'. Harold Macmillan, at this stage attached to Eisenhower's headquarters, said with some condescension that the role of the British was to run the American empire in the same way as 'the Greek slaves ran the operations of the Emperor Claudius'. Not only did the Greeks, in Macmillan's view, have better brains than the Romans; they were also better at fighting.

Alexander's appreciation of the American II Corps which had been defeated at the Kasserine Pass was, 'soft, green and untrained . . . I handed them a victory on a plate, but their hands were too weak to take it'. Eisenhower, Bedell Smith, his Chief of Staff, and Patton, the Corps Commander, 'are not professional soldiers, not as we understand that term'. But he stressed that the British must be careful not to imply any superiority: the two nations must suffer together and conquer together.[1]

Not all Britons were so circumspect. The American Ralph Ingersoll, planning OVERLORD on the Anglo-American staff of COSSAC (Chief Of Staff to the Supreme Allied Commander), reported that his countrymen were frankly told by their allies, many of whom had served with American units in Africa, ' "But you chaps simply haven't the commanders. Look how long it took us to find Montgomery – and you have only just begun your war" . . . They really believed this.'[2]

COSSAC was headed by the British Lieutenant-General Frederick Morgan, whose title was 'Chief of Staff to the Supreme Allied Commander (Designate)'. It was a pretty nebulous body, with Morgan acting as a Chief of Staff to an SAC who did not yet exist. Its responsibility was to plan the invasion of north-west Europe. Within COSSAC, support was divided between landing on the Pas de Calais and to the north of the Cotentin peninsula. The split was on a national basis: the Americans were for the second option, the British for the first, and Morgan did not think much of either. Mountbatten resolved the deadlock by inviting the planners to his HQ at Largs in Scotland, where the American view prevailed. Morgan presented the plan, which Churchill immediately named OVERLORD, in May 1943.

Difficulties and tensions between the British and American components of COSSAC persisted. The Americans had a sense of inferiority when they dealt with their British counterparts, whom they recognised to be able and intelligent and, above all, more experienced.[3] The Americans represented an army that had never fought a battle.

As well as having military experience, the British officers were well versed in the techniques of politics and obstruction. According to the Americans the British deployed a variety of techniques to ensure that their wishes prevailed. Rank was pulled, there was a delicate manipulation of agenda, American newcomers were seduced by a charm offensive, and if that failed to work were neutralised by being sent home on some pretext. Added to all that, the plan for OVERLORD, 113 pages long with ten maps, was written exclusively in British military terms, and frequently left the Americans bemused. 'To maintain' meant 'to keep in repair' to the Americans, but as a British military term of art meant 'to supply'. 'Lift' was not a verb: it meant the fleet required to move forces and supplies to France. 'Hard' was not an adjective but a noun, meaning a beach paved to accept the loading and unloading of landing craft.

It seems clear that the British were concerned to obscure who was to be in charge of the invasion. While there was to be a Supreme Allied Commander, the British emphasised that he would not actually command. His function was largely to be political, presiding over an Anglo-American military authority, and negotiating with the governments in exile in Britain. Military decisions would be made by the Combined Chiefs.[4] The Americans had no difficulty in concluding that if in any event even two of the three Commanders-in-Chief were British, OVERLORD could be varied or even postponed at Churchill's whim. In fact Morgan argued that since the ultimate superiority of American power dictated that the Supreme Commander would be American, all three Commanders-in-Chief should be British. He pointed out that the British Commanders had a monopoly of experience in waging the war.

On his recovery from his pneumonia, just after Montgomery's success at Wadi Akarit, where 6,000 prisoners were taken, Churchill was astounded to learn that Eisenhower had decided not to follow up the expected success in Tunisia with an immediate invasion of Sicily – because he had discovered that there were not just the expected six Italian divisions there, but also two German divisions. He was following the advice of an appraisal by the British Joint Planning Committee, but Alexander and others had already rejected it. Churchill was horrified at the reaction to a mere two divisions. His comment was perceptive: 'This is an example of the fatuity of planning staffs playing upon each other's fears, each service presenting its difficulties at the maximum, and Americans and Englishmen vying with each other, in the total absence of one directing mind and commanding willpower'. That is not just Churchilliage: it is a fair assessment of the conservative inclinations of a series of different agencies yoked together, no one of them wishing to be responsible for accepting a necessary risk.

Churchill's philosophy in regard to the Joint Planning Committee encapsulates precisely his feelings in relation to the British Chiefs of Staff. If the Chiefs of Staff had not been faced with his directing mind and commanding willpower, the war would not have been won as it was, however infuriating and exhausting his presence could be.

His energising arguments won the day and the British Chiefs of Staff, and the American Joint Chiefs, agreed with him: the landings were to go ahead. But difficulties remained. The British Chiefs decided that the landing craft earmarked for cross-Channel landings would be required for Sicily and that accordingly if Sicily went ahead it would do so at the expense of any cross-Channel venture in 1943. This was not what the Americans wanted. On the one occasion that 'Jakey' Devers, the senior American member of COSSAC, was invited to dine with Churchill, the Prime Minister told him that Sicily was going to be a cheap victory. 'That's what the world wants, cheap victories.' Devers is reported to have replied, 'If you will forgive me, sir, I think that's bunk. I think one squad of soldiers on the Channel coast of France will mean more to the world than two armies ashore in Sicily'.[5]

Churchill decided that to force Sicily forward he had to meet FDR again: another example of a conference decision requiring clarification and confirmation. He left for America and the Third Washington Conference on board the *Queen Mary* and on 7 May heard the news of the capture of Tunis and then Bizerta. On 10 May the church bells rang, or possibly rang again, depending on whether or not General Kennedy's recollection was accurate. All North Africa was now in Allied hands and 240,000 prisoners had been taken. Alex signalled to the Prime Minister: 'Sir, it is my duty to report that the Tunisian campaign is over. All enemy resistance has ceased. We are masters of the North African shores.'

38

TRIDENT

When Churchill, *en route* for his meeting with Roosevelt, heard that a German submarine was going to cross the *Queen Mary's* path, he ordered that a machine-gun be put in his lifeboat. He told Averell Harriman, 'I won't be captured. The finest way to die is the excitement of fighting the enemy.' Then a pause and the disarming touch that made him so irresistible: 'It might not be so nice if one were in the water and they tried to pick me up'.

Despite his age and encroaching infirmities, Churchill loved these high-level trips and conferences. But one must not lose sight of the fact that they were absolutely necessary for the effective prosecution of the war. Some American planners were now arguing strenuously for the Pacific and not Sicily for summer 1943. Indeed landing craft for Sicily were no longer being transferred from the Far East. Churchill told Hopkins that he was 'conscious of the serious divergences beneath the surface' before he left for this Washington conference, TRIDENT. But he still had a stock of goodwill with FDR and once at the White House he was able to persuade the President that Sicily should proceed and should be followed by the invasion of Italy, HUSKY. He did not have to do a great deal of persuading. Sicily had been more or less agreed on at Casablanca, and was logically pretty inevitable.

A lot of ground that had already been covered at Casablanca was covered again at TRIDENT, partly because Admiral Leahy, Chairman of the American Chiefs, had been absent from the earlier conference. More generally, the Americans, sensitive to the feeling that they had been outmanoeuvred at earlier meetings, had begun to gain confidence and to speak out. They were as well represented as the British and backed up by rows of aides and assistants. The record was very much in mind, and the result was unproductive and formal. Best results were achieved when the Chairman of the day proposed an adjournment to an off-the-record meeting of the Chiefs alone. The process tended to reduce tensions. It was frequently necessary.

From now on these high-level meetings were increasingly fraught and difficult. The 76-year-old Secretary for War, Stimson, was particularly difficult. He personalised the argument and claimed that Churchill was obsessed by a Balkan strategy to redress the historical record of the Dardanelles. He did not reduce mutual confusion by conflating ROUNDUP and SLEDGEHAMMER, and referring repeatedly to 'Operation Roundhammer'.

An unwelcome feature of TRIDENT was a renewed attempt, led as usual by Admiral King, to displace Germany First with a Pacific policy which would be followed until victory in the east, even if Britain were out of the war by then. The atmosphere was not pleasant. Americans charged the British with being half-hearted about ROUNDUP; Britons said that there was not much hope for ROUNDUP since American soldiers were not arriving in Britain at the agreed rate – by now there should have been 80,000; there were only 15,000. Even Marshall said that it might be better to put the Pacific first if Britain intended to 'waste time in the Mediterranean'.[1] But at the end of the day Germany remained first, even though all that could be done for the moment would be in North Africa or from its shores. There was neither time before the autumnal storms nor available resources to mount ROUNDUP, now transmuting into OVERLORD, in 1943. In the event Sicily, HUSKY, did not conclude until August 1943, the month originally planned for OVERLORD. The decision at TRIDENT was for a definite launch of OVERLORD in May 1944.

That left the Allies with the question of what to do in the meantime. The answer was to be Italy, which forward troops could already see from Sicily. It was an obvious decision, but it exacerbated tensions between Britain and America. A major division in strategic thinking led to exasperation and a growing conviction among the Americans that Britain was not really onside, and that her views must often simply be ignored and overridden.

It was agreed at TRIDENT that if Italy had fallen by the end of August (which proved to be a vain hope), further operations would be in that theatre, the Balkans or southern Europe.

Back in Britain the War Cabinet was always much bolder when they did not have to deal with Churchill face to face. While he was in Washington he decided on a military occupation of the Azores, which belonged to Portugal, Britain's traditional ally but neutral in this war.

There was quite a prolonged battle on the point, which Eden and the Cabinet won, preferring diplomacy to military occupation.

As everyone expected, Stalin reacted angrily to the news that there would be no cross-Channel landing in 1943. Churchill suggested a meeting, ideally at Scapa Flow. Roosevelt did not reply immediately to this proposal, but when Churchill said he would write direct to Stalin if he heard nothing more, the President jumped in to forestall the initiative. He said that he had only just received Stalin's letter, which was quite simply not the case.

Roosevelt was crystal-clear that he would not be attending a meeting in Britain. America's remarkable sensitivity to any suggestion that they were being manipulated by their closest allies continued to make a meeting on British soil unthinkable. In any event, Roosevelt had other ideas in mind. He had wanted for some time to meet Stalin independently and to achieve an 'intimate understanding' with him.[2]

In May 1943 Roosevelt's emissary, Joseph E. Davies, told Stalin that his boss and Churchill did not see eye to eye on everything. They differed, for example, on colonialism. He tried to arrange a meeting à deux between Stalin and Roosevelt in Alaska. Churchill discovered this at the end of June 1943.

He had to accept that increasingly his relationship with Roosevelt was not going to be an exclusive one, but he was entirely against a one-to-one Roosevelt–Stalin meeting, which he said bore no comparison to his meeting with the Russian leader in 1942 'on an altogether lower level'. Roosevelt simply claimed that it was not his idea at all, but Stalin's: 'I did not suggest to U[ncle] J[oe] that we meet alone'; it had all been 'Uncle Joe's' idea. More baloney: from intelligence sources Churchill knew this was not true. But Uncle Joe put an end to the whole matter by writing again to both men in such bitter terms that the idea of a meeting disappeared.

In the course of his visit Churchill had also to deal with the fact that America had broken her agreement to exchange information regarding the atomic project.

Churchill was concerned that America planned to attack Sardinia after Sicily and before Italy, an exercise which would consume time and resources without any significant benefit. But despite all the problems and untruths, by the time TRIDENT concluded on 25 May he had got much of what he had come for. It says much for his magnanimity and the breadth of his outlook that these divergences and differences did not colour his view of his allies or narrow the width of his vision. That vision remained large, romantic, idealistic and hopeful. He felt that the future would be marked by closer and closer convergence with America. At a lunch in the British Embassy in the course of TRIDENT, he said that there could be little hope for the future without the 'fraternal association' of Britain and the United States:

> I should like the citizens of each, without losing their present nationality, to be able to come and settle and trade with freedom and equal rights in the territories of the other. There might be common passport, or a special form of passport or visa. There might be some form of common citizenship . . .

He developed these ideas further in a speech at Harvard on 6 September 1943.

Now he flew to Algiers to put heart into Eisenhower and the American planners. There Churchill's thinking was based on the information then coming from Ultra, which indicated that Germany planned to pull out of Italy and retire to the Alps. The flaw in the strategy which he advocated was that Germany was to change her position. Just a few months later, in October 1943, Hitler told Kesselring to defend Italy south of Rome. Churchill's plan at Algiers was not to move through Italy into the Balkans, but rather to use the country as a base. Eisenhower listened to his arguments over dinner and on the following day agreed that if Sicily went well, then the next attack should indeed be on mainland Italy. Critics who claim that Churchill did not have a coherent Mediterranean Strategy should observe a policy of coherent Mediterranean opportunism. What he urged at Algiers was part of it.

The opportunity to reflect on broad issues of strategy was often interrupted by difficulties among his French allies. But while Churchill was at Algiers there was a brief rapprochement between Giraud and de Gaulle when they became co-presidents of the FCNL. Churchill told Roosevelt in a telegram of 4 June, 'The bride and bridegroom have at last physically embraced. I am entertaining the new committee at lunch today, but I will not attempt to mar the domestic bliss by any intrusions of my own'.

The First Quebec Conference: QUADRANT

Intensive bombing on Sicilian airfields began on 3 July 1943 and landings were scheduled for 10 July. Churchill sat up through the night, playing bezique, but periodically breaking off to say, 'So many brave young men going to their deaths tonight. It is a grave responsibility.'

Even before Sicily had been captured he decided that he had to return to see Roosevelt again to consolidate the Italian venture. He wanted to see Italy occupied at least as far as Rome, and then used as a base to liberate the Balkans. Events were encouraging: Mussolini fell from power on 25 July and the news was greeted in Britain with great enthusiasm. The news reached Chequers where the Prime Minister was watching cartoon films. Fitzroy Maclean was present and reported that Churchill rose to relay the news '[a]s the squawking of Pluto and the baying of Donald Duck died away'.[1] In public Churchill played the news down: the real enemy had never been Mussolini, but Hitler. All the same, he told Roosevelt that he would be happy to deal with any non-fascist government in Italy that would allow the Allies to enter the country and to fight the Germans from there.

He boarded the *Queen Mary* on 4 August and, with the usual large contingent of some 300 persons, sailed for the conference in Quebec, with a side-trip to Hyde Park.

At Quebec he was told by Alex that the whole of Sicily had now been captured: 'The last German soldier was flung out of Sicily and the whole island is now in our hands.' But the campaign had not gone altogether smoothly. There had been disputes between Monty and Patten, as Monty tried to take over routes of advance that had been assigned to the latter. As so often, this lack of diplomacy did not tend to Montgomery's benefit. Patten did not go out of his way thereafter to assist him, and moved independently towards Palermo. Monty's heart was not wholly in the Sicilian campaign. He considered Italy to be an irrelevance and was not upset to leave Italy at the end of 1943 and come back to

England to command 21st Army Group. Eisenhower's control of Sicily was very loose, and Alexander was too sensitive to political issues to restrain Patten, who wanted the kudos of capturing notable towns rather than strategic features. Because the British Eighth Army and Seventh US Army did not, as planned, operate together, the Germans were able to escape from the island.

The purpose of QUADRANT, the First Quebec Conference, then, was to assess the Mediterranean situation and Italy in particular. Churchill was very apprehensive that the United States was not prepared to follow up Sicily with a serious Italian campaign. At TRIDENT the decision had been that resources were to be concentrated on OVERLORD, but the speed of events after HUSKY encouraged the British to hope that this decision might now be reconsidered. Churchill was pre-empted by the American Secretary of War, Stimson, who had just returned from a European tour, and got at the President first. The burden of the Anglophobe Stimson's report was that the British were entirely un-committed to a massive landing:

> The difference between us is a vital difference of faith . . . We cannot now rationally hope to come to be able to cross the Channel and come to grips with our German enemy under a British commander. His Prime Minister and his Chief of the Imperial General Staff are frankly at variance with such a proposal. The shadows of Passchen-daele and Dunkerque still hang too heavily over the imagination of these leaders of his Government. Though they have rendered lip-service to the operation, their hearts are not in it, and it will require more independence, more faith, and more vigor than it is reasonable to find in any British commander to overcome the natural difficulties of such an operation carried out in such an atmosphere of his government.

The American chiefs feared that FDR might be nobbled by the Prime Minister when he visited Hyde Park before the conference proper. They need not have worried: the President accepted Stimson's position. It was now inevitable that there would be an American commander for OVERLORD, and that there would be no significant retention of troops in Italy.

But Churchill did secure an important concession from Roosevelt at the conference: there would at least be no immediate troop movements from Italy – indeed Alexander would be allowed landing craft for an

Istrian landing. That did not mean that there were not heated discussions. In the light of HUSKY's success Britain had imposed a standstill on naval movements in the area. The Americans took serious exception to this unilateral breach of the TRIDENT decision, and it was soon countermanded.

Again, Brooke said that the British did not mean to divert divisions from OVERLORD, but then qualified that statement: there would be no diversions – *except* to the extent that this would pull German divisions away from the landing area. This provoked such bitterness that the CIGS, who was chairing the conference, proposed a break for an off-the-record meeting of the Chiefs alone. Here the air was cleared a bit, as he told the Americans that there had to be more of an atmosphere of trust. The Americans thought that Britain was against OVERLORD; the British thought the Americans were so rigidly wedded to it that they would ignore the possibility of capitalising on success elsewhere. Brooke sought to demonstrate that Britain was fully committed to the landings, but believed that success would obviously depend in part on the strengths of the opposing forces in the theatre. Operations in the Mediterranean would reduce German strength in the north, and thus OVERLORD and the Mediterranean were not mutually exclusive but mutually dependent. This was phase two of Brooke's Mediterranean Strategy, and he had great difficulty in getting Marshall to accept it. At the end of the day he appeared to do so, but many of Marshall's compatriots continued to suspect that Britain would still try to slip out of the commitment.

The misunderstandings, the allegations of bad faith, were all the more regrettable in that they flowed from no more than a difference of emphasis. Almost all on the British side had worries about OVERLORD, although some were less ready than others to share them with the Americans. When Churchill expressed his concerns in a minute to the COS on 19 October 1943,[2] Brooke agreed with him. There was a general concern that victories in the Mediterranean were not being followed up. There seemed to be a real risk that they would be thrown away by a premature conflict on the Atlantic seaboard, which Germany, with her logistical advantages there, would easily win. But no one doubted that ultimately the last great offensive of the war would take place there.

The outcome of the Quebec conference after some sharp disagreements and hard bargaining was a series of compromises. Essentially the Americans saw Churchill's advocacy of Italy as hiding a desire to avoid a cross-Channel landing in its entirety. For the Americans the main Allied effort in 1944 should consist of landings on the Atlantic coast of France, and this was to be reflected in any 1943 decisions about the Mediterranean theatre. The American Chiefs also wanted to draw pressure away from the Channel coast by landings in the south of France. This was agreed to, and would later prove a source of considerable dissension. Churchill increasingly felt that the Italian campaign was fulfilling the same object in a more logical way, and a way that offered possibilities of subsequent development.

Italy was downgraded, in order to limit its drain on supplies, by confining the advance to the line Pisa–Ancona. Operations in the Balkans were to be similarly limited to supplying partisans and the minor use of commando forces. On the other hand Churchill secured Roosevelt's agreement to leaving Japan aside until Germany had been defeated. The primacy of the German war, so important for Britain, could still not be taken for granted.

A Supreme Commander had to be chosen for the cross-Channel invasion, and it was now that the promise to Brooke was revoked, apparently on a whim, and without consulting or warning Brooke: 'Not for one moment did he realise . . .'

Churchill's motives for agreeing so readily to the change, indeed pretty well suggesting it, were complex. He feared that the European landings might be a disaster akin to one of the great First World War offensives, and he preferred that an American commander should take the blame. If Roosevelt had declined the proposal that the commander should be American, no one could blame Britain for what happened. Secondly, he reckoned that if the OVERLORD Commander were American, then the Mediterranean commander would be British and he was very anxious that he should have an intimate control over events in the Mediterranean. When it was rumoured that Marshall, the assumed commander of OVERLORD, might be in charge of the Mediterranean as well, Churchill moved fast to scupper the scheme, which would have conflicted with the principle of equality between the Western allies as well as taking the Mediterranean out of his portfolio.

The American perception that Churchill was not wholly committed to OVERLORD increasingly informed their approach to planning and its legacy was to detach them from the closest of cooperation even on other issues for the rest of the war. After the war the view remained in America that Britain – or at least the Prime Minister – would always have shelved a full-scale invasion given the chance. The view is wrong: the only real divergence was on a question of timing and scale. Of course, if an alternative that was certain of success and cheaper in lives had turned up, Churchill would have preferred it.

It is worth remembering that there were others whose views were even stronger than his. Smuts managed to persuade the King that the Mediterranean was a more promising sphere of activity, and Churchill was summoned to a dinner at the palace with the King and Smuts on 14 October to discuss the question. He had already told Smuts and now told the King that 'There is no possibility of our going back on what is agreed. Both the US and Stalin would violently disagree with us'. Even among the Chiefs of Staff it was felt that a doctrinaire commitment to OVERLORD was neglecting opportunities that might exist elsewhere – for instance in the Balkans. At a meeting of the Chiefs of Staff on 19 October (Smuts present) there was little dissension. Brooke spoke of the dangers of fighting on the basis of 'lawyer's contracts', and Churchill summed up saying that 'It was clear that if we [and not the Americans] were in a position to decide the future strategy of the war we should agree

(i) To reinforce the Italian theatre to the full.

(ii) To enter the Balkans.

(iii) To hold our position in the Aegean Islands.

(iv) To build up our airforces and intensify our air attacks on Germany.

(v) To encourage a steady assembly in this country of United States troops, which could not be employed in the Pacific owing to the shortage of shipping, with a view to taking advantage of the softening in the enemy's resistance due to our operations in other theatres, though this might not occur until after the spring of 1944.[3]

Behind all of this was the feeling that OVERLORD was too inflexible, that its planning required an unnecessarily early withdrawal of troops and landing craft from the Mediterranean, and that although it might be possible to establish a bridgehead in Northern France, the German lines of communication were so good that there could be a repulse on a far, far greater scale than that of Dieppe. These concerns were reflected in a long telegram Churchill sent to Roosevelt on 23 October.[4]

Churchill's reservations about OVERLORD have to be seen against the fact that at the time of the Quebec Conference the resources allocated to

the invasion were scanty. Morgan's planners had been allowed very
limited numbers of men and quantities of shipping. Any possibility of
attacking a substantial port had been discounted, and all that was
envisaged was an invasion of Normandy by three divisions on a front of
thirty miles. A landing on this scale was fraught with risk. Early in 1944,
much more substantial operations were planned by Ike and Monty. At
Quebec, Churchill prevailed on Marshall to accept an increase to four
and a half divisions, but it was hardly surprising that he was apprehensive about an assault on the Atlantic Wall with such meagre
resources.

When the Quebec Conference ended on 24 August, Churchill was
dismayed to hear that Eden, Brooke, Portal and Mountbatten were all
to fly home on the same flying boat. He told Eden, 'I don't know what I
should do if I lost you all. I'd have to cut my throat. It isn't just love,
though there is much of that in it, but you are my war machine.
Brookie, Portal, you and Dickie, I simply couldn't replace you.'

After the end of the conference, Churchill spent some more time in
America, partly on holiday at a fishing camp in the Laurentian
Mountains, partly at Washington, and partly in Boston, where he
received an honorary degree from Harvard. He remained closely in
touch with the conduct of the war. Italy's new Prime Minister, Pietro
Badoglio, signed an armistice with the Allies on 23 September 1943,
but before then Mussolini had been rescued from prison and established
a new fascist government at Lake Garda on 15 September.

Eventually Italy was invaded. Landings of British and Canadian
forces at Messina took place on 2 September and a week later Allied
troops landed at Salerno; on the other hand, on the previous night the
Germans occupied Rome.

Exasperation in the Aegean

Churchill was increasingly applying his mind to post-war issues. What was to be done with Germany? Was it to be divided, and if so how? On 5 September he wrote to Smuts, saying, 'I think it inevitable that Russia will be the greatest land power in the world after this war will have rid her of the two military powers, Germany and Japan, who in our lifetime have inflicted upon her such heavy defeats.' He hoped that there would be 'a friendly balance with Russia at least for the period of rebuilding'. Beyond that he was not so sure.[1]

At the same time, he was involved in more immediate strategic planning. He agreed with Roosevelt on 9 September that if Allied troops enjoyed speedy success in Italy, substantial aid could go to the partisans and the Balkans. He remained convinced of the utility of operations in that area. Roosevelt responded with the generalisation that 'we should be prepared to take advantage of any opportunity that presented itself'. Whether that meant much is debatable.

The landings at Salerno by Clark's Fifth Army went badly, and the invading troops were almost repulsed. Churchill was horribly reminded of Gallipoli. He telegraphed to Alexander with his memories of defeat at Suvla Bay where Sir Ian Hamilton had remained remote from the action. 'I feel it my duty to set before you this experience of mine from the past'. Alexander had already risen to the occasion and was on the beachhead. He quietly told Clark that his Corps commander, Ernest J. Dawley, appalled him: 'I do not want to interfere with your business, but I have some ten years' experience in this game of sizing up commanders. I can tell you definitely that you have a broken reed on your hands, and I suggest you replace him immediately.'

The Prime Minister left Halifax for the Clyde on 14 September, on board the battleship *Renown*. Among those on board was Dudley Pound. He was suffering from brain cancer and his health was poor and deteriorating. He handed Churchill his letter of resignation as they travelled by train to London. At Euston Station he was met by an ambulance, which took him to the Royal Masonic Hospital. Churchill visited him there on 8 October, on his way to Chequers, and at the King's request placed the insignia of the Order of Merit in his hands. Pound could not speak, but recognised the Prime Minister and grasped his hand. He died on 21 October, Trafalgar Day.

The First Sea Lord, A.V. Alexander, nominated the obvious successor, Admiral of the Fleet Sir Andrew Cunningham. Churchill tried hard to resist Cunningham's appointment. 'Winston never forgave ABC for Alexandria', said Admiral Royer Dick, who served with ABC throughout the war.[2]

Cunningham was independently minded, and had shown this when Churchill interfered at the time of Crete, but after Sir Bruce Fraser, the Admiral commanding the Home Fleet, had turned down the appointment ('I believe I have the confidence of my own fleet. Cunningham has the confidence of the whole navy'). Cunningham got the job, tolerated but not liked. He was, like Wavell and Auchinleck, spectacularly tongue-tied: a handicap in dealing with an articulate virtuoso.

At sea, Cunningham had performed well; now, on land he proved disappointing. He and Churchill never got on. He prided himself on his independent mind. He criticised Churchill for allegedly not truly understanding the use of sea-power and he cannot have relished the fact that Churchill certainly did give pre-eminence in his strategic thinking in the Second World War to the army and considered moreover that the navy was a particularly closed and conservative profession.

Soon after reaching London, Churchill had to face claims in the Commons that the delay in the landings on mainland Italy had been due to negotiations about Badoglio's appointment. He explained the need for time to prepare landing craft. 'When I hear people talking in an airy way of throwing modern armies ashore here and there as if they were bales of goods to be dumped on a beach and forgotten, I really marvel at the lack of knowledge that still prevails of conditions of modern war'. His response was delicious. What he was saying was exactly what the Chiefs so often said about him.

Difficulties with the Chiefs continued. One of the high points in the turbulent relationship arose early in the following month, when he proposed on 7 October that the island of Rhodes should be seized. The Joint Planning Committee had submitted a plan on 6 October for an attack on the island, which involved moving forces out of the adjacent island of Kos. Churchill was excited by the adventure and called for his plane to be prepared so that he could fly to Tunis and obtain troops from Eisenhower.

No one shared his enthusiasm. Brooke despaired: 'I can control him no more. He has worked himself into a frenzy of excitement about the Rhodes attack, has magnified its importance so that he can no longer see anything else and has set himself on capturing this one island even at the expense of endangering his relations with the President and the Americans and the future of the Italian campaign. He refused to listen to any arguments or to see any dangers.' Roosevelt vetoed the proposal and forbade any switching of resources from Italy or OVERLORD. Churchill responded by saying that the Rhodes landing craft would be back in Britain nearly six months before they would be needed for OVERLORD. Roosevelt was unmoveable. Churchill's secretary, Marian Holmes, recorded his sense of frustration: 'The PM said he had had a bad day, a very bad day. In a rather confiding way he said, "The difficulty is not in winning the war; it is in persuading people to let you win it – persuading fools". He seemed distressed and said he felt "almost like chucking it in". He had been trying to persuade the Americans to invade Rhodes'.[3]

The aphorism about winning the war naturally goes with what he said to Brooke on 1 April 1945 about allies: 'There is only one thing worse than fighting with allies, and that is fighting without them!' But on both occasions he was not just throwing around *bon mots*. He was genuinely frustrated and even hurt that opportunities, as he saw it, were being lost. If they had been rejected after due discussion he would have accepted the position easily enough. What was so galling was that repeatedly for the rest of the war America would not even give proper consideration to arguments that he put to her.

How important the Dodecanese were, either in themselves or as a diversion of men and materials from other projects, must be very questionable. When Churchill heard that Jumbo Wilson was in favour of occupying them he was excited by the opportunity. It was just the sort of combined naval and army operation that appealed to his sense of history. He ignored Wilson's warning that nothing could be done immediately because of lack of resources. He sent a personal signal: 'Good. This is the time to play high. Improvise and dare.' The Chiefs of Staff were told, 'Here is a business of great consequence to be thrust through by any means . . . Immense prizes at little cost, though not at little risk'. The Germans certainly thought the islands were important enough to merit counter-action.

The appeal of the venture to Churchill seems to have had much to do with eighteenth-century history and derring-do. He sent a signal to Wilson on 13 September: 'The capture of Rhodes by you at this time with Italian aid would be a fine contribution to the general war. Let me know what are your plans for this. Can you not improvise the necessary garrison out of the forces in the Middle East? What is your total ration strength? This is the time to think of Clive and Peterborough and of Rooke's men taking Gibraltar'.

That historical allusion pretty well sums up the Dodecanese caper, Churchill's last romantic frolic. It offered little prospect of altering the outcome of the war, and was not without its moments of farce. Major the Earl of Jellicoe arrived at the headquarters of Admiral Campioni, the Italian commander of Rhodes, bringing a personal letter from Jumbo Wilson. Fearing capture when he landed on the island, he had swallowed it, leaving him suffering from acute thirst and nausea. When he asked Campioni to throw in his lot with the British he had difficulty in making himself understood as a result of the obstruction in his throat. A high price was paid for these adventures in terms of British losses, and those Italians who supported the attempted seizure and were captured were summarily shot.

The Dodecanese scheme was pretty much Churchill's own, and is one of his failures. The pity about it, after the needless loss of life, is that it was not a good issue on which to test the American connection. Pushing hard for a fairly obviously flawed operation lost him credibility and goodwill in the States, and meant that less attention was paid thereafter to better proposals.

The Dodecanese issue rankled with Churchill. After the war he criticised Ike as having been 'obdurate' and 'unreasonable' in the matter and he said of Roosevelt that 'This was the only ungenerous act which I experienced in our long military partnership'. He was unfair to Ike, who had done what he could for Churchill at the time. Opposition to the plan stemmed as much from his own Chiefs of Staff as from FDR's advisers.[4] Brooke allowed himself to be exceptionally critical of Churchill in relation to the Dodecanese, but he too could be excited by Mediterranean opportunism and opportunities in the Balkans.[5]

On 24 October Alexander was at Eisenhower's headquarters, and expressed doubts about OVERLORD. He recorded his worries about the expected strength of German resistance. Eisenhower summarised the meeting in a lengthy document. It consisted of four parts, the first three expressive of the doubts and dangers, but the fourth part consisting of an optimistic conclusion. Churchill forwarded only the three unfavour-able bits to Eden, who was in Moscow, for use in negotiations with Stalin. The Americans discovered what he had done and were furious. Stimson said it revealed 'how determined Churchill is with all his lip service to stick a knife in the back of OVERLORD'. Hopkins and Roosevelt were equally angry, the latter describing what Churchill had done as 'improper'.[6]

In contrast with OVERLORD, Italy continued to seem to Churchill to be full of potential. According to Cadogan, he was prepared to resign if the Italian campaign were deprived of adequate resources. He may have threatened to do so, but he would never have carried out his threat. He was conscious that he could get away with as much as he did over Italy only because there was a preponderance of British forces on the battlefield. Things might be different later. He told the War Office in November 1943 that he wished to say to the Americans that 'We will match you man for man and gun for gun on the battlefront' in OVERLORD. In the event, American forces on all fronts did not equal those of Britain until a month after D-Day.

Eden's mission to Moscow was to try to persuade Stalin that it might be well to capitalise on the Italian opportunities by delaying the cross-Channel landing. It was bitterly galling for Churchill and the Chiefs of Staff, who were at one with him on this matter, to see troops being removed from Italy, where there was a job to be done, in contemplation of cross-Channel landings whose outcome would be doubtful. It was to this sort of situation that Churchill referred when he talked about battles being 'governed by lawyers' agreements made in all good faith months before, and persisted in without regard to the ever-changing fortunes of war'.

Two British divisions in Sicily, which could have been used in Italy, were moved back to Britain in October for use in OVERLORD, still more than six months away. Another two divisions were about to go, together with four American divisions. Allied landing craft which could have been used as part of an assault on Rome were also about to be transferred until Eisenhower declared that without these landing craft his advance on Rome would be delayed until January or February 1944: the American Joint Chiefs gave the landing craft a stay of execution of just one month. The effect of the withdrawals was to reduce Allied strength in Italy from twenty-three divisions to eleven, and the ratio of Allied to German troops from 24:10 to 14:10.

As the cross-Channel landings approached, so the tensions between the allies increased. When and where and indeed whether the landings should take place mattered greatly to Churchill and Roosevelt; but the issue was of far greater importance to the third ally, Stalin, whose people continued to pour out their blood on an unimaginable scale, and for whom a second front was not an academic issue to be debated among strategists. Fairly amazingly, there had not yet been any meeting at which the Big Three were all present. Churchill had shuttled back and forth across the Atlantic and to Moscow, but Roosevelt and Stalin had never met.

It was now impossible to postpone a meeting further. The three great allies agreed to meet at Teheran at the end of November 1943.

Teheran

The relationship between Prime Minister and President was now more complicated than in the hands-across-the-sea days of ARCADIA. While the joshing and joviality still appeared on the surface, currents of suspicion and exasperation flowed below. The advisers and experts who swam in these deeper waters were particularly aware of these disturbances. On both sides there was a mood of distrust and suspicion.

Before Churchill and Roosevelt could meet Stalin at Teheran to consider the global conspectus, they had to sort out their internal difficulties over Italy. They agreed to have preliminary talks at Cairo – though a shorter meeting than the Prime Minister wanted.

On 11 November, suffering from a heavy cold and sore throat, and feeling ill because of his inoculations for cholera and typhoid, Churchill once again boarded the *Renown*. While they were at sea it was calculated that by then Churchill had travelled 111,000 miles since the outbreak of war. In the course of talks with service chiefs while docked at Algiers, it was said that the Chiefs of Staff system was a good one. Churchill responded, 'Not at all. It leads to weak and faltering decisions – or rather indecisions. Why, you may take the most gallant sailor, the most intrepid airman, or the most audacious soldier, put them at a table together – what do you get? The sum total of their fears!'[1]

His next stop was Malta, where he was so ill that he spent two days in bed. He commiserated with Jumbo Wilson about the loss of Leros in the Dodecanese, where 5,000 British soldiers had been taken prisoner: 'Like you, I feel this is a serious loss and reverse, and, like you, I have been fighting with my hands tied behind my back'.

The two Western leaders met at Cairo on 25 November 1943. A proposal for an American European Chief was renewed and again repulsed. Churchill therefore assumed that Marshall would command OVERLORD and that Eisenhower would replace him in Washington as Chief of Staff. It was a complete surprise to learn, in the course of a sightseeing drive with Roosevelt in Cairo, that the President needed Marshall beside him in Washington, and that Eisenhower would command OVERLORD.

Roosevelt handled the change of Supreme Commander badly. A secret memorandum from Hopkins for the President dated 4 October 1943 treated the appointment of Marshall as a given, but went on to argue that he should have command of all the Allied forces at OVERLORD, American and British, on land, sea and air. Only the Russians would not be under his command. Marshall would have had enormous powers and responsibilities, of which OVERLORD itself would only be one component.

Hopkins had been prepared to concede direct command of OVERLORD itself to Montgomery 'in order to satisfy the British' but only 'in order to get our main objective of Marshall's command over the whole business.'² Inevitably, Churchill vetoed this proposal: he wanted the Mediterranean for Britain. After Churchill pretty well volunteered at Quebec that the Supreme Commander would be an American, there was no doubt in anyone's mind that the American would be Marshall. The choice seemed an inevitable one. In America Marshall's standing was unchallenged, even by Macarthur, and he was highly regarded in Britain, both at Cabinet level and by popular opinion. At this stage in the war he was infinitely better known to the British public than Eisenhower. From the point of view of the United States, they could rely on Marshall not to be pushed around by the British: Roosevelt was firmly of the view that Churchill did not greatly like Marshall because the latter could always get the better of him.

After Quebec, Marshall was indeed told that he would have the command, though retaining the office of Chief of Staff. Eisenhower would come back to Washington as Acting Chief of Staff. Mrs Marshall started to move their furniture out of the Chief of Staff's residence.

But Marshall's colleagues in Washington were not as keen to see the removal go ahead. King and Arnold seemed to have been motivated more by admiration than by envy, wanting to keep their colleague working with them in Washington. Admiral Leahy agreed. As King said, 'We have the winning combination here in Washington. Why break it up?' But until Teheran Marshall remained the prospective Supreme Commander. It was only on Sunday 5 December that things changed. On that day, Roosevelt made a momentous decision against the advice of his Chiefs of Staff, and of Hopkins and Stimson, and contrary to the preferences of Stalin and Churchill. He told Marshall that if he let him leave Washington 'I could not sleep at night with you out of the country'. Marshall took the decision with magnificent stoicism, although he was being deprived of the historic culmination of his career. He 'recalled saying that I would not attempt to estimate my capabilities; the President would have to do that; I merely wished to make clear that whatever the decision, I would go along with it wholeheartedly; that the issue was too great for any personal feeling to be considered'.[3] After Teheran and Cairo, Roosevelt flew to Tunis. When he met Eisenhower there he said, 'Well, Ike, you'd better start packing'. Ike thought he was referring to his move to Washington as Acting Chief of Staff.

The British view was that Ike was an inexperienced man, a political figurehead, and would not be the true military commander. The assumption sounds arrogant and condescending, but it was widely held. As Brooke said, 'We inserted under him one of our own commanders to deal with the military situations'. This was the 'stratosphere policy', which had been applied in the Mediterranean theatre. Rightly or wrongly, British senior officers had retained a fairly low opinion of their American counterparts from a professional point of view. Further, it seemed important for Britain, partly to inspire popular confidence, and partly simply to win the war, that Montgomery was seen to be the commander of the Allied land forces during the assault phase.

On the main issue at Cairo, Italy, Churchill received significant support from Eisenhower. Ike now wanted to make Italy a central part of Allied strategy, even wanting to go beyond Rome to 'the valley of the Po. In no other area could we so threaten the whole German structure including France, the Balkans and the Reich itself. Here also our airpower will be closer to vital objectives in Germany'. He went so far as to argue for the postponement of OVERLORD, wanting to continue 'the maximum possible operations in an established theatre.' Churchill could have written the script; but nothing was agreed before it was time for him and Roosevelt to fly on to Teheran.

When he arrived there, Churchill was too tired to dine with the other two. Roosevelt took advantage of his absence and arranged a meeting with Stalin for the following morning, an hour before the Big Three were due to meet. It was made perfectly clear to Churchill that FDR intended to deal with Stalin as an independent party, and he declined to consult with Churchill before his early morning meeting. Jacob recorded that Churchill was deeply upset by what he regarded as a disavowal of the concept of the English-speaking peoples as a combined force for good.[4]

The President's action did indeed conflict with many of his genial assurances. Churchill was to say, 'I realised for the first time what a very *small* country this is. On one hand the big Russian bear with its paws outstretched – on the other the great American elephant – & between them the poor little English donkey – who is the only one who knows the right way home'.[5] His position was invidious. Roosevelt, said Cadogan, 'promises everything that Stalin wants in the way of attack in the West, with the result that Winston, who has to be more honest, is becoming an object of suspicion to Stalin'.[6]

Roosevelt and his advisers came to Teheran determined to be done with British obstructions to OVERLORD once and for all. Relations between the two staffs had been poor enough at the pre-summit meeting in Cairo, but OVERLORD had not been the major topic there, and at Teheran the approach was not to debate but to manoeuvre. Roosevelt insisted that there should be no agenda. He opened the conference by setting out the OVERLORD plan to Stalin. Stalin grabbed at it: 'Make OVERLORD the basic operation for 1944'. Churchill was presented with a *fait accompli* and if he appeared unenthusiastic Stalin questioned Britain's courage. All this was achieved at an opening meeting so casually arranged that Marshall was not even aware of it; he had gone off sightseeing.

Hap Arnold noted how Stalin's manner towards the British, formerly reasonably cordial, was now 'half-humorous, half-scathing'.[7] At the plenary meeting on the second day, Roosevelt began by ignoring his British ally and talking exclusively to the Soviet delegation. Then he made jokes at the expense of Britain. Stalin smiled more and more at Churchill's discomfiture, and eventually he and Roosevelt openly burst out laughing.[8] It is clear that while Churchill frequently saw Stalin in an idealised light, and believed that he and the Russian got on well, Stalin had no great liking for him.[9] It was all very petty and mean-minded and far removed from the heroic aspirations of the early years of the war. No wonder Churchill told Moran that he was 'appalled by his own impotence' at Teheran.[10]

Brooke believed that Averell Harriman, now US ambassador to Russia, was briefing against Britain. Certainly, according to Elliot Roosevelt, his father came to the conference with the intention of indicating to Stalin that he regarded Churchill as something of an amusing irrelevance, and went to the conference dinner on 29

November with the intention of taking Stalin's side 'in any joshing dispute'. This culminated in Stalin's pretending to favour executing 50,000 key German personnel so that Germany could not embark on another war. According to Elliot Roosevelt, Churchill, affected by the number of toasts consumed as this prodigious meal, failed to recognise a joke and leaped to his feet to protest. The President intervened: 'As usual it seems to be my function to mediate this dispute. Clearly there must be some sort of compromise between your position, Mr Stalin, and that of my good friend the Prime Minister. Perhaps we could say that, instead of summarily executing fifty thousand war criminals, we should settle on a smaller number. Shall we say forty-nine thousand, five hundred?' Elliot Roosevelt says that he himself suggested it was all academic as between them the Allies would kill the 50,000 criminals and a good deal more in the course of the fighting. He claimed that he was attacked by Churchill for deliberately damaging relations between the allies, and that there were no more invitations to Chequers.[11]

Eden tried to defuse the situation and explain that it was a joke, but Churchill walked out and had to be pursued by Stalin and Molotov who brought him back to the table. In his history Churchill referred to Elliot Roosevelt's 'intrusion', and said that although he consented to return, he 'was not then, and am not now, fully convinced that all was chaff and there was no serious intent lurking behind.'[12]

Roosevelt had no embarrassment about the way he treated Churchill at the conference. 'The biggest thing achieved at Teheran', he said according to Elliot Roosevelt, 'was in making it clear to Stalin that the US and Great Britain were not allied in one common bloc against the Soviet Union. I think we've got rid of that idea, once and for all.'[13]

Privately, Churchill was very upset by Roosevelt's desertion at Teheran.[14] While he did not blame Roosevelt directly for distancing himself, he did speak of a climate of opinion among the American camp 'which seemed to wish to win Russian confidence even at the expense of coordinating the Anglo-American war effort'. It was very far from the way he thought things should be handled.

By now Roosevelt was thinking increasingly of the mechanics of regulating world affairs after the war. He wanted to make sure that Britain did not create a western European alliance, which would encourage Russia to form a bloc of eastern European nations. Such a series of alliances would militate against the success of the new, post-war organisation. He wanted to encourage understanding between Britain and Russia. At the same time, he personally wanted to charm

Stalin, and convince him that there was no concerted Anglo-American line against Russia. It was for this reason that he had initially refused to meet Churchill at Cairo ahead of the main conference and subsequently capitulated only to the extent of spending one day with him. At Teheran itself he did not see Churchill on his own until the fifth day. He spoke quite frankly to Stalin about his own differences with Britain. He also indicated his acquiescence in Stalin's territorial ambitions.[15] His policy, taken together with his failure to understand those ambitions, created ideal conditions for Stalin to pursue them.

On 28 November FDR, rather surprisingly, talked of an Allied advance to the north of Italy, and thence to the Danube. But in reality so far as America was concerned any attempts to delay or avoid OVERLORD were a waste of time. Whatever arguments Churchill put forward, Roosevelt had bought in to the unshakeable American belief that the deployment of very large numbers of troops in a major confrontation with the enemy was the way to win the war with a minimum loss of American lives. Marshall held strongly to this traditional American theory. He had been on Pershing's staff on the Western Front in the First World War, and looked on British efforts at the Dardanelles, in Salonika and in Palestine, for example, as wasteful dissipations of force.[16] Britain, and in particular Churchill, took a different view, conditioned by a different historical experience. Churchill had fretted throughout the First World War, frustrated and angered by what he saw as an unimaginative, attritional approach, that eschewed any flash of strategic insight in favour of leaving huge armies standing in the mud and 'chewing barbed wire in Flanders'.

Everything in Churchill's experience, as well as his nature, combined to urge him away from a strategy he had so deplored. As General Hollis observed, '[T]he memory of one million dead from the British Empire in the First World War – largely as a result of stupid frontal attacks and no imagination – hung heavily over every proposal. Their memory was the unseen visitor at every conference I attended.'[17]

Roosevelt thought moreover, not entirely fancifully, that Churchill's views were partly based on his concerns about the shape of post-war Europe. The prospect of Russian domination did not particularly interest the President, and certainly did not distress him unduly.[18]

Stalin of course preferred landings in Normandy to having western troops in competition with him in central Europe: he argued strongly against postponement of OVERLORD. At a full meeting on the afternoon of 30 November, it was agreed that OVERLORD should proceed as planned, in May 1944. With Stalin and Roosevelt in favour, that outcome had never really been in doubt. Stalin asked Churchill whether he really believed in OVERLORD. The reply was, 'It will be our stern duty to hurl across the Channel against the Germans every sinew of our strength'.

On the following day, 1 December, the talk was about what was to happen to Poland. Churchill was conscious that the invasion of Poland was the cause of the present war, and opinion at home in the United Kingdom took the fate of Poland very seriously indeed. On the other hand, he had much experience of dealing with the Poles in exile in London, and was conscious that 'we should never get the Poles to say they were satisfied. Nothing would satisfy the Poles'. He proposed to tell the London Poles that they would be wise to accept a deal by which they would receive about 300 square miles of Germany but would lose the city of Lvov to Russia. The minutes recorded that 'he was not prepared to make a great squawk about Lvov'. Roosevelt said, 'I don't care two hoots about Poland. Wake me up when we talk about Germany'.[19]

Roosevelt's Chief of Staff, Admiral Leahy, criticised the way Poland had been settled. Roosevelt's reply was not good enough: 'I know it, Bill – I know it. But it's the best I can do for Poland at this time'.[20]

His lack of interest in Poland was bizarre, given the reason for the outbreak for the war, and indeed its initial moral justification. It also represented a considerable move from his position in January 1942 when Stalin demanded of Eden that the West should recognise the 1941 frontiers of Russia, including the Baltic States and Poland up to the Curzon Line. Roosevelt and Hull responded with a reversion to Wilsonian principles of self-determination: there was to be no repetition of the secret territorial agreements of the First World War settlements at Paris and Versailles. Harry Hopkins conveyed this message to Churchill during his visit to London in April 1942, following up what Hull had already said.[21] But by Teheran, Roosevelt had privately told Stalin that the United States *did* accept Russia's claim to Poland as far as the Curzon Line. As far as the government of Poland was concerned, he was happy to leave matters on the vague basis that he hoped that Russia, Britain and the Poles themselves could sort something out.

He went further than failing to defend Poland's frontiers and autonomy: together with King Saud he tried to establish a Jewish state in Poland. Churchill insisted on Palestine. The President's final caprice was a spur of the moment decision. On the basis of liking the look of the young Shah of Persia, who made a formal, protocol visit with the present of a little rug for Eleanor, Roosevelt had a memorandum for discussion drawn up at top speed, guaranteeing Iran's independence and her control of her own economic interests – a remarkable intrusion into affairs that affected Britain greatly, and America not at all.[22]

On 2 December, Churchill flew to Cairo and tried, not for the first time, to persuade the Turkish president, İnönü, to join the Allies. İnönü declined to do so. By 9 December Churchill was feeling very ill but nonetheless flew on to Tunisia. Brooke recalled that '[He] sat on his suitcase in a very cold morning wind, looking like nothing on earth.' When he reached Eisenhower, near Carthage, intending to fly on to Italy, he gave up. He told Eisenhower, 'I am afraid I shall have to stay with you longer than I had planned. I am completely at the end of my tether and I cannot go on to the Front until I have recovered my strength.' By 12 December his temperature was 101 degrees and pneumonia was diagnosed. Against the advice of his doctors, he continued to work. Clementine flew out to be with him. Churchill received the news with emotion, but when Charles Wilson told her how pleased he had been, 'she smiled whimsically. "Oh, yes," she said, "he's very glad I've come, but in five minutes he'll forget I'm here." '[23]

Her husband told their daughter, Sarah, 'If I die, don't worry – the war is won'. He could see something appropriate about dying among the ruins of Carthage.

42

Marrakech and de Gaulle

At Carthage Churchill was very ill indeed. He was unable to leave his sickbed till 24 December when he had a conference about the provision of landing craft for Anzio. On the following day, Christmas Day, he had his first meal out of bed and he entertained the five Commanders-in-Chief to lunch. That evening there was a cocktail party, which he attended as if he had never been ill. By the following day he was well enough to dictate the doctors' medical bulletin for them. Despite their orders, he flew from Carthage to Marrakech on 27 December and remained there until 14 January.

Even at his illest – he had suffered a mild heart attack as well as pneumonia – he continued to work and control events. On New Year's Eve he gave a party for all ranks. After joining in singing *Auld Lang Syne*, he was heard to bellow to his wife, 'There's a wasp in my punch!'[1] And when he eventually was able to return to London and went to see the King, he disdained Sir Thomas ('Tommy') Lascelles' suggestion that he might use the lift. 'Lift?' he retorted, and 'Winston', Nicolson reported, 'ran up the stairs two at time. When he reached the top, he turned to Tommy and cocked a snook.'[2]

De Gaulle was unfortunately close to the sickbed, and did nothing to assist convalescence by declining to work with colleagues tainted by a Vichy past. Churchill refused to see him, and only backed down reluctantly when urged to do so by Harold Macmillan who as Plenipotentiary Minister was with his chief in Marrakech: 'He really is a remarkable man. Although he can be so tiresome and pigheaded, there is no one like him. His devotion to work and duty is quite extraordinary'.

In November of the previous year, Churchill and Roosevelt had been very upset by the Free French arrest in Beirut of the Lebanese President, Prime Minister and several Ministers, accompanied by the suspension of the constitution. This seemed to Churchill a foretaste of the kind of leadership that de Gaulle would bring to France. Now, at Carthage, the Prime Minister heard that the FCNL had arrested three of the PM's protégés, Boisson, Peyrouton and Flandin. It is surprising that in all these circumstances and despite his weakness Churchill was even prepared to contemplate inviting de Gaulle to his villa. Macmillan was a sensitive observer. He recorded in his diary, 'Churchill feels about de Gaulle like a man who has quarrelled with his son'. To achieve a meeting Macmillan had to effect some delicate manoeuvres and diplomatic finesse. But de Gaulle had all sorts of resentments and slights to rehearse. Churchill had stopped in Algiers without visiting him, neither Churchill nor Roosevelt had told him what had happened at Teheran, and so on, at great length. The invitation that Macmillan negotiated was declined. There was then the usual series of exchanges. They would be tedious to enumerate. They must have irritated and exhausted Churchill in his weakened condition.

He rang Macmillan repeatedly 'in a state of great anxiety and emotion' to find out what the latest developments were. At length the general accepted the invitation with extremely bad grace: tactfully Macmillan told Churchill that he had accepted it 'with pleasure'. Even at that, there were further explosions before the meeting, when Churchill discovered that de Gaulle had forbidden a visit from General de Lattre de Tassigny, who had been invited for later in the week. His immediate reaction, from which Duff Cooper had to prise him, was to cancel his meeting with de Gaulle.

When the meeting did eventually take place, it began over lunch, with Duff and Diana Cooper, Clementine, Diana Churchill and others present. The lunch went well and there was a splendid Churchillian stage whisper to Duff Cooper: 'I'm doing rather well, aren't I? Now that the General speaks English so well, he understands my French perfectly'. Even de Gaulle, who heard the aside as he was intended to do, managed to laugh.

The after-lunch exchanges did not go so well. Churchill tried to impress on de Gaulle that he had to avoid creating a division in France between opponents and supporters of the Vichy regime. De Gaulle continued to infuriate and Churchill's wonderful response goes to the heart of his notion of working with more powerful allies: 'Look here! I am the leader of a strong, unbeaten nation. Yet every morning when I wake my first thought is how I can please President Roosevelt and my second thought is how I can conciliate Marshal Stalin. Your situation is very different. Why then should your first waking thought be how you can snap your fingers at the British and Americans?' By the following day, de Gaulle had absorbed enough of what Churchill had told him to invite the Prime Minister to review French troops in Marrakech.

43

Italy and OVERLORD

The Anzio landing, designed to lead to the capture of Rome, was approved by Roosevelt on 29 December, while Churchill was still at Marrakech. It was hard to scrape together sufficient landing craft, and the process involved delaying the transfer of some to Britain by a month. The landings took place on 22 January, when Churchill was back in London. He was full of exciting proposals for follow-ups to Anzio – the Dalmatian Coast or Northern Italy. But the landings went badly: 'We hoped to land the wildcat that would tear the bowels of the Boche. Instead we have stranded a vast whale with its tail flopping about in the water.'

Alexander was failing to bind the Allied armies together. He was not impressed by the American performance and there was jealousy between his two Army Commanders, the American Clark and the British Leese. Clark had no great love of the British and thought that Alex was biased in favour of Leese. He was anxious to reach Rome before his British counterpart and had the American weakness of thinking in terms of seizing headline objectives rather than those that were militarily significant. On Bastille Day, Leese's resentment of Clark and his self-promotion led to his walking out of the French celebrations.[1]

In course SHINGLE, the Anzio landings, moved into DIADEM, the attack on Rome, via an assault on the Gustav Line, and the three battles of Monte Cassino. Shortly after the liberation of Rome, Badoglio, the unappealing ex-fascist leader whom Churchill had incautiously accepted as leader of the Provisional government, was toppled and replaced by Ivanoe Bonomi, whose father loved the works of Sir Walter Scott. Churchill was not enthusiastic, but acquiesced in the appointment. Attlee complained that all this had been done without reference to the War Cabinet. Churchill, most unconvincingly, said that it would have caused 'great inconvenience' to call a meeting of the War Cabinet on a Sunday afternoon.

The Germans fought with very great skill in Italy. Their tactics were flexible and their staff work impressive. They were very far from a spent force. Contrary to everything that Churchill and others had expected, under the stimulus of Speer's reforms German production increased, despite all that strategic bombing had done.

By contrast, the British economy was increasingly weak. British exports were only 30 per cent of what they had been in 1938 and over half of her balance of payments deficit was funded by the United States. Economic issues were another strand of the tensions between the two English-speaking allies. There were oil rivalries in the Middle East. Churchill telegraphed to Roosevelt on 4 March 1944: 'Thank you very much for your assurances about no sheep's eyes at our oilfields in Persia and Iraq. Let me reciprocate by giving you the fullest assurance that we have no thought of trying to horn in upon your interests or property in Saudi Arabia.'[2] There was also friction in regard to aviation and post-war bases and routes.

By the end of January 1944, with slow progress in Italy, the American planners were seriously concerned about implementation of OVERLORD. The full quota of landing craft required for the operation had not yet been built, and many of those that were available were being used for the Italian landings as part of what they regarded as a jaunt personally dreamed up by Churchill, a campaign that never made military sense.[3] Just how the repeated postponements of OVERLORD frustrated the Americans is emphasised by the words with which Marshall chose to end his paper on the strategic concept of the whole war: '[I]t was our purpose to avoid the creation in Italy of a vacuum into which the resources of the cross-Channel campaign would be dissipated as the Germans had bled themselves in the North African campaign'.

Some of the reasons the Americans gave for British reluctance to press on with OVERLORD were fanciful: a desire, for instance, to preserve the youth of the aristocracy from the losses they had experienced in the First World War. But there was a genuine puzzlement among the Americans on COSSAC that even the arrival of the V-weapons did not encourage the British to get on to the Continent and stop them at source. Ralph Ingersoll, an American on the staff of COSSAC from the start:

It still seems sufficient testimony to the courage and character of the British that the very live threat of national disaster by pilotless planes and rockets did not appear to sway a single British officer's determination to let nothing hurry or distract him in his politics or planning.

It is not as if the capability of the V-weapons were underestimated or taken lightly . . . But the British remained unhurried.[4]

But even on an American calculation the chances of successful invasion were poor. Ingersoll himself says that in the summer of 1943 the odds were on the Germans, and that '[T]he net of the *experienced* military advice . . . was certainly against hasty invasion of northwest Europe'. The emphasis is his, and it represents a significant qualification.[5]

Churchill was at very great pains in his history of the war to say that he had *not* opposed the idea of the sort of landing which OVERLORD was, and it is perfectly true that he was not against such landings in principle and did not dispute that the war could only be finished by a direct assault on Fortress Europe. That is not to say that he was enthusiastic about the prospect of such an operation. He was always anxious to see Germany's strength and perhaps her economy eroded before risking the assault. His attritional–peripheral approach meant that he never did feel quite certain that the time was right for OVERLORD.

His views were typical of those that had become prevalent in Britain after 1918, the view that the First World War had been an anomalous British adoption of the alien approach of Clausewitz and Napoleon. It has been argued that his aversion to a major European land campaign was *not* based on the First World War experience.[6] This view is based on the absence of references to the First World War in the correspondence between Churchill and Roosevelt. Be that as it may, it is perfectly clear from innumerable other references to that war that it *did* weigh heavily with Churchill.

Memories of the earlier war were not, however, the only restraining factor. His reservations also stemmed from the fact that he was far from confident that heavy losses, which he was always prepared to contemplate where necessary, would result in a decision.[7]

The fact that the war ended with frontal attacks on Germany from the east and west does not necessarily mean that America was right and Churchill wrong. By 1944 – if the landings went well, a major hypothesis – America could bring so much materiel to bear that the outcome was inevitable. But that does not necessarily mean that the strategy was subtle and inspired. A similar strategy had won the First World War, but at enormous cost and only after prolonged stalemate. Churchill and Lloyd George had been the most outspoken critics of that strategy. Thus Churchill had written of Third Ypres in *The World*

Crisis: '[I]n Flanders the struggle went on. New divisions continued to replace those that were shattered. The rain descended and the mud spread. Still the will-power of the commander and the disciplines of the army remained invincible . . . Ceaselessly the Menin Gate of Ypres disgorged its stream of manhood . . .'[8]

For Churchill the personification of military negativism was William Robertson, CIGS for most of the First World War. Just before Marshall visited Britain in July 1942, he had been studying Robertson's *Soldiers and Statesman*. Dill telegraphed Brooke to say that Marshall had marked up Chapter 3 of Volume One, in which Robertson stressed the importance of concentration on the decisive point and the mistake, as he saw it, and as American theorists were to see it, of diversion of resources to the Dardanelles. The War Office in Britain, who started to study Robertson's book with great interest found that the same chapter carried the message that service chiefs must speak their minds and not acquiesce in political decisions.[9] The man whom Churchill saw as the epitome of poor soldiering ('He had no ideas of his own . . . He represented professional formalism expressed in the plainest terms.') was the man Marshall looked to as his exemplar.

Dill and particularly Brooke were roused to fury by Churchill's attacks on the generals and his criticism of what he saw as their defeatism. They resented it, perhaps inordinately and unnecessarily, when he accused their profession of cowardice and said that firing squads should be sent out to North Africa. This was partly because he had a fairly poor opinion of the quality of the British Army, both at its higher levels and through the ranks. The bearing of the British troops did not always impress. The retreat to Dunkirk, the Battles of Crete, and North Africa, pre-Montgomery, showed instances of poor performance alongside examples of great courage and sustained discipline. Many observers thought that the bloodletting of the Great War had deprived the army of a generation of natural leaders, and that the quality of the 1939 army as a whole bore no relation to the highly trained and professional BEF of 1914.

There was something behind Churchill's criticisms. Wavell and Auchinleck made much of the training that their troops required before they could face action and Wavell confirmed that his men had not displayed soldierly qualities.[10] The Prime Minister noted the surrender in Malaya and Singapore to much smaller Japanese forces. There were many instances of German victories in North Africa over larger units. Tobruk was taken by a force half the size of the garrison. By the end of the Desert War, the Eighth Army was fairly spent. There were many other pieces of evidence available to the Prime Minister.[11] He had not been impressed by the army's performance in Norway. Even before the fall of Singapore he wrote to Violet Bonham-Carter, saying that 'our soldiers are not as good fighters as their fathers were. In 1915 our men fought on even when they had only one shell left and were under a fierce barrage. Now they cannot repel dive-bombers. We have so many men in Singapore, so many men that they should have done better.'

His reservations about the army's performance were shared by others. Eden and Cadogan had similar views. Even Brooke wrote in his diary when Singapore fell, 'If the army cannot fight better than it is doing at present we shall deserve to lose our Empire!' Brooke was no less apprehensive than Churchill about OVERLORD. He wrote in his diary that he was 'torn to shreds with misgivings . . . The cross-Channel operation is just eating into my heart . . .' It might prove 'the most ghastly disaster of the war'. America, with her belief in the invincibility of large numbers, and with a limited experience of the events of the previous war, did not understand how genuine and how reasonable such apprehensions were.

44

ANVIL and the Vienna Alternative

Bad as they may have been, the difficulties and rows in autumn 1943 about the movement of divisions from Italy for OVERLORD were not as fierce as the battles that took place in spring 1944, as the allies clashed over switching resources from Italy to ANVIL, the French Mediterranean landings. Churchill was never at all enthusiastic about ANVIL. It seemed to do what Italy did, but not as well. After the fall of Rome, it seemed to him and Alexander that there were huge Italian opportunities to be seized.

He saw the possibility of reaching the Ljubljana Gap and Vienna. Brooke was also for keeping up the pressure on the Germans in Italy – in his case, simply in order to tie up as many Germans on that front as possible. The effectiveness of this strategy can be and has been questioned. At the high point in 1944 there were 1,677,000 Allied forces, land and air, in the Mediterranean, compared with 411,000 under Kesselring in Italy.[1] Who then was drawing in the other's forces, Kesselring or Alexander? The answer is in part that the Allies in the Mediterranean theatre were not only there for Italy. It is true that looking at Italy alone by June 1944 Allied troops outnumbered Kesselring by two to one, but that does not necessarily mean that the investment was unprofitable: even if it did not actually draw Germans away from Normandy, and did not absorb one German soldier for every Allied soldier, the Italian campaign kept Kesselring's army out of the way.[2]

But while persistence in the Italian campaign did tie up German troops in that theatre, it did not prevent Germany from increasing her strength in the west at the same time as maintaining or even increasing her strength in Italy. By June 1944 there were twenty-eight German divisions, with a real strength of twenty-three, in Italy, as against an Allied strength, according to Liddell Hart, of thirty divisions. Bryant's claim for Brooke (presumably with the latter's agreement) was that the continued offensive in Italy, first, was essentially Brooke's achievement and secondly, drew German forces away from OVERLORD. The first claim cannot be substantiated. It is true that at Casablanca Brooke had pressed for the Mediterranean but Churchill's keenness to get on with ROUNDUP at that time was a brief enthusiasm. The Mediterranean involvement was primarily due to Churchill. The answer to the second claim lies simply in the fact that the continued campaign merely retained German troops which could otherwise have gone to Normandy.[3]

Churchill and Brooke were not separated over ANVIL. At Teheran Brooke had been conscious that Stalin, wanting a free hand in the Balkans, wished to see the Allies out of Italy. Brooke wanted the Italian campaign continued – and continued without a diversion of resources to ANVIL. In the spring of 1944 he and Dill pressed hard to convince the Americans that it was important that the Italian campaign continued. Brooke wanted Germany to continue to be tied in to the Italian front. He calculated that if the campaign continued, at least eighteen German divisions would be held on that front. He could not induce Marshall to understand, let alone accept, that ANVIL would weaken Allied pressure on the Italian front. Kennedy too saw how Alexander was helping OVERLORD, and that the Mediterranean landings would bring that to an end.[4]

Brooke resented the wind-down of Italy; but he acquiesced earlier than Churchill did. Conversely, on 25 October 1943, he had complained in his diary that the build-up in Italy was slower that he had expected because of 'the Americans who have put us in this position with their insistence to abandon the Mediterranean operations for the very problematical cross-channel operations. We are now beginning to see the full beauty of the Marshall strategy! It is quite heartbreaking when we see what might have been done this year if our strategy had not been distorted by the Americans.'

On 1 November 1943 Brooke had prepared for a further Combined Chiefs meeting, 'and the stink of the last one is not yet out of my nostrils!' His diary entry, even from him, is remarkable:

I now unfortunately know the limitations of Marshall's brain and the impossibility of ever making him realize any strategical situation or its requirements. In strategy I doubt if he can ever see the end of his nose. When I look at the Mediterranean I realize only too well how far I have failed in my task during the last 2 years! If only I had had sufficient force of character to swing those American Chiefs of Staff and make them see daylight, how different the war might be. We should have been in a position to force the Dardanelles by the capture of Crete and Rhodes, we should have the whole Balkans ablaze by now, and the war might have been finished in 1943!! Instead, to satisfy American shortsightedness we have been led into agreeing to the withdrawal of our forces form the Mediterranean for a nebulous 2nd Front, and have emasculated our offensive strategy!! It is heartbreaking.[5]

The difference between Brooke on the one hand and Churchill and Alex on the other is that the CIGS did not subscribe to the Vienna Alternative. Once it was clear that ANVIL was to go ahead he was for accepting the position. The Vienna Alternative he flatly rejected on the grounds of terrain and time of year. Brooke's diary for 28 March gives a picture of the Prime Minister as a very old and tired man (but again and again he proved himself capable of rebounding from exhaustion into exuberant vitality). 'We found him in desperately tired mood. I am afraid that he is losing ground rapidly. He seems quite incapable of concentrating for a few minutes on end, and keeps wandering continuously. He kept yawning and said he was feeling desperately tired.'

It may have been exhaustion that caused Churchill to overreact to a minor government defeat on the following day, 29 March. It was the Conservatives and not the Labour Party who revolted. They did so over a proposal for equal pay for men and women teachers and on this minor matter the government lost by just one vote – because Sir George Harvie-Watt was in his bath. Churchill insisted on a vote of confidence on this trivial issue. Harold Nicolson queried whether he was not going over the top. 'No. Not at all. I am not going to tumble round my cage like a wounded canary. You knocked me off my perch. You have now got to put me back on my perch. Otherwise I won't sing.' He won the vote with a majority of over 400. The PM had no embarrassing sense that he had taken a sledgehammer to a nut. He wrote to Randolph, 'I was sure you would be interested in the House of Commons racket. I am the child of the H. of C., and when I was molested by a bunch of cheeky boys I ran for succour to the old Mother of Parliaments and she certainly chased them out of the backyard with her mop.'[6]

It was perhaps as well to demonstrate to the Americans and the world that Parliament, as much as the country, was solidly behind him. In any event, he was concerned about the government's lack of authority in the

House – to the extent, indeed, that he contemplated taking on the
Foreign Secretaryship (which he was already doing in an acting capacity
while the Foreign Secretary was ill), in addition to Defence and his
duties as Prime Minister, so that Eden could concentrate on managing
the difficult House.[7]

On 12 April he pointed out to Marshall that even if there had still
been no breakout from the Anzio beachhead, or link-up with the rest of
the army in Italy, eight German divisions had been pulled down to the
Italian front. As a result he was able to obtain an agreement that no
further troops would be withdrawn for the moment. Even as late as
August 1944, after D-Day, Churchill was trying to have ANVIL forces
diverted to Brittany. Marshall and the Joint Chiefs would have none of
it. Churchill described Arnold, King and Marshall as 'one of the
stupidest strategic teams ever seen'. But 'they are good fellows and
there is no need to tell them this.' Just as well. The extent of the
difference in views about Italy as opposed to OVERLORD was so great at
this time that he drafted a cable to FDR threatening resignation on
account of 'absolutely perverse strategy'. He did not send it.[8]

In reality, he had a high opinion of Marshall and had been far from
happy that the Supreme Command at OVERLORD had been given to
Eisenhower, whom he liked, but did not particularly respect.

The loss of Churchill's battle over ANVIL meant that nearly 40 per
cent of the American Fifth Army in Italy was removed from the theatre,
together with elements of air support and materiel. How successful the
Allies would have been in Italy, even at full strength, remains debatable,
but the more of them there were, the more Germans there would have
had to be there too.

The Americans thought that Churchill was against the Normandy
Second Front because of his 'incurable' preference for 'eccentric
operations'. In Robert Sherwood's *Roosevelt and Hopkins*, the American
position is put at its lowest: 'It was certainly no fault of Churchill's that
two American Expeditionary Forces went into France, north and south,
in the summer of 1944'. Sherwood's book displeased Churchill and he
was very touchy indeed about any suggestion that he had not en-
thusiastically supported the idea of a Second Front. The reasons for his
views were more complicated than the Americans allowed. Like the
Chiefs of Staff, Churchill still feared the capacity of the Wehrmacht. On
9 April 1944 he told Cadogan, 'This battle has been forced on us by the
Russians and the United States military authorities.' He told Roosevelt
in November 1943, 'Unless there is a German collapse, the campaign of

1944 will be the most dangerous we have undertaken and personally I am more anxious about its success than I was about 1941, 1942 and 1943.'[9]

There were reasonable grounds for his apprehensions. After all, if Dieppe had been a disaster and the Anzio landings a failure, what could realistically be expected of a landing in France? After the war, Marshall referred to Churchill's weakness for the 'soft underbelly': 'The soft underbelly had chrome-steel base-boards.' But it might be thought that the base-boards of the Atlantic Wall would be stronger still. And if Kesselring could hold up the Allies in Italy repeatedly, when Alexander had a superiority over the Germans of two or three to one, what could be expected in France, where the Allies did not even have a toehold?

The extent to which OVERLORD, the largest and most ambitious amphibious landing in history, involved unquantifiable elements is reflected in a little episode recalled by Goronwy Rees. Rees was one of Montgomery's staff officers. (Incidentally, he thought very highly of Monty, and found that – on military matters – he thought hard about what he was doing, something he found to be rare among generals.) Montgomery asked him for an estimate of casualties during the initial phases of the landings. After much work Rees tabulated his calculations and presented his figures to the Commander in Chief. 'Thank you, very good, very good. But you see, it won't do. If our casualties are as big as this, we can't do the operation at all. We haven't got the reserves to replace the casualties. Divide Major Rees's calculations by half.'[10]

On the eve of the invasion Brooke wrote, 'It is very hard to believe that in a few hours the cross-Channel invasion starts! At the best it will fall so very, very short of the expectation of the bulk of the people, namely all those who know nothing of its difficulties. At the worst it may well be the most ghastly disaster of the whole war.'[11]

That Italy *vs* ANVIL absorbed so much of Churchill's time in the spring and summer of 1944 does not mean that he had no time for battle with the Chiefs. There were some long meetings and difficult passages. At the beginning of August 1944, for example, there were two days of seven-hour meetings that contained exchanges such as:

PM (to CIGS) It is no good losing your temper.
CIGS I am not losing my temper. But I am in despair that the PM will not give the decision he has been pressed for for over six months.
PM It has now been proved wise not to have given a decision before, and the delay has done no harm.[12]

There were stresses, too, between Britain and America over South East Asia at this time. Churchill complained to Clementine in August 1944 that there were still too many British forces 'mis-employed for American convenience' in Burma, at the expense of the recapture of Singapore.[13]

A minor clash arose from Churchill's enthusiasm for opportunism, reflected in a proposal of 2 February 1944 that Bordeaux be seized by a *'coup de main'* on D plus 20 or D plus 30. The Chiefs of Staff vetoed this suggestion out of hand. But that was a minor skirmish compared to a major battle in the spring of 1944. The conflict between Churchill and the Chiefs in regard to British strategy in South East Asia in 1944 has been described as 'perhaps their most serious disagreement of the war'.[14]

He wanted Britain to follow the European war with a Far Eastern campaign conceived from an Indian perspective and designed to recover Britain's lost eastern possessions, focused separately from the American campaign against Japan. On 20 March 1944 he told the Chiefs that it was his 'duty, as Prime Minister and Minister of Defence' to rule that the Bay of Bengal was to remain the 'centre of gravity for the British and Imperial war effort against Japan'. He wanted Britain to advance through the Bay of Bengal towards Malaya; the Chiefs wanted to join with the Americans in moving from Australia.

Unanimously the Chiefs insisted on joining the American advance in Japan through the Pacific. This issue brought the Chiefs closer to resignation than any other in the war.[15] The issue was only truly resolved when it became academic in the light of the detonation of the atomic bomb. From the political and practical point of view, the Chiefs were no doubt correct, but from the point of view of a strategic defence of Britain's national interests, Churchill's position is understandable.

D-Day: De Gaulle Remains
Below the Level of Events

As the prospect of returning to the European mainland came closer, there was increasing pressure on the British government, both in Parliament and in the country at large, to say how liberated France would be administered and with what authority in France Britain would deal. On 3 May 1944, for example, Anthony Eden faced difficult questioning on these points in the Commons.

Churchill's difficulty was that while he had his own reservations about de Gaulle and the Free French, Roosevelt's views were very much stronger. De Gaulle was out of Britain at this stage and Churchill wanted to bring him back so that he could be closer to events. Roosevelt also wanted him back in England, but not for a fleeting visit, rather to be corralled there until after D-Day. Churchill chose to delay the invitation until at or about the time of D-Day itself. When he spoke in the Commons on 24 May he tried to explain that the allies had not recognised the French Committee of Natural Liberation as the government or even the provisional government of France because they could not be certain that it was truly representative of the French nation – a very fair point. He was able to say that de Gaulle had now been invited to pay a visit 'in the near future' and that he had just heard from Duff Cooper that the general would accept.

His speech was a particularly statesmanlike one but he did not carry the House with him. His old friend, Harold Nicolson 'the Member for Paris', made a particularly strong interjection: 'I cannot fully explain either to myself or to others the true nature of the policy adopted by His Majesty's government towards France . . .' That was not surprising. There were many others who spoke in the same sense and they were supported in the press over the course of the next few days. Churchill was losing important public support and in the face of all this criticism he made several appeals to Roosevelt to allow de Gaulle's people

recognition. He met with little success. On 27 May Roosevelt un-
helpfully wrote saying that he was hopeful that Churchill could
persuade de Gaulle to assist in the liberation of France 'without being
imposed by us on the French people as their government. Self-
determination really means absence of coercion'. Another rebuff followed shortly: 'I think I can only repeat the simple fact that I cannot
send anyone to represent me at the de Gaulle conversation with you'.

After Giraud had been forced out of the French Committee of
National Liberation at the end of 1943, Churchill had faced growing
pressure to recognise the FCNL as provisional rulers of France. America
would certainly not go that far. They declined to recognise the Conseil
as the official representative of France. The *Alice in Wonderland* solution
arrived at during the QUADRANT conference in Quebec in 1943 was for
America and Britain to issue separate statements, each setting out quite
different positions in regard to the Conseil.

After much toing and froing and semantic brouhaha the United
States did no more than 'accept' the FCNL. Britain chose to recognise
the Committee in a rather circular formula as 'administering those
French territories which acknowledged its authority'. Churchill could
still refer to de Gaulle, whom he had 'raised as a pup' as 'a budding
Führer'. 'There is nothing this man will not do if he has armed forces at
his disposal.' As Foreign Secretary, Eden was much more in favour of de
Gaulle, arguing that to contain a post-war Germany, there had to be a
strong France and strong French morale. He argued so strongly for de
Gaulle that Churchill warned him that they might be coming to a
break.[1]

De Gaulle did nothing to make life easier for Churchill. On 26 May
the FCNL unilaterally announced that it was now the Provisional
government of the French Republic. The combination of de Gaulle's
pretensions and Roosevelt's prejudices meant that the whole issue gave
Churchill enormous concerns, and they were compounded by the fact
that Roosevelt's Supreme Commander, Eisenhower, wanted a French
Provisional government ready to put in place following OVERLORD,
something with which his President would not agree.

All or most of these worries were caused by Roosevelt, but when a de
Gaulle visit to Washington was set up for the beginning of July 1944,
the President made the swiftest of turnarounds. He continued to regard
de Gaulle as 'a narrow-minded French zealot with too much ambition
for his own good and some rather dubious views on democracy'. He still
believed that de Gaulle would 'crumble and that the British supporters

of de Gaulle will be confounded by the progress of events . . . [O]ther parties will spring up as the liberation goes on and . . . de Gaulle will become a very little figure'. More succinctly, 'He is a nut'.[2]

But de Gaulle had successful meetings with Marshall, King, Henry Morgenthau, Cordell Hull (with whom he actually got on well) and the Mayor of New York, Fiorello La Guardia. He received a triumphant reception in New York and in Canada there were also great demonstrations of support. When he returned to Algiers on 13 July he learned that the American government now recognised his Committee as the de facto sole administration of France. Life would have been infinitely simpler for Churchill if Roosevelt had not taken so long to come to an inescapable conclusion; but he was, at base, always a politician rather than a statesman.

That American visit lay ahead; now, as D-Day approached, Churchill did his best to make de Gaulle's visit memorable. When he landed at London airport a band played the Marseillaise. He was handed a personal letter from Churchill, 'My Dear General de Gaulle, welcome to these shores!' He was taken to Churchill's headquarters in a special station near Portsmouth where, according to Eden, there was only one bath and one telephone ('Mr. Churchill seemed to be always in the bath and General Ismay always on the telephone'). He walked down the railway line with Eden. Churchill, with his sense of history, was on the track to greet the general with outstretched arms, but de Gaulle did not respond to his embraces.

A sour petulance was as usual the general's response to great events. He was greatly taken up with minor questions such as the American issued foreign currency that was to be used in France: *'Allez, faites la guerre, avec votre fausse monnaie!'* De Gaulle complained about lack of official recognition. Churchill had to tell him that if he were not careful, the United States would disown the FCNL, in which case Britain would be with the Americans. Churchill had to say that in a dispute between the French National Committee and the United States, Churchill would always side with the United States. De Gaulle said he was well aware of that fact. Poor Churchill was not helped by Bevin who joined in with a booming intervention. He told de Gaulle that when Churchill said that Britain would always side with America, he spoke for himself only, and not the government. Churchill was indeed distinctly on his own in siding with the President against France, and de Gaulle knew it. Bevin, Attlee and Eden were for a more independent approach, and so was the bulk of parliamentary opinion. Churchill's awareness of his vulnerability led him to bluster. He telephoned Eden on 6 June: 'Again soon after midnight W. rang up in a rage because Bevin and Attlee had taken my view. Argument continued for forty-five minutes, perhaps longer. I was accused of trying to break up the government, of stirring up the press on the issue. He said that nothing would induce him to give way, that de Gaulle must go. There would be a Cabinet tomorrow. House of Commons would back him against de Gaulle and me and any of the Cabinet who sided with me, etc. FDR and he would fight the world.'

De Gaulle was particularly annoyed by Churchill's suggestion that he should go to see Roosevelt. He did not like the idea of submitting himself as a candidate for approval. 'The French government exists. I have nothing to ask, in this sphere, of the United States of America or of Great Britain.'[3]

Duff Cooper gives a wonderful picture of that evening at Churchill's headquarters and of de Gaulle's failure to rise to the level of events:

Anthony [Eden] tells me about his bitter battles on behalf of de Gaulle. The Prime Minister had invited de Gaulle to come over here for the big battle with France. On 4 June Winston and he [Eden] had gone down in a special train to near Portsmouth where they waited. De Gaulle and his party came there by car and Anthony went to meet them. They then lunched on the train and Winston produced champagne and drank to the health of France. Roosevelt had said that de Gaulle was not to be told of the operations but Winston ignored that, told him everything, took him across to see Eisenhower and forced the latter to show him the maps. Not one word of thanks from de Gaulle. Winston, feeling rather hurt, said to him, 'I thought it only fitting that you should be present with us today'. 'I see,' said de Gaulle glumly, 'I was invited as a symbol' . . . Anthony was almost beside himself, feeling that Winston was deeply moved emotionally by the thought of the occasion, and that de Gaulle's ungraciousness would make him dislike the man all the more. Finally Winston asked de Gaulle to dine with him. 'Thank you – I should prefer alone with my staff.' 'I feel chilled,' Winston said to Anthony.[4]

He walked away, back along the railway track, a stiff, solitary figure. Even with a return to French soil so imminent – perhaps because of its very imminence – de Gaulle was more difficult than ever, no more ready than in the past to see the importance of Allied unity. Instead he focused on the most trivial of details. Ike told him that as Supreme Allied Commander he would shortly be broadcasting to the French population. De Gaulle: 'You, broadcast a proclamation to the French people? By what right? And what will you tell them?' When de Gaulle was asked to make his own speech to the French people he declined to do so in the order envisaged, after the Heads of State and Eisenhower. 'If I were to broadcast, it could only be at a different hour and outside the series'.[5]

On the following evening, ahead of the landings, de Gaulle was again asked to broadcast to France. The conditions he set were wrongly understood by Churchill as amounting to a refusal, and great diplomacy was needed by the Free French ambassador, Pierre Viénot, to reconcile the two men. At the very time that OVERLORD was being launched, Churchill was preoccupied by the stand-off. 'I so beat up this poor man [Viénot] – de Gaulle of course would not come himself – that he practically collapsed. All his sympathies were with me. He was ashamed of de Gaulle.' Eventually de Gaulle made his speech. Churchill then ordered that he be sent back to Algiers, 'in chains if necessary. He must not be allowed to enter France.' Eden prevailed on him to withdraw this demand.[6]

The triviality of de Gaulle's reaction to events is amazing. Cadogan's response was 'It's a girls' school. Roosevelt, PM, and – it must be admitted – de Gaulle all behave like girls approaching the age of puberty. Nothing to be done'. De Gaulle kept it up. Two hundred French liaison officers were not allowed to accompany the embarkation because there had been no agreement about their duties.

When he came to make his broadcast he referred to his organisation as quite simply *'le gouvernement Français'*; Eden had seen the text in advance but let it through with a grin. 'I'll have trouble with the Prime Minister about this, but we'll let it go.' In fact, Eden was engaged in a very difficult pair of parallel dialogues with Churchill and de Gaulle. He was trying to explain to Churchill that Britain had either to break with de Gaulle, and thus France, or agree with him. 'There is no middle course. We must point this out to the President and tell him that de Gaulle must be supported'. Simultaneously, he and Duff Cooper worked on de Gaulle to try to induce him not to distance his Committee from the Allies. De Gaulle's fixation with national independence is reflected in a remark which he made to Eden over dinner on 7 June: 'The General . . . continued to complain about our dependence on American policy. I retorted that it was a fatal mistake in national policy to have too much pride'. De Gaulle did not accept that advice, then or ever.

The wisdom of keeping de Gaulle on a short lead was underlined by what happened when he was allowed a day trip to France on 14 June: when he got to Bayeux, without any warning and without any agreement he undercut American attempts to establish a civil administration by appointing his own man, François Coulet, as Commissioner of the Republic for the Liberated Territory of Normandy.

When he was allowed on French soil for longer he became even more outrageous. He insisted that General Leclerc's Second Armoured Division, which had been trained in Britain and was partly composed of French elements of the British Eighth Army, should be allowed to be the first unit to reach Paris. He himself followed Leclerc into the capital where he made the famous speech at the Hôtel de Ville: 'Paris [has been] liberated by itself, liberated by its people with the help of the armies of France, with the help and support of the whole of France, of France that is fighting, of France alone'.[7] He was of course working to restore self-respect and to rewrite the history of the years since 1940, but there was something a little mean-minded in the way he did it, just as when he ordered British SOE officers whenever he met them to leave the country they had been fighting to defend: 'You have no place here'.[8]

His fiction prevailed. Until recently French histories of the war made little reference to the role of the Americans in the liberation and less, or none, of that of the British.

The Return to Europe

Accounts of Churchill's exhaustion have to be read with caution. The diaries of his intimates are full of entries recording what a shadow he was of his former self, how lacking in vitality he was, how aged. A few pages on they record how wonderfully renewed and vigorous he is. He had enormous powers of rehabilitation. Just six months after D-Day he was rushing off to Greece from a family Christmas, eating by the light of hurricane lamps with shells exploding all round him – and enjoying the adventure hugely.

But at this time, in the early summer of 1944, after nearly five years of war, he was showing unmistakable symptoms of exhaustion. One of the symptoms, strangely, was to talk more and not less at Cabinet meetings. He became discursive, monopolised the meeting and prevented discussion of much of the agenda.

Part of the reason was simply that what had been his overwhelming preoccupation – fighting for victory – had now essentially been achieved. As he said, it was now a straight run in – 'even the Cabinet could do it on their own'. After the Quebec Conference he said to Charles Wilson, 'I have a very strong feeling that my work is done. I have no message. I had a message'. Now Lyttelton told Eden that 'the Cabinet was on the verge of mutiny about late hours and length of sittings'. Eden remonstrated unavailingly. At a Defence Committee meeting on 6 July 1944, Brooke exploded insubordinately: 'If you would keep your confidence in your generals for even a few days, I think we should do better . . . I have listened to you for two days on end undermining the Cabinet's confidence in Alex until I felt I could stand no more. You ask me questions, I gave you answers. You didn't accept them and telegraphed Alex who gave the same answers.' It was not the Prime Minister's best evening. Eden described it as deplorable, and A.B. Cunningham, always ready to be critical of Churchill, described him as 'very tired and too much alcohol.'[1]

Generals could be difficult, even hurtful. Monty refused to let the Prime Minister address his troops ahead of D-Day. The accounts of the incident originate from Montgomery himself and may not be accurate as far as their details are concerned. In one account, 'Monty runs through the battles he's won in the past two years, Alamein, Tripoli, Mareth, Wadi Akarit, the assault upon Sicily, the invasion of the Italian main-land . . . Did the Prime Minister wish to . . . come between a general and his men, his own staff in fact? "I could never allow it – never", Monty pronounced. "If you think that is wrong, that can only mean you have lost confidence in me" '.[2] In another account, Churchill gave in to Monty, in tears. Even if neither account is wholly accurate, the Prime Minister was not allowed to address the troops. It was, as he well knew, a historic occasion, a *Henry V* opportunity. He would have loved it, and would have done something wonderful, inspiring the men and adding to his country's literary heritage. It is doubtful that he could have done any damage beyond upstaging Monty.

The scale of Anglo-American bombing ahead of D-Day worried Churchill. The high numbers of French and Belgian civilian casualties seemed unacceptable. Eisenhower did not agree and the matter went to Roosevelt. Churchill asked that if the estimate of collateral casualties were above a certain level, raids should not take place. Roosevelt declined to intervene. Churchill told Air Chief Marshal Sir Ralph Tedder, the British Air Commander in Chief and Eisenhower's Deputy, 'You're piling up an awful load of hatred'.[3]

The finality of Roosevelt's word on such matters is surprising, given that as late as D-Day British troops were still more numerous than Americans. By the end of the war, American deployment was 80 per cent, but at D-Day 57 per cent of the troops were British. All the same, America did not spare Churchill the knowledge that they were the masters now.

The final battle between Britain and America over ANVIL, scheduled for 15 August, took place in the middle of June. Britain had very persuasive evidence from Enigma decrypts that Germany would not defend herself against an attack in the south of France as strongly as she would defend herself against attacks from Italy. This was supported by a further decrypt received on 28 June, which revealed that Hitler had ordered the defence of the Apennines, whatever the cost. The British Chiefs of Staff and Churchill were at one in seeing huge attractions in an amphibious landing near Trieste, coupled with renewal of the Italian advance. The result would be to pull away more German divisions from

Normandy, assisting the breakout far more than a successful landing on the French Mediterranean coast. Churchill and the Chiefs were supported by an enthusiastic General Wilson, in command of British forces in the Middle East, who wanted to carry out an amphibious assault at the top of the Adriatic, pushing on east to Zagreb and then Austria and the Danube. Even Brooke was positive: 'Now we have the most marvellous information, indicating clearly the importance Hitler attaches to Northern Italy.'

The Enigma decrypts, referred to always as 'Boniface', a code for a code, were downplayed by America, and indeed Marshall dismissed the value of Boniface with a mistaken reference to what this intelligence had said ahead of D-Day.

Brooke, Portal and Cunningham telegraphed to the American Chiefs on 28 June: It would be a 'grave strategic error not to take advantage of destroying the German forces at present in Italy and thus drawing further reserves on to this front'. Their approach was reinforced by Churchill, telegraphing to Roosevelt to remind him of approving noises about Istria which the President had made at Teheran. Roosevelt responded speedily but negatively, saying that his political survival would be in doubt if any setback in Normandy could be attributed to the transfer of forces to the *Balkans*. There had been no mention of the Balkans. Did Roosevelt even understand what was being put to him? His slip may have been a Freudian one: the Americans had by now developed an allergic reaction to the very word 'Balkans'. When Harold Macmillan was discussing the capture of Rome with American top brass, he sensed that some of them were warming to Alexander's plans. But there was an interjection from Marshall: ' "Say, where is this Ljubljana? If it's in the Balkans we can't go there." I told him it was practically in Austria and he seemed relieved.'[4] Macmillan took the trouble to mark the 'a' of 'can't' to show how Marshall pronounced it. For some reason it is Butler, rather than Macmillan, who is always described as 'feline'.

Churchill responded tactfully to the President, making the point that there was no question of doing anything in the Balkans, and returned again to what Roosevelt had said to him at Teheran.

The President remained uninterested, proposing putting the dispute to Stalin. Stalin would obviously have sided with the President, quashing any idea of Allied activity in the areas of Eastern Europe which he was about to seize. Churchill explained this to the President and decided that, as so often, a meeting would be needed to resolve the problem. A flying boat and a bomber were made ready for the journey to the States, but Roosevelt would not even discuss the matter. 'What can I do, Mr. President, when your Chiefs of Staff insist on casting aside our Italian offensive campaign, with all its dazzling possibilities . . . ? I am sure that if we could have met, as I so frequently proposed, we should have reached a happy agreement.' A poignant observation.[5]

Even in hindsight Churchill thought ANVIL (or DRAGOON as it became, allegedly because Britain had been dragooned into it[6]) had been a mistake. In September he told Colville that he thought that although an undistinguished minority would argue that there should have been an invasion in 1943, the grand strategy, the movement through TORCH, HUSKY and so on to OVERLORD, would be highly approved. But ANVIL (as it is convenient to continue to refer to the operation) had been a pure waste: it had not helped Eisenhower at all, and by reducing Alexander's armies, had allowed the Germans to transfer troops from Italy to the invasion zone.[7] Churchill always regarded emasculation of the Italian campaign in favour of ANVIL 'as the major error of our Allied strategy', a view which was not contradicted by the Memoirs of Mark Clark, the Senior American Commander in Italy.[8]

Although Churchill had accepted from Teheran onwards that there was to be a massive cross-Channel landing in May (or June) 1944, he had continued to see it slightly differently from the Americans. As late as February 1944 he advocated a revived study of JUPITER, an attack on Norway to supplement OVERLORD although at the cost of drawing resources away from it. Brooke and the others always dismissed his interest in Norway with a sneer, but Brooke himself had talked of 'spelling OVERLORD with the letters T-Y-R-A-N-T'.[9]

If OVERLORD had been supplemented by attacks from Scandinavia and the southern French Atlantic coast, or by 'rolling up Europe from the South-East, and joining hands with the Russians', as Churchill advocated to Dominion Prime Ministers in May 1944, the war would not have concluded with a massive thrust on a single front. What the result would have been will never be known, but what is clear is that the offensive on the western front, as it did take place, was seriously flawed. This book is intended to be a survey of grand strategy, and not tactics, but, briefly, there were huge losses in the hard fighting to escape from the *bocage* of Normandy, advances at many stages were slow and often stalled, and casualties were so much higher than expected that two British divisions had to be disbanded and American troops moved from the Pacific theatre.

Apart from many individual mistakes, a series of problems flowed from the fact that the concept was of one great frontal advance. The Americans repeatedly threw themselves forward in hugely costly attacks, and tended to try not to lose face by breaking off unprofitable actions. Conversely, the Germans were able to concentrate their resources in defence, notably by deploying new troops in 'the Miracle of the West'.

That still lay ahead, but in the meantime America found the continued British enthusiasm for Italy tiresome. They were also irritated by what they regarded as unacceptable stratagems. For instance, just forty-eight hours before the American Seventh Army set sail from Italy and Corsica for the South of France, the British Chiefs communicated with the British Theatre Commander in the Mediterranean, telling him to consider abandoning the attack and diverting the troops to Brest. Apart from the practical issues, the constitutional irregularity of the request offended the Americans. The responsible body was not the British Chiefs, but the Combined Chiefs. The British Chiefs did copy their letter – but not to the Combined Chiefs, simply to their opposite numbers in Washington. There was a very sharp reaction. The Americans were technically correct.

The Second Quebec Conference

ANVIL opened on 14/15 August, despite all Churchill's efforts. He had opposed the diversion of resources from Italy not only because that theatre was dominated by Britain, but also because of his awareness of the strategic desirability of limiting the influence of the Russians in the Balkans and Eastern Europe after the war. His vision was never shared by the Americans. It was his defeat over ANVIL that prompted his famous, not entirely facetious, remark that he would leave the matter to history, but that he intended to be one of the historians.

While we shall never know what a full-scale continuation of the Italian campaign might have done, it can certainly be said that ANVIL did not contribute much to victory or even to the success of the Normandy campaign. As late as December 1944, when he was Supreme Commander in the Mediterranean, Alexander was still arguing strongly for an advance from Italy into Austria and Yugoslavia. By then the plan was unrealistic and Brooke was angered by Alex's interference and support of what he was by now describing as 'Winston's strategic ravings'.

Churchill received no more support on the issue from his man in the Mediterranean. When Wilson succeeded Eisenhower as Supreme Allied Commander in the Mediterranean he pursued a policy of neutrality in the dispute between America and ANVIL on the one hand and Britain and Italy/the Balkans, on the other. While that was constitutionally correct, Churchill was disappointed to be supported neither by his CIGS nor the SAC Mediterranean.

A continuation of the Italian campaign at full strength had really been killed off long before OVERLORD began, but in early August there did remain a slight prospect that ANVIL might be cancelled and its resources transferred to landings in Brittany. This would have supported the flank of the Normandy campaign and would have assisted Montgomery greatly. Churchill planned to consult with Montgomery on 5 August, but had to divert because of fog. He found that Eisenhower, who had been for the plan, had very speedily changed his mind, although his Chief of Staff, General Bedell Smith, had not. The Prime Minister asked Hopkins to support Brittany. He flew back to Montgomery's headquarters, but cut short his visit rather than distract Monty at the height of the battle, and returned to Britain to receive a message from Hopkins saying that he was sure that the President would not agree. The British Joint Staff Mission in America argued the case with their American counterparts but 'could not budge them'. Roosevelt confirmed to Churchill that there was to be no change of plan. That was regrettable: Brittany made more sense that the Riviera.

All this flying around had not exhausted the 69-year-old Churchill. He now went on to Algiers and then to Italy to be with Alex. In Algiers he had a brief meeting with Randolph, who was recuperating from the results of a plane crash in Yugoslavia. Randolph pressed him to countermand a recent decision not to meet de Gaulle: de Gaulle was the frustrated leader of a defeated country whereas Churchill 'as the unchallenged leader of England, the main architect of victory can afford to be magnanimous without fear of being misunderstood'.[1] Magnanimity was of course one of Churchill's most evident qualities, and it was its very absence in de Gaulle that so disappointed him. He told Eden in June 1944, 'remember there is not a scrap of generosity about this man'. To Roosevelt: 'I am sure he will make all the mischief he can'. He was not much more enthusiastic about other future European allies: he told the Foreign Office in November 1944, 'The Belgians are extremely weak, and their behaviour before the war was shocking. The Dutch were entirely selfish and fought only when they were attacked, and then only for a few hours'.[2]

On 12 August, possibly by way of an amend for many slights, Roosevelt invited Churchill but not Stalin to a meeting in Quebec for the following month. Before he left for this, the Second Quebec Conference, Churchill dashed around the Mediterranean basin, swam in his beloved sea and told the Chiefs of Staff that if Alex could break through into the Po Valley, he still favoured a move into the Adriatic. He continued to have his eye on Vienna, and had told Alex that if the war should end prematurely he was to dash for the city with armoured cars.

On his return to London ahead of the Quebec trip his exertions took their toll and he succumbed again to pneumonia. As he recovered he tried – in vain – to persuade Roosevelt to join him in appealing to Stalin to support the rising in Warsaw. Stalin was simply standing back and allowing the Nazis to suppress the rising. Churchill wanted to tell him that if he did not at least allow allied aircraft to use Soviet bases to bring in supplies for the insurgents, allied support to Russia would be reduced or withdrawn. Roosevelt was not prepared to do this or indeed anything else: he was secretly asking Stalin for use of airbases to allow America to bomb Japan. Churchill did all he could, but had to confess to Smuts that he had less and less influence.[3] The Polish Underground Army in Warsaw was loyal to the London government-in-exile, and Churchill recalled no occasion when the War Cabinet was so angry with its allies.[4]

On 5 September Churchill set off from Greenock on the *Queen Mary*, taking with him a nurse and a penicillin expert. When he discovered that American servicemen on board were going to lose a week's leave because their departure had been delayed on his account, he at once telegraphed Roosevelt asking if the week could be reinstated. 'It would be a pleasure to me if this could be announced before the end of the voyage and their anxiety relieved.' This was one request to which Roosevelt felt able to agree.

Difficult discussions about the Far East took place at a staff conference on board the *Queen Mary* on 8 September 1944. Churchill was realistic about the life left in the German enemy. He was very perturbed about the prospect of moving troops from Italy to the Far East at a very early date, on the assumption that a German collapse was imminent.

He was also occupied on the voyage with another dispute, this one with Attlee and the War Cabinet over increased pay to be given to troops for fighting in the Japanese War. He had already said that he considered the proffered terms to be inadequate, and was accordingly furious that the War Cabinet proposed nonetheless to publish them in his absence. A violent reply to Attlee's telegram was dictated, but a more temperate one followed. Eden's 'aid and friendship' was invoked. The Prime Minister was entitled to some consideration 'when I am absent on public duty of highest consequence'.[5]

At the conference, the American Secretary of the Treasury, Henry Morgenthau, argued for punitive de-industrialisation of Germany postwar: the great factories of the Ruhr would be closed, as would the shipyards. His plan had been discussed at length by the President and the Treasury Secretary. Churchill's immediate reaction – of humanity and honour – was typical: 'I'm all for disarming Germany, but we ought not to prevent her living decently. There are bonds between the working classes of all countries and the English people will not stand for the policy you are advocating. I agree with Burke. You cannot indict a whole nation. What is to be done should be done quickly. Kill the criminals, but don't carry on the business for years.' What happened next is not clear. He changed his mind, accepted Morgenthau's plan for what he called the 'pastoralization' of Germany, subject to some minor alterations. Moran says Churchill was persuaded by arguments from Cherwell;[6] or he may have felt that his first duty was to his own: Britain had been offered a three billion dollar loan from Morgenthau on generous terms.

At this point Eden turned up, and when he arrived at the conference he attacked the plan vigorously. Apart from anything else, he was satisfied that in the long term the destruction of factories and industrial equipment and the flooding of mines could not work to Britain's economic interest. Churchill did not much like being opposed publicly by his Foreign Secretary. Eden was told that they had to choose between 'our own people' and the Germans: he was referring to Britain's economic distress. In his history of the war Churchill says, 'We had much to ask from Roosevelt and Morgenthau'. When he dictated a telegram for the War Cabinet two days later, he referred to the benefits which Britain might receive from the pastoralisation of Germany, and an agreement with Roosevelt was initialled that same day.

Further reflection brought Churchill back to his original opposition to an essentially inhumane arrangement; by then, fortunately for history and humanity, the Americans themselves had ditched the plan: it was vetoed by Stimson and Hull. The whole episode was not a prepossessing one. Churchill concedes that he 'had not had time to study the terms of the memorandum in detail', in which case he should not have initialled it. Roosevelt, too, distanced himself from the plan – 'I dislike making plans for a country we do not yet occupy' – in which case *he* should not have initialled it.

Breakout: Allies at Loggerheads

By the time Churchill reached Greenock again on 26 September, the news of the failure at Arnhem reached him. Generally the Allied breakout from Normandy had not been going well. British forces had reached Brussels but Boulogne, Calais and Dunkirk were still in German hands, and Metz had been retaken. The Russians were moving much faster: Bulgaria had surrendered to Russia on 9 September, and Romania had changed sides.

The original concept of Normandy was of a drive west to capture the ports on the Cherbourg and Brittany peninsulas. Then the armies would regroup on the Seine before the next phase. In the event Patton saw opportunities in wheeling east. Bradley and Montgomery agreed on 3 August, and 60,000 Germans were trapped at Falaise. Montgomery was persuaded by Bradley to close the pincers round the Falaise–Argentan gap further west than planned, so that parts of the German army were allowed to escape. Patton now had the chance to press on forward and, disobeying Bradley, did just that. The Allies pushed on towards Paris and Brussels until the German counter-attack in the Ardennes and stalemate.

There was dispute about the nature of their advance. Montgomery and Bradley argued for a narrow thrust into Germany with a force of forty divisions, directed north of the Ardennes towards the Ruhr. Eisenhower, on the other hand wanted an attack on a broad front. There were political tensions. America suspected that Britain wanted Germany and Russia to fight each other to a standstill; the British suspected America of trying to do a deal with Russia in exchange for a declaration of war against Japan.

Relations between Monty and Patton had been bad ever since the American attended a post-North Africa debriefing as an observer. Patton said afterwards that there had been too much talk and the comment was relayed to Montgomery, who said, 'The next time I see

Georgie Patton, I'll have just three things to say to him: "Get out of my way; take your troops back and train them, and leave me your petrol" '. This was well known at American Headquarters, and it rankled. After the liberation of France Patton toyed with sending Monty, who was far in his rear, a five-gallon can of petrol with a suitable message.

The two men approached matters in very different ways and the Americans generally were surprised by the caution of the British commanders after D-Day. Monty was always Brooke's favourite, rather than Churchill's, and the Prime Minister was annoyed when Montgomery became bogged down before Caen. The Germans, whose principles of command had been taken as models by the British before the war, understood better what Montgomery was doing, although they too criticised his failure to capitalise on success. Without the experience of the reverses in North Africa – or indeed of the huge losses in the First World War which the British generals had seen – Americans could too easily misunderstand such incidents as the hesitation before the attack on Walcheren Island, when according to American lore Ike had to order Montgomery to attack.

When the Allied advance stalled, Churchill came to the view that Monty's narrow-fronted attack might have delivered speedier results.

On his way back from Italy to England, Montgomery had been told by Eisenhower that he would command all the land forces, including the Americans, until Ike moved from England to France. Then Bradley would be given command of 12th US Army Group and Montgomery would command 21st Army Group, consisting of First Canadian and Second British Armies. This changeover took place on 1 September 1944 and Ike assumed operational command. Monty was promoted field marshal to counter the 'demotion' that was perceived in Britain.

Although the change in the system of command had been envisaged from the start, that fact had never been highlighted. The War Office only learned that it had taken place from a letter from Montgomery of 21 August 1944. He reported that at a staff meeting at Supreme Headquarters Allied Expeditionary Force (SHAEF) the previous day it had been decided both to change the command and to send part of his forces east to the Saar. Montgomery had not been present at this meeting. At the suggestion of de Guingand, his Chief of Staff, he was consulted before the decision was implemented. He argued, of course, that to change the system of command was a bad and unnecessary idea, and that the quickest way to win the war was to sweep north, clear the coast and then advance into the Ruhr. Eisenhower listened, but overruled him. Neither the Chiefs of Staff nor Churchill could interfere with a decision that had overwhelming political support from America. The Director of Military Operations, speaking for the War Office, suspected that the war was lengthened thereby by some six months.[1]

Relations between the two armies were at their worst after American forces experienced the fierce German onslaught in the Ardennes and were brought to a halt in the snow of the Bulge. The British press said that the Americans simply could not cope, and there was great pressure for Monty's appointment as a permanent Ground Force Commander. Monty himself had put the idea forward as early as September, and Churchill almost certainly supported it. Eisenhower was widely thought to have proved indecisive in August, and the British Chiefs had in any case never intended that SHAEF should exercise day-to-day military control. Eisenhower declined the suggestion, but his response was in an unfortunately defensive tone, rehearsing what the Americans had done since D-Day.

Churchill considered that Eisenhower had suffered 'a strategic reverse'. He told Smuts that 'before the offensive was launched we placed on record our view that it was a mistake to attack against the whole front and that a far greater mass should have been gathered at the point of desired penetration. Montgomery's comments and predictions beforehand have in every way been borne out.' He went on to remind Smuts however that as the British armies were only about half the size of the American, soon to be little more than a third, 'it is not as easy as it used to be for me to get things done'.[2]

As always, Montgomery's prodigious arrogance did him no favours. The promotion to Field Marshal to placate the British press meant that he formally outranked Ike, as he would continue to do until the latter's promotion towards the end of the war. As long as he did so, he declined to visit the Supreme Commander, but insisted that Ike attend on him, which he usually did. Monty happily flew to see his subordinates, but refused to fly to Ike's HQ. It was the duty of a Supreme Commander to visit his forward commanders. No wonder that while Brooke thought Montgomery 'the finest tactical general we have had since Wellington', he added, with a shake of his head, 'but on some of his strategy, and especially on his relations with the Americans, he is almost a disaster'.[3] Monty did not even make the suggestion to Ike that he become Ground Force Commander personally: he sent his Chief of Staff, Freddie de Guingand, on his behalf.

After Bradley's breakthrough in the Ardennes at Bastogne, there was a physical gap between the American armies, and to fill it Montgomery was given command of the First and Ninth American Armies. The arrangement was explicitly a temporary assignment, and the two armies were to revert to American control once the crisis in communication was over. But British public opinion never thought that would happen; nor, almost certainly, did Monty. He might indeed have secured his prize if he had not yet again displayed a disastrous lack of tact. He gave a press conference on 7 January 1945 at which he patronised the Supreme Commander, indicated that he personally had always found him a charming fellow and deprecated the criticism of him that was so widespread. The suggestion was that there could be room for them both, although Ike's role would be no more than that of a figurehead. It was a spectacular performance. It put a complete end to any hope of Monty's becoming Ground Force Commander, and there was feeling that his command might be at an end.

The antipathy among the Allied generals came into the open. Bradley was prepared to resign rather than serve under Monty, and Patton had undertaken to go with him.[4] Bradley too called a press conference. He declared publicly that Monty's command of First and Ninth Armies was only temporary. And he went further and said not only that Monty had not won the Battle of the Ardennes, but also that he *could* not have done so because he played no part in it until the final stages and even then only on the northern end and not where it was won, at Bastogne.

The British press represented Bradley's intervention as an insult to Montgomery, and public opinion was outraged; but the facts were incontrovertible and Churchill, who had not intervened until now, was obliged to contact Eisenhower and apologise for his field marshal; he said the trouble had all been stirred up by a group of his friends who were frankly 'an embarrassment to the British Government'.[5] American military opinion was not impressed by Montgomery's attempted coup and they saw Churchill's intervention as a belated and unconvincing move to distance himself from it.

Montgomery's appalling failure to comprehend how other people's minds work was doing as much damage to inter-allied relations now as in Sicily in 1943, and Churchill had to exercise some diplomacy to undo the damage. Montgomery had made a whole series of cack-handed interventions in Eisenhower's plans. Back in August 1944, when Montgomery had pressed Eisenhower to allow him to make a pencil thrust into the heart of Germany with a consequent diversion of American resources to support him, Eisenhower, who was far from the compliant cipher that the British had earlier thought him, rejected the plan perfectly clearly.

Montgomery appeared to acquiesce, but in fact continued to press his position so strongly that Eisenhower flew up to the British Commander's Advanced Headquarters on 10 September. In Eisenhower's aircraft Montgomery was so intemperate in his language that Eisenhower, with commendable restraint, leaned forward and put his hand on Montgomery's knee, saying 'Steady, Monty! You can't speak to me like that. I'm your boss'. Montgomery replied, 'I'm sorry, Ike'.

This was not the first time Eisenhower had been unhappy with Montgomery. He was uncharacteristically infuriated by what he regarded as undue timidity in GOODWOOD, the planned breakout at Caen. Here he was unfair. To the Americans the Germans at Caen simply had to be smashed, with the usual American application of force to force. Montgomery's position was a little subtler. He knew that Caen was defended more heavily than any other sector, and, rather than waste troops in a great attritional assault, he drew more German forces in, so as to make a breakout elsewhere easier. By the end of June there was only half a panzer division and 140 tanks on the American front, as opposed to seven and a half armoured divisions and over 700 tanks at Caen. And yet the Americans promoted the myth that it was they who had had to help out Montgomery. It is not easy to feel sorry for the man, but occasionally it happens.

While Churchill was also displeased by Montgomery's performance at GOODWOOD, he was not as angered by that as by Montgomery's refusal to allow him to visit his Forward Headquarters while he was engaged in fighting the battle. 'Haig had allowed him in the last war . . . He would make it a matter of confidence, etc. etc.', recorded Brooke, who warned Monty that he had better perform an about-turn. He did, and Churchill was mollified by his visit.

On 10 October Montgomery put up a paper entitled *Notes on Command in Western Europe*. He argued, not for the first time, for a single thrust and a single ground commander (himself) and he did so in insubordinate terms that positively invited his dismissal. The paper concluded,

15. I do not believe we have a good and sound organisation for command and control.
16. It may be that political and national considerations prevent us having a sound organisation. If this is the case I would suggest we say so. Do not let us pretend we are all right, whereas actually we are very far from being all right in this respect.[6]

Eisenhower responded by cutting Montgomery down to size: 'This is no longer a Normandy beachhead!' Montgomery's reply was not taken at face value: 'You will hear no more on the subject of command from me'. On 30 December 1944 Marshall told Eisenhower to make no concessions 'of any kind whatsoever'. Ike had in fact made no concessions and had no intention of doing so now, but he had had enough. He drafted a reply to Marshall that would have meant the end of Montgomery's career. Freddy de Guingand got wind of the fact that his chief was about to be axed, dashed to Eisenhower's headquarters and secured a brief delay, then rushed back through the snow to Montgomery who, stunned, drafted a letter of apology. But he still did not really understand: he was as cocky and imperceptive as ever at the press conference on 7 January.

It was not only Montgomery however who felt that things could be better done than the Americans were doing them. The British Chiefs and Americans such as Bedell Smith were concerned about Eisenhower's hands-off approach. A deputation of American generals including Bedell Smith and Whiteley made representations to the Supreme Commander. On 24 November 1944 the British Chiefs, under conditions of great secrecy, discussed bringing Marshall over to review the problem. When Marshall was present at a Combined Chiefs meeting on 1 February 1945 he declined to cramp Eisenhower's style, but did criticise Monty. Brooke had no choice but to knuckle under, reflecting as usual that 'Marshall clearly understood nothing of strategy'.[7]

'The Naughty Document'

Churchill's thoughts were increasingly turning to the shape of post-war Europe. As they did so, his mood became more and more one of foreboding. He sensed that as one war was coming to an end the seeds of a future conflict were being sown. He decided he must go to see Stalin. His visit caused worries in America, where there was increasing concern about European territorial arrangements that were not based on self-determination.

The situation in Eastern Europe was becoming very fluid. By 1 October 1944 Finland and Bulgaria were no longer part of the Axis powers; both had been occupied by Russia. The Red Army had moved through Estonia, Latvia and Lithuania. Russia was in possession of large parts of Poland, Hungary and Yugoslavia. She was on the frontiers of Greece and Turkey. British forces were in Greece.

Churchill pressed Roosevelt to be allowed to discuss 'spheres of influence' in the Balkan area – a form of words that caused alarm and panic in Washington. Roosevelt was less politically committed on the issue than some of his advisers and he drafted a cable in which he proposed to give Churchill an implied mandate to speak for the United States – he himself could not be present at the meeting with Stalin because of the upcoming Presidential election. Hopkins spotted the cable and recognised its political implications, and on his initiative the cable never left the White House. Churchill was told very distinctly, first, that Averell Harriman would be present as an observer on behalf of the President and, secondly, that Harriman had no power to speak on behalf of the President. Churchill could talk to Stalin as much as he wanted, but he could not make any arrangements of which the United States might disapprove.

Once the State Department and Cordell Hull knew what was being suggested about spheres of influence, Roosevelt had to say that he was unwilling to approve such arrangements.[1] Churchill was angry: he was conscious that someone had to do something to limit Russian ambitions, and to date the Americans had done nothing.[2] Roosevelt gave some ground. *Temporary* arrangements might be made, and matters would be reviewed in three months time, but that would be the limit.[3]

Roosevelt may have wanted to allow for the development of American business interests, or to avoid what he regarded as undemocratic arrangements: whatever the reason he did not want British and Russian spheres of influence in the Balkans. But Churchill went off to Moscow with a free hand for three months at least, and as a result of Roosevelt's indecisive stance he thought that the President was more or less acquiescing in his policy. He had, after all, written to the President saying that 'somebody must have the power to plan and act'; he had asked the President to trust him and give the arrangements three months' trial. Roosevelt appeared to have done that. The State Department on the other hand thought that spheres of influence had been knocked on the head once and for all. Hull was not aware that on 12 June Roosevelt had agreed to give Churchill's ideas about spheres of influence during the war a temporary trial. At Moscow Churchill thought he was acting in accordance with Roosevelt's permission; the State Department thought he was doing exactly what he had been told not to.

There was plenty of room for misunderstanding. Prime Minister and President were corresponding simultaneously at this time on a number of major issues: OVERLORD, the status of de Gaulle's *Comité*, recognition of the new Italian government and zones of occupation, all as well as spheres of influence. Minor matters such as FDR's gift of two electric typewriters were also dealt with. Issues were not disposed of one by one: Churchill generally replied by return, but Roosevelt did not. His letter of 10 June 1944, for example, was in response to Churchill's message of 31 May. Since then Churchill had sent eleven other messages and drafted a twelfth, which was not sent. The decision on spheres of influence was therefore not clear-cut and decisively stated.

The Prime Minister had told the Commons on the day he reached London on his return from Quebec that he could not 'conceive that it is not possible to make a good solution whereby Russia gets the security which she is entitled to have, and which I have resolved that we shall do our utmost to secure for her, on her western frontier, and, at the same time, the Polish nation have restored to them that national sovereignty and independence for which, across centuries of oppression and struggle, they have never ceased to strive'. And so, on 9 October in

Moscow, as they had done at Teheran, he and Stalin discussed making the Curzon Line Poland's eastern frontier, with pressure being brought on the Poles to agree. The talk then turned to what was to happen in southern Europe and the Balkans. He explained that he did not want to talk of 'spheres of influence', a phrase which would shock the Americans, but that if he and Stalin were in agreement, he thought he could sell the agreement to them.

This *Realpolitik* resulted in 'The Percentages Agreement', some scribbles on little more than the back of an envelope, in which Churchill proposed that Romania be 90 per cent a Russian interest and 10 per cent British; Greece 90 per cent British 'in accord with the USA' and 10 per cent Russian; Yugoslavia and Hungary 50 per cent each; Bulgaria 75 per cent Russia and 25 per cent the others. Stalin looked briefly at the list, ticked it and passed it back. It lay on the table until Churchill said, 'Might it not be thought rather cynical if it seemed we had disposed of these issues, so fateful to millions of people, in such an off-hand manner? Let us burn the paper'. Stalin: 'No, you keep it'.

The British ambassador's original draft account of the incident is good: 'PRIME MINISTER then produced what he called a "Naughty document" showing a list of the Balkan countries and the proportion of interest in them of the Great Powers. He said the Americans would be shocked if they saw how crudely he had put it. Marshal Stalin was a realist. He himself was not sentimental while Mr. Eden was a bad man.'[4]

Churchill did keep it and the remarkable document can still be seen. He tried to mitigate its brutality in a letter to Stalin that he dictated two days later: 'These percentages which I have put down are no more than a method by which in our thoughts we can see how near we are together, and then decide upon the necessary steps to bring us into full agreement'. If they were made public they might appear quite crude, and even callous, but they provided a framework which would avoid bloodshed and 'our broad principle should be to let every country have the form of government which its people desire'. Averell Harriman told Churchill that Roosevelt and Secretary of State Cordell Hull repudiated this letter, and it was never sent.

Churchill realised later that he had forgotten all about Albania, which was now divided 50–50. But Molotov wanted Hungary, which had been 50–50 to be 80–20 for Russia. Eden agreed to this. A gloss was put on the agreement when it was relayed to the War Cabinet. It was 'only an interim guide'. It would be reviewed at the great Peace Conference which would settle affairs at the end of the war, a conference which never took place.

The agreement was a diplomatic triumph for Churchill. He had truly no alternative but to make the concessions he did, and Stalin had no need to make his concessions. He may have felt that what he was getting was a fairly free hand in Poland, where Churchill had been making reasonably conciliatory noises;[5] and it may have helped that Churchill gave the impression that he was speaking for America, which he was not.

In fact, the Percentages Agreement was particularly unacceptable to Washington because it followed on negotiations in which there had been profound misunderstandings between London and Washington. Eden and the Soviet ambassador in London, Gusev, had reached a broad agreement in May 1944 that Moscow could deal with Romania after the war, providing that London could deal with Greece. America had been unhappy that this might be part of a process of splitting the Balkans up into Russian and British spheres of influence. On his return to the United States from Teheran, Roosevelt had reported to Congress that private arrangements and notions such as the balance of power and spheres of influence were at an end. Spheres of influence smacked of imperialism. Spheres of influence in the Pacific for the Americans were one thing; spheres of influence for other countries elsewhere another.

The Polish government-in-exile in London joined Churchill and Stalin in Moscow. Churchill described them in a telegram to the King: 'Our lot from London are, as Your Majesty knows, a decent but feeble lot of fools, but the delegates from Lublin [the Soviet nominees] seem to be the greatest villains imaginable'. The Poles proved intransigent and when Churchill met the London Poles on 15 October, he ended up shouting, 'I will have nothing more to do with you. I don't care where you go. You only deserve to be in your Pripet Marshes.' Despite a violent attack of diarrhoea, and then a temperature that rose above 100 degrees, bringing two doctors and two nurses from Cairo, he continued to shuttle between the Poles, described by Oliver Harvey as 'Like the Bourbons expecting everything to come back to them', and Stalin. No agreement was reached, but the discussions were academic to the extent that Stalin was insisting in any event that his puppets, the Lublin Poles, would have the majority in the future Polish government.

Russia was still not at war with Japan, but at the conference Stalin gave an undertaking to Churchill that cheered the Americans, and promised to declare war on Japan the day that Germany was defeated.

With that promise, Churchill returned to London, telling the Commons on his return that, 'I have not hesitated to travel from court to court like a wandering minstrel, always with the same song to sing, or the same set of songs'. Harold Nicolson said he was 'superb. Cherubic, pink, solid and vociferous.'

Churchill told the Commons that his purpose as a troubadour was to secure 'the unity of the Allied Powers'. His efforts were not approved of by the Foreign Office, which felt that in December 1944 he was pursuing a policy of appeasement towards his allies. This was the *Economist*: 'Let an end be put to the policy of appeasement which, at Mr. Churchill's personal bidding, has been followed, with all the humiliations and abasements it has brought in its train, ever since Pearl Harbor removed the need for it'. This view, developed by subsequent historians, is founded on the premise that there could have been a negotiated peace with Germany which would have meant that Lend-Lease did not drain away all Britain's resources and that she did not emerge as a minor and impoverished nation in a world dominated by America and Russia. In reality, there was no alternative: Roosevelt had committed Britain to a policy of unconditional surrender, Britain could not negotiate a separate peace from her allies and Churchill could only achieve the best results for Britain by working as closely and amicably as possible with those allies.[6]

Allies Accelerating Apart. Christmas in Athens

Hopkins warned the British just before the 1944 Presidential election that they were unwise to hope, as they did, for a Democratic victory. The Republicans were not interested in foreign policy and would leave Britain with a free hand in India, Europe and the Middle East. He knew that after the elections Roosevelt would be homing in on these issues: 'You will find him right in in [*sic*] all these questions with his own views and you will have to pay attention to them'.

He was right: until now Roosevelt had been interested primarily in winning the war. Now, with the election won, and for what remained of his life, he was trying to form the shape of a post-war world. In the second role he was much further from Britain than he had been in his first. Furthermore, Roosevelt's re-election coincided, more or less, with the replacement of Hull by Ed Stettinius. Although Hull had been no friend of Britain, State Department and President now worked much more closely together, and there was a concerted policy of shaping the post-war world in a way that would restrict Britain's influence and tend to favour Stalin. Halifax noted that there was a 'desire for a brand new 100 per cent American foreign policy, not tied to Britain's apron strings'. This was reflected in American interference in Italy and Greece, where Britain till now had enjoyed a fairly free hand, and was thought to have used it to favour the right. Stettinius blamed Churchill for precipitating the developing crisis in Greece by vetoing the appointment of Papandreou, as Prime Minister. Papandreou led the Greek socialists.

Greece was indeed Churchill's major concern in this last winter of the war. As a result of the Percentages Agreement he now had the luxury of regarding Greece as his responsibility. Stalin was in agreement on that; America was not. Churchill's Greek policy of December 1944 marked a further low point in the increasingly different political positions of the two allies.

Churchill tried to contact Hopkins by telephone on 9 December. The transatlantic line was particularly bad, and Hopkins could not work out what the problem was. On the following day he heard that Admiral King had ordered Admiral Hewitt, the American Commander of the Mediterranean Fleet, not to permit any troop landing craft to be used to transfer supplies to Greece. Hopkins realised that King was interfering in a political issue. While America was right to keep its troops out of Greece, she could not withdraw cooperation on the matter of transport. From a command point of view, in any case, Hewitt was under the command of General Wilson, and orders should not have been given to him without consultation with the Combined Chiefs. Hopkins was able to defuse the problem by getting King to withdraw his order and by persuading the British ambassador, Halifax, to urge that Churchill should not raise the matter with the President.

But even the benevolent Hopkins thought that 'the British government had messed up the whole [Greek] thing pretty thoroughly.'[1] All of this came on the heels of a remark by Churchill in the course of the Polish debate in the House of Commons, when he said that 'all territorial changes must await the Conference at the peace table after victory has been won, but to that principle there is one exception, and that exception is, change that is mutually agreed'. This fairly innocent observation caused a storm in the States, reviving accusations that Roosevelt had had to face ever since Placentia Bay, allegations that the big powers intended to carve the world up. Eden had to make a correction.

The freedom Churchill had been given by Stalin was remarkable in that the issue in Greece was a communist challenge to the established government. By the beginning of December there were extensive reports of violence by communists in Athens. Policemen were being murdered and police stations were being seized. Churchill voiced his concerns to Clementine, from whom he now received one of her interfering letters. She urged her 'Darling Winston, Please do not before ascertaining full facts repeat to anyone you meet today what you said to me this morning i.e. that the communists in Athens have shown their usual cowardice in putting the women & children in front to be shot at – because altho' communists are dangerous, indeed perhaps sinister people, they seem in this war on the continent to have shown personal courage. I write this only because I may not see you till tomorrow & I am anxious (perhaps over-anxious).' She then added, '*Tout savoir, c'est tout comprendre; tout comprendre, c'est tout pardoner.*'

Churchill paid no attention. He telegraphed the British commanding officer in Greece, General Scobie: 'Do not hesitate to fire at armed males in Athens who assail British authority or Greek authority with which we are working'. Scobie took 1,800 communist prisoners. Because Colville's telegram had omitted the key code word, 'Guard', to signify that it was a purely British matter and was not to be seen by the Americans, the telegram, with phrases like 'Treat Athens as a conquered city', reached the White House. It was then leaked to the press, notably to Drew Pearson, an anti-British columnist on the *Washington Post* who had a mole either in the White House itself or in the State Department. The instruction to Scobie to act as if he were in a 'conquered city' in particular provoked great indignation about intolerable quasi-imperialism when it appeared in the press.

There were protests on both sides of the Atlantic and Churchill demanded that a debate on the subject be treated as a vote of confidence. 'Democracy is no harlot, to be picked up in the street by a man with a tommy-gun.' If the vote went against him he would accept his dismissal; otherwise action against dissidents would continue. Two hundred and seventy-nine voted for the government; 30 were against it. It was a Friday and there was only a two-line whip, so the result was not a bad one for the Prime Minister. Churchill made light of the event in a letter to Hopkins of 10 December 1944 for Roosevelt's eyes: 'Do not be misled by our majority yesterday. I could have had another 80 by sending out a three line whip instead of only two. On Fridays, with the bad communications prevailing here, members long to get away for the weekend. Who would not?'[2] But James Stuart, the Chief Whip, told Colville that the Greek issue was the first one on which he had seen the House 'really irritated and impatient' with Churchill.[3]

Churchill's letter of 10 December was addressed to Hopkins because he needed his help in mollifying Roosevelt. A day later he wrote to him again, thanking him for his 'mediation'.[4] It was needed. American opinion was inflamed. On 10 December the British Embassy in Washington reported that, 'suspicion of British despotism in Europe is now thoroughly awakened'.[5] Roosevelt was furious: 'Greece. British troops. Fighting against the guerrillas who fought against the Nazis for the last four years. How the British can dare such a thing! The lengths to which they will go to hang on to the past!'[6]

From Canada, Mackenzie King was equally unhelpful, telegraphing to ask that no Canadian troops be deployed, and that he should be allowed to announce the fact publicly. According to Lascelles, 'Winston sent him a strongly-worded rebuke for his poltroonery', and the following day Mackenzie King telegraphed to say that he had been misunderstood, and had never intended to make a public announcement.[7]

Alexander had moved to Greece from Italy and found the situation serious. Macmillan was also in Athens and, with the British ambassador, Reginald Leeper, recommended the appointment of Archbishop Damaskinos as regent, with a government under him acceptable to the Commons. But Churchill still had reservations about a government which might well lean to the left.

By 22 December he decided that he had to go to Greece to sort things out himself. On 23 December he arrived at Chequers, where the family were settled for Christmas, but told Clementine that he would not be staying. She took the news badly and retired to her room in what her daughter, Mary, described as 'floods of tears'.[8]

Clementine's reaction was an unnecessary burden. Refuelling at Naples on Christmas Day, Churchill sent her a telegram: 'Love and many thoughts for you all at luncheon today. I'm sorry indeed not to see the tree.' He also had to worry about the American dimension. He sent a telegram to Roosevelt: 'Anthony and I are going out to see what we can do to square this Greek entanglement. We cannot abandon those who have taken up arms in our cause, and must if necessary fight it out with them.' Sir Leslie Rowan described this famous journey as 'one of his most courageous and lonely acts'.[9] Churchill almost alone apprehended what was really happening in Greece. America totally misread the situation, and so did most of the British press and the political left. It is bizarre that the one person who shared a true understanding of the situation was Stalin, and it is all the more to his credit that he kept his word and allowed Churchill to frustrate his plans. It is thus thanks to Stalin that Greece remained on the Western side of the Iron Curtain.

Churchill read too much into this instance of Stalinist fidelity, and for quite some time cited it as evidence that Russia could be trusted to keep her word. He referred to Stalin in a message to Eden on 3 December as 'That great and good man' and on 11 December said, 'I am increasingly impressed, up-to-date, with the loyalty with which, under much temptation and very likely pressure, Stalin has kept off Greece in accordance with our agreement'.[10]

The visit to Athens was exciting as well as productive. Part of Churchill's time was spent on board the cruiser *Ajax*. There was a fancy-dress party and Archbishop Damaskinos in his black robes and tall hat was briefly mistaken for one of the partygoers. Shellfire and machine-gun fire continued constantly. British fighters strafed communist positions. The Admiral's barge, carrying Churchill, was almost hit by shellfire as it approached the shore. In a conference room at the Greek Foreign Ministry proceedings were conducted by the light of hurricane lamps and with background noise from rocket fire. Back on the *Ajax*, Churchill was delighted to authorise the captain to return fire. As he slept, or tried to sleep, depth charges were exploded continuously throughout the night, against the risk of a submarine attack.

By the time he left, the framework for a stable government had been established. The Archbishop appeared able to form an administration and was prepared to do so with or without communist participation. Churchill was reassured, as he told Roosevelt, that the Archbishop was not at all 'Left Wing in communist sense'. He saw the United States ambassador and was very frank to him about what he considered to be the inadequate support given by America in the whole affair.

He was very moved by the suffering and privation he observed in Athens. He took the opportunity of telling Roosevelt, in his telegram of 28 December, that 'the poor people [were] all pinched and only kept alive by rations we are carrying to them, often at loss of life'. Britain had lost 'over 1,000 men . . . The vast majority of the people long for a settlement that will free them from the communist terror.'

He was impressed also by the courage of the women on the embassy staff and requested that fifteen of them be given the British Empire Medal in the New Year's Honours List. The proposal was vetoed by the Palace, where Lascelles facetiously referred to the 'Fifteen Brave Ladies'.[11]

As always when he was away from Clementine, he sent her countless letters and on his way home tried to mollify her about his absence over Christmas: 'Hope to be with you at dinner tomorrow. I was feeling lonely.' Clementine may have felt guilty: she was awaiting him at Bovingdon Airbase when he arrived on 29 December.

Later on the same day he found that the exiled King George II of Greece was unwilling to appoint Damaskinos as regent. At 1.30 a.m. on the following morning he saw the King and told him that 'if he did not agree, the matter would be settled without him, and that we would recognise the new government instead of him'.

Ultimately, Damaskinos was able to form a government from which the communists were excluded. Churchill was reasonably pleased with what he had achieved. He told Clementine that 'I am sure in Greece I found one of the best opportunities for wise action that this war has tossed to me from its dark waves'.

But there was much criticism both in America and in London. H.G. Wells attacked him bitterly and daftly, in phrases that owed everything to caricature and nothing to reality:

> His ideology, picked up in the garrison life of India, on the reefs of South Africa, the maternal home and the conversation of wealthy conservative households, is a pitiful jumble of incoherent nonsense. A boy scout is better equipped. He has served his purpose and it is high time he retired on his laurels before we forget the debt we owe him. His last associations with the various European Royalties who share his belief in the invincible snobbishness of mankind and are now sneaking back to claim the credit and express their condescending approval of the underground resistance movements that have sustained human freedom through its days of supreme danger, are his final farewell to human confidence.[12]

There was criticism in the *Manchester Guardian* and in *The Times*, where one leader declared that 'There is no ground for pride or satisfaction in the knowledge that British troops have been engaged in house-to-house operations in a working-class suburb of Athens'. But the Labour members of the War Cabinet and the Labour Party generally, though not a young Major Dennis Winston Healey (who had been the military Landing Officer for the British assault brigade on the beach at Anzio),[13] at the Party Conference[14] were entirely supportive.

Foreign policy and the communist threat caused ongoing trouble in Parliament and the War Cabinet through the later months of 1944, when a decision had to be made between seeing Franco as an undisposed-of dictator, or as a bastion of capitalism. Churchill took the latter view, but was faced by a powerful attack from an alliance of Attlee, Eden and Hoare (now Lord Templewood), which only failed to be more serious because Attlee chose not to press it.[15]

Yalta

On 20 January 1945, the day on which Hungary signed an armistice with the Allies and the Red Army entered Germany, Churchill received a letter from Attlee, complaining in moderate tones that the Prime Minister was protracting Cabinet meetings with long soliloquies without having read the papers under discussion. Churchill's hurt and anger were compounded when he went to Clementine for support and she told him that Mr Attlee was quite right to have written as he did and that she admired him for doing so. Deflated and depressed, Churchill lay in bed all day. But his natural elation could not be long suppressed and eventually he bounded out of bed and telling his staff that they should 'cast care aside' and 'not bother about Attler or Hitlee', took them all off to watch Bette Davis in *Dark Victory*.

The next meeting of the Big Three was to be held at Yalta. Churchill went in no triumphalist mood. He wrote to Clementine on 1 February telling her how saddened he was by the plight of German women and children fleeing before the advancing Red Army. 'I am clearly convinced that they deserve it; but that does not remove it from one's gaze. The misery of the whole world appals me, and I fear increasingly that new troubles may arise out of those we are successfully ending.'

He saw agony and suffering throughout the world, and he saw it increasing and not diminishing as victory approached, because a common purpose between the Allies was giving way to a new spirit of conflict. This was the theme of Yalta for him, and part of that theme was that his convictions were not shared with Roosevelt. The sense of frustration and despair that was engendered remained with him for the rest of his life. That is why at the end of that life he saw his career as one of failure and not of success. The war from which the West emerged victorious was for him a tragedy.

Churchill met Roosevelt at Saky in the Crimea on 3 February. The President could not leave his jeep, and Churchill walked beside it as he inspected a guard of honour, 'as in her old age an Indian attendant accompanied Queen Victoria's phaeton', said Cadogan. 'The President looked old and thin and drawn; he had a cape or shawl over his shoulders and appeared shrunken; he sat looking straight ahead with his mouth open, as if he were not taking things in.' All the observers at the conference made similar remarks, Hopkins, Cunningham and Eden among others. Cunningham said that the President did not appear to know what he was talking about. It was left to Churchill to defend the interests of the West.

He described Roosevelt's arrival at Saky. He was a 'tragic figure . . . He could not get out of the open motorcar, and I walked at his side while he inspected the guard.' Moran diagnosed hardening of the arteries of the brain, and questioned the President's will or capacity for judgement and analysis.[1] Even at the Second Quebec Conference in September 1944 Colville had noticed that the President's eyes were glazed and that he had said 'nothing impressive or even memorable.'[2] At Yalta, desperately ill, he sat through many meetings in silence. Moran said that Churchill found the President no longer seemed able to take an intelligent interest in the war and often seemed not even to read the papers he gave him. 'We have moved a long way since Winston, speaking of Roosevelt, said to me in the garden at Marrakech, "I love that man", [but] he is still very reticent in criticism'.[3] The problem was that Roosevelt's prejudices grew stronger as his intellect grew weaker. Hopkins told Moran on the way to the conference, 'You will find us lining up with the Russians'.

There was no concerted planning between the Western allies. Eden told Hopkins that they were going into 'a decisive conference and had so far neither agreed what we would discuss nor how to handle matters with a Bear who would certainly know his mind'.[4]

Churchill himself had been unwell on the way to Yalta, remaining in bed in his aeroplane at Malta for six hours, but his intellect and wit were as sharp as ever: when he shouted at his valet, 'Sawyers, where's my hot-water bottle?' Sawyers replied 'You are sitting on it, sir. Not a very good idea'. 'It's not an idea', said the Prime Minister. 'It's a coincidence.'[5]

The first plenary session of what was to be the last meeting of the original Big Three began on 4 February. At the dinner that night Churchill made the very reasonable observation that 'he was constantly being "beaten up" as a reactionary but that he was the only one of three representatives present who could be thrown out of office at any time by the votes of his own people'.

Yalta was to settle the face and nature of Europe for half a century, but its decisions were reached very speedily. The plenary sessions concluded on 9 February, although a number of separate meetings took place thereafter. The biggest question to be discussed was Poland. Again, Roosevelt took little interest in this matter. He said, 'Coming from America,' he took 'a distant view of the Polish question; the 5 or 6 million Poles in the United States were mostly of the second generation'. Later he said that 'Poland has been a source of trouble for over five hundred years'. Churchill's reply was more humane: 'We must do what we can to put an end to those troubles'.

Stalin continued to insist on a preponderance of power for the Lublin Poles. Churchill managed to obtain an agreement to free general elections in Poland. On that basis, Britain 'would salute the government that emerged without regard to the Polish government in London'. Stalin agreed and said that the elections could be held within a month. These sentences summarise very briefly negotiations that were long, difficult and tense, but in essence Stalin's undertaking was the basis of the resolution to the Polish question which Churchill took back to London. It was an undertaking in which he had to believe. Only time would show that it was an undertaking that would not be honoured.

Churchill's interest in Poland was very real. When he returned to Parliament, and faced criticisms of a sell-out, he wrote to Roosevelt, 'I have based myself in Parliament on the assumption that the words of the Yalta Declaration will be carried out in the letter and spirit' . . . [I]f we do not get things right now, it will be soon be seen by the world that you and I by putting our signatures to the Crimea settlement have underwritten a fraudulent prospectus.'[6] After Yalta Roosevelt declined to press Stalin on the issue until Churchill hit on the device of querying the viability of the inaugural United Nations Conference at San Francisco, a project that was dear to the President, if the way to unity had not been paved by a clarification of Stalin's intentions. Stalin's reply was not wholly satisfactory, and the conduct of his armies as they moved towards Germany pointed up the problems that lay ahead, but neither Roosevelt nor, initially, Truman shared Churchill's appreciation of events.

De Gaulle had been excluded from Yalta. Churchill said that his presence 'would have wrecked all possible progress, already difficult enough'.[7] The exclusion still rankles in France, which sees Yalta as a carve-up by Russia and the Anglophone world. For her own self-respect, France cut and pasted pictures to make the absent de Gaulle appear to sit beside the Big Three. But Churchill went out of his way to ensure that France had a zone of occupation in Germany, and a seat on the Control Commission, a concession to a largely non-combatant nation which seemed remarkable at the time and for which he had to fight hard. It was intended to contribute to the rehabilitation of post-war France – all the more necessary as the Foreign Office expected America to desert post-war Europe as they had done in 1918.[8]

Churchill's generosity was all the more remarkable in view of the fact that relations between Britain and France were going through yet another very low phase at this time. Looking beyond the war, Churchill and the French Foreign Office at the Quai d'Orsay wanted a British–French alliance. De Gaulle would not consider it, despite all that Britain did for her at Yalta – in the face of considerable opposition from both the Americans and the Russians. Far from showing gratitude, in French proceeded to occupy Stuttgart, which was not even in their zone.

When there was a serious outbreak of violence in the Levant which required British intervention, de Gaulle saw the whole matter as yet another Machiavellian attempt by the British to seize a French possession. He summoned Duff Cooper, now ambassador in Paris, on 4 June 1945 and told him, 'I admit that we are not in a position to wage war against you at the present time. But you have insulted France and betrayed the West. This cannot be forgotten'.[9] And yet it was Churchill alone who insisted on a special role for France in the Levant. When Roosevelt and Stalin agreed that the peace should be made by the Great Powers only, Churchill's response was that 'The eagle should permit the small birds to sing and care not whereof they sang'.

The new United Nations Organisation was discussed at Yalta. Indeed, for America, the Pacific war and the United Nations were the main point of Yalta. Stalin was well aware of that, and used America's preoccupations to gain his own objectives. The United Nations would be run by a Security Council dominated by the Great Powers, but Churchill did his best to enhance the position of the Lesser Powers. He and Roosevelt agreed that the Soviet Union would have three seats in the assembly, one for itself, one for Byelorussia, and one for the Ukraine, a concession that caused dismay when it was revealed to the American public.

Stalin promised Churchill that he would persuade Tito, in Yugoslavia, to give undertakings regarding the future of that country. He was reassuring: 'when he made a statement he would carry it out'. Earlier there had been a short discussion of Greece where Stalin told

Churchill 'he did not wish to interfere'. Churchill said he was 'much obliged'.

Debate still continues on how far the West, Churchill and an American delegation led by an ailing President, sold out to Stalin at Yalta. There were certainly substantial concessions to ensure that Russia confirmed what Stalin had promised to Churchill in Moscow, and would break the neutrality treaty and participate in the war against Japan. Eden warned that concessions to Russia in the east could only be made at the cost of friction with China. Churchill thought that this was far outweighed by the 'thousands of millions of pounds' which Britain would save as a result of an early end to the Japanese war. He was deluded about the extent to which he could trust Stalin and he continued to overrate his reliability, even if he was more realistic than Roosevelt. As late as 1956–7, Churchill was still saying, referring back to the Percentages Agreement of 1944, that Stalin always kept his word.[10] In the immediate aftermath of Yalta he said, 'Poor Neville Chamberlain believed he could trust Hitler. He was wrong. But I don't think I'm wrong about Stalin.' He told Colin Coote, 'If only I could dine with Stalin once a week there would be no trouble at all'.[11]

Roosevelt's final move at Yalta was to have the Big Three sign a 'Declaration on Liberated Europe' which purported to commit them to 'free elections' and 'self-government' for 'liberated peoples'. What did he imagine he was doing? Apologists have suggested that he was tricking Stalin into giving a pledge which could later be used against him if need be, but the argument is far too elaborate. Roosevelt knew very well that there was no question of free elections where Stalin's writ ran, and he was either playing politics or, as seems more likely, simply failing to think through the reality of a piece of idealistic bombast.

There was nothing really surprising in Stalin's behaviour at and after Yalta. Russia had carried the real burden of fighting Germany. It was her armies that defeated Germany and it was unrealistic to think that Stalin would not expect to be rewarded. During the war Churchill had often spoken in the strongest, minatory terms about Soviet expansionism. It is clear that part of his mind was focusing on the spread of communism in post-war Europe. Greece was one case in point; his worry about Spain, if Franco were to fall, was another. He tried to persuade himself that one way of containing Soviet expansionism was to limit it by deals done with Russia reinforced by the strength of his personal relationship with Stalin. But for most of the war the issue was very much subsidiary to the primary aim of defeating Hitler: the real showdown could be postponed until victory had been achieved.

The problem was that now that victory was imminent, he could not induce Roosevelt to address the problem in concert with him. Roosevelt thought the problem less pressing than that of detecting and destroying British spheres of influence. Back in May 1944, he had told Harriman, then ambassador in Moscow, 'that he didn't care whether the countries bordering Russia were communized'.[12] For Churchill there were two levels of concern about Russia after Yalta. One was in relation to Poland and the other in relation to other instances of Soviet aggrandisement. Of the two, Poland was much more acute, largely because of its symbolic importance and the peculiar interest which the ex-Chamberlainites right took in it. Poland had much less significance for Roosevelt.

Yalta was a messy compromise from which no one nation emerged triumphant. But it is wrong to say, as de Gaulle and the French did, that but for Yalta Europe would not have been divided up into two armed camps. President George W. Bush at Riga in 2005 described the conference as 'an attempt to sacrifice freedom for the sake of stability',[13] but he was as far adrift as the largely Conservative backbenchers who, after Yalta, put down an amendment to the motion before the House, regretting 'the decision to transfer to another power the territory of an ally'. Yalta was in any event intended only to be a provisional arrangement ahead of the great Peace Conference. It merely recognised facts.

In the course of the history of the parliamentary truce which Churchill later called 'the Grand Coalition' there was a number of occasions on which the participants recognised the historic nature of the bond that held them together, apart from and above the level of party rancour and strife. One such occasion was at the conclusion of the Yalta Conference, when the Cabinet in London reviewed and approved what the Prime Minister and Foreign Secretary had achieved in the Crimea. At Attlee's suggestion a telegram was sent to them: 'War Cabinet send their warmest congratulations to you and the Foreign Secretary on the skill and success with which you have conducted discussions at Crimean Conference and on the most satisfactory result you have achieved, and wish you a safe journey home'.[14]

On his way home from Yalta Churchill asked his pilot to circle the island of Skyros, on which lay the body of Rupert Brooke whom he had known well in the earlier war: his vivid sense of place as well as of history was always with him. He then made a stop in Athens, where the peace he had established still held. He visited the Regent, Archbishop Damaskinos, and went on to Constitution Square. There he was greeted by a crowd that Harold Macmillan estimated at 40,000. Macmillan and Churchill too had never seen anything like the reception he received, a vindication of what he had done the previous December, and perhaps the intervention of 1941 was also remembered. He received the Freedom of the city that is the birthplace of democracy and the cradle of oratory.

After his travels in the eastern Mediterranean, Churchill arrived in London on 19 February, in much better health than when he had left for Yalta. One of the aspects of the conference which had been specifically noted with approval by the War Cabinet before he left the Crimea was the agreement on 'the difficult matter of Poland'; but he returned to be greeted by a mood of great hostility to the Yalta agreement as it touched that country. The Chief Whip, James Stuart, had already warned Eden by telegram of what might be expected.[15]

There still remained a small band of right-wing Conservatives, supporters of Chamberlain who had never reconciled themselves to Churchill. These Jacobites found a rallying point in Poland. Having been attacked in the past by Churchill as appeasers, they now attacked him for the same reason. They may have been sincere. Chips Channon said that 'The conscience of the gentlemen of England and of the Conservative Party has been stricken by our failure to support our pledged word to Poland'.[16] It was a bit rich that Churchill should have been accused of appeasement by what was very much the Munich Second Eleven, and he might well have been bitter. In fact his main reaction was to appreciate the humour of the situation. Harold Nicolson said that 'Winston is as amused as I am that the warmongers of the Munich period have now become appeasers, while the appeasers have become warmongers'.[17] Lord Dunglass, Chamberlain's Parliamentary Private Secretary at Munich, and later Lord Home, spoke against Yalta. Lord Cranborne, the Dominion Secretary, later Lord Salisbury, told Churchill on 3 April that the Polish aspect of Yalta was 'a fraud which will very soon be exposed'. Four government Ministers abstained in the vote and two resigned. The rebellion was easily quashed: only 25 Conservatives voted against their government. On 3 April, Churchill told 'C', the Head of British Intelligence, to find out if some of the Tory rebels were in the pay of the Polish government in exile.[18]

The rebels were unreasonable. As Eden told Colville on his return to London, 'the Tories had no right to complain about Poland. The PM had not sold the pass. On the contrary the Curzon Line was a boundary proposed as fair by H.M.G. after the last war.'[19] Cadogan took a similar view: 'The PM and Anthony are well satisfied – if not more – and I think they are right. Of course Poles in London, and extreme right-wing MPs, criticise and grumble. All I can say is that, in the circumstances, I think we did much better by Poland than I, at least, could have thought possible before we left.'[20]

Of course everything depended on Stalin, and there were no sanctions that could be applied to him at Yalta, given America's position. But Churchill committed himself, as he told Roosevelt, to advising Parliament if 'the spirit of the Yalta declaration' were not applied 'in the business of setting up a new Polish government etc'.[21]

In the debate Churchill said that he was sure that Russia wanted 'to live in honourable friendship and equality with the western democracies. I feel also that their word is their bond.' Later, when he wrote the history of the war, he glossed that statement by saying that: 'I felt bound to proclaim my confidence in Soviet faith in order to procure it. In this I was encouraged by Stalin's behaviour about Greece.'[22] But even at the time, Churchill's eyes were open. He wrote to the Prime Minister of New Zealand, 'The proof of the pudding is in the eating. We are only committed on the basis of full execution in good faith of the terms of the published communiqué.'[23] He told the War Cabinet that if Stalin did not implement his undertakings in regard to the Polish elections, Britain's commitment would be at an end.

Very soon, alas, Churchill's hopes were dispelled when Stalin failed to implement the Yalta agreement in relation both to Poland and to Romania. On the basis of the Percentages Agreement and Greece, Churchill wanted Roosevelt to tackle Stalin on these breaches of the agreement. That did not happen.

Churchill's message to Roosevelt of 13 March 1945 captures his mood of frustration:

> We can of course make no progress at Moscow [regarding Poland] without your aid, and if we get out of step the doom of Poland is sealed . . . A month has passed since Yalta and no progress of any kind has been made . . . I do not wish to reveal a divergence between the British and the United States Governments, but it would certainly be necessary for me to make it clear [to the House of Commons] that we are in presence of a great failure and an utter

breakdown of what was sorted out at Yalta, but that we British have not the necessary strength to carry the matter further and that the limits of our capacity to act have been reached.[24]

Roosevelt's reply was simply to deny that any divergence existed. His responses over Poland were drafted by the State Department, but he saw them and approved them. He accepted the State Department line that America had to continue to work with Russia.

Between 8 and 18 March, Churchill sent no less than ten telegrams to Roosevelt, urging him to stiffen his resolve against the Soviets. On 6 April 1945 Roosevelt telegraphed from Warm Springs, Georgia, in more encouraging terms than hitherto. He was in 'general agreement' with Churchill. 'We must not permit anybody to entertain the false impression that we are afraid'. Soon the allied armies will be 'in a position to permit us to become "tougher" than has here before appeared advantageous to the war effort'.[25] The message has sometimes received more attention than it deserves.[26] On the face of it, as the editor of the Churchill–Roosevelt correspondence says, 'For the first time during the war Roosevelt seemed to place politics ahead of military cooperation with the Soviet Union'. But it really centred on the narrow issue of allegations from Stalin about an understanding between Alexander and the German Kesselring at Berne. It was drafted by Leahy to support Harriman and received scant attention from Roosevelt.[27] It did not signal a momentous change in American foreign policy.

Roosevelt was sadly in no condition to exercise any restraint on Stalin. He was far sicker than Wilson had been at one stage in Paris in 1919, and the consequences for the world were more serious. Churchill described himself later at Yalta 'talking to a friendly but darkening void'. Hopkins doubted if the President had heard more than half of what went on around the table and told Churchill that hardly any of the President's final messages to him were truly his.[28] He was suffering from congestive heart disease, high blood pressure, chronic anaemia and a consequent inadequate blood supply to the brain. It was tragic that this great and vigorous man, in domestic matters the most effective President of the twentieth century, inventive, innovative and original, should end his career baffled and deluded in the midst of foreign policy matters of which he knew little. Four days after sending his telegram from Warm Springs came that 'terrific headache'. The President suffered his fatal cerebral haemorrhage and died on 12 April 1945.

How far Roosevelt, in full vigour, would have behaved differently we shall never know. Even before his final decline he had tended to a more idealistic interpretation of Stalin than Churchill and indeed seemed to regard the Russian leader as closer to him than the imperialist English aristocrat. His penultimate message to Churchill of 11 April 1945, for which he *was* personally responsible, said that 'I would minimise the general Soviet problem as much as possible, because these problems, in one form or another, seem to arise every day, and most of them sort themselves out . . .'[29]

There was a fear, not just on Roosevelt's part, but shared by his advisers, even Hopkins who parted company with Churchill on this issue, that what the Prime Minister was trying to do was to restore the 'unsavoury *status quo ante*'.[30]

The Disintegration of Unity

In these last months Churchill had only limited control over the fighting. On 22 February 1945 he tried to have Alexander appointed as Deputy Theatre Commander in France. Eisenhower would have none of it. The concept of British generals pulling the strings, while Americans occupied honorific positions, the stratosphere theory, had completely gone. Churchill was reduced to a plaintive response: 'I am sure you would not wish to deny us the kind of representation on your Staff in respect of military matters which is our due'.[1] The Americans had jettisoned the principle of equality of command.

Increasing suspicions about Stalin prompted Churchill to press Eisenhower to push towards Berlin, and to capture it before the Russians got there: 'I deem it highly important that we should shake hands with the Russians as far to the east as possible'. He received no support from Roosevelt. Eisenhower was worse. He not only departed from directly targeting Berlin, but he told Stalin what he was doing. To make matters worse, he did so without informing his British deputy, Tedder, or the combined Chiefs. Eisenhower's innocence contrasted with Stalin's deviousness. The Russian played along with American naïvety, cabling Eisenhower to say that Berlin had 'lost its former strategic importance' and that he would only send some second-rate forces, sometime in May. Simultaneously, however, he sent Zhukov and Koniev off to the city in a race of savage rivalry. Churchill was furious on a number of counts, and not only because Berlin was being handed over to the Soviets. A coding error in the telegram led him for some time to understand that Montgomery was to play a negligible part in the advance. Additionally he was annoyed about Tedder. Tedder was supposed, in his view, to promote British interests at Supreme Head-quarters, whereas Churchill felt he had gone native. He wrote a savage attack on Tedder for the Chiefs of Staff, which Brooke thought outstandingly wrong-headed: 'He must have been quite tight when dictating it'. But Brooke and the Chiefs of Staff were as angry as Churchill about Eisenhower's change of plan.

This was Churchill's last great argument with Eisenhower. On Churchill's eightieth birthday Eisenhower was prompted to write to a friend on the subject of greatness. He concluded that Churchill 'came nearest to fulfilling the requirements of greatness in any individual that I have met . . . I have known finer and greater characters, wiser philosophers, more understanding personalities, but no greater man.'[2]

While the Prime Minister was travelling back from Yalta to London, the bombing of Dresden had begun. Dresden arose out of a revived Joint Intelligence Committee proposal for Operation THUNDERCLAP, designed originally to destroy German morale as the war came into its final phase. THUNDERCLAP had been intended for Berlin; the revived plan was for raids on Chemnitz, Leipzig and Dresden, critical points in the German transport system, together with targets that would assist the Soviet offensive in the east. The Americans were all for the raids. Portal and Sir Archibald Sinclair, the Secretary of State for Air, wanted to concentrate on oil targets. It was Churchill, heading for Yalta, who insisted that revised THUNDERCLAP go ahead. It would put him in a stronger negotiation position with Stalin. Dresden was targeted at the specific insistence of the Russians at a time when they were suspicious of allied intentions.

Colville found Harris alone in the Great Hall at Chequers on the night that thirty-six hours of bombing ended. He asked him what the news was of Dresden. Harris replied, 'There is no such place as Dresden'.[3]

The material damage and loss of life, the fires and terror of Dresden, were appalling, but Germany was able to make it seem even worse. They inflated the losses. They stigmatised it as an inhumane assault on the civilian population of a town that was without strategic significance, although the city contained critical elements of Germany's war industry and was an important railway junction. In his famous speech in the House of Lords on 14 February 1943, Dr George Bell, the Bishop of Chichester, had denounced the bombing policy; Richard Stokes attacked it in the Commons. As early as 28 March 1945, Churchill, appalled by what the policy amounted to, sent the Chiefs of the Air Staff a memorandum in which he referred to Dresden as 'a serious query against the conduct of allied bombing'. The Air Chiefs were horrified by Churchill's turn-around, and a further memorandum was sent in substitution on 1 April 1945 with a call simply for the review of bombing policy 'in our own interests'. Another minute, of 19 April, consisted simply of the sentence, 'What was the point of going and blowing down Potsdam?' On 6 April bomber command was told to stop attacking industrial centres.

It remains difficult to know how the moral, humane and military arguments should have been balanced at the height of these hectic days, and it was difficult for the West alone to gauge proportionality. At this time there was never more than 25 per cent of the Wehrmacht in the West.

On 29 April, just two months after the champagne toasts at Yalta, dismayed by what he saw happening in Poland and Yugoslavia, Churchill sent an important appeal to Stalin:

> There is not much comfort in looking into a future where you and the countries you dominate, plus the Communist Parties in many other States, are all drawn up on one side, and those who rallied to the English-speaking nations and their associates or Dominions are on the other. It is quite obvious that their quarrel would tear the world to pieces, and that all of us leading men on either side who had anything to do with that would be shamed before history . . . [Do] not, I beg you, my friend Stalin, underrate the divergences which are opening about matters which you may think are small to us, but which are symbolic of the way the English-speaking democracies look at life.[4]

On the same day, Russia set up a Provisional Austrian government without consulting the West, who were not allowed to send representatives to Vienna.

Churchill protested against the Austrian *démarche*. On this occasion he was supported by the new President, Truman. Truman did not however support him on 30 April, when Churchill heard that Eisenhower had told the Soviet High Command that he would advance no further than Linz and that indeed the Americans would withdraw up to 140 miles from their present positions in Germany once the war was ended, in order to comply with the Yalta agreement which the Russians were already being seen to dishonour.

Truman, for all that he had recognised the likelihood of succeeding to the Presidency, had taken no trouble to prepare for the eventuality so far as knowledge of foreign affairs was concerned. On his succession he claimed to know what was required on the domestic front, but no more than that: a serious omission in the circumstances. He could of course learn nothing of what Roosevelt had been thinking. Even Stettinius, who had been drafting much of Roosevelt's paperwork latterly, did not know what subtleties, qualifications and evasions had been lodged in the late President's mind.

By degrees Truman came to see what the reality of the situation was. He saw the world in black and white and fairly simple terms, and that was no bad thing when looking at the rights and wrongs of what Stalin was doing. On 14 April in just his second message to Churchill, he said that Stalin must understand that the Lublin Poles could not dictate who should negotiate the new government of Poland. On 15 April Churchill told Eden that he had wanted a lead from the United States and now it had come.[5]

The aspect of American foreign policy which certainly did remain constant as between Roosevelt and Truman was the desire for the conference in San Francisco to pave the way for the establishment of the United Nations Organisation. This had been at the heart of Roosevelt's later foreign policy. The comparison between Roosevelt's intervention in the Second World War and Wilson's in the First World War is obvious: both justified intervention not as involvement in the power-politics of the old world but as, and only as, part of a scheme to replace that dirty system with a more idealistic world order. Wilson's aims had been thwarted and discredited when the negotiations at Versailles proceeded on the basis of European business as usual; America turned its back on the League of Nations and watched as Europe descended into the squalor of fascism and appeasement. Roosevelt was clear that things must never be the same again, and between his final election success and his death his policy was directed to avoiding a return to the old order. To sell the United Nations settlement to America, Roosevelt needed to be able to convince American opinion that the new organisation had no taint of secret deals and covert spheres of influence. Roosevelt's thoughts about foreign policy can only be understood by studying these last few months of his life.

Truman was no less committed to the United Nations solution: it was such a significant part of US foreign policy that he could not have done otherwise. But he, as Roosevelt was not, was influenced by those such as Leahy, who saw the inescapable reality, 'that a Europe dominated by a single overwhelming power spelled danger to American security'.[6] Thus the post-war settlement resulted not in the global New Deal, which Roosevelt's critics on the right had feared, but in American military imperialism. Far from continuing with Roosevelt's determined efforts to conciliate the Soviets and base the United Nations at all costs on Three Power unity, Truman told Molotov that he was going to go on with his plans for San Francisco, and the Russians could do what they wanted. 'I gave it to him straight' he said, with a 'one-two to the jaw'. Molotov went white, and said 'I have never been talked to like that in my life' and Truman replied, 'Carry out your agreements and you won't get talked to like that'.[7]

Events were moving at a great pace. On 29 April the German armies in Italy surrendered unconditionally to Alexander. Mussolini was caught and executed and on 1 May Hitler committed suicide. On 7 May Jodl signed the German instrument of surrender. Fighting was to stop at midnight on 8 May. Captain Pimm brought the news to Churchill when he awoke. 'For five years you've brought me bad news, sometimes worse than others. Now you've redeemed yourself.'

On 7 May also, Churchill managed to encourage Ike to enter Prague before the Russians. He did so, but promptly withdrew as soon as Soviet troops arrived. Even more reprehensibly, some five weeks later, on 14 June, Eisenhower ignored an appeal from Churchill and withdrew his troops from central Germany and Czechoslovakia despite the fact that Russia was putting Polish leaders arrested near Warsaw on trial in Moscow.

Eighth May was VE Day. From San Francisco, Eden, always decent and fair and not without some nobility, sent a telegram to his chief: 'All my thoughts are with you today, on this day which is so essentially your day. It is you who have led, uplifted and inspired us through the worst days. Without you this day could not have been.'[8] When Churchill spoke to the crowds in Whitehall from the balcony of the Ministry of Health and declared, 'This is your victory', the crowd roared back, 'No – it is yours'.

Four days earlier, as it became clear that the end of the war was imminent, Ismay had written: 'My dear Prime Minister, Your Defence Office, with intense pride and – if we may be so bold – with deep affection offer their most grateful congratulations to their Chief, whose superb leadership has today been crowned with a triumph which only History will be able to measure'.[9] That was a tribute from the Ministry of Defence.

On the eve of VE Day, the Prime Minister and the Chiefs of Staff posed in the garden of No.10 for a group photograph. Churchill himself had put out a tray of glasses and a bottle of champagne. He did not overlook such practical arrangements: for VE Day itself he personally checked in advance with Scotland Yard and the Ministry of Food that there were adequate supplies of beer in the capital. He toasted the Chiefs as 'The Architects of Victory',[10] drinking to each man in turn. The Chiefs failed to toast their great leader in response.

Ismay ranked below the Chiefs and it was not for him to take the initiative. He 'hoped that they would raise their glasses to the chief who had been the master-planner; but perhaps they were too moved to trust their voices'.[11] Brooke's diary is very matter-of-fact about the occasion and discloses no pent-up emotion. In any event, he had seen his master in tears often enough to dispel any concern about appearing unmanned. Joan Bright, Ismay's assistant, recalled later, 'it was a sad example of human imperceptiveness that neither the Chief of the Imperial Staff, nor the First Sea Lord, nor the Chief of the Air Staff saluted him in a toast . . . Whatever the reason it was an opportunity missed that the Grand Old Man, who had been the architect of the victory that they were marking, did not receive a tribute from his three closest military advisers.'[12]

On 14 May the customary breadth of his spirit was again displayed when he thought to send messages to three French Prime Ministers who had been his colleagues in the dark days before the fall of France and who had been prisoners of the Germans: Léon Blum, Édouard Daladier and Paul Reynaud. Another telegram went to Harry Hopkins, whose visit before America entered the war had meant so much: 'Among all those in the Grand Alliance, warriors or statesmen, who struck deadly blows at the enemy and brought peace nearer, you will ever hold an honoured place'.[13]

Potsdam

On 12 May, foreshadowing his Fulton speech, the Prime Minister telegraphed to Truman: 'An Iron Curtain is drawn down upon [the Soviet] front. We do not know what is going on behind. There seems little doubt that the whole of the region Lübeck-Trieste-Corfu will soon be completely in their hands.' Once the Americans withdrew from central Europe and Czechoslovakia, as they threatened shortly to do, 'A broad band of many hundreds of miles of Russian-occupied territory will isolate us from Poland'. He pressed Truman to come with him to a further meeting with Stalin before allied forces had left Europe and could no longer exercise any influence on Russia. It was agreed that they would meet at Potsdam.

In response to Tito's occupation of the Italian province of Venezia Giulia, Truman sent Churchill on 12 May what was described as a 'most robust and encouraging telegram'. The President declared that he had 'come to the conclusion that we must decide now whether we should uphold the fundamental principles of territorial settlement by orderly processes against force, intimidation or blackmail'.[1]

As Sir Martin Gilbert put it, the telegram 'confirmed a harmony of Anglo-American interests towards Russia which had not existed during Roosevelt's wartime Presidency'[2] and Churchill certainly looked forward to Potsdam in the expectation that he would find Truman more of his mind than FDR had latterly been. But in his 12 May telegram Truman also made it clear that there was to be no suspicion of the English-speaking allies 'ganging up': he would therefore not visit Churchill in London, as invited, and travel together with him to Potsdam. He offered to make a London visit afterwards. Even that offer was significant and welcome, though the visit never took place: Roosevelt had repeatedly talked of accepting a visit to Britain, but had been scrupulously careful to avoid it because of the implications of old-world chumminess.

But it is important to remember that despite his realism, Truman remained the man that Roosevelt had chosen as his Vice President. On 10 May he wrote to Eleanor Roosevelt, talking of how difficult the Russians were, but adding that 'the difficulties with Churchill are very nearly as exasperating as they are with the Russians'.[3] Truman believed that only America, not Russia and equally not Britain, had the confidence of the smaller nations, and he reassured Russia by sending Joseph E. Davies, the pro-Russian former US ambassador to the Soviet Union, as envoy to London ahead of the Potsdam meeting. Davies was known not only for his sympathy for the Soviets, but also for his contempt for British imperialism. Churchill and Davies did not get on well. The exchanges between them reflected that fact.

By now Churchill was profoundly dispirited. America talked of withdrawing from Europe while all sorts of issues remained outstanding. The Russians were all-powerful. They could drive Britain off the Continent with ease: they had a majority of two to one over the Western allies, and that would increase if the Americans left. The victorious Prime Minister told Brooke that he had never in his life been 'more worried by the European situation than he was at present'.[4]

With the military victory in Europe won, the question of the continuation of the coalition with Labour and the Liberal Party came into question. Churchill certainly wished it to continue, subject to a referendum of the people. Attlee probably shared this wish. He asked that Churchill, in his letter proposing a continuation, commit the government to implementation of social reforms. Churchill had no difficulty in agreeing. But the view of the Labour Party in conference at Blackpool was that it was time for the coalition to finish. The Grand Coalition, as Churchill liked to call it, came to an end. At his own expense he distributed commemorative medals to all its members at a farewell party. With the tears running down his cheeks, he told his Cabinet colleagues, 'The light of history will shine on all your helmets'. He now led a Conservative caretaker government until a general election could take place and its results were known.

The fruits of victory for Churchill were tainted by the bitter awareness that all his efforts over the last five years might have resulted in winning one war only to see the world punished in another, even more disastrous than the German conflict. On 18 May he met the Soviet ambassador, Gusev, and gave him a fierce talking-to. He complained about Soviet secrecy. He told the ambassador that demobilisation of the Royal Air Force was being postponed. On the previous day he had indeed ordered that the British Air Forces should be kept intact and all German aircraft in allied hands were to be preserved in operational condition.

He instructed the planners to prepare Operation UNTHINKABLE. The purpose of UNTHINKABLE was to assess the feasibility of imposing the allied will on Russia in relation to Poland and it assumed a hypothetical start of hostilities against the former Russian ally as soon as 1 July 1945.

UNTHINKABLE remained unmentionable until 1954, when Churchill told his constituents at Woodford: 'Even before the war had ended and while the Germans were surrendering by hundreds of thousands, and our streets were crowded with cheering people, I telegraphed to Lord Montgomery directing him to be careful in collecting the German arms, to stack them so they could easily be issued again for the German soldiers whom we should have to work with if the Soviet advance continued'.[5] Challenged on the point, he could not find the telegram to which he referred. There was amusement and embarrassment and Churchill said, 'I made a goose of myself at Woodford'. But later Montgomery claimed that while there had been no telegram, there had been an oral instruction from Churchill, as a result of which very large numbers of weapons were accumulated until he asked for a specific order, confirming or rescinding his oral instructions. When no such order came, he arranged for destruction of the weapons.

As well as being unmentionable, UNTHINKABLE was pretty well un-doable, but the planners tried their best on paper, with the assumed use of German troops. The allies would have to go far further into the Soviet Union than the Germans had been able to do in 1942. Brooke said that the project was 'fantastic and the chances of success quite impossible. There is no doubt that from now onwards Russia is all-powerful in Europe.'[6] On 9 June 1945, as UNTHINKABLE was out of the question, Churchill asked the planners how 'we could defend our island' assuming an American abandonment of Europe. He was back to 1940.

Ultimately Truman was to be a greater enemy of the Russians than Roosevelt had ever been, but for the moment an initial spell of belligerence was followed by a return to conciliation. When Churchill first met Truman at Potsdam on 15 July 1945 he asked him squarely whether the President thought that the states that Russia now con-trolled were 'free and independent or not'. Truman dodged the question and simply replied that while he did not want to see these states degenerate into mere Soviet satellites, he did not want to impede Stalin's legitimate requests. He had no wish to be Churchill's agent.

Before adopting this more conciliatory tone towards Russia, Truman had been suggesting a joint display of force over Trieste, to check Tito's acquisitiveness. 'If we stand firm on this issue, as we are doing on Poland, we can hope to avoid a host of other similar encroachments', he said to Churchill. The latter commented to Alex that 'This action if pursued with firmness may well prevent a renewal of the World War'.[7]

But after the Trieste affair, Truman was increasingly influenced by Joseph E. Davies, now back from his role as Envoy to London. Davies advocated a policy of appeasement to avoid a breakdown in US–Soviet relations. Truman told Davies that Churchill was causing him as much difficulty as Stalin; when Davies visited Churchill he had concluded and reported to the President that Churchill was 'more concerned over preserving England's position in Europe than in preserving peace', a simplistic caricature of the Prime Minister's position. He further said that Churchill's position had directly accounted for the Soviet attitude since Yalta.

The President's name was eventually to be commemorated in history in the policy of containment of communism known as the Truman Doctrine. The journey to that declaration from a philosophy of détente was a long one in terms of theory, but a short one in terms of time. The evolution of the doctrine began as early as February 1946 with the 'Long Telegram' to the US Treasury from George F. Kennan, the Deputy Chief of Mission of the United States to the USSR, which properly analysed the nature of Soviet communism and distinguished it from social democracy. Kennan went on from that to predict accurately the development and nature of what turned out to be the Cold War. He expanded his thesis in an anonymous piece, the 'X Article', more formally 'The Sources of Soviet Conduct', in the July 1947 issue of *Foreign Affairs*; but even before then Truman had endorsed the new policy in his Declaration of 12 March that year. Churchill was aware of the irony: what immediately prompted the Declaration was the continuing Greek Civil War. Truman said it was now 'the policy of the United States to support free peoples who are resisting attempted subjugation by armed minorities or outside pressures'. How different from December 1944 when Churchill made his lonely and dangerous Christmas visit to Athens, in the face of ill-informed and facile hostility from the United States. If his perception of the true nature of militant communism had been shared by the naïve and blinkered White House of that time, how different the postwar years might have been.

Churchill had been furious to discover from Davies that Truman wanted a one-to-one meeting with Stalin before the Big Three summit at Potsdam. He had done very much for the United States: he had supported 'unconditional surrender' rather than making peace with Hitler. He expected a special relationship in return. Davies took it much amiss that Churchill should be so 'violent and bitter' about the Soviets. Churchill told the President that the British government would not 'attend any meeting except as equal partners from its opening', and Truman backed down.

But a month later, taking the Davies line, he told Churchill that he could see no reason for not implementing the Yalta agreement on occupation zones in Germany. To fail to implement it would harm Soviet–American relations. 'This', said Churchill, 'struck a knell in my breast'. There were 3 million American soldiers in Europe and only 1 million British: 'I had no choice but to submit . . . Soviet Russia was established in the heart of Europe. This was a fateful milestone for mankind'.

The general election was held on 5 July. The service vote had to be collected from the theatres throughout the world in which British servicemen and women were based and to enable the vote to be brought in and counted there was a three-week delay between the date of the election and the announcement of the results. During the break Churchill took a week's holiday in Biarritz. Colville describes him in the sea, floating 'like a benevolent hippo'. France provided a team of detectives who had been kitted out by *la Sûreté* in old-fashioned bathing costumes. Together with Churchill's own detective, the team swam round and round the Prime Minister, creating a *cordon sanitaire.* Their efforts were indeed necessary, because they succeeded in keeping at bay a flaxen-haired French countess who hoped to enlist Churchill as her protector to avoid the consequences of enthusiastic collaboration. In the event her golden locks escaped the scissors of unofficial justice, and she got off with a short spell of imprisonment.[8]

Churchill flew on to Berlin, and the conference, on 15 July. Among those who were there to meet him was Attlee, attending the conference as an observer pending the outcome of the election. Churchill met and liked Truman. He surveyed the ruins of Hitler's chancellery. All the Germans who were watching, except for one old man, began to cheer. 'My hate had died with their surrender and I was much moved by their demonstrations, and also by their haggard looks and threadbare clothes.'

The first plenary session took place on 17 July. There were private meetings as well as formal ones. Stalin told Churchill that he had started smoking cigars. Churchill said that if a picture of Stalin smoking a cigar could be 'flashed across the world, it would cause an immense sensation'. He pressed on Truman a continuation of the closest of relations between Britain and America. He was dissatisfied with the cold response: such relations would have to be carried out within the context of the United Nations. He said that was not what he wanted. If a man proposed marriage to a woman it was 'not much use if he were told that she would always be a sister to him'.

He wanted a continuation of provision of reciprocal facilities, for instance in regard to bases for fuelling operations. He wanted, in effect, in a real, tangible form, a special relationship. Truman did agree to a suggestion that the combined Chiefs of Staff should be kept going until conditions were more stable, but later Churchill was told that if there were any disagreement, the United States would make the final decision.

The planners had told the President about Britain's 'melancholy' financial position. Britain 'had spent more than half her foreign investments for the common cause *when we were alone*, and now emerged from the war with great external debt of three thousand million pounds' (my emphasis). Truman said to Churchill on 18 July at Potsdam that he would do his best to help, but that he might have domestic difficulties. A month later, when Churchill was out of office, Truman abruptly terminated Lend-Lease. At the 18 July meeting the President had referred to the 'immense debt' that America owed to Britain 'for having held the fort at the beginning . . . If you had gone down like France, we might well be fighting the Germans on the American coast at the present time.'[9]

At the second plenary session that day, Churchill pressed Stalin about Poland. Stalin told him that the Provisional government had not refused to hold free elections. Truman brought the proceedings to an end when Churchill felt there were still points to discuss. After the war he told Colville that to please the new President Eisenhower he had excised from his history the fact that 'the United States, to please Russia, gave away vast tracts of Europe – the British General Election had occupied too much of his attention which should have been directed to stemming this fatal tide . . . [Truman was] bewildered by responsibilities which he had never expected.'[10] That evening he dined with Stalin, and the Russian leader reassured him that the central European nations, like Poland, would have free elections.

On 23 July Churchill heard the news of the successful test of the atomic bomb. As at the news of Pearl Harbor, he was jubilant: this time because the Russians need not be involved in the Japanese War. As at the news of Pearl Harbor, Brooke failed to share his vision: 'I tried to crush his over-optimism based on the result of one experiment, and was asked with contempt what reason I had for minimizing the results of these discoveries'.

There was little to celebrate about Potsdam. The British Chiefs of Staff were angered when they found that they were to be excluded from devising the strategy for the war in the Pacific: all Marshall was prepared to do was to let them know what was to happen. Finally he gave way only to the extent that the United States Chiefs would consult with the British, while retaining the right to make the final decisions. The days of the Combined Chiefs were at an end.

Churchill did secure some modest gains in negotiations with Stalin: Britain and America were allowed to share with Russia in occupying Vienna, and satisfactory territorial arrangements were made in relation to Persia and Turkey. But that was all. He tried yet again, but unsuccessfully, to argue for a democratic future for Poland. By now he had to resist claims from a communist Poland for aggrandisement in the west, where earlier the London Poles had sought to extend their frontiers to the east.

In subsequent discussions Churchill continued to press Stalin and the Polish Communist Leader, Bierut, for the return of Silesia to Germany. They refused, but Bierut told him that Poland would follow 'the English model' of democracy and would be 'one of the most democratic countries in Europe'. Neither Churchill nor Truman attached any value to such assurances and when the ninth plenary session ended at 12.15 p.m. on 25 July no agreement had been reached and the matter was deferred 'until a later agreement'.

There was now a break of forty-eight hours while Attlee and Churchill left to hear the outcome of the vote in London. Stalin had told Churchill that there would be a Conservative majority of eighty. Eden reported that the Conservative Party predicted a majority of about seventy. But when Churchill and Attlee went in separate jeeps to a British victory parade in Berlin on 21 July, Churchill's secretary, John Peck, noticed that the Prime Minister was getting markedly less cheers than the Labour leader. Mountbatten had dined with Churchill at Potsdam on 24 July and was told that the Prime Minister had great plans in store for him. Mountbatten had been in India when the British troops were voting and he wrote later, 'It was a mournful and eerie feeling to sit there talking plans with the man who seemed so confident that they would come off, and I felt equally confident that he would be out of office within twenty-four hours'.

On his first night back in London, Churchill woke up before dawn with 'a sharp stab of almost physical pain', a premonition of defeat. Before noon that morning it was evident that there was to be a Labour landslide. On 27 July, Attlee returned to Potsdam as Prime Minister. Churchill remained in London. He had feared when he woke at dawn on the previous day that 'The knowledge and experience I had gathered, the authority and goodwill I had gained in so many countries would vanish'.

Epilogue

On 26 October 1951, at the age of seventy-six, Churchill returned to power. He finally resigned from office, with great reluctance, on 5 April 1955. The last piece of political advice he gave, as he said goodbye to those Ministers who were not in the Cabinet, was, 'Never be separated from the Americans'.

His second Ministry is now regarded as having been a productive and valuable one. His main ambition in these years, and the desire which was part of the cause of his reluctance to leave the scene, was to attempt to secure world peace, to reduce the tension which had brought Britain and America to the brink of war with their Russian wartime ally. He had hoped that his personal links with Stalin might allow him to act as a peacemaker, and proposed to President-Elect Eisenhower in February 1952 that they both go to Moscow. Eisenhower declined. When Stalin died on 9 March of that year, he felt that it might be possible to establish an understanding at a meeting with his successors. That meeting never took place, and his last great plan of reducing world tension and exorcising the spectre of atomic war was thwarted, largely by his former colleague, Eisenhower, with the assistance, at home, of his long-time deputy, Anthony Eden.

Churchill had been made a Knight of the Garter in 1953, a distinction he had declined in 1944 when the King reported that his Prime Minister 'became all blubby'. Lascelles said that then 'they seem to have fallen on each other's necks, in an ecstasy of fraternal devotion'.[1] The honour had been proffered again after the 1945 election, but despite much pressure Churchill would not accept it in view of the decision of the electorate.[2]

He was offered a dukedom by the Queen at the time of his resignation in 1955. Dukedoms for commoners were long in abeyance, and without his knowledge his Secretary and the Queen's had discussed the matter in advance, so that the Queen could be assured that there was

no risk that he would accept. In the event he found himself momen-
tarily tempted and hesitated before declining. He reported, 'And do you
know, it's an odd thing, but she seemed almost relieved'.[3] He remained
a Member of the House of Commons until 1964, when he was eighty-
nine. He died on 24 January 1965. Three hundred thousand people
walked past his coffin as he lay in state at Westminster Hall. He received
the first State Funeral that a commoner had received since the death of
the Duke of Wellington. The Queen broke with precedent and awaited
the arrival of her greatest subject.

Countless historians have felt constrained to describe him as, under
God, the saviour of his country, which he was. No Prime Minister of
Great Britain, indeed no Minister of any sort, has done more for his
country, and it is inconceivable that any ever will. What was said of the
younger Pitt can be said even more truly of Churchill: 'He saved his
country by his efforts and the world by his example'. He was a great
man. His faults were only the product of an abundance of vigour and
enthusiasm. The scale and range of his abilities was matched by a
profound sense of humanity and magnanimity. His nobility was the
reflection of the belief that mankind was itself noble, endowed with a
duty and a destiny.

Clementine Churchill, a popular figure in her own right as a result of
her war work, was created a Baroness in May 1965. Despite the wealth
which her husband's writings, particularly his history of the Second
World War, brought to him and to family trusts, she lived latterly in
straitened circumstances. She declined offers of assistance. She died on
12 December 1977.

De Gaulle was a caretaker President of France under the Fourth
Republic from September 1944 to 20 January 1946. He returned to the
Presidency under the Fifth Republic. The constitution of that Republic
was his creation and modern France is substantially shaped by his ideas
and his concept of the role that his country should play in the world.
On 16 May 1967, when Britain sought to join the community of
European powers whose formation Churchill had been one of the first
to urge, de Gaulle refused the requests of Harold Macmillan, with
whom he had worked in North Africa, complaining that Britain was too
close to America to be a true European. On 10 January 1966 de Gaulle
was the only world statesman who wrote to Clementine on the first
anniversary of her husband's death in terms which greatly moved her:
*'Voici venir le triste et émouvant anniversaire. Laissez-moi vous dire, qu'en
portent en cette occasion ma pensée sur la grande mémoire de Sir Winston*

*Churchill, je ressens, mieux que jamais, la dimension de sa personalité . . .
Je voudrais que vous sachiez aussi de quel coeur ma femme et moi-même
partageons le chagrin où vous a laissée, ainsi que les vôtres, la disparition de
votre si cher et si glorieux mari*'.[4]* He continued to write every year until
January 1970. Ten months later he was dead.

During the Cold War, America sought to defend herself by
establishing her front line on the east, rather than the west, of the
Atlantic. She established countless military bases throughout Britain.
The special relationship between Britain and America was talked of
more than it had been before. There was however little evidence of its
actual existence. When Britain, along with France, invaded Suez in
1956, Eisenhower, who had earlier said he would not force a withdrawal, changed his position and told his wartime colleague, Eden,
that if the adventure were not ended America would withdraw her
support of the pound sterling. As a result of the scale of Britain's war
debts to the United States that support was essential. On 3 November
1956 Eden wrote to Eisenhower, 'If you cannot approve, I would like
you at least to understand the terrible decisions we have had to make. I
remember nothing like this since the days when we were comrades
together in the war.'[5] Eisenhower failed to respond to this plea from
his old comrade, and three days later the Chancellor of the Exchequer,
Harold Macmillan, who had also worked closely with Eisenhower in
North Africa, was told by America that they would only save Britain
from collapse by supporting a loan application to the International
Monetary Fund if Britain were to agree to a ceasefire that same night.
To America the Suez venture smacked of imperialism and Britain's
economic weakness meant that it could be stopped. In the first week
of November alone, Britain lost $100 million from her currency
reserves. In these circumstances Britain had no choice but to withdraw. Anthony Eden resigned from office, his fragile health broken by
years of strain.

In the Vietnam War, Britain's Prime Minister, Harold Wilson,
declined to provide military support to the United States. President
Lyndon B. Johnson complained that even a single piper would have
been enough. In the Falklands War, America provided valuable

* 'As this sad anniversary approaches, and my memory turns to Sir Winston, I am
more than ever conscious of the scale of his personality. I should like you to know that,
and to know also how deeply my wife and I share with you and your family your grief
over the loss of a very dear and wonderful husband.'

intelligence support for Britain, but nothing more, despite the warm personal relationship which existed between President Reagan and Margaret Thatcher.

When George W. Bush became President he telephoned Tony Blair. He told him it was his first phone call to a foreign leader and he referred to the special relationship between the English-speaking peoples.[6] Soon he was to request Britain's help in Afghanistan and Iraq.

It had long been evident that the special relationship only mattered – indeed only existed – when both parties wanted it to. But the phrase still leaps easily to the lips of the petitioner.

APPENDIX I

Codenames for Principal Military Operations

ANVIL	Invasion of South of France Summer 1944 (later DRAGOON)
BATTLEAXE	Attempt to clear Cyrenaica, June 1941
BREVITY	Unsuccessful attempt to relieve Tobruk, May 1941
BOLERO	Build-up of United States forces in Britain, ahead of invasion
COMPASS	Successful operation in the Western Desert under O'Connor, December 1940
CRUSADER	Eighth Army offensive, North Africa, November 1941– February 1942
DIADEM	Allied attack on Rome
DRAGOON	Final name for ANVIL
GYMNAST	Landings in French North Africa (later known as TORCH)
HUSKY	Landings in Sicily
JUPITER	Contemplated invasion of Norway
OVERLORD	Invasion of North-west Europe, Summer 1944
ROUNDUP	Contemplated substantial invasion of Europe for 1943
RUTTER	Dieppe Raid, 1942
SHINGLE	The Anzio landing
SLEDGEHAMMER	Contemplated small-scale landing in Europe for 1942
TORCH	Anglo-American landings, French North Africa, formerly GYMNAST

APPENDIX II

Principal War Conferences

Atlantic Conference, Placentia Bay, Newfoundland, 9–12 August 1941 (WSC, FDR)

ARCADIA, **First Washington Conference**, 22 December 1941–14 January 1942 (WSC, FDR)

Second Washington Conference, 20–25 June 1942 (WSC, FDR)

Moscow Conference, 12–17 August 1942 (WSC, JS, Harriman)

Casablanca Conference, 14–24 January 1943 (WSC, FDR with de Gaulle and Giraud in walk-on parts)

TRIDENT, **Third Washington Conference**, 12–27 May 1943 (WSC, FDR)

QUADRANT, **First Quebec Conference**, 17–24 August 1943 (WSC, FDR, Mackenzie King)

First Cairo Conference, 22–26 November 1943 (WSC, FDR, Chiang Kai-shek)

Teheran Conference, 28 November–1 December 1943 (WSC, FDR, JS)

Second Cairo Conference, 4–6 December 1943 (WSC, FDR, Inönü)

OCTAGON, **Second Quebec Conference**, 12–16 September 1944 (WSC, FDR)

Moscow Conference, 9 October 1944 (WSC, JS)

Yalta Conference, 4–11 February 1945 (WSC, FDR, JS), preceded by preparatory **Malta Conference** (WSC, FDR)

Potsdam Conference, 17 July–2 August 1945 (interrupted by declaration of the results of the British general election) (WSC, HST, JS, Attlee)

APPENDIX III

Outline Chronology of Churchill's War

1939

3 September	Britain and France declare war on Germany.
3 September	Churchill First Lord of the Admiralty.
3 October	Roosevelt announces that USA will remain neutral.

1940

28 March	Britain and France agree not to sign separate peace with Germany.
9 May	Norway Debate vote.
10 May	Hitler invades France.
10 May	Chamberlain resigns. Churchill appointed Prime Minister.
26–28 May	Cabinet debates peace overtures.
27 May	Evacuation from Dunkirk begins.
28 May	Belgium surrenders.
10 June	Mussolini declares war on the Allies.
14 June	German Army enters Paris.
15 June	USA rejects France's appeal for help against Germany.
17 June	Pétain negotiates an armistice with Germany.
22 June	France signs armistice with Germany and is divided into two zones.
28 June	Churchill recognises de Gaulle as leader of the Free French.
3 July	Royal Navy destroys bulk of the French fleet at Mers-el-Kébir.
10 July	Luftwaffe launches Battle of Britain.
23 August	The Blitz begins.
25 August	Royal Air Force bombs Berlin.
2 September	Destroyers for Bases Agreement.
13 September	Graziani and Italian Army advance into Egypt.
15 September	'The culminating date' in the Battle of Britain.
25 September	Dakar.
12 October	Hitler postpones Operation Sealion.
28 October	Italy invades Greece.
5 November	F.D.R.'s third Presidential victory.
9 December	O'Connor opens COMPASS

1941

22 January	Britain captures Tobruk.
9 February	O'Connor at El Agheila.
22 February	Britain undertakes to support Greece.
7 March	British Army invades Italian-controlled Ethiopia.
11 March	Master Lend-Lease Act passed by US Congress.
24 March	Rommel enters the Desert War.
6 April	Italian Army in Ethiopia surrenders to Allied forces.
21 April	Greece surrenders to Germany.
24 April	Evacuation from Greece.
25 April	Rommel enters Egypt.
8 June	Syria invaded by British and Free French forces.
15 June	Wavell opens BATTLEAXE.
21 June	Auchinleck replaces Wavell.
22 June	Hitler launches Operation Barbarossa.
14 July	Armistice in Syria with Vichy France.
9–12 August	Atlantic Conference, Placentia Bay.
12 August	German Army advances on Leningrad.
7 December	Pearl Harbor.
8 December	US declares war on Japan.
10 December	Japan sinks *Prince of Wales* and *Repulse*.
11 December	Germany and Italy declare war on US.
22 December	ARCADIA opens.
24 December	Free French seize St. Pierre and Miquelon.
25 December	Hong Kong surrenders.

1942

21 January	Rommel opens his second offensive.
8 February	Japanese troops land on the north-west corner of Singapore.
15 February	Singapore surrenders.
23 April	Luftwaffe bombs Exeter, Bath and other cities.
30 May	Harris orders the first 1,000-bomber attack on Germany at Cologne.
14 June	Rommel defeats Ritchie at Gazala.
20–25 June	Second Washington Conference.
21 June	Rommel captures Tobruk.
8 August	Auchinleck dismissed. Montgomery appointed to command Eighth Army.
12–17 August	Churchill in Moscow.
19 August	Dieppe raid.
30 August	Rommel defeated by Montgomery at Alam Halfa.
23 October	Montgomery opens Second Battle of El Alamein.
8 November	TORCH landings in North Africa.
11 November	Admiral Darlan surrenders French North Africa to Eisenhower.
11 November	Germany occupies Vichy France.

12 November	Britain recaptures Tobruk.
24 December	Darlan assassinated.

1943

18 January	Luftwaffe renews air attacks on London.
12–24 January	Casablanca Conference.
23 January	Eighth Army enters Tripoli.
25 February	British and US military aircraft begin round-the-clock bombing of Nazi Germany.
7 May	Allies capture Tunis.
12–27 May	TRIDENT.
13 May	Last Germans surrender in Tunisia.
27 May	Jean Moulin holds the first meeting of the Conseil National de la Résistance in Paris.
10 July	Invasion of Sicily.
25 July	Mussolini falls from power.
17–24 August	QUADRANT.
3 September	Eighth Army lands in Italy.
15 September	Mussolini restored to power at Lake Garda.
23 September	Badoglio signs armistice with the Allies.
13 October	General Mark Clark and 5th Army capture Naples.
13 October	Badoglio declares war on Germany.
18 November	Intensive bombing of Berlin by the RAF begins.
28 November	Teheran Conference.
28 December	Churchill, Roosevelt and Stalin meet at Teheran.

1944

22 January	Anzio landings begin.
6 March	United States Air Force begin daylight air attacks on Berlin.
26 May	French Council for National Liberation declares itself the Provisional government of France.
4 June	Allies capture Rome.
6 June	D-Day.
13 June	First V1 Rocket bomb lands on Britain.
9 July	Allied troops capture Caen in Normandy.
1 August	Warsaw rising.
14 August	Allied troops land on the French Mediterranean coast.
24 August	Allies enter Paris.
8 September	First V2 Rocket lands on Britain.
11 September	Allied troops enter Germany.
12–16 September	OCTAGON.
9 October	Churchill in Moscow.
7 November	FDR's fourth Presidential victory.
25 December	Churchill in Athens.

1945

4 February	Churchill, Stalin and Roosevelt meet at Yalta Conference.
27 March	Last V2 Rocket lands on Britain.
12 April	Roosevelt dies. Truman President.
29 April	German forces in Italy surrender to the Allies.
1 May	Hitler commits suicide.
2 May	Berlin surrenders.
4 May	All military forces in Germany surrender to the Allies.
8 May	General Jodl signs the official surrender of Germany.
8 May	VE Day.
17 July	Potsdam Conference opens.
23 July	Atomic bomb tested.
26 July	Churchill resigns, following British general election.

Bibliographical Note

I have not thought it worthwhile to compile a bibliography. This book is the product of forty years' reading of books by and about Churchill, prompted by a present from my parents in 1968 of the collection of essays edited by Sir John Wheeler-Bennett, *Action this Day: Working with Churchill* – still stimulating and valuable. The literature surrounding Churchill is vast. Zoller's *Annotated Bibliography of Works about Sir Winston S. Churchill* runs to 432 pages. Much that is of importance is contained in slim volumes which stand apart from the more magisterial studies, and thus even a select bibliography would be too extensive to be helpful.

Some, but certainly not all, the works I have found most useful are referred to in the References that follow, where a full bibliographical record is given in the first reference to each book.

For a full bibliography, reference may be made to Zoller's compilation. The Churchill Centre's website (www.winstonchurchill.org) is also helpful.

Despite what I have said about the significance of the slim volumes, I must record the importance of the most magisterial of all, the great series of the official biography, begun by Randolph Churchill with Sir Martin Gilbert's assistance, then written jointly by the two men, and finally, and for the most part, by Sir Martin Gilbert alone. These eight volumes are authoritative and painstakingly researched, but eminently readable, at times gripping. Their companion volumes of documents are of enormous assistance to the historian, and it is a matter of regret that they currently extend only to the end of 1941. The whole is an outstanding biographical achievement, on a scale that is unlikely to be repeated.

References

Chapter 1

1. Private communication, *The Churchill Centre*.
2. Quoted, John Ramsden, *Man of the Century: Winston Churchill and his Legend since 1945* (London: Harper Collins, 2002). Quotation from pbk edn, p. 196.
3. David Reynolds, *In Command of History: Churchill Fighting and Writing the Second World War* (London: Allen Lane, 2004).
4. Quoted, Ramsden, *Man of the Century*, pbk edn, p. 199.
5. See Ramsden, *Man of the Century*, pbk edn, p. 202.
6. See, for example, Robert Blake and William Roger Louis (eds), *Churchill, A Major New Assessment of his Life in Peace and War* (Oxford: Oxford University Press, 1993). There are other well-researched critical studies, such as David Carlton *Churchill and the Soviet Union* (Manchester: Manchester University Press, 2000) and Tuvia Ben-Moshe, *Churchill: Strategy and History* (Boulder, CO: Lynne Rienner Publishers, 1991).
7. Howard, 'The End of Churchillism? Reappraising the Legend', in *Foreign Affairs*, September/October 1993.
8. C. Zoller, *Annotated Bibliography of Works about Sir Winston Churchill* (New York: M.E. Sharpe in association with the Churchill Centre, 2004), chapter 2; updated by personal communication from the Churchill Centre.

Chapter 2

1. See John Colville, *The Fringes of Power, Downing Street Diaries, 1939–55* (London: Hodder and Stoughton, 1985), p. 123.
2. A. Roberts *The Holy Fox: A Biography of Lord Halifax* (London: Weidenfeld & Nicholson, 1991), p. 199.
3. Quoted, F. Smith, Earl of Birkenhead, *Halifax: the Life of Lord Halifax* (London: Hamish Hamilton, 1965), p. 454.
4. M. Gilbert, *Winston S. Churchill*, vol. 6 (London: Heinemann, 1983), p. 313.
5. W. Churchill, *The Second World War*, vol. 1 (London: Cassell, 1948), p. 526.
6. See, for example, Blake, 'How Churchill became Prime Minister' in Blake and Louis, *Churchill*, p. 272.

7. Colville in J. Wheeler-Bennett (ed.), *Action this Day: Working with Churchill, Memoirs by Lord Normanbrook and others* (London: Macmillan, 1968), p. 49.
8. R. James (ed.), '*Chips', The Diaries of Sir Henry Channon* (London: Weidenfeld and Nicholson, 1967), p. 242.
9. N. Nicolson (ed.), *Diaries and Letters of Harold Nicolson 1939–45* (London: Collins, 1967), 30 April 1940.
10. Quoted, A. Roberts, *Eminent Churchillians* (London: Weidenfeld & Nicholson, 1994), p. 141 *et seq.*

Chapter 3

1. Colville, *The Fringes of Power*, p. 195.
2. M. Soames, *Clementine Churchill* (London: Cassell, 1979). Quotation from pbk edn, p. 386.
3. J. Colville, *The Churchillians* (London: Weidenfeld & Nicholson, 1981), p. 115.
4. Colville, *The Fringes of Power*, p. 336.
5. Colville, *The Fringes of Power*, p. 238.
6. Colville, *The Churchillians*, p. 21.
7. Colville, *The Fringes of Power*, p. 273.

Chapter 4

1. Quoted, Colville, *The Fringes of Power*, p. 122.
2. *Daily Herald*, 21 May 1940.
3. J. Kennedy, *The Business of War, The War Narrative of Major-General Sir J. Kennedy* (London: Hutchinson, 1957), p. 80.
4. For an excellent account of the political constraints at this period, see L. Olson, *Troublesome Young Men: The Rebels who Brought Churchill to Power and Helped Save England* (New York: Farrar, Straus and Giroux, 2007), especially chapter 19.
5. Quoted, David Reynolds, 'Churchill & the British "Decision" to Fight on in 1940', in R. Langhorne (ed.), *Diplomacy and Intelligence during the Second World War: Essays in Honour of F.H. Hinsley* (Cambridge: Cambridge University Press, 1985), pp. 149 & 297.
6. Churchill to Chamberlain 10 May 1940, quoted D. Reynolds, *From World War to Cold War: Churchill, Roosevelt, and the International History of the 1940s* (Oxford: Oxford University Press, 2006), p. 77.
7. See M. Gilbert, *The Churchill War Papers*, vol. 2, (London: Heinemann, 1994), p. 49.
8. Chamberlain Papers.
9. See Gilbert, *Churchill*, vol. 6, p. 828 *et seq.*
10. Soames, *Clementine Churchill*, p. 299 *et seq.*
11. Quoted, Gilbert, *Churchill*, vol. 6, p. 835.
12. Churchill to J.A. Spender Churchill papers, 20/29, quoted, M. Gilbert, *The Churchill War Papers*, vol. 3 (London: Heinemann, 1999), p. 895.

13. See Gilbert, *War Papers*, vol. 3, p. 912 *et seq*; Hansard, 9 July 1941.
14. Gilbert, *War Papers*, vol. 3, p. 883 *et seq*.
15. Churchill to Clement Attlee and Lord Cranborne, Churchill Papers, 20/50, quoted by Gilbert, *War Papers*, vol. 3, p. 1717; Hansard, 29 April 1941.
16. C. Cross (ed.), *Life with Lloyd George: the Diary of A.J. Sylvester 1931–45* (London: Macmillan, 1975), p. 281.

Chapter 5

1. Quoted P. Addison, *Churchill: The Unexpected Hero* (Oxford: Oxford University Press, 2005), p. 57.
2. W. Churchill, *The World Crisis* (London: Thornton Butterworth, 1923), Part 3, Chapter 10.
3. A. Marder, *From The Dreadnought to Scapa Flow: the Royal Navy in the Fisher Era 1904–19* (Oxford: Oxford University Press, 1965), vol. 1, p. 255.
4. Quoted Addison, *Churchill: The Unexpected Hero*, p. 73.
5. Colville, *The Fringes of Power*, p. 403.
6. Quoted Martin Gilbert, *Churchill*, vol. 5 (London: Heinemann, 1976), p. 687.
7. Quoted M. Gilbert, *Continue to Pester, Nag and Bite: Churchill's War Leadership* (Toronto: Vintage Canada, 2004) published in the UK as *Winston Churchill's War Leadership*, p. 7.
8. D. Stafford, *Churchill and Secret Service* (London: John Murray, 1997). Quotation from pbk edn, p. 397.
9. See, for a fascinating exploration of Churchill's interest in intelligence, Stafford, *Churchill and Secret Service*.
10. Quoted Gilbert, *Winston Churchill's War Leadership*, p. 48.

Chapter 6

1. Churchill, *The Second World War*, vol. 2 (London: Cassell, 1949), p. 157 *et seq*.
2. See J. Lukacs, *Five Days in London, May 1940* (London: Yale University Press, 1999).
3. R. Jenkins, *Churchill*, (London: Macmillan, 2001), p. 610.
4. Ismay to Robert Sherwood, quoted Reynolds, *In Command of History*, p. 172.
5. See Halifax, Diary, 6 June 1940 quoted, Reynolds, *From World War to Cold War*, p. 82.
6. Chamberlain, Diary, 26 May 1940 quoted, Reynolds, *From World War to Cold War*, p. 81.
7. See David Reynolds, 'Churchill the Appeaser? Between Hitler, Roosevelt and Stalin in World War Two', in Michael Dockrill and Brian McKercher (eds), *Diplomacy and World Power: Studies in British Foreign Policy, 1890–1950* (Cambridge: Cambridge University Press, 1996), p. 197 *et seq*.
8. Reynolds, *In Command of History*, p. 171.
9. See Colville, *The Fringes of Power*, pp. 140–1 (27 May 1940).

10. A.J.P. Taylor, 'The Statesman', in A.J.P. Taylor, R.R. James, J.H. Plumb, A. Storr and B. Liddell Hart, *Churchill: Four Faces and the Man* (London: Allen Lane the Penguin Press, 1969), p. 36.
11. Cabinet papers, 65/13, quoted, Gilbert, *The Churchill War Papers*, vol. 2, p. 181.
12. Lukacs, *Five Days in London: May 1940*, p. 2.
13. D. Dilks (ed.), *The Diaries of Sir Alexander Cadogan 1938–1945*, (London: Cassell, 1971), 27 May 1940.
14. C. Hill, *Cabinet Decisions on Foreign Policy: the British Experience October 1938 – June 1941* (Cambridge: Cambridge University Press, 1991), p. 185.
15. Quoted, J. Jackson, *The Fall of France: The Nazi Invasion of 1940* (Oxford: Oxford University Press, 2003). Quotation from pbk edn, p. 209 *et seq.*
16. See Reynolds, *From World War to Cold War*, pp. 113, 114.
17. Quoted, Gilbert (ed.), *Churchill*, Companion Vol. 3, Part 2, pp. 1494.
18. Robert Lloyd George, *David and Winston* (New York: Overlook Press, 2008), p. 235.
19. See David Reynolds, 'Churchill & the British "Decision" to Fight on in 1940', in Langhorne, *Diplomacy and Intelligence during the Second World*, p. 153.

Chapter 7

1. Lloyd George, *David & Winston*, p. 231.
2. Churchill, *The Second World War*, vol. 2, p. 13.
3. Dilks (ed.), Cadogan *Diaries*, p. 301.
4. Ben-Moshe, *Churchill: Strategy and History*, p. 333.
5. Quoted, Stafford, *Churchill and Secret Service*, pbk edn, pp. 398–9.
6. Quoted G. Best, *Churchill & War* (London: Hambledon and London, 2005), pp. 169–70.
7. A.J.P. Taylor, 'The Statesman', in Taylor *et al.*, *Churchill: Four Faces and the Man*, p. 36.
8. Basil Liddell Hart, 'The Military Strategist', in Taylor *et al.*, *Churchill: Four Faces and the Man*, p. 197.
9. See Brian Bond, 'Alanbrooke & Britain's Strategy', in Lawrence Freedman, Paul Hayes and Robert O'Neill (eds), *War, Strategy, & International Politics: Essays in honour of Sir Michael Howard* (Oxford: Oxford University Press 1992), p. 179.
10. Quoted, Stafford, *Churchill and Secret Service*, pbk edn, p. 223.
11. Stafford, *Churchill and Secret Service*, pbk edn, p. 229.
12. Rowan in Wheeler-Bennett, *Action this Day*, p. 250.
13. Churchill to Lord Woolton and Robert Hudson, 14 June 1941 Churchill papers, 20/36, quoted, Gilbert, *The Churchill War Papers*, vol. 3, p. 802 – an 'Action this Day' memorandum.
14. Hansard, 7 May 1941.
15. Gilbert, *The Churchill War Papers*, vol. 2, p. xxv.
16. Quoted, Gilbert, *The Churchill War Papers*, vol. 2, p. 426.

Chapter 8

1. Quoted Reynolds, *In Command of History*, p. 147.
2. See Antoine Capet, 'France in Churchill's *The Second World War*' in P. Chassaigne and M. Dockrill, *Anglo-French Relations 1898–1998: From Fashoda to Jospin*. Studies in Military and Strategic History Series (Basingstoke: Palgrave, 2002), p. 125–37.
3. Churchill, *The Second World War*, vol. 2, p. 45 *et seq.*
4. Churchill, *The Second World War*, vol. 2, p. 189.
5. Churchill, *The Second World War*, vol. 2, p. 43.
6. See G. Corrigan, *Blood, Sweat and Arrogance and the Myths of Churchill's War* (London: Weidenfeld & Nicholson, 2006), p. 236.
7. Gilbert, *Churchill*, vol. 6, p. 442.
8. E. Spears, *Assignment to Catastrophe*, vol. 2 (London: Heinemann, 1954), p. 76.
9. R. Tombs, *That Sweet Enemy* (London: Heinemann, 2006), p. 557.
10. Spears, *Assignment to Catastrophe*, vol. 2, p. 210.
11. Spears, *Assignment to Catastrophe*, vol. 2, p. 216.
12. See F. Kersaudy, *Churchill and de Gaulle* (London: Collins, 1981). Quotation from pbk ed, p. 65 *et seq.*
13. Spears, *Assignment to Catastrophe*, vol. 2, p. 218 *et seq.*
14. Colville, *The Fringes of Power*, p. 160.
15. Tombs, *That Sweet Enemy*, p. 560.
16. Colville, *The Fringes of Power*, p. 158.
17. Churchill, *The Second World War*, vol. 2, p. 181.
18. See J. Jackson, *The Fall of France: The Nazi Invasion of 1940* (Oxford: Oxford University Press, 2003). Quotation from pbk edn, p. 12 *et seq.*
19. Jackson, *The Fall of France*. Quotation from pbk edn, p. 69 *et seq.*
20. Churchill, *The Second World War*, vol. 2, p. 40 *et seq.*

Chapter 9

1. Kersaudy, *Churchill and de Gaulle*, pbk edn, p. 54.
2. Spears, *Assignment to Catastrophe*, vol. 2, p. 139.
3. Charles de Gaulle, *Mémoires de Guerre, L'Appel*, vol. 1 (Paris: Plon, 1954), p. 71.
4. See Corrigan, *Blood, Sweat and Arrogance*, p. 275.
5. E. Spears, *Two Men who saved France: Pétain and de Gaulle* (London: Eyre and Spottiswoode, 1996), p. 164.
6. De Gaulle, *L'Appel*, p. 275 *et seq.*
7. Colville, *The Fringes of Power*, 13 December 1940.
8. See S. Roskill, *Churchill and the Admirals* (London: Collins, 1977). Quotation from p. 157, pbk edn.
9. Quoted, Roskill, *Churchill and the Admirals*, p. 156, pbk edn.
10. Roskill, *Churchill and the Admirals*, p. 122, pbk edn.
11. D. Wragg, *Sink the French: the French Navy after the Fall of France 1940* (Barnsley: Pen and Sword Maritime, 2007), p. 142.

12. See Capet in Chassaigne and Dockrill, *Anglo-French Relations 1898–1998*, p. 125–37.
13. Colville, *The Fringes of Power*, p. 185
14. Quoted, Gilbert, *Churchill*, vol. 6, p. 642 *et seq.*
15. Quoted, Gilbert, *Churchill*, vol. 6, p. 830.
16. Colville, *The Fringes of Power*, p. 311.

Chapter 10

1. Roskill, *Churchill and the Admirals*, p. 160, pbk edn.
2. Quoted, A. Danchev, '"Dilly-Dally", or Having the Last Word: Field-Marshal Sir John Dill and Prime Minister Winston Churchill', in *Journal of Contemporary History* vol. 22, no.1 (January 1987), p. 22.
3. Quoted, Roskill, *Churchill and the Admirals*, p. 118, pbk edn.
4. Personal communication to Roskill, quoted Roskill, *Churchill and the Admirals*, p. 120, pbk edn.
5. Letter to John Colville, quoted, Colville, *The Churchillians*, p. 147.
6. See Reynolds, *In Command of History*, p. 183.
7. Reynolds, *In Command of History*, p. 184.
8. Colville, *The Fringes of Power*, p. 195.
9. Quoted, Stafford, *Churchill and Secret Service*, pbk edn, p. 229.
10. See Stafford, *Churchill and Secret Service*, pbk edn, p. 230.
11. Stafford, *Churchill and Secret Service*, pbk edn, p. 231–3.

Chapter 11

1. James Leutze (ed.), *The London Observer, The Journal of General Raymond E. Lee, 1940–41* (London: Hutchinson, 1971), p. 10.
2. M. Soames (ed.), *Speaking for Themselves: The Personal Letters of Winston and Clementine Churchill* (London: Doubleday, 1998); 6 April 1945, quotation from pbk edn, p. 523.
3. See Jacob in Wheeler-Bennett, *Action this Day*, p. 198.
4. Churchill papers, 20/49, quoted, Gilbert, *War Papers*, vol. 3, p. 38.
5. Jacob in Wheeler-Bennett, *Action this Day*, p. 185.
6. Reynolds, *In Command of History*, p. 191.
7. Quoted by Alex Danchev, 'Field-Marshall Sir John Dill', in J. Keegan (ed.), *Churchill's Generals* (London: Weidenfeld & Nicholson, 1991), pbk edn, p. 58.
8. A. Cunningham, *A Sailor's Odyssey* (London: Hutchinson, 1951), p. 231.
9. Quoted Gilbert, *Winston Churchill's War Leadership*, p. 55.
10. Colville, *The Fringes of Power*, p. 309.

Chapter 12

1. See, for example, Basil Liddell Hart, 'The Military Strategist', in Taylor *et al.*, *Churchill, Four Faces and the Man*, p. 189.

2. Quoted Michael Dewar, 'Field-Marshall Lord Wilson', in Keegan, *Churchill's Generals*, pbk edn p. 169.
3. Quoted B. Pitt, *Churchill and the Generals* (London: Sidgwick & Jackson, 1981), pbk edn p. 65.
4. Quoted, Pitt, *Churchill and the Generals*, pbk edn p. 66.
5. See R. Lamb, *Churchill as War Leader – Right or Wrong?* (London: Bloomsbury, 1991), p. 88 *et seq.*
6. Kennedy, *The Business of War*, pp. 83 and 85.
7. C. Barnett, *The Desert Generals* (London: Kimber, 1960), p 44.
8. Reynolds, *In Command of History*, p. 233.
9. Kennedy, *The Business of War*, p. 85.
10. See Roskill, *Churchill and the Admirals*, p. 182 pbk edn.
11. Churchill, *The Second World War*, vol. 3, p. 101.
12. Quoted, Churchill, *The Second World War*, vol. 3, p. 108–9.
13. PREM 3/288/7, Wavell to Viscount Cranborne, 31 October 1942.
14. Quoted Michael Dewar, 'Field-Marshall Lord Wilson', in Keegan, *Churchill's Generals*, pbk edn, p. 171.
15. Churchill papers, 20/37, quoted, Gilbert, *The Churchill War Papers*, vol. 2, p. 426.
16. See Keegan, 'Churchill's Strategy', in Blake and Louis, *Churchill*, p. 335.
17. See James Leasor, *War at the Top: based on the experiences of General Sir Leslie Hollis* (London: Joseph, 1959), p. 148 *et seq.* and G. von Blumentritt *et al.*, *The Fatal Decisions* (London: Joseph, 1956).
18. Leasor, *War at the Top*, p. 151.
19. Quoted Michael Dewar, 'Field-Marshall Lord Wilson', in Keegan, ed, *Churchill's Generals*, p. 173.

Chapter 13

1. See Reynolds, *In Command of History*, p. 240.
2. Quoted, Stafford, *Churchill and Secret Service*, pbk edn, p. 223.
3. Kennedy, *The Business of War*, pp. 106, 109.
4. See Reynolds, *In Command of History*, p. 517 *et seq.*
5. Kennedy, *The Business of War*, p. 165.
6. Kennedy, *The Business of War*, p. 115.
7. Kennedy, *The Business of War*, p. 146.
8. Kennedy, *The Business of War*, p. 115.
9. Kennedy, *The Business of War*, p. 356.
10. Quoted Addison, *Churchill, The Unexpected Hero*, p. 182.
11. Quoted Reynolds, *From World War to Cold War*, p. 108.
12. Quoted Reynolds, *In Command of History*, p. 231.
13. Quoted, Alex Danchev, 'Field-Marshal Sir John Dill', in Keegan, (ed) *Churchill's Generals*, pbk edn, p. 57.
14. Quoted, Alex Danchev, 'Field-Marshal Sir John Dill', in Keegan, (ed) *Churchill's Generals*, pbk edn, p. 57.

15. Alex Danchev, 'Field-Marshal Sir John Dill', in Keegan, (ed) *Churchill's Generals*, pbk edn, p. 58.
16. See Danchev, '"Dilly-Dally", or Having the Last Word', p. 28.
17. Quoted Danchev, 'Field-Marshal Sir John Dill', in Keegan, *Churchill's Generals*, pbk edn, p. 56.
18. See Lamb, *Churchill as War Leader – Right or Wrong?*, p. 98 *et seq.*
19. Hansard, 7 May 1941, quoted, Gilbert, *The Churchill War Papers*, vol. 3, p. 628.
20. Colville, *The Fringes of Power*, pp. 395, 397.
21. Harold Nicolson, *Diaries*, 10 June 1941.
22. See J. R. M. Butler, *Grand Strategy*, vol. 2 *(History of the Second World War, United Kingdom Military Series, vol. 3)* (London: 1964).

Chapter 14

1. Oliver Lyttelton, *The Memoirs of Lord Chandos* (London: Bodley Head, 1962), p. 248.
2. See Sheffield, 'Lieutenant-General Sir Adrian Carton Wiart and Major-General Sir Louis Spears', in Keegan, *Churchill's Generals*.
3. *Chicago Daily News*, 27 August 1941.
4. Churchill, *The Second World War*, vol. 2, p. 451.
5. FO 371/28545, Eden to W. Churchill, Note on C. de Gaulle, 1/9/41.
6. Harold Nicolson *Diaries* 20 January 1941.
7. Harold Nicolson *Diaries* 27 February 1941.
8. Quoted Dilks (ed.), Cadogan *Diaries 1938–1945*, p. 302.

Chapter 15

1. See Kennedy, *The Business of War*, p. 106 *et seq.*
2. Danchev, 'Field-Marshal Sir John Dill', in Keegan, *Churchill's Generals,* p. 59.
3. See Brig. Bernard Fergusson, Introduction to Kennedy, *The Business of War*, p. xvi.
4. Churchill, *The Second World War*, vol. 3, p. 217.
5. Churchill, *The Second World War*, vol. 3, p. 354.
6. Communication from Auchinleck to Correlli Barnett, quoted, Barnett, *The Desert Generals*, p. 73.
7. Reynolds, *In Command of History*, p. 257.
8. For example, those of Olivia Manning. *Cairo in the War* by Artemis Cooper (London: Hamish Hamilton, 1992), not a novel, vividly portrays the highly charged, cosmopolitan character of the capital in which so many remarkable individuals took refuge.
9. Barnett, *The Desert Generals*, p. 111.
10. Quoted Pitt, *Churchill and the Generals*, p. 99.
11. Quoted, Stafford, *Churchill and Secret Service*, pbk edn, p. 285.

Chapter 16

1. Quoted P. Warner, *Auchinleck: The Lonely Soldier*, (London: Buchan & Enright, 1981), pbk edn, p. 166 *et seq.*
2. Quoted Warner, *Auchinleck: The Lonely Soldier*, pbk edn, p. 172 *et seq.*
3. Kennedy, *The Business of War*, p. 226.
4. See Kennedy, *The Business of War*, pp. 242–4.
5. Churchill, *The Second World War*, vol. 4 (London: Cassell, 1951), p. 306.
6. H. Ismay, *The Memoirs of Lord Ismay* (London: Heinemann, 1960), p. 162.
7. James, *Chips*, p. 334.
8. C. Moran, *Winston Churchill: The Struggle for Survival 1940–1965* (London: Constable, 1966), p. 42.
9. See Colville in Wheeler-Bennett, *Action this Day*, p. 60.
10. Personal communication to Correlli Barnett, quoted, Barnett, *The Desert Generals*, p. 215.
11. See A.J.P. Taylor, 'The Statesman', in Taylor *et al.*, *Churchill: Four Faces and the Man*, p. 42.

Chapter 17

1. Reynolds, *In Command of History*, p. 257.
2. Kennedy, *The Business of War*, pp. 162, 179.
3. James Leasor, *War at the Top*, p. 149.
4. See Danchev, ' "Dilly-Dally", or Having the Last Word', pp. 21–44.
5. Marshall to Churchill, 7 November 1944, Marshall Papers, 64/43, Marshall Research Foundation, Lexington, Virginia.
6. Kennedy, *The Business of War*, p. 284.
7. Quoted, Fraser, *Alanbrooke* (London: Collins, 1982), p. 202.
8. See Reynolds, *In Command of History*, p. 406.
9. Fraser, *Alanbrooke*, p. 553.
10. A. Danchev and D. Todman (eds), *War Diaries 1939–1945: Field Marshal Lord Alanbrooke* (Berkeley: University of California Press, 2001), p. 249.
11. See, e.g. A. Danchev and D. Todman (eds), *War Diaries, 1939–1945: the War Diaries of Field-Marshal Lord Alanbrooke* (London: Weidenfeld & Nicholson, 2001), 13 March, 21 April and 27 October 1941.
12. Leasor, *War at the Top*, p. 226.
13. Leasor, *War at the Top*, p. 243.
14. Leasor, *War at the Top*, p. 168 *et seq.*
15. Danchev and Todman, *War Diaries 1939–1945: Field Marshal Lord Alanbrooke*.
16. Danchev and Todman, *War Diaries 1939–1945: Field Marshal Lord Alanbrooke*, p. xxxiii.
17. Kennedy, *The Business of War*, p. 204.
18. Ismay, *The Memoirs of Lord Ismay*, p. 175.
19. Danchev and Todman, *War Diaries 1939–1945: Field Marshal Lord Alanbrooke*, p. 566.

20. Fraser, *Alanbrooke*, p. 211.
21. Danchev and Todman, *War Diaries 1939–1945: Field Marshal Lord Alanbrooke*, p. 544.
22. Moran, *Winston Churchill: The Struggle for Survival 1940–1965*, p. 713.
23. Danchev and Todman, *War Diaries 1939–1945: Field Marshal Lord Alanbrooke*, p. 712 *et seq.*
24. Ismay, *The Memoirs of Lord Ismay*, p. 159.
25. Quoted Addison, *Churchill, The Unexpected Hero*, p. 241.
26. Gilbert, *Churchill* vol. 6 (London: Heinemann, 1988), p. 1232.
27. Quoted, Dilkes (ed.), Cadogan *Diaries 1938–1945*, p. 301.

Chapter 18

1. See Reynolds, *From World War to Cold War*, p. 294, referring to Mira Wilkins, *The Maturing of Multi-national Enterprise: American Business Abroad from 1914–1970*, pp. 29–30.
2. R.R. James (ed.), *Winston S. Churchill, His Complete Speeches*, vol. 4 (New York and London: Chelsea House Publishers in association with R.R. Bowkes, 1974).
3. Cabinet Memorandum 29 June 1927, quoted, Phillips O'Brien, 'Winston Churchill and the US Navy', in R.A.C. Parker (ed.), *Winston Churchill: Studies in Statesmanship* (London: Brassey, 1998), p. 34.
4. Gilbert, *Churchill*, Companion vol. 5, part 1, p. 1033.
5. Gilbert, *Churchill*, Companion vol. 5, part 1, pp. 342, 348.
6. See John Gooch, 'Hidden in the Rock', in Freedman *et al.*, *War, Strategy, & International Politics*, p. 157.
7. John Gooch, 'Hidden in the Rock', in Freedman *et al.*, *War, Strategy, & International Politics*, p. 172 – and see generally.
8. R. Ingersoll, *Top Secret* (S.I: Partridge, 1946), p. 60.
9. Woodrow Wilson to Colonel House, 21 July 1917, quoted Arthur S. Link (ed.), *The Papers of Woodrow Wilson*, vol. 43 (Princeton, NJ: Princeton University Press, 1966–94), p. 238.

Chapter 19

1. Reynolds, *From World War to Cold War*, p. 31.
2. Quoted, Reynolds, *From World War to Cold War*, p. 29.
3. Quoted B. McKercher, *Transition of Power: Britain's loss of Global Pre-Eminence to the United States, 1930–1945* (Cambridge: Cambridge University Press, 1999), p. 269.
4. Quoted Reynolds, *From World War to Cold War*, p. 310.
5. Quoted Reynolds, *From World War to Cold War*, p. 170.
6. Quoted McKercher, *Transition of Power*, p. 294.
7. H. Ickes, *The Secret Diary of Harold L. Ickes*, vol. 3 (New York: De Capo, 1974), p. 511.

8. J. Burns, *Roosevelt: The Lion and the Fox,* vol. 1 (New York: Harcourt, Brace, 1956), pbk edn, p. 458 *et seq.*
9. See McKercher, *Transition of Power,* p. 264.
10. Colville, *The Fringes of Power,* 5 March 1941.
11. Quoted McKercher, *Transition of Power,* p. 302.
12. F. Kimball, (ed.), *Churchill and Roosevelt. The Complete Correspondence,* vol. 1 (Princeton, NJ: Princeton University Press, 1984), C-22X.
13. See Reynolds, *In Command of History,* p. 113.

Chapter 20

1. Kimball, 'Churchill and Roosevelt', in Blake and Louis, *Churchill,* p. 297.
2. See D. Bercuson and H. Herwig, *One Christmas in Washington: The Secret Meeting between Roosevelt and Churchill that Changed the World* (Toronto, ON: McArthur, 2005), p. 49.
3. Kimball, *Churchill and Roosevelt. The Complete Correspondence,* C–9X.
4. Dilks (ed.), Cadogan, *Diaries,* p. 284.
5. Kimball, *Churchill and Roosevelt. The Complete Correspondence,* R–4x.
6. Quoted Reynolds, *In Command of History,* p. 200.
7. Churchill to Ismay, quoted in Reynolds, *From World War to Cold War,* p. 95.
8. Kimball, *Churchill and Roosevelt. The Complete Correspondence,* C–20x.
9. Gilbert, *Churchill,* vol. 6, p. 974.
10. See D. Reynolds, *The Creation of the Anglo-American Alliance, 1937–41: A Study in Competitive Cooperation* (London: Europa, 1981), p. 126.
11. Cabinet Minute, quoted in Reynolds, *From World War to Cold War,* p. 95.
12. Bernard M. Baruch Papers, quoted Reynolds, *From World War to Cold War,* p. 95.
13. Quoted W. Kimball, *The Juggler: Franklin Roosevelt as Wartime Statesman* (Princeton, NJ: Princeton University Press, 1991), p. 7.

Chapter 21

1. Kimball, *Churchill and Roosevelt. The Complete Correspondence.* Vol. 1, C-43X.
2. Kimball, *Churchill and Roosevelt. The Complete Correspondence,* pbk edn, p. 88.
3. Quoted Gilbert, *Winston Churchill's War Leadership,* p. 60.
4. Addison, *Churchill, The Unexpected Hero,* p. 178.
5. Kimball, *Churchill and Roosevelt. The Complete Correspondence,* C–11x.
6. Kimball, *Churchill and Roosevelt. The Complete Correspondence,* R–5x.
7. R. Sherwood, (ed.), *The White House Papers of Harry L. Hopkins,* vol. 2 (London: Eyre and Spottiswoode, 1948), p. 796.
8. Churchill, *The Second World War,* vol. 3, p. 19 *et seq.*
9. Colville, *The Fringes of Power,* p. 160.
10. Colville, *The Fringes of Power,* p. 331.

11. D. Stafford, *Roosevelt & Churchill, Men of Secrets* (London: Little, Brown, 1999), quotation from pbk edn, p. 54.

12. D. Hart-Davis, *King's Counsellor. Abdication and War: the Diaries of Sir Alan Lascelles* (London: Weidenfeld & Nicholson 2006), p. 251.

13. Colville, *The Fringes of Power*, p. 345.

14. Eric Seal, quoted in M. Gilbert, *Churchill: A Life* (London: Heinemann, 1991), p. 689.

15. Quoted Addison, *Churchill: The Unexpected Hero,* p. 178.

16. Stafford, *Roosevelt & Churchill, Men of Secrets,* pbk edn, p. 59.

17. See Kathleen Burk, 'American Foreign Economic Policy & Lend-Lease' in A. Lane and H. Temperley, *The Rise & Fall of the Grand Alliance, 1941–45,* (London: Macmillan Press; St Martin's Press, 1995), p. 52 *et seq.*

18. C. Ponting, *1940: Myth & Reality* (London: Hamilton, 1990), p. 212.

19. Kimball, *Churchill and Roosevelt. The Complete Correspondence*, pbk edn, Vol 1, p. 88.

20. Gilbert, *Churchill*, vol. 6, p. 972 *et seq.*

21. R. Skidelsky, *John Maynard Keynes: Fighting for Britain, 1937–1946* (London: Macmillan, 2000), p. 103.

22. See A.J.P. Taylor, 'The Statesman', in Taylor et al., *Churchill: Four Faces and the Man,* p. 44.

23. Colville, *The Fringes of Power*, p. 229.

24. See Kathleen Burk, 'American Foreign Economic Policy & Lend-Lease' in Lane & Temperley, *Rise & Fall of the Grand Alliance,* p. 43 *et seq.*

25. Colville in Wheeler-Bennett, *Action this Day,* p. 96.

26. PREM, WSC to Halifax, 10 January 1942, fo. 364; quoted, J. Charmley, *Churchill's Grand Alliance: The Anglo-American Special Relationship 1940–57* (London: Hodder & Stoughton, 1995), p. 49.

27. PREM 4/17/1, Cherwell to WSC, December 1940, fos. 82/85; quoted, Charmley, *Churchill's Grand Alliance,* p. 23.

28. Quoted Charmley, *Churchill's Grand Alliance,* p. 49.

29. Sayers, *Financial Policy*, Table 5, quoted Burk, 'American Foreign Economic Policy & Lend-Lease' in Lane & Temperley, *Rise & Fall of the Grand Alliance,* p. 57 *et seq.*

30. See Charmley, *Churchill's Grand Alliance,* p. 135.

Chapter 22

1. W. Harriman and E. Abel, *Special Envoy to Churchill and Stalin, 1941–1946* (New York: Random House, 1975), p. 75.

2. Quoted Gilbert, *Churchill. A Life,* p. 705.

3. Elliot Roosevelt, *As He Saw It* (New York: Duell, Sloan and Pearce, 1946), p. 44.

4. Quoted Reynolds, *In Command of History,* p. 260.

5. Roosevelt, *As He Saw It,* pp. 36, 38.

6. Quoted Moran, *Winston Churchill: The Struggle for Survival 1940–1965,* pp. 742–3.

7. See Reynolds, *In Command of History*, p. 260.
8. See Gilbert, *Churchill*, vol. 6, p. 1161.
9. Quoted, Gilbert, *Churchill*, vol. 6, p. 1163.
10. Quoted Reynolds, *In Command of History*, p. 261.
11. See Gilbert, *Churchill. A Life*, pp. 705, 706.
12. Quoted Gilbert, *Churchill*, vol. 6, p. 1167.
13. H. Macmillan, *The Blast of War 1939–1945* (London: Macmillan, 1967), p. 415.
14. Sherwood, *The White House Papers of Harry L. Hopkins*, vol. 2, p. 364.
15. Bercuson & Herwig, *One Christmas in Washington*, p. 29 *et seq.*
16. Sherwood, *The White House Papers of Harry L. Hopkins*, vol. 2, p. 374.

Chapter 23

1. Danchev and Todman (eds), Alanbrooke, *War Diaries 1939–1945*, p. 209.
2. 30 November 1941. Kimball, *Churchill and Roosevelt. The Complete Correspondence*, C–135x.
3. Quoted, Roskill, *Churchill and the Admirals*, pbk edn, p. 126.
4. See Attlee to Churchill, 20 December 1941, Churchill papers, 20/23, quoted, Gilbert, *War Papers*, vol. 3, p. 1654.
5. See Reynolds, *The Creation of the Anglo-American Alliance, 1937–1941*, p. 54 *et seq.*
6. Quoted Gilbert, *Churchill*, vol. 6, p. 1177.
7. Quoted Reynolds, *The Creation of the Anglo-American Alliance, 1937–41*, p. 56 *et seq.*
8. H. Stimson and M. Bundy, *On Active Service in Peace and War* (New York: Harper & Brothers, 1948), 18 November 1940.
9. See Reynolds, *The Creation of the Anglo-American Alliance, 1937–41*, p. 218.
10. Quoted, Reynolds, *The Creation of the Anglo-American Alliance, 1937–41*, p. 219.

Chapter 24

1. Gilbert, *Winston Churchill's War Leadership*, p. 18.
2. Fraser, 'Field-Marshal Viscount Alanbrooke', in Keegan, *Churchill's Generals*, p. 93.
3. Colville, *The Fringes of Power*, p. 418.
4. Colville, *The Fringes of Power*, p. 489.
5. Fraser, 'Field-Marshal Viscount Alanbrooke', in Keegan, *Churchill's Generals*, pbk edn, p. 93.
6. Fraser, *Alanbrooke*, p. 217.
7. *Daily Telegraph*, 28 May 1981.
8. Gilbert, *Churchill*, vol. 7, p. 53.
9. Stafford, *Churchill and Secret Service*, pbk edn, p. 275.
10. Alex Danchev, 'Being Friends: The Combined Chiefs of Staff and the Making

of Allied Strategy in the Second World War', in Freedman *et al.*, *War, Strategy and International Politics,* p. 208.

11. Quoted Bercuson and Herwig, *One Christmas in Washington,* p. 138.
12. Churchill papers, 20/36, quoted, Gilbert, *War Papers,* vol. 3, p. 1623.
13. Reynolds, *In Command of History,* p. 270.
14. Quoted Bercuson and Herwig, *One Christmas in Washington,* p. 170.
15. Lamb, *Churchill as War Leader – Right or Wrong?,* p. 165.

Chapter 25

1. Quoted Bercuson and Herwig, *One Christmas in Washington,* p. 245.
2. Reynolds, *From World War to Cold War,* p. 244.
3. Cordell Hull, *The Memoirs of Cordell Hull,* vol. 2 (London: Hodder and Stoughton, 1948), pp. 1473–4.
4. Quoted, Bercuson and Herwig, *One Christmas in Washington,* p. 223.
5. Quoted, Bercuson and Herwig, *One Christmas in Washington,* p. 224.
6. Bercuson and Herwig, *One Christmas in Washington,* p. 175.
7. See Danchev, 'Being Friends', in Freedman *et al.*, *War, Strategy, & International Politics,* p. 196 *et seq.*
8. Quoted, R. Overy, *Why the Allies Won* (London: Jonathan Cape, 1995), pbk edn, p 306.
9. H. Nicholas (ed.), *Washington Dispatches 1941–1945: Weekly Political Reports from the British Embassy* (London: Weidenfeld & Nicholson, 1981), p. 257 *et seq* (9 October 1943).
10. Dill to Wavell, 9 January 1942, Wavell Family Papers.
11. Quoted, Bercuson and Herwig, *One Christmas in Washington,* p. 250.
12. See M. Stoler, *The Politics of the Second Front: American Planning and Diplomacy in Coalition Warfare, 1941–43,* (Westport, CT and London: Greenwood Press, 1977), p. 7.
13. Quoted Bercuson & Herwig, *One Christmas in Washington,* p. 261.

Chapter 26

1. Churchill, *The Second World War,* vol. 4, p. 43.
2. Nicolson, *Diary,* 17 December 1941.
3. Quoted J. Charmley, *Churchill: The End of Glory: A Political Biography* (London: Hodder and Stoughton, 1993), p. 479.
4. J. Wheeler-Bennett, *King George VI: His Life and Reign* (London: Macmillan; St. Martin's Press, 1958), p. 537.
5. Quoted J. Barnes and D. Nicholson (eds), *The Leo Amery Diaries* (London: Hutchinson, 1980), 23 December 1941, p. 755.
6. Channon, *Diary,* 27 January 1942, p. 318.
7. Hansard, 25 March 1942.
8. Harold Nicolson, *Diaries,* 16 February 1942.
9. See Reynolds, *In Command of History,* p. 341.
10. See Reynolds, *In Command of History,* p. 341.

11. Kimball, *Churchill and Roosevelt. The Complete Correspondence*, C–37.
12. Danchev and Todman, *War Diaries 1939–1945: Field Marshal Lord Alanbrooke*, p. 343.
13. W. Churchill, *Secret Session Speeches* (London: Cassell, 1946), p. 53 *et seq.*
14. See Carlton, *Churchill and the Soviet Union*, chapter 5.
15. Colville, *The Fringes of Power*, p. 309.
16. Quoted Gilbert, *Churchill*, vol. 7, p. 62.
17. P. French, *Liberty or Death: India's Journey to Independence and Division* (London: HarperCollins, 1997). Quotation from pbk edn, pp 142, 144.
18. Quoted Gilbert, *Churchill*, vol. 7, p. 89.
19. Hansard, 29 April 1941.
20. Colville, *The Fringes of Power*, p. 288.

Chapter 27

1. Roskill, *Churchill and the Admirals*, pbk edn, p. 142.
2. Quoted, Roskill, *Churchill and the Admirals*, pbk edn, p. 143.
3. Quoted, Roskill, *Churchill and the Admirals*, pbk edn, p. 134.
4. Quoted, J. Colville, *The Churchillians*, p. 144.
5. Quoted Roskill, *Churchill and the Admirals*, pbk edn, p. 134.
6. See appendix 17 in C. Webster and N. Frankland *The Strategic Air Offensive against Germany*, vol. 4 (London: Imperial War Museum in association with Battery Press, 1961), p.231 *et seq.*
7. J. Keegan, *Churchill* (London: Weidenfeld & Nicholson, 2002), p. 137.
8. Carver, 'Churchill and the Defence Chiefs', in Blake and Louis, *Churchill*, p. 368.
9. J. Burns, *Roosevelt: The Soldier of Freedom* (New York: Harcourt Brace Jovanovich, 1970), p. 552.
10. Roskill, *Churchill and the Admirals*, pbk edn, p. 139.
11. Captain G.H. Roberts, quoted Roskill, *Churchill and the Admirals*, p. 297.

Chapter 28

1. F. Pogue, *George C. Marshall: Ordeal and Hope, 1939–1942* (New York: Viking Press, 1966), p. 319 *et seq.*
2. See Kimball and Rose, 'Churchill and D-Day: Another View', in *Finest Hour*, Journal of the Churchill Centre and Societies, Autumn 2004, number 124, p. 31 *et seq.*
3. Ismay, *The Memoirs of Lord Ismay*, p. 249.
4. See Danchev and Todman, *War Diaries 1939–1945: Field Marshal Lord Alanbrooke*, p. 247 *et seq.*
5. Churchill, *The Second World War*, vol. 4, p. 289 *et seq.*
6. Sherwood, *The White House Papers of Harry L. Hopkins*, vol. 2, p. 598.
7. See Reynolds, *From World War to Cold War*, p. 59.
8. Luce, 'The American Century' in *Life*, 17 February 1941, p. 61 *et seq.*
9. Quoted, Reynolds, *The Creation of the Anglo-American Alliance, 1937–41*, p. 251.

10. Charmley, *Churchill's Grand Alliance: The Anglo-American Special Relationship 1940–57*, p. 130.

Chapter 29

1. See Danchev and Todman, *War Diaries 1939–1945: Field Marshal Lord Alanbrooke*, p. 281.
2. Gilbert, *Churchill*, vol. 6, p. 1144.
3. Leasor, *War at the Top*, p 184.
4. Cunningham, *A Sailor's Odyssey*, p. 468.
5. Professor David Jablonsky, US Army War College, at Churchill Centre Conference, 2006.
6. Hart-Davis, *King's Counsellor*, p. 129.
7. Sherwood, *The White House Papers of Harry L. Hopkins*, vol. 2, p. 604.

Chapter 30

1. Hart-Davis, *King's Counsellor*, p. 60.
2. Stafford, *Roosevelt & Churchill, Men of Secrets*, pbk edn, p. 220.
3. Richard Symons, *The Making of Pakistan* (London: Faber & Faber 1950), p. 74.
4. Quoted Charmley, *Churchill's Grand Alliance: The Anglo-American Special Relationship 1940–57*, p. 90.
5. R. Dallek, *Lyndon B. Johnston: Portrait of a President*, (Oxford: Oxford University Press, 2004). Quotation from pbk edn, p. 201.
6. Stafford, *Roosevelt & Churchill, Men of Secrets*, pbk edn, p. 221.
7. Charmley, *Churchill's Grand Alliance: The Anglo-American Special Relationship 1940–57*, p. 61.

Chapter 31

1. Harold Nicolson, *Diaries*, 2 July 1942.
2. Harold Nicolson, *Diaries*, 2 July and 9 September 1942.
3. Bullock, A., *The Life and Times of Ernest Bevin*, vol. 2 (London: Heinemann, 1967), p. 300, but see Danchev 'Waltzing with Winston' in Paul Smith (ed.), *Government and the Armed Forces in Britain, 1856–1990* (London/Rio Grande: Hambledon P., 1996), p. 199.
4. Moran, *Winston Churchill: Struggle for Survival, 1940–1965*, p. 72.
5. See Warner, *Auchinleck The Lonely Soldier*.
6. Quoted, Warner, *Auchinleck The Lonely Soldier*, pbk edn, p. 179.
7. Quoted, Warner, *Auchinleck The Lonely Soldier*, pp. pbk edn, 314, 315.
8. Reynolds, *In Command of History*, p. 306.
9. Jacob's Diary, quoted in A. Bryant, *The Turn of the Tide, 1939–1943: A Study Based on the Diaries and Autobiographical Notes of the Field Marshal Viscount Alanbrooke* (London: Collins, 1957), p. 451.
10. Moran, *Winston Churchill: The Struggle for Survival 1940–1965*, p. 53.

11. Reynolds, *In Command of History*, p. 306.
12. Harold Nicolson, *Diaries*, 6 November 1941.

Chapter 32

1. C. De Gaulle, *Mémoires de Guerre: vol. 2 L'Unité 1942–44* (Paris: Plon, 1956), p. 33.
2. Quoted, Kersaudy, *Churchill & De Gaulle*, pbk edn, p. 211.
3. Hart-Davis, ed, *King's Counsellor*, p. 132.
4. FO 371/31950, C. Peake to W. Strang, 31/10/42, quoted Kersaudy *Churchill & De Gaulle*, pbk edn, p. 216.
5. Kimball, *Churchill and Roosevelt. The Complete Correspondence*, R–123/1, quoted, Reynolds, *From World War to Cold War*, p. 175.
6. See, for example, Moran, *Winston Churchill: The Struggle for Survival 1940–1965*, p. 62.
7. Moran, *Winston Churchill: The Struggle for Survival 1940–1965*, p. 55.
8. See Kimball and Rose, 'Churchill and D-Day: Another View', in *Finest Hour*, Journal of the Churchill Centre and Societies, Autumn 2004, number 124, p. 32.
9. Kimball, *Churchill and Roosevelt. The Complete Correspondence*, R–210.
10. Reynolds, *In Command of History*, p. 326.
11. See D. Reynolds, *Summits: Six Meetings that shaped the Twentieth Century* (New York: Basic Books, 2007), p. 112.
12. See Reynolds, *In Command of History*, p. 309.
13. See Reynolds, *In Command of History*, p. 345 *et seq.*
14. Ronald Lewin, *Montgomery as Military Commander* (London: Batsford, 1971), p. 81.
15. See Kennedy, *The Business of War*, p. 272.

Chapter 33

1. Pitt, *Churchill and the Generals*, pbk edn, p. 139.
2. Dilks (ed.), Cadogan *Diaries*, p. 475.
3. Barnett, *The Desert Generals*, p. 256.
4. Quoted, Pitt, *Churchill and the Generals*, p. 151.
5. See Basil Liddell Hart, 'The Military Strategist', in Taylor *et al.*, *Churchill: Four Faces and the Man*, p. 193.
6. J. Harvey (ed.), *Diplomatic Diaries of Oliver Harvey 1937–40* (London: Collins, 1970), vol. 2, 2 October 1942, p. 165.

Chapter 34

1. Churchill papers, 9/152, quoted, Gilbert, *War Papers*, vol. 3, p. 1103.
2. Kimball, *Churchill and Roosevelt. The Complete Correspondence*, R–210.
3. Churchill, *Secret Session Speeches*, p. 95.

4. Stafford, *Churchill and Secret Service*, pbk edn, p. 294.
5. FO 954/8, Eden to Halifax No.42 8/1/43.
6. Quoted Reynolds, *In Command of History*, pp. 332, 333.
7. See Charmley, *Churchill's Grand Alliance: The Anglo-American Special Relationship 1940–57*, p. 74.

Chapter 35

1. Macmillan, *The Blast of War 1939–1945*, p. 243.
2. Elliot Roosevelt, *As He Saw It*, p. 100.
3. Danchev 'Being Friends', in Freedman *et al.*, *War, Strategy, & International Politics*, p. 208 *et seq.*
4. See Lamb, *Churchill as War Leader – Right or Wrong?*, p. 217 *et seq.*

Chapter 36

1. Macmillan, *The Blast of War 1939–1945*, p. 248.
2. H. Giraud *Un Seul But, la Victoire: Alger 1942–44* (Paris: René Julliard, 1949), p. 91, *et seq.*
3. Quoted Kersaudy, *Churchill & de Gaulle*, pbk edn, p. 246.
4. R. Sherwood, *Roosevelt & Hopkins* (New York: Harper, 1948), p. 685.
5. Quoted H. Adams, *Harry Hopkins: A Biography* (New York: Putnam's, 1977), p. 311.
6. Sherwood, *The White House Papers of Harry L. Hopkins*, vol. 2 p. 643.
7. Macmillan, *The Blast of War 1939–1945*, p. 341 *et seq.*
8. Quoted, Gilbert, *Churchill*, vol. 7, p. 346.
9. Macmillan, *The Blast of War 1939–1945*, p. 345.
10. Macmillan, *The Blast of War 1939–1945*, p. 353.
11. Reynolds, *In Command of History*, p. 324.
12. Ismay, *The Memoirs of Lord Ismay*, p. 290.
13. Kersaudy, *Churchill & de Gaulle*, pbk edn, p. 266.
14. A. Eden, *The Eden Memoirs: The Reckoning Part 3* (London: Cassell, 1965), p. 386.
15. PREM 3 181/2, FDR to WC No.228, 17/06/43.

Chapter 37

1. See Brian Holden Reid, 'Field-Marshal Earl Alexander' in Keegan, *Churchill's Generals*, pbk edn, p. 114.
2. Ingersoll, *Top Secret*, p. 74.
3. Ingersoll, *Top Secret*, p. 13.
4. Ingersoll, *Top Secret*, p. 25.
5. Ingersoll, *Top Secret*, p. 30.

Chapter 38

1. Pitt, *Churchill and the Generals*, p. 170.
2. W.A. Harriman and Elie Abel, *Special Envoy to Churchill & Stalin 1941–46* (New York: Random House, 1975), p. 216 *et seq.*

Chapter 39

1. Quoted, Stafford, *Churchill and Secret Service*, pbk edn, p. 309.
2. See Gilbert, *Churchill*, vol. 7, p. 533.
3. Quoted Reynolds, *In Command of History*, p. 380.
4. Reynolds, *In Command of History*, pp. 380, 381.

Chapter 40

1. Quoted Gilbert, *Churchill. A Life*, p. 753.
2. Ollard, 'Churchill and the Navy' in Blake and Louis, *Churchill*, p. 390.
3. Quoted, Gilbert, *Churchill. A Life*, p. 755.
4. See Reynolds, *In Command of History*, p. 378.
5. See Correlli Barnett, 'Anglo-American Strategy in Europe' in Lane & Temperley, *The Rise & Fall of the Grand Alliance, 1941–45*, p. 183 *et seq.*
6. Reynolds, *In Command of History*, p. 382.

Chapter 41

1. Quoted Gilbert, *Churchill. A Life*, p. 758.
2. Quoted Adams, *Harry Hopkins*, p. 337.
3. See Sherwood, *The White House Papers of Harry L. Hopkins*, vol. 2, p. 793 – and earlier for background to this decision.
4. Jacob, in Wheeler-Bennett, *Action this Day*, p. 209.
5. M. Potter (ed.), *Champion Redoubtable: the Diaries and Letters of Violet Bonham-Carter 1914–1944* (London: Weidenfeld & Nicholson, 1998), pp. 312–13.
6. Dilks (ed.), Cadogan *Diaries*, p. 580.
7. H. Arnold, *Global Mission* (New York: Harper & Bros, 1949), p. 468.
8. See Overy, *Why the Allies Won*, pbk edn, p. 301 *et seq.*
9. See Carlton, *Churchill and the Soviet Union*, p. 102.
10. Moran, *Winston Churchill: The Struggle for Survival 1940–1965*, p. 102.
11. Elliot Roosevelt, *As He Saw It*, p. 188 *et seq.*
12. Churchill, *The Second World War*, vol. 5, p. 330.
13. Elliot Roosevelt, *As He Saw It*, p. 206.
14. Lady Soames in American television series, 'The American Experience. The Presidents. F.D. Roosevelt'.
15. Carlton, *Churchill and the Soviet Union*, p. 107.
16. Ismay, *The Memoirs of Lord Ismay*, p. 252.

17. Leasor, *War at the Top*, p. 239.
18. Elliot Roosevelt, *As He Saw It*, p. 184 *et seq.*
19. Quoted, Halifax, Diary, 18 December 1943.
20. See Charmley, *Churchill's Grand Alliance: The Anglo-American Special Relationship 1940–57*, p. 141.
21. See K. Sainsbury, *Churchill & Roosevelt at War: The War They Fought and the Peace They Hoped to Make* (Houndmills: Macmillan, 1994), p. 61.
22. Elliot Roosevelt, *As He Saw It*, p. 192 *et seq.*
23. Moran, *Winston Churchill: The Struggle for Survival 1940–1965*, p. 152.

Chapter 42

1. Moody, J., *From Churchill's War Rooms: Letters of a Secretary, 1943-45* (Stroud: Tempus, 2007), p. 88.
2. Nicolson (ed.), Harold Nicolson *Diaries*, vol. 2, p. 346.

Chapter 43

1. See Brian Holden Reid, 'Field-Marshal Earl Alexander' in Keegan, *Churchill's Generals*, pbk edn, p. 119 *et seq.*
2. Quoted Reynolds, *In Command of History*, p. 414.
3. Ingersoll, *Top Secret*, p. 50.
4. Ingersoll, *Top Secret*, p. 72.
5. Ingersoll, *Top Secret*, p. 55.
6. See Ben-Moshe, *Churchill, Strategy & History*.
7. See Ben-Moshe, *Churchill, Strategy & History*, p. 263 *et seq.*
8. Churchill, *The World Crisis*, vol. 2, p. 1212 *et seq.*
9. Kennedy, *The Business of War*, p. 254.
10. See Corrigan, *Blood, Toil, Tears & Sweat*, p. 370 *et seq.*
11. See Ben-Moshe, *Churchill, Strategy & History*, p. 266 *et seq.*

Chapter 44

1. Quoted, Correlli Barnett, 'Anglo-American Strategy in Europe' in Lane & Temperley, *The Rise & Fall of the Grand Alliance, 1941–45*, p. 182 *et seq.*
2. But see Basil Liddell Hart, 'The Military Strategist', in Taylor et al., *Churchill: Four Faces and the Man*, p. 194.
3. See Brian Bond, 'Alanbrooke & Britain's Strategy' in Freedman et al., *War, Strategy, & International Politics*, p. 190 *et seq.* and references therein to Liddell-Hart and John Ehrman.
4. See diary for 23 June 1944, Kennedy, *The Business of War*, p. 333.
5. Danchev and Todman (eds), *War Diaries 1939–1945: Field Marshal Lord Alanbrooke*, p. 465.
6. Quoted, Gilbert, *Churchill*, vol. 7, p. 722.

7. Colville, *The Fringes of Power*, p. 479.
8. See Reynolds, *From World War to Cold War*, p. 126.
9. Quoted Reynolds, *From World War to Cold War*, pp. 122,123.
10. Television interview with John Morgan, 1978, quoted J. Harris (ed.), *Goronwy Rees: Sketches in Autobiography* (Cardiff: University of Wales Press, 2001), note, p. 394.
11. Danchev and Todman (eds), *War Diaries 1939–1945: Field Marshal Lord Alanbrooke*, p. 554, 5 June 1944.
12. Kennedy, *The Business of War*, p. 337.
13. Quoted, Addison, *Churchill, The Unexpected Hero*, p. 204.
14. See John Ehrman, *Grand Strategy. August 1943–September, 1944* (*History of the Second World War United Kingdom Military Series*, vol. 5) (London: 1956), p. 425.
15. See Danchev and Todman (eds), *War Diaries 1939–1945: Field Marshal Lord Alanbrooke*, entry for 21 March 1944, p. 533.

Chapter 45

1. See Reynolds, *In Command of History*, p. 411 *et seq*.
2. Quoted Kersaudy, *Churchill & de Gaulle*, pbk edn, p. 364.
3. Quoted, Tombs, *That Sweet Enemy*, p. 590.
4. Harold Nicolson, *Diaries*, 5 July 1944.
5. See Kersaudy, *Churchill and de Gaulle*, pbk edn, p. 349.
6. Reynolds, *In Command of History*, p. 412 *et seq*.
7. Quoted, Tombs, *That Sweet Enemy*, p. 593.
8. Tombs, *That Sweet Enemy*, p. 593.

Chapter 46

1. Quoted, Gilbert, *Churchill*, vol. 7, p. 844.
2. N. Hamilton, *Monty: The Making of a General 1887–1942*, vol. 2 (London: Hamilton, 1981), p. 592.
3. See Gilbert, *Winston Churchill's War Leadership*, p. 88.
4. Macmillan, *The Blast of War 1939–1945*, p. 503.
5. See Gilbert, *Churchill: A Life*, p. 780 *et seq*.
6. Ambrose, 'Eisenhower and the Second World War', in Blake and Louis, *Churchill*, p. 402.
7. Colville, *The Fringes of Power*, p. 507.
8. See Reynolds, *In Command of History*, p. 451.
9. Alanbrooke, *War Diaries*, 24 November 1943.

Chapter 47

1. Quoted Gilbert, *Churchill: A Life*, p. 787.
2. See Reynolds, *In Command of History*, pp. 453, 454.

3. Quoted, Stafford, *Churchill and Secret Service*, pbk edn, p. 357.
4. See Reynolds, *In Command of History*, p. 457.
5. Quoted, Gilbert, *Churchill*, vol. 7, p. 952.
6. Moran, *Winston Churchill: The Struggle for Survival 1940–1965*, p. 178.

Chapter 48

1. Kennedy, *The Business of War*, p. 350 *et seq.*
2. Quoted Reynolds, *In Command of History*, p. 446.
3. Hamilton, *Monty*, vol. 2, p. 799.
4. Ingersoll, *Top Secret*, p. 215.
5. Ingersoll, *Top Secret*, p. 216.
6. Ronald Lewin, *Montgomery as Military Commander: the making of a General 1887–1942* (London: Batsford 1971), p. 308.
7. See Danchev and Todman (eds), *War Diaries 1939–1945: Field Marshal Lord Alanbrooke*, pp. 628, 653.

Chapter 49

1. 10 June 1944. Kimball, *Churchill and Roosevelt. The Complete Correspondence.* R–557.
2. 11 June 1944. Kimball, *Churchill and Roosevelt. The Complete Correspondence.* C–700.
3. 12 June 1944. Kimball, *Churchill and Roosevelt. The Complete Correspondence.* R–560.
4. Quoted G. Ross (ed.), *The Foreign Office & the Kremlin: British documents on Anglo-Soviet relations 1941–45* (Cambridge: Cambridge University Press, 1984), p. 177.
5. See Carlton, *Churchill and the Soviet Union*, for the Polish thesis.
6. See C. Barnett, *The Collapse of British Power* (London: Eyre Methuen, 1972), pp. 588, 592; Charmley, *Churchill: The End of Glory*, pp. 559–61; Reynolds, *From World War to Cold War*, p. 100 *et seq.*

Chapter 50

1. Sherwood, *The White House Papers of Harry L. Hopkins,* vol. 2, p. 833.
2. Kimball, *Churchill and Roosevelt. The Complete Correspondence.* C–849/1.
3. Colville, *Fringes of Power*, 19 December 1944.
4. Kimball, *Churchill and Roosevelt. The Complete Correspondence.* C–850/1.
5. Nicholas, ed, *Washington Dispatches 1941–45.*
6. Elliot Roosevelt, *The Way He Saw It*, p. 222.
7. Hart-Davis, ed, *King's Counsellor*, p. 279.
8. Soames, *Clementine Churchill*, pbk edn, p 518.
9. Rowan in Wheeler-Bennett, *Action this Day*, p. 258.
10. See Reynolds, *In Command of History*, p. 463.

11. Hart-Davis, *King's Counsellor*, p. 282.
12. Quoted Gardner, *Churchill in his Time*, p. 266.
13. Dennis Healey was born on 30 August 1917, when Churchill was Minister of Munitions.
14. Stafford, *Churchill and Secret Service*, pbk edn, p. 359.
15. See Carlton, *Churchill and the Soviet Union*, p. 123 *et seq*.

Chapter 51

1. Moran, *Winston Churchill: The Struggle for Survival 1940–1965*, p. 179.
2. Colville, *The Fringes of Power*, p. 514.
3. Moran, *Winston Churchill: The Struggle for Survival 1940–1965*, p. 226.
4. Eden, diary 2 February 1945, in Eden, *The Reckoning*, p. 512.
5. Moran, *Winston Churchill: The Struggle for Survival 1940–1965*, p. 224.
6. Quoted Norman A. Graebner, 'Yalta, Potsdam and Beyond', in Lane & Temperley, *The Rise & Fall of the Grand Alliance, 1941–45*, p. 228 *et seq*.
7. See Reynolds, *In Command of History*, p. 465.
8. See Reynolds, *Summits*, p. 115.
9. E. Woodward, *British Foreign Policy in the Second World War* (London: HMSO, 1962), vol. 3, p. 86.
10. See Reynolds, *In Command of History*, p. 507.
11. Quoted Reynolds, *In Command of History*, p. 417.
12. Memorandum of Conversations with the President, 21 October–19 November 1944, Averell Harriman Papers, Library of Congress.
13. See White House website, http://www.whitehouse.gov/news/releases/2005/05/20050507-8html
14. Quoted, Gilbert, *Churchill*, vol. 7, p. 1215.
15. Gilbert, *Churchill*, vol. 7, p. 1223.
16. Channon, *Diary*, 28 February 1945.
17. Harold Nicolson, *Diaries*, 27 February 1945.
18. Reynolds, *In Command of History*, p. 469.
19. Colville, *The Fringes of Power*, 19 February 1945.
20. Dilks (ed.), Cadogan *Diaries*, p. 719.
21. Quoted, Gilbert, *Churchill*, vol. 7, p. 146 *et seq*.
22. Quoted Reynolds, *In Command of History*, p. 469.
23. Quoted Gilbert, *Churchill: A Life*, p. 826.
24. Kimball, *Churchill and Roosevelt. The Complete Correspondence*. C–910.
25. Kimball, *Churchill and Roosevelt. The Complete Correspondence*. R–736.
26. See Charmley, *Churchill's Grand Alliance: The Anglo-American Special Relationship 1940–57*, p. 155.
27. Kimball, *Churchill and Roosevelt. The Complete Correspondence*, pbk edn, vol. 3, p. 617.
28. Reynolds, *In Command of History*, p. 473.
29. See Reynolds, *In Command of History*, p. 474
30. Sherwood, *The White House Papers of Harry L. Hopkins*, vol. 2 p. 829.

Chapter 52

1. Quoted Reynolds, *From World War to Cold War,* p. 128.
2. Ambrose, 'Eisenhower in the Second World War' in Blake and Louis, *Churchill,* p. 404.
3. Colville, *The Churchillians,* p. 150.
4. Quoted, Gilbert, *Churchill,* vol. 7, p. 1320.
5. See Charmley, *Churchill's Grand Alliance: The Anglo-American Special Relationship 1940–57,* p. 162.
6. McClain, 'The Role of Admiral W.D. Leahy in United States Foreign Policy', PhD thesis, quoted Charmley, *Churchill's Grand Alliance: The Anglo-American Special Relationship 1940–57,* p. 143.
7. There must be doubt about the accuracy of the precise words, quoted by Charmley, *Churchill's Grand Alliance: The Anglo-American Special Relationship 1940–57,* p. 166.
8. Quoted, Gilbert, *Churchill,* vol. 7, p. 1351.
9. Alanbrooke, *War Diaries,* 4 May 1945.
10. An ever-green formula: see Walter Reid, *Architect of Victory: Douglas Haig.*
11. Ismay, *The Memoirs of Lord Ismay,* p. 394.
12. J. Astley, *The Inner Circle: A View of War at the Top* (London: Hutchinson, 1971), p. 206.
13. Quoted, Gilbert, *Churchill,* vol. 8, p. 4.

Chapter 53

1. Quoted, Gilbert, *Churchill,* vol. 8, p. 8.
2. Gilbert, *Churchill,* vol. 8, p. 8.
3. Quoted Charmley, *Churchill's Grand Alliance: The Anglo-American Special Relationship 1940–57,* p. 175.
4. Alanbrooke, *War Diaries,* 11 June 1945.
5. R. James (ed.), *Winston Churchill: His Complete Speeches, 1897–1963,* vol. 8 (New York: Chelsea House Publishers 1974), pp. 8604–5.
6. Alanbrooke, *War Diaries,* 24th May 1945.
7. Quoted Reynolds, *In Command of History,* pp. 477, 478.
8. Colville, *The Fringes of Power,* p. 410.
9. Quoted, Gilbert, *Churchill,* vol. 8. p. 67.
10. Colville, *The Fringes of Power,* p. 658.

Epilogue

1. Hart-Davis, *King's Counsellor,* p. 276.
2. Hart-Davis, *King's Counsellor,* p. 343.
3. Colville Papers, quoted Gilbert, *Churchill,* vol. 8, p. 1124.
4. Quoted, Soames, *Clementine Churchill,* pbk edn, p. 733.
5. Eden to Eisenhower 5/11/56 National Archives PREM 11/1177.
6. A. Campbell, *The Blair Years* (London: Arrow Books, 2007).

Index

offensive operations, Churchill as
    champion of 71–4
Onassis, Aristotle 20
operations *see* military operations
OVERLORD (invasion of North-west Europe,
    1944) 73, 115, 116, 286–90, 291–2,
    294–5, 306, 308, 319
  D-Day 298, 301
  planning for 211, 213, 255–6, 260,
    271, 272–3
  Quebec conference, planning at
    264–7
  Teheran conference, planning at
    275–8, 280, 281
Owen, Frank 197
Oxford Dictionary of National Biography
    39

Pacific 245
  reverses in theatre 202–3
Pahlavi, Mohammad Reza, Shah of
    Persia 282
Papandreou, Georgios 323
Park, Air Vice-Marshall Keith 70
Patton, General George S. 255, 263–4,
    312–13, 315
Pearl Harbor, and reaction to 169–70,
    175
Pearson, Drew 325
Peck, John 33, 351
Peirse, Air Marshall Sir Richard 67
people, identification with 125
Pershing, General John J. 280
Persia 91, 93, 107, 111, 224, 282, 287,
    351
Pétain, Marshal Henri Philippe Omer
    8, 48, 50, 52–3, 54, 58, 97
Peyrouton, Marcel 284
Phillip, Terence 19
Phillips, Admiral Tom 171
Phillips, Ambassador William 216
Pimm, Captain Richard 196, 343
Placentia Bay summit 114, 160–67
pneumonia 254, 257, 282–3, 309–10
Poland 281, 341, 342
  cost of war for 158
  post-war future for 318, 320, 321,
    331, 334–5, 336–7, 341, 342

Potsdam discussions on 345, 347,
    348, 350, 351
  Yalta discussions on 331, 334–5,
    336–7
political insecurity 21–8, 192–7
political vulnerability 192–7, 219
Ponting, Clive 8
Portal, Air Chief Marshall Sir Charles
    F.A. 45, 67, 176, 178, 201, 245,
    268, 305
post-war arrangements
  'Percentages Agreement' and spheres
    of influence 318–22
  Poland, post-war future for 318, 320,
    321, 331, 334–5, 336–7, 341, 342
  Roosevelt's interest in shaping post-
    war world 323
  spheres of influence 318–19, 320, 322
  see also Potsdam conference; Quebec
    conference (September 1944); Yalta
    conference
Potsdam conference (July–August 1945)
    347–52
Pound, Admiral A. Dudley Pickman
    Rogers 45, 59, 65–6, 71, 171, 176,
    178, 184–5, 198–9, 202–3, 269–70
power, tenuousness of 11–16
Pownall, Henry 47
Prime Minister
  second premiership (1951–55) 5–6,
    353
Prime Minister, appointment as 12–13
Prytz, Bjorn 38
publications 3–10

Quebec conference (August 1943) 156,
    207, 208, 263–8
Quebec conference (September 1944)
    310–11

Rashid Ali, Prime Minister of Iraq
    90–91
Reagan, Ronald 356
Rees, Major Goronwy 295
Reith, John C.W., Baron Reith of
    Stonehaven 5
Reod, Mrs Helen OM 217
Reves, Emery and Wendy 20